# Academic Writing
# in a Second Language:
# Essays on
# Research and Pedagogy

# Academic Writing in a Second Language: Essays on Research and Pedagogy

*edited by*

**Diane Belcher**
Ohio State University

*and*

**George Braine**
University of South Alabama

**Ablex Publishing Corporation**
**Norwood, NJ**

Printed in the United States of America

**Library of Congress Cataloging-in-Publication Data**

    Academic writing in a second language : essays on research and pedagogy / Diane Belcher and George Braine, editors.
      p.  cm.
    Includes bibliographical references and index.
    ISBN 1-56750-115-X. — ISBN 1-56750-116-8 (pbk.)
    1. English language — Study and teaching — Foreign speakers.
    2. English language — Rhetoric — Study and teaching.  3. Second language acquisition.  I. Belcher, Diane Dewhurst, 1951-    .
    II. Braine, George.
    428'.007 — dc20                   94–13814
    PE1128.A2 A22 1994             CIP

Ablex Publishing Corporation
355 Chestnut Street
Norwood, New Jersey 07648

# Contents

# Contributors

Diane Belcher is Acting Director of the ESL Composition Program at Ohio State University. Her reviews and articles on second language writing have appeared in *English for Specific Purposes, The Modern Language Journal, The Rhetoric Society Quarterly,* and other journals.

Philippa J. Benson is a PhD candidate in Rhetoric at Carnegie Mellon University. She developed and runs the Writing Clinic at the university's ESL Center. She has also taught in China.

Joel Bloch is an Assistant Professor at Lake Superior State University in Sault Ste. Marie, Michigan, where he teaches composition and linguistics. He has taught in China, Canada, Israel, and Ukraine.

George Braine is Assistant Professor of English at the University of South Alabama. He has taught ESL and EFL in Sri Lanka, Oman, and the United States for over 20 years.

Christine P. Casanave is Associate Professor of English at Keio University's Fujisawa campus in Japan. Her research and writing interests include second language reading and writing, disciplinary socialization, and the professional development of language educators.

Lan Chi graduated from teacher training college in China, where she was an English teacher and factory worker. She works as a document coordinator for a large law firm in Pittsburgh.

Ulla Connor is Professor of English at Indiana University at Indianapolis, where she directs the ESL Program and the ESL teacher training program. She has published widely on second language reading and writing. She is coeditor of *Writing Across Languages: Analysis of L2 Text* and *Coherence in Writing: Research and Pedagogical Perspectives.*

Alister Cumming is Associate Professor of Curriculum and Head of the Modern Language Centre at the Ontario Institute for Studies in Education. His research focuses on writing in a second language and curriculum evolution in second language education. He is currently editor of *Language Learning.*

Tony Dudley-Evans is Senior Lecturer and Director of the English for Overseas Students Unit at the University of Birmingham. He has published widely in the area of English for Specific Purposes and is currently the coeditor of the journal *English for Specific Purposes.* He recently coedited *Economics and Language* (Routledge).

Jan Frodesen directs the ESL program in the Department of Linguistics at the University of California, Santa Barbara. She was previously on the faculty of UCLA Writing Programs. She is coauthor of *Grammar Dimensions: Form, Meaning, and Use, Book 4.*

Naomi Fujishima received her MA in TESOL from the Monterey Institute of International Studies. She teaches in the Intensive English Program at Kwansei Gakuin University in Nishinomiya, Japan.

Peggy A. Heidish is the Director of the ESL Center at Carnegie Mellon University, where she specializes in the training and testing of ITAs. She created and teaches the ITA workshop and developed and runs the ITA testing program.

Christine Holten is a lecturer in the Department of TESL/Applied Linguistics at the University of California, Los Angeles. She supervises and teaches ESL composition and literature courses and also teaches graduate courses in second language writing and teaching methodology.

Sally Jacoby is a PhD candidate in Applied Linguistics at the University of California, Los Angeles. Since 1978, she has developed rhetoric- and grammar-based curricula for EST/ESP students in academic and scientific settings.

Ann Johns is Professor of Linguistics and Writing Studies at San Diego State University, where she serves on the integrated curriculum committee. She has published widely in English for Academic Purposes and is coeditor of *Coherence in Writing: Research and Pedagogical Perspectives* and coeditor of the journal *English for Specific Purposes.*

Melinda J. Kramer is Professor of English at Prince George's Community College, where she teaches business communication, argumentation, and composition. She is the author of the *Prentice Hall Handbook for Writers*.

David Leech is a PhD candidate in Applied Linguistics at the University of California, Los Angeles. He has taught ESL and EFL in China, Saudi Arabia, and the United States.

Ilona Leki is Professor of English and Director of ESL at the University of Tennessee. She is the coeditor of the *Journal of Second Language Writing* and *Reading in the Composition Classroom: Second Language Perspectives*. She is also author of *Understanding ESL Writers: A Guide for Teachers*.

Peter Master is Associate Professor of Applied Linguistics at California State University, Fresno. He is the Review Editor of the journal *English for Specific Purposes,* the coeditor of *The CATESOL Journal,* and the editor of "Issues in ESP" in *TESOL Matters*.

Maureen Mathison is Assistant Professor in the Rhetoric and Composition Program and the Communications Department at the University of Utah. Currently, she is a Charles Phelps Taft Postdoctoral Fellow at the University of Cincinnati.

Paul Prior is Assistant Professor of English at the University of Illinois at Urbana-Champaign, where he directs the WAC program for teaching assistants through the Center for Writing Studies. He has also taught EFL in Saudi Arabia.

Melanie Schneider is Assistant Professor of Education and Linguistics at Beloit College, where she also directs the TESL Program. Her research and teaching interests include teacher education, second language acquisition, and the development of writing abilities.

Diane Tedick is Assistant Professor of Second Languages and Cultures Education at the University of Minnesota. She works with graduate students and preservice and inservice teachers of ESL and foreign languages.

# Acknowledgments

We are especially grateful to Ilona Leki and Tony Silva for advice and encouragement at several crucial early stages of this project. At the latter end of the editing process, some much-appreciated suggestions and moral support came from Barbara Dobson, Liz Hamp-Lyons, Alan Hirvela, Terence Odlin, and John Swales. Throughout this endeavor, our spirits and commitment have been sustained by the contributors to this volume, a remarkable group of scholar–teachers whose intellectual curiosity and interest in students' welfare make us proud to be part of their community of practice. Some aspects of this project, such as photocopying and postal costs, were funded by an Arts and Sciences Support and Development Award from the University of South Alabama. For their immense patience with our years-long preoccupation with this volume, we thank our children — Roy, Vera, and Claire — and our always supportive spouses, Fawzia and Jim.

# Introduction

**Diane Belcher**
*Ohio State University*

**George Braine**
*University of South Alabama*

Although academic writing is inherently a cognitive as well as a social process, it will be readily apparent to anyone who glances at our table of contents or at the abstracts accompanying each chapter in this volume that our interests extend beyond the composing processes of individual writers to the contexts of learning in which those composing processes take place. It would be difficult to say whether our students first led us to look outside our own classrooms, to "take the social turn" as Trimbur (1994, p. 108) calls it, or if our sense of what was outside led us to look with concern at our students. What is clear is that many of us have felt compelled to be less "myopic" (Ackerman, 1993, p. 361) in our writing classes for nonnative speakers of English who will soon be or already are expected to speak authoritatively in postsecondary academic communities. If one accepts the Mina Shaughnessy (1977) view of academic discourse—as useful ways of talking about and to the world—then there seems little reason to keep the intellectual customs and even some of the domain-specific literacies outside the purview of the second language writing classroom (Ackerman, 1993).

Yet our enthusiasm for mapping out potential access routes for our students to the "privileged language of public life" (Bartholomae, 1985, p. 9) should not be assumed to imply a naive view of academic literacy practices as neutral, value-free, and nonexclusionary. We are well aware of how marginalized academic discourse can make nonnative speakers feel at Anglophone institutions of higher learning. Canagarajah (1993) sees many second language college students faced with the dilemma of being forced to choose between allegiance to their native culture—hence being judged "unfit" for the academy—and membership "at whatever psychological and social costs" in the academy, whose discourse will afford them "only negative subject positions," the appearance of being cognitively deficient or deviant (p. 303). Given the gatekeeping that guards entry into postsecondary institutions and the elaborate socialization rituals of their disciplinary discourse communities, it is certainly easy enough to find testimonials to the elitism and oppressiveness of academic discourse.

The response, however, of many who have felt excluded from the "culture of power," as Delpit (1988, p. 285) calls white Anglophone academia, has been not to evade it but to "encounter" it (Trimbur, 1994, p. 114). Feminists have not only created their own academic subculture but have met the dominant academic culture on its own turf. Steinitz and Kanter (1991), both feminists, see no other choice for women but to learn "to advocate for themselves in the competitive, conflict-laden society where, unfortunately, we continue to live" (p. 139). In the same vein, Kirsch (1993) observes that writing teachers who attempt to resist the competitive values of "masculine" academic discourse by limiting discourse in their own classrooms to expressive writing do a disservice to students, male and female, who must move on without experience into the academic argumentative fray. Delpit (1988) argues similarly for students of color. In her view, ignoring the culture of power by concentrating instead on development of an autonomous self makes sense only for those students whose code is already that of the dominant culture. According to Delpit, minority parents more often than not want their children to learn the spoken and written language, the discource patterns, and the presentation of self that will enable them to be competitive in the larger society.

For many nonnative-speaker college students, both the adversarial ethos, or the "literary Darwinism" (Frey, 1990) that feminists complain of, and the privileged code of Anglophone academic discourse can present enormous obstacles to "encountering" academic discourse. Ballard and Clanchy (1991) note that students from Southeast Asia who pursue degrees in Australia generally bring with them a "reproductive" approach to learning that valorizes respect for teachers and texts and prizes rote learning and memorization. In Australia, these students are confronted with a "speculative" educational tradition that expects them to question what they have learned to revere. In the United Kingdom, Richards and Skelton (1991) have found African and Middle Eastern postgraduate students likely to evaluate subject matter less often and less critically than their British counterparts, and thus to have a much "more difficult entree into the charmed circle of the British academic community" (p. 40). And in the United States, Rouzer (1993) has suggested that "epistemological optimism" may go far to explain Chinese students' reluctance to adopt the skeptical stance toward others' knowledge claims that is considered essential scholarly rigor by many Western academics.

What is perhaps most astonishing about these felt (by teacher and student) differences in learning styles and discourse roles (for more on these see Basham, Ray, & Whalley, 1993; Mangelsdorf, Rosen, & Taylor, 1990; and Matalene, 1985) is that so many second language students appear undaunted by them. To many of their teachers, they appear not to share Canagarajah's (1993) understandable fear and loathing of potential ideological domination but to be eager to use the voices and codes of academic authority. Raimes (1993), for example, observes that in her 25 years of teaching students from the world over she has seen no real evidence that "*all* ESOL students face conflicts when writing for the academy" (p. 309). Raimes adds that with many students coming from totalitarian regimes where they "have spent their lives resisting domination" (p. 310), they certainly would not have needed any prompting from a teacher to resist the strictures of Western ideology if they desired to do so. Whether this apparent lack of resistance stems from traditions of reverence for learning, fear of academic failure, a desire to participate in increasingly English-speaking international research communities (Swales, 1990), or perhaps dreams, like those of many feminists, of championing their causes in arenas of power, it is obvious to many ESL/EFL (hereafter ESL) teachers that their students welcome guidance through the mystifying labyrinth of academic discourse. There is much less agreement, however, as Spack (1988b) has noted, over the form this guidance should take.

The approach to demystification of Anglophone academic discourse that many of the contributors to this volume have taken, as may be apparent by now, is neither a sociotherapeutic one (Spellmeyer, 1993) of open resistance to academic oppression (as advocated, for example, by Benesch, 1993) nor a psychotherapeutic approach committed to helping students find some "unified or stable subjectivity" (Trimbur, 1994, p. 113). It is, rather, an approach informed by a belief in the power of explicit cognitive awareness of the texts, subtexts, and contexts of academic discourse to enable individuals to join the collectivist endeavors that academic communities are without loss of the "home perspectives" that Bizzell (1982, 1986) has often spoken of. This academic discoursal consciousness raising does not attempt to "unlock the door to the entire academic universe" (Spack, 1988a, p. 708). It does attempt instead to promote a sense of "socio-rhetorical community," a shared awareness of the rules of academic games and the strategies that successful players use (Swales, 1990, 1993). While we obviously cannot teach all of the "passwords" (Noddings, 1984, p. 2) privileged by insiders in the academic community, we can teach some subset of them, and through these, a feeling for how they function rhetorically, the intentions they can serve, and the messages readers can construct from them. In this way, it is hoped, students will begin to see how their own words can function as passwords in the academy for their own purposes.

One of the often-mentioned advantages of such an explicit presentation and explication of the rules of the academic culture of power is that it makes learning the rules easier. Delpit (1988) sees an obvious analogy between academic initiation and her own experiences in Alaskan Native communities. Delpit has found that without the luxury of long-term immersion, adapting to village life is easier, both "psychologically and pragmatically" (p. 283), if a member of the community tells her directly of the preferred dress code, interaction styles, taboo words and actions, and other such matters. Likewise, Williams and Colomb (1993), citing Swales' work, argue that explicit teaching of the forms of academic discourse — of its genres — may in turn reveal social context to students, just as social context reveals genres. They suggest that the forms themselves may be heuristic, even generative of disciplinary knowledge — or as Cintron (1993) observes, that they not only direct but enable seeing.

For many teachers, however, a more compelling reason for explicit teaching of academic discourse is not just that it can promote participation in academia, but that it can promote critical participation (Bazerman, 1992; Herndl, 1993). Farr (1993) has pointed out that explicit teaching of "essayist literacy," as many have referred to academic discourse (e.g., Scollon & Scollon, 1981), is far more likely than implicit pedagogical models to facilitate open debate over the value of the traditional forms of academic discourse. To Williams and Colomb (1993), teachers who choose not to focus their students' attention on the forms of academic discourse risk hiding from students and themselves the "ideological commitment and consequences" (p. 262) of particular genres. Bazerman (1992), too, observes that oppressioin of the self is less likely to occur when discourse is held up for inspection than when it is learned implicitly "as a matter of getting along" (p. 64). Christie (1987) argues even more forthrightly: "Capacity to recognize, interpret, and write genres is capacity to exercise choice" (p. 32).

To enhance the likelihood that explicit teaching of academic discourse will actually promote critical and empowering participation in academic discourse communities, it is, at risk of stating the obvious, necessary for teachers themselves to believe that critical judgment can and should be exercised when using academic discourse and that this discourse is a source of power for its users, even when they are students. If academic discourse is presented in a framework that highlights its variability, which is both cause and effect of its epistemic nature (how it helps us see our world) and its transformative capabilities (how it helps us shape our world), then the very real privileges that students can enjoy as consciously purposeful users of this privileged discourse should become much more apparent to them.

## THE VARIABILITY FACTOR

Whether viewed synchronically or diachronically, variability is one of the most salient features of academic discourse (Bazerman, 1992). Just from the synchronic perspective alone, we see academic discourse varying from university to university, department to department, and professor to professor. As Casanave (this volume) and Prior (1991) note, the local interactions of academic communities constitute multitudes of microsocieties. There are, however, also global communities that crisscross demographic boundaries, united by the likemindedness that Swales (1990) speaks of, the common epistemology, methodology, and social ontology (Berkenkotter & Huckin, 1993; Killingsworth, 1992) that biologists, historians, or mathematicians around the world share. Yet even these global communities are marked by as much difference as sameness. The discourse of some social scientists can look more like that of natural scientists than like that of other social scientists (Belcher, 1993). The positivist experimentalists in the field of education, for example, may have more in common with empiricists in other disciplinary communities than with the self-reflexive, postmodernist cultural critics of their own. The "classroom" genres of any disciplinary community may also differ in marked ways from its professional, or "authentic" (Johns, this volume), genres, the former more likely being exercises in problem-solving methods rather than actual problem solving (on differences between the two see Berkenkotter & Huckin, 1993; on similarities see Walvoord & McCarthy, 1991).

Given this enormous synchronic variability — numerous content domains, ideological camps within those domains, and practitioners with various degrees of socialization — attempts to characterize academic discourse with some limited set of descriptors, such as impersonal, or "author-evacuated" (Geertz, 1988, p. 9), objective, and colorless, are not so much inaccurate as accurate only for some academic genres. As Elbow's (1991) opening statements in his "Reflections on Academic Discourse" demonstrate, academic prose can be highly personalized, unabashedly subjective, and remarkably vivid: "I love what's in academic discourse: learning, intelligence, sophistication — even mere facts and naked summaries of articles and books; I love reasoning, inference, and evidence; I love theory. But I hate academic discourse" (p. 135). For Elbow, the most reasonable pedagogical approach to this difficult-to-define discourse (both normative and innovative at the same time as Ritchie, 1989, among others, has noted) is to teach "the principle of discourse variation" (p. 152): that different readers, within the academy and without, have different expectations and reactions. This seems indeed a humane way of preparing students for the realpolitik of academic "discourse disparity" (Swales, 1993). As Delpit (1988) has pointed out, while the conventions are arbitrary, they are also politically charged. One passes exams, is awarded degrees, or gains tenure by exhibiting the ideologies and methodologies valued by particular communities. Yet if students can attain "a critical distance on the discourse" (referred to less sanguinely by Bizzell, 1986, p. 39), they may see more clearly where they can exercise the "choice" that Christie (1987) speaks of.

When experienced firsthand, and especially when students are unprepared for it and unreflective about it, discourse diversity can certainly be bewildering and even threatening (Chiseri-Strater, 1991; McCarthy, 1987). A diachronic view of academic discourse may give students more of the "distance" they need in order to appreciate their rights as critical consumers of the conventions that universities teach them, despite the tight reign held on classroom discourse by some faculty. The textbook windows on disciplinary discourse that students usually look through, especially at the undergraduate level, reveal little of historical change (Bazerman, 1992; Myers, 1992). From the textbook vantage point, disciplinary discourse communities are far more likely to look like "purveyors of hegemonic univocality" than the "locales of heteroglossic contention" that Bazerman (1992, p. 63) and others assert they are (e.g., Dillon, 1991; Harris, 1989). Even when students are exposed to the "authentic" genres of their fields of study, however, they may not understand on their own that genres are not stable entities. Students in the natural sciences are not likely to know that the apparently static conventions of the primary research report have evolved over the last few centuries (Bazerman, 1988), with notable modifications in even the last few decades (Huckin, 1987), in response to the changing needs and values of the scientific community. In fields where the "heteroglossic contention" is more conspicuous, the human sciences — that is, the humanities and social sciences — students may not realize that not only do diametrically opposed ideologies coexist in their fields, but they may transform each other over time. In anthropology, for example, the attacks of Geertz (1988) and others (see Nelson, Megill, & McCloskey, 1987) on traditional ethnography, on the Western scientific objectification of "primitive," dominated peoples, resulted in a transformed and revitalized methodology, a new approach to ethnographic study with appeal to practitioners throughout the human sciences (Bazerman, 1992). Those who were once lone voices in the wilderness are now heralded as leaders of the ethnographic renaissance.

For students, however, the price for innovation is likely to be much higher than for those who are already insiders. Innovative students run the risk of being judged as ignorant or incompetent outsiders. As Bridwell-Bowles (1992) and others have noted of their own innovative ventures, not until they reached the safe haven of tenure did they feel secure enough to move away from the conventions they were trained in. Yet it does appear to be the case that as more and more of the formerly excluded enter the academy, as students and then academics, the pressure for change and, to some extent, the tolerance of change in academic discourse communities are on the rise (Aisenberg & Harrington, 1988; Kirsch, 1993). For many who have recently attained positions of authority in the academy—women, minorities, nonnative speakers, and others—there is not just a feeling of freedom to experiment with nontraditional discourse strategies in their own writing, but a sense of obligation to bring about change. As Delpit (1988) says of herself: "I place myself to influence as many gatekeeping points as possible. And it is there that I agitate . . . pushing gatekeepers to open their doors to a variety of styles and codes" (p. 292; see also Land & Whitley, 1989).

## ACADEMIC DISCOURSE AS EPISTEMIC

Of course, the fear of many writing researchers and teachers of both native and nonnative speakers is that students, no matter how determined, will not be able to add their voices to the academic conversation even in their own classrooms—that in fact their own voices will be irretrievably lost as a result of their initiation into the academic discourse community. Many cite Shaughnessy's (1977) observation (e.g., Courage, 1993) that college both "beckons and threatens" students from outside the dominant culture by offering them the means to improve the quality of their lives while taking from them "their distinctive ways of interpreting the world, . . . assimilat[ing] them into the culture of academia without acknowleding their experience as outsiders" (p. 292). To Bizzell (1987), the danger of academic initiation seems even greater: "empowering" students to succeed academically may blind them to their original goals. Others see academic literacy as paradoxically narrowing and widening students' field of view, as simultaneously "oppressive and emancipatory" (Kraemer, 1991). The novice academic writer learns to see his/her world through a microscope, a telescope, statistical analysis, or problematizing critical reading, to construct meaning for others wearing the same types of lenses, and in doing so s/he sees the world (the old in the context of the new) and communicates with it in a way s/he may never have before. McGinley and Tierney (1989) note that the more complex and diverse combinations of forms of reading and writing that schools can offer students are, in effect, different "traversal routes" through "topical landscapes," resulting in multiple, critical perspectives rather than a single dominant one. For Harris (1989), introducing students to new ways of talking about the world can create a "useful dissonance" for them, a complication and enrichment of language use. Viewing academic literacy as requiring abandonment of outsider loyalties for insider member ship is too simplistic and "misleading" according to Harris because "one is always already committed to a number of conflicting beliefs and practices" (p. 19). Entering the academic discourse community is not a matter of leaving one community for another, but rather a "reposition[ing] . . . in relation to several continuous and conflicting discourses" (p. 19). For nonnative speakers, however, this repositioning can be an extremely painful process—one that feels initially like loss even if it ultimately amounts to gain.

Nonnative speakers themselves have provided the most compelling accounts of the pain of initiation into Anglophone academia—accounts that attest to the epistemic nature of the new linguistic and rhetorical conventions that may seem on the surface more stylistic than formative. Shen (1989) observes that when he was urged in English composition and literature classes at an American university to just "write what *you* think" and "be yourself," he felt the need to redefine his "ideological and logical identities":

> By such a redefinition I mean not only the change in how I envisioned myself, but also the change in how *I* perceived the world. The old "I" used to embody only one set of values, but now it had to embody multiple sets of values. To be truly "myself," which I knew was a key to my success in learning English composition, meant *not to be my Chinese self* at all. That is to say, when I write in English I have to wrestle with and abandon (at least temporarily) the whole system of ideology which previously defined me in myself. . . . I had to put aside an ideology of collectivism and adopt the values of individualism. (p. 461)

Although Shen sees the change he underwent as "profound," he nevertheless views it as welcome, as adding a new dimension to his world view. Rodriguez's (1982) experience growing up as the socioeconomically disadvantaged child of Mexican immigrants in the United States was quite different from Shen's experiences as an international college student, yet there are congruences. When Rodriguez realized as a child in elementary school that to develop a public identity he had to learn "to speak the public language of *los gringos,*" his sense of change in himself and his relationship with his family was also profound: "Gone was the desperate, urgent, intense feeling of being at home; rare was the experience of feeling myself individualized by family intimates" (p. 23). Yet for Rodriguez, too, the gain, "the calming assurance that I belonged in public" (p. 22), was equally profound. Similarly, Lu (1987, 1992), who had to cope with two vastly different approaches to literacy as a child in the People's Republic of China—her parents' individualistic, liberal literary preferences and her Marxist teachers' determined rejection of "bourgeois individualism"—

argues that in fact struggling with such conflicting influences provides opportunities for self-development – development, for example, of greater tolerance of ambivalence or multiple world views that the student not confronted with such dissonance may not have.

That becoming an insider in Anglophone academia does not require cultural conversion is especially well illustrated by Kraemer's (1991) account of literary theorist and Calcutta native Gayatry Chakravorty Spivak's participation in a panel discussion at a Modern Language Association Convention. When asked why students should be encouraged to enter the academic community, why they should become like the academics who teach them, Spivak responded by dramatically standing up, calling attention to her sari and her purple spiked hair, and exclaiming, "I don't want them to be like me. Look at me!" (p. 54) in obvious reference to the unique identity she had forged for herself. Certainly, Spivak, Lu, Rodriguez, and Shen all exemplify an enlargement of identity that insider academic status can achieve with outsider sensitivities.

## TRANSFORMATIONS

If contact with the academic discourse community transforms the self in some way, it is also true that the community itself is changed by those who join it (Bizzell, 1988; Kraemer, 1991), and in fact the ultimate goal of the community is, essentially, change. Although universities as institutions may resist change, members of the academic community, as Brodkey (1987) has pointed out, are more accepting. Brodkey cites the acceptance of such major theoretical changes as quantum physics and transformational grammar, despite the substantial reconceptualization of research issues and methods that acceptance entailed. The change that members of academic communities can effect is not just intellectual, not just internal to the academy. Bazerman (1992) sees participation in the academy as a "means to individual and group influence in the constant reproduction and reshaping of our society" (p. 62). Not only does the academic community welcome the engagement of those interested in change, in identifying and addressing problems social and otherwise, it also "thoroughly depends on alternative perspectives," as Kraemer (1991, p. 57) and others have observed (e.g., Kaufer & Geisler, 1989). Novelty is at the heart of academic discourse: introducing, critiquing, building on, rejecting new knowledge claims; for classroom academic discourse, appreciation, if not eventual production, of disciplinary novelty is the pedagogical goal. There is perhaps no more dramatic an example of the extent to which novelty is prized and rewarded in academic discourse communities than the reception of Watson and Crick's (1953) "A structure for deoxyribose nucleic acid." Although their findings were not radically different in import from those that Avery had very conservatively announced in standard technical detail almost a decade earlier, Watson and Crick's stylistically bold and brief paper so caught the imagination of the scientific community that almost overnight an entirely new field of study, molecular biology, was established, with far-reaching effects for society at large (Halloran, 1984; but see also Berkenkotter & Huckin, 1993; Miller, 1992).

Undeniably, academic communities, even while valorizing change, also resist it. New knowledge claims and the discourse that constructs them can fall on deaf ears — as indeed did geneticist Barbara McClintock's. For decades, McClintock's fellow scientists rejected her novel claim of genetic transposition, a claim that, if accurate, meant that DNA was not, as Watson and Crick had asserted, completely in control but itself subject to reprogramming in higher, multicellular organisms (Keller, 1983, 1985). Fellow scientists also rejected McClintock's novel approach to her subject, her empathic involvement as an observer: ". . . . I wasn't outside, I was down there. I was part of the system" (Keller, 1985, p. 165). But it is at least to the credit of the scientific community, as Horning (1993) points out, that McClintock always had a lab and the fellowship of a small number of supporters, and that when more of her fellow academics eventually learned to read her unique interweaving of verbal and visual arguments, they accorded her the acclaim, the Nobel prize, that she deserved. Bizzell (1988) has remarked that there are always oppositional discourses in the academy: ". . . . people working out their relations to the changing historical circumstances are creating them all the time" (p. 152). To Bizzell, the challenge is to convince others that this opposition is what "normal" intellectual life is all about and to persuade students to participate in it. For teachers of nonnative speakers, the challenge is to convince their students not only that the academy is the forum that their outsider perspectives deserve, but that their outsider perspectives are what the academy needs.

## ACADEMIC WRITING IN A SECOND LANGUAGE

Our aim throughout this volume is to help make the Anglophone postsecondary academic discourse community feel more "beckoning" than "threatening" to nonnative speakers of English. All of the contributions to this volume have been motivated by the authors' involvement as teachers and researchers with ESL students and fellow ESL teachers at the authors' own and other postsecondary institutions. While it would certainly be gratifying if our reflections on academic literacy issues, our research findings, and our pedagogical suggestions were found to be relevant to our readers' own teaching environments, it would be far more gratifying if our volume encouraged readers to learn more about the wider social contexts in which their students function when they leave their ESL classrooms. We urge this "social turn" not because we see ESL programs as service units that should cater to the rest of the university community's needs, but because we feel that through greater contact with the intellectual and sociopolitical diversity of the academic community that we and our students are part of, our understanding of both our students and of the academic discourse that they must somehow become conversant in can be enriched. We do not feel that we are overly optimistic in also expecting the rest of the academic community's understanding of second language writers, in turn, to be enriched through contact with those of us who specialize in teaching nonnative speakers of English.

In the first section of our book, "Issues," all four of the chapters offer commentary on what can be seen as variations on a single theme — what Schneider and Fujishima (this volume) have aptly labeled the "isolationist tendencies in higher education" (p. 21). In Schneider and Fujishima's own chapter, they recount a cautionary tale of an ESL graduate student who made little progress as a language learner and in his academic program possibly as a result of his narrow focus on his subject-area classes, a focus that excluded most of his surroundings — both the larger university community and disciplinary subcultures. Schneider and Fujishima raise troubling questions about the academic community's role in this student's stalled career (or that of any student like him). Had his instructors, both ESL and subject-area, taken a less compartmentalized view of their student, either as a language learner or as a subject-area specialist-in-training, had they communicated with each other, they might have arrived at some effective intervention strategies that could have saved the student from academic failure.

In Chapter 2, Leki highlights similar isolationist tendencies at the undergraduate level. ESL undergraduates in Leki's study proved largely unable to predict how writing and subject-area faculty would respond to ESL student writing. Perhaps not surprisingly, Leki also found little agreement among faculty at her university in their responses to ESL writing. Possibly the most disturbing of Leki's findings is the degree of confidence that some faculty expressed in the universality of their judgments — their belief that their own definition of "good writing" was the norm of the entire academic community. Leki does not ask for greater faculty agreement on some uniform, context-free standard of good writing, but instead for a greater awareness of the diverse assumptions about writing that faculty throughout any campus are likely to hold and for better preparation of students for this diversity.

In the latter two chapters in Part I, Prior and Casanave focus on the need for EAP (English for academic purposes) reseachers to take a much more contextualized look at academic discourse than they have previously. Prior notes that his own attempts to understand student writing and faculty feedback in graduate seminars in a number of fields convinced him of the necessity of detailed ethnographic research designs and a sociohistoric perspective on discourse and knowledge. Prior feels that such an approach is essential if students are to be viewed as "full subjects working to achieve their social, intellectual, and affective goals within complex, emergent streams of situated activity rather than as 'academic dopes' endlessly re-encoding the abstract rules and conventions of monologic discourses" (p. 78). Like Prior, Casanave, in Chapter 4, argues against simplistic characterizations of academic socialization. Rejecting popular conceptualizations of disciplinary communities as monolithic and unchanging, Casanave finds that to understand how students are socialized in their degree programs and as disciplinary writers, one should consider the microsociety the students inhabit: the students' interactions with their teachers, would-be mentors, and fellow students as well as with the training the students receive and writing tasks they are assigned. In the sociology graduate program that Casanave investigated, successful socialization appears to be the result of a student's ability to "try on different disciplinary personae" without feeling obliged to make a commitment (p. 108), a strategy that, Casanave notes, can empower a student to experiment, resist, and, "if necessary, continue looking" (p. 108). Less successful socialization, however, may not indicate inability but rather unwillingness to participate in such game-playing, and may point as well to a disciplinary community's, or a microsociety's, limited responsiveness to a student's personal goals.

In Part II, the researcher–contributors look at various corners of the academic world, corners which often strike students as too far-flung to share any commonalities (Flower, 1990; Haas, 1994). Most of the chapters in this section point to common strategies that may indeed serve students well as readers and writers in many of the new disciplinary terrains that they feel less than prepared for.

In Chapter 5, Braine presents the results of his analysis of the writing tasks in seventeen undergraduate courses in the natural sciences and engineering, some of the most popular fields for ESL students. Although Braine found the tasks to be quite different from those in most writing classes, the writing strategies called for in the experimental report genres so common in these scientific and technical fields are those that many ESL writing teachers already commonly teach — summarizing and paraphrasing. At the graduate level, however, when students are often assumed to have already progressed beyond simple knowledge display, they may need more than summarizing and paraphrasing skills to begin to enter into dialogue with experts in their fields. In Chapter 6, Belcher suggests that graduate students across the curriculum may well be persuaded of the advantages of critical thinking habits in their approach to the established knowledge of their fields if they are exposed to genres such as book reviews and article comments that conspicuously reveal some of the social dynamics of their disciplines. Belcher observes that the common linguistic and rhetorical strategies and even common evaluative criteria (e.g., regarding audience) that she has found in the review genres of numerous disciplines can function heuristically for students, encouraging both a critical mind-set and a critical voice.

In Chapter 7, Connor and Kramer consider the challenges that both ESL and NES (native English speaker) graduate students in business management face when they write in response to relatively long readings. The primary reading strategy that Connor and Kramer found the more successful ESL and NES business graduate students employing—rhetorically purposeful reading, or reading with the writing task in mind: "analysis, evaluation, and arguing an original point of view" (p. 171)—is one that may prove helpful to students in any class in which they must read to write.

If ESL students feel that their ability to control sentence-level grammar is challenged each time they enter a new subject area, Master's study, in Chapter 8, suggests that this feeling is understandable and, in fact, probable given the universe of new lexical items and discourse conventions that students are confronted with when they enter a new domain. Master focuses on an aspect of English grammar especially subject to lexical and discourse considerations—article usage. Despite their status as merely "local errors," problems with article use may be particularly irritating to non-ESL faculty, given the high frequency of articles in English and the faculty's likely lack of understanding of the difficulties that the article system poses for learners of English. Although Master looks at students in one field—applied linguistics—he proffers a consciousness-raising strategy that students might use in any discipline. Rather than extensive formal instruction in rules and practice with exercises, Master's students were provided with feedback on article errors in their own writing along with a brief discussion of those errors, and were also asked to keep a log of their errors. Not only does this approach, which appeared to make a marked difference in the students' control of articles, look promising for other troublesome grammatical structures, but it may also be a strategy that non-ESL faculty could be taught to facilitate.

Another source of strain on writers in institutional settings is actually a function of time—the obvious time constraints of placement exams and in-class midterms and finals, as well as qualifying and other field-specific exams, but also the less obvious de facto time limits on out-of-class writing, when students must juggle heavy course loads with family, job, and other commitments. One of the main findings of Tedick and Mathison's rhetorical analysis of holistically-scored timed student writings may help students face the pressure of writing within a limited window of time with more confidence. In Chapter 9, Tedick and Mathison discuss their observation that the essays in their study (composed by ESL graduate students in a variety of fields) that more often received the highest holistic scores were those that were also the best "framed," in other words, those providing context that established reader expectations and development that met those expectations. Tedick and Mathison also found that the topics of the most effectively framed essays were more often field-specific rather than general. For teachers and administrators involved in assessment of second language writing proficiency, one implication is that giving students an opportunity to write on topics for which they already possess an organized body of knowledge may be more likely to reveal their ability to "frame." For ESL students, especially at the graduate level, the good news is that knowledge they already have can enable their use of a very reader-friendly rhetorical strategy.

Perhaps the most intimidating and, for second language learners, the most perplexing of all the prospects a student may face when writing in academic settings is that of a plagiarism accusation. That source-use conventions vary from culture to culture has long been suspected by experienced ESL practitioners. In Chapter 10, Bloch and Chi look specifically at citation practices in two disciplinary and national cultures: natural and social science journals published in the People's Republic of China and in the United States. What Bloch and Chi have discovered may be reassuring to some students, especially those in the "hard" sciences: that Chinese citation practices in the natural sciences have already moved much closer to the Western model, while clear differences remain in Chinese and American English social science citations. Bloch and Chi suggest that when giving Chinese ESL students source-based writing tasks, we should assume neither total ignorance of source text use nor familiarity with our own preferred (most probably humanities-based) conventions. By reminding us that Chinese students come from a culture that has its own millennia-old rhetorical traditions, but an overlay of recent Western influence in certain domains as well, Bloch and Chi help us understand why what may strike us as good common academic sense (if not ethics), practices such as explicit acknowledgement of sources, explicit commentary on sources, or privileging of recently published sources, can look to many of our students more like the arbitrary, culture-bound, discipline-constrained preferences that they may in fact be.

All the chapters in "Pedagogy," Part III of our volume, describe and reflect on actual curricula and writing assignments, as well as classroom, tutorial, and computer lab activities developed by the authors. These pedagogical practices are not presented as models of what second language college-level writing instruction should be everywhere, but as examples of what some ESL specialists and students interested in academic literacy are attempting at their institutions in Canada, the United Kingdom, and the United States.

In Chapter 11, Johns introduces us to an adjunct program (ESL classes linked with subject-area courses) designed for at-risk students at San Diego State University. Johns' observation that undergraduates must cope with two rather different types of academic genres — as writers, classroom genres such as essay exams and summary/critiques; as readers, authentic genres, that is, texts produced by professionals — informs a major component in the San Diego State adjunct courses: the "Academic Task Portfolio." Through student collection and analysis of the students' own responses to reading and writing assignments, the adjunct program hopes to make what may be formidable new genres less so by encouraging the students to expect and be open to differing text styles and to feel free to question faculty about such matters as their organizational and citation convention preferences.

Dudley–Evans at the University of Birmingham and Benson and Heidish at Carnegie Mellon University have focused their efforts on designing materials and activities for ESL graduate students — writers who are confronted almost immediately in their degree programs with very cognitively demanding academic writing tasks. The ESL program whose development Dudley–Evans has overseen provides students with a dual global and local, product- and process-oriented perspective on academic discourse. "Common-core" instruction offers the insights of Dudley–Evans and other genre analysts on the rhetorical moves of common academic text types that are often less than rhetorically transparent to students. Field-specific classes, collaboratively taught by an ESL and a subject-area specialist, show students how a particular discipline adapts these common moves and other conventions to its own research writing goals. The actual writing process is nurtured in writing clubs — groups of peers who gather together to offer each other supportive criticism. Across the Atlantic at Carnegie Mellon, where most of the graduate programs are in the natural sciences and technology, Benson and Heidish have developed conferencing strategies for their ESL writing clinic that could easily be transferred to the writing classroom. The Benson and Heidish approach is grounded in a strong sense of the need to convince second language technical writers that technical writing is indeed a process, to bolster their confidence in themselves as technical experts and writers, and to make them explicitly aware of American pedagogy in order to increase their understanding of the communicative functions of strategies commonly used in American academic discourse.

Frodesen's course for ESL graduate students at the University of California, Los Angeles, as described in Chapter 14, was designed for the extremely heterogeneous class, that having students in disciplines as distinctly different as the arts and engineering and at any stage of their degree programs. Working with a student/teacher negotiated syllabus, Frodesen invited students to choose the writing assignments most relevant to their research interests, to take the initiative with prospective mentors by requesting information and advice from faculty on writing and publishing, and to seek peer feedback on their writing through the use of student-designed peer response forms. Frodesen's account of her course makes a persuasive case for the learning-centered approach as a means of promoting greater student self-direction and responsibility, and, as a result, engagement, than a more teacher-centered class would be likely to.

Jacoby, Leech, and Holten's EAP writing course, which, like Frodesen's, was developed at UCLA, had a more homogeneous group of students in mind – undergraduate science majors. While their course directs student attention to one genre – the experimental report – its pedagogical aim, not unlike those of other contributions in this volume, is to teach the process of experimental report writing. The Jacoby, Leech, and Holten course deconstructs the experimental report text by presenting it as a series of progressively more challenging stages in the report-writing process, starting with what many experienced science writers find the easiest aspect of their research to verbalize, their methodology, and moving toward the most rhetorically demanding, introduction and discussion. Impressed on the students at every stage of the process is the degree of decision-making that writers of science are responsible for – the intent obviously being not only to help the students become more rhetorically-conscious writers, aware of how they can influence readers, but also more rhetorically-conscious readers, aware of how scientific texts attempt to influence them.

The final chapter of the volume departs from all the others by emphasizing the cognitive more than the social aspects of writing. Arguably, however, Cumming's chief concern should be that of students and teachers, no matter what their particular academic milieu: how to make composing more than mere knowledge telling. Without knowledge transforming, writing, as Cumming argues, is just "a kind of translation from one medium to another," with no consolidation of old and new ideas or synthesis of the writer's own earlier thoughts and fresh insights (pp. 380–381). Cumming's overview of various pedagogical approaches to fostering knowledge-transforming composing strategies as well as his discussion of actual attempts to model the expertise of highly proficient adult ESL writers through the use of "thinking prompts" in computer, tutorial and classroom settings in Canada should be of interest to all of us who equate writing with thinking and see transformation, whether of personal knowledge in undergraduate writing or of both public and personal knowledge through graduate student writing, as the ultimate goal of academic discourse.

# REFERENCES

Ackerman, J. (1993). The promise of writing to learn. *Written Communication, 10,* 334–370.

Aisenberg, N., & Harrington, M. (1988). *Women of academe: Outsiders in the sacred grove.* Amherst: The University of Massachusetts Press.

Ballard, N., & Clanchy, J. (1991). Assessment by misconception: Cultural influences and intellectual traditions. In L. Hamp-Lyons (Ed.), *Assessing second-language writing in academic discourse* (pp. 19–35). Norwood, NJ: Ablex.

Bartholomae, D. (1985). Inventing the university. In M. Rose (Ed.), *When a writer can't write* (pp. 93–116). New York: Guilford.

Basham, C., Ray, R., & Whalley, E. (1993). Cross-cultural perspectives on task representation in reading-to-write. In J. Carson & I. Leki (Eds.), *Reading in the composition classroom: Second language perspectives* (pp. 299–314). Boston, MA: Heinle & Heinle.

Bazerman, C. (1988). *Shaping written knowledge: The genre and activity of the experimental article in science.* Madison: University of Wisconsin Press.

Bazerman, C. (1992). From cultural criticism to disciplinary participation: Living with powerful words. In A. Herrington & C. Moran (Eds.), *Writing, teaching, and learning in the disciplines* (pp. 61–68). New York: Modern Language Association.

Belcher, D. (1993). ESP and the human sciences. *CATESOL News, 25, 5,* 16.

Benesch, S. (1993). ESL, ideology, and the politics of pragmatism. *TESOL Quarterly, 27,* 705–717.

Berkenkotter, C., & Huckin, T. (1993). Rethinking genre from a sociocognitive perspective. *Written Communication, 10,* 475–509.

Bizzell, P. (1982). Cognition, convention, and certainty: What we need to know about writing. *PRE/TEXT, 3,* 213–243.

Bizzell, P. (1986). Foundationalism and anti-foundationalism in composition studies. *PRE/TEXT, 7,* 37–56.

Bizzell, P. (1987, July). Context, convention and canon: Some uses of the concept of "discourse community." Paper presented at the Penn State Conference on Rhetoric and Composition, State College, PA.

Bizzell, P. (1988). Arguing about literacy. *College English, 50,* 141–153.

Bridwell-Bowles, L. (1992). Discourse and diversity: Experimental writing within the academy. *College Composition and Communication, 43,* 349–368.

Brodkey, L. (1987). *Academic writing as social practice.* Philadelphia, PA: Temple University Press.

Canagarajah, A. S. (1993). Up the garden path: Second language writing approaches, local knowledge, and pluralism. Comment on Ann Raimes's "Out of the woods: Emerging traditions in the teaching of writing." *TESOL Quarterly, 27,* 301–306.

Chiseri-Strater, E. (1991). *Academic literacies: The public and private discourse of university students.* Portsmouth, NH: Heinemann.

Christie, F. (1987). Genres as choice. In I. Reid (Ed.), The place of genre in learning: Current debates (pp. 22–34). Deakin University (Australia): Centre for Studies in Literacy Education.

Cintron, R. (1993). Wearing a pith helmet at a sly angle: Or, can writing researchers do ethnography in a postmodern era? *Written Communication, 10,* 371–412.

Courage, R. (1993). The interaction of public and private literacies. *College Composition and Communication, 44,* 484–496.

Delpit, L. (1988). The silenced dialogue: Power and pedagogy in educating other people's children. *Harvard Educational Review, 58,* 280–298.

Dillon, G. (1991). *Contending rhetorics: Writing in academic disciplines*. Bloomington: Indiana University Press.

Elbow, P. (1991). Reflections on academic discourse: How it relates to freshmen and colleagues. *College English, 53,* 135–155.

Farr, M. (1993). Essayist literacy and other verbal performances. *Written Communication, 10,* 4–38.

Flower, L. (1990). Negotiating academic discourse. In L. Flower, V. Stein, J. Ackerman, M. Kantz, K. McCormick, & W. Peck (Eds.), *Reading-to-write: Exploring a cognitive and social process* (pp. 221–252). New York: Oxford University Press.

Frey, O. (1990). Beyond literary Darwinism: Women's voices and critical discourse. *College English, 52,* 507–526.

Geertz, C. (1988). *Works and lives: The anthropologist as author*. Stanford, CA: Stanford University Press.

Haas, C. (1994). Learning to read biology: One student's rhetorical development in college. *Written Communication, 11,* 43–84.

Halloran, M. (1984). The birth of molecular biology: An essay in the rhetorical criticism of scientific discourse. *Rhetoric Review, 3,* 370–383.

Harris, J. (1989). The idea of community in the study of writing. *College Composition and Communication, 40,* 11–22.

Herndl, C. (1993). Teaching discourse and reproducing culture: A critique of research and pedagogy in professional and non-academic writing. *College Composition and Communication, 44,* 349–363.

Horning, B. (1993). The controversial career of Evelyn Fox Keller. *Technology Review, 96,* 59–68.

Huckin, T. (1987, March). *Surprise value in scientific discourse*. Paper presented at the Conference on College Composition and Communication, Atlanta, GA.

Kaufer, D., & Geisler, C. (1989). Novelty in academic writing. *Written Communication, 6,* 286–311.

Keller, E. F. (1983). *A feeling for the organism*. New York: W. H. Freeman & Co.

Keller, E. F. (1985). *Reflections on gender and science*. New Haven, CT: Yale University Press.

Killingsworth, M. J. (1992). Discourse communities—Local and global. *Rhetoric Review, 11,* 110–122.

Kirsch, G. (1993). *Women writing the academy: Audience, authority, and transformation*. Carbondale: Sourthern Illinois University Press.

Kraemer, D. (1991). Abstracting the bodies of/in academic discourse. *Rhetoric Review, 10,* 52–69.

Land, R., & Whitley, C. (1989). Evaluating second language essays in regular composition classes: Toward a pluralistic U.S. rhetoric. In D. Johnson & D. Roen (Eds.), *Richness in writing: Empowering ESL students* (pp. 284–293). New York: Longman.

Lu, M. (1987). From silence to words: Writing as struggle. *College English, 49,* 437–447.

Lu, M. (1992). Conflict and struggle: The enemies or preconditions of basic writing? *College English, 54,* 887–913.

McCarthy, L. P. (1987). A stranger in strange lands: A college student writing across the curriculum. *Research in the Teaching of English, 21,* 233–265.

McGinley, W., & Tierney, R. (1989). Traversing the topical landscape. *Written Communication, 6,* 243–269.

Mangelsdorf, K., Roen, D., & Taylor, V. (1990). ESL students' use of audience. In G. Kirsch & D. Roen (Eds.), *A sense of audience in written communication. Written communication annual* (Vol. 5, pp. 231–247). Newbury Park, CA: Sage.

Matalene, C. (1985). Contrastive rhetoric: An American teacher in China. *College English, 47,* 789–808.

Miller, C. R. (1992). Kairos in the rhetoric of science. In S. Witte, N. Nakadake, & R. Cherry (Eds.), *A rhetoric of doing: Essays in honor of James Kinneavy* (pp. 310–327). Carbondale: Southern Illinois University Press.

Myers, G. (1992). Textbooks and the sociology of scientific knowledge. *English for Specific Purposes, 11,* 3–17.

Nelson, J., Megill, A., & McCloskey, D. (1987). *The rhetoric of the human sciences: Language and argument in scholarship and public affairs.* Madison: University of Wisconsin Press.

Noddings, N. (1984). Caring: A feminine approach to ethics and moral education. Berkeley: University of California Press.

Prior, P. (1991). Contextualizing writing and response in a graduate seminar. *Written Communication, 8,* 267–310.

Raimes, A. (1993). The author responds. *TESOL Quarterly, 27,* 306–310.

Richards, K., & Skelton, J. (1991). How critical can you get? In P. Adams, B. Heaton, & P. Howarth (Eds.), *Socio-cultural issues in English for academic purposes* (pp. 124–140). London: Modern English Publications and The British Council.

Ritchie, J. S. (1989). Beginning writers: Diverse voices and individual identity. *College Composition and Communication, 40,* 152–174.

Rodriguez, R. (1982). *Hunger of memory.* Boston: Godine.

Rouzer, J. (1993). Epistemological optimism and the teaching of ESL to Chinese. *The Ohio TESOL Newsletter, 17,* 8–9.

Scollon, R., & Scollon, S. B. (1981). *Narrative, literacy and face in interethnic communication.* Norwood, NJ: Ablex.

Shaughnessy, M. (1977). *Errors and expectations: A guide for the teacher of basic writing.* New York: Oxford University Press.

Shen, F. (1989). The classroom and the wider culture: Identity as a key to learning English composition. *College Composition and Communication, 40,* 459–466.

Spack, R. (1988a). The author responds to Johns. . . . *TESOL Quarterly, 22,* 707–708.

Spack, R. (1988b). Initiating ESL students into the academic discourse community: How far should we go? *TESOL Quarterly, 22,* 29–51.

Spellmeyer, K. (1993). *Common ground: Dialogue, understanding, and the teaching of composition.* Englewood Cliffs, NJ: Prentice Hall.

Steinitz, V., & Kanter, S. (1991). Becoming outspoken: Beyond connected education. *Women's Studies Quarterly, 19,* 138–153.

Swales, J. (1990). *Genre analysis: English in academic and research settings.* Cambridge, UK: Cambridge University Press.

Swales, J. (1993). Discourse community and the evaluation of written text. In J. Alatis (Ed.), *Georgetown University round table on languages and linguistics* (pp. 316–323). Washington, DC: Georgetown University Press.

Trimbur, J. (1994). Taking the social turn: Teaching writing post-process. *College Composition and Communication, 45,* 108–118.

Walvoord, B., & McCarthy, L. P. (1991). *Thinking and writing in college: A naturalistic study of students in four disciplines.* Urbana, IL: NCTE.

Watson, J. D., Crick, F. H. C. (1953, April 25). A structure for deoxyribose nucleic acid. *Nature, 171,* 737–738.

Williams, J., & Colomb, G. (1993). The case for explicit teaching: Why what you don't know won't help you. *Research in the Teaching of English, 27,* 252–264.

# PART I

# Issues

# CHAPTER 1

# When Practice Doesn't Make Perfect: The Case of a Graduate ESL Student

**Melanie L. Schneider**
*Beloit College*

**Naomi K. Fujishima**
*Kwansei Gakuin University*

The academic problems of foreign students in the United States are often viewed by higher education faculty and the public alike as language problems.[1] While proficiency in English greatly affects the academic success of foreign students, this study proposes that familiarity with the larger university culture and disciplinary subcultures, including accepted patterns of interaction, is also essential. Focusing on one graduate student who experienced only limited academic success, this study raises questions and suggests reasons for this student's difficulties, which occurred despite high levels of motivation and discipline. It also raises questions about policy decisions affecting foreign students, communication between academic programs, and curriculum needs for graduate ESL students.

## INTRODUCTION

Growing numbers of foreign students are attending U.S. colleges and universities: 419,585 foreign students, a record number, were enrolled in 1991–1992, approximately half in graduate programs and half in undergraduate programs (Watkins, 1992). Accompanying this increase in numbers has been a recent call for research on the kinds of academic tasks and

---

[1]Although foreign students include both native and nonnative English speakers from outside the United States, for the purposes of this article, *foreign students* will refer to nonnative speakers only.

cultural knowledge that contribute to the academic success of foreign students (Ballard, 1984; Johns, 1988; Reid, 1989; Spack, 1988). Underlying this research is the belief that achieving success at the postsecondary level involves more than control of the English language; it also involves familiarity with the writing conventions of the university culture and disciplinary subcultures in which the second language learner participates. In fact, Ballard (1984) argued that while a student is "inducted" into a particular discipline through lectures, discussions, readings, and laboratory work, "it is through *written* assignments that the success of his acculturation is most commonly judged" (p. 43; emphasis in original).

Although many foreign students succeed in their academic studies, as determined by the satisfactory completion of their degree programs, others do not. It is easy to dismiss the failures of this second group of learners as due to one or more of the following: lack of motivation, inadequate preparation, poor discipline, or a negative attitude. But what about the learners who appear to be promising students, who appear to be highly motivated, and well-disciplined but still are not succeeding. What factors may account for this lack of progress? What effects do such stalled efforts have on these learners and on their prospects for academic success?

This chapter provides an account of one foreign student's struggle to enter the academic discourse community at a graduate professional school in the United States. Although apparently strong in quantitative reasoning, this student, a native speaker of Chinese, experienced repeated difficulties in expressing himself adequately in spoken and written English. Through analyses of journal entries, classroom writing samples, and interviews with his ESL and content teachers, the learner's perspective and his teachers' perspectives on the above questions are described and compared. Four main factors are identified as possible explanations for this student's limited academic success: English language proficiency, sensitivity to socio-linguistic norms, motivation for learning, and learner strategies. In addition, other personal factors, such as obligation to family, are considered.

Several case studies of unsuccessful adult learners of English, focusing on affective and social variables, have suggested that the amount and the kind of interaction are at the heart of successful second language acquisition in adults (Schmidt, 1983). These studies include Shapira's study (1978) of Zoila, a 25-year-old Guatemalan Spanish speaker who experienced little improvement in her acquisition of English grammar during 18 months; Kessler and Idar's study (1979) of a Vietnamese mother and child, in which they found little change in the English language development of a Vietnamese mother as compared to her child over a 6-month period; and Cazden, Cancino, Rosansky, and Schumann's study (1975) of six adult learners, in which Alberto, a 33-year-old Costa Rican, clearly made the least progress as a second language learner. A common thread underlying all of these studies is the assumption, based on the acculturation model of second language acquisition (Schumann, 1978), "that if communicative needs were greater and psychological and social distance less, much greater control of the grammatical structures of the target language could have been acquired without formal instruction" (Schmidt, 1983, p. 139).

Schmidt's study (1983) of Wes, a 33-year-old native speaker of Japanese who emigrated to Hawaii, challenged this assumption. Wes, an artist, exhibited very low social and psychological distance from native speakers of English but still showed negligible progress in grammatical competence over a 3-year period. Schmidt interpreted these findings to mean that Wes was strongly motivated to communicate his ideas in English in social and business transactions, not to control the grammar. Schmidt's study of Wes thus provided a test case for Schumann's acculturation model of second language acquisition (SLA).[2]

Unlike these earlier case studies, which focused on spoken English, this study examines both the spoken and written development of an adult learner of English in an academic setting. It also does not focus on Schumann's acculturation model, but considers a related variable, type of motivation, as one way to partially account for sluggish SLA and subsequently, limited academic success.

## THE CASE OF A GRADUATE ESL STUDENT: ZHANG[3]

The subject of this study, Zhang, is a 30-year-old native speaker of Chinese from Taipei, Taiwan. He completed a B.S. degree in agricultural economics from Chinese Culture University in Taiwan in 1986. He spent the next two years completing his military service in the Taiwanese equivalent of the Marine Corps. Following his military service, Zhang worked for two years as a manager for a trading company in Taiwan. During Zhang's undergraduate years, his older brother was completing an M.A. in International Policy Studies at the Monterey Institute of International Studies (MIIS), a graduate professional school in Monterey, California. Following his brother's footsteps, Zhang applied to MIIS in early 1990 for admission to the

---

[2]In Schumann's (1978) acculturation model, social and affective variables combine into a single variable, acculturation, which is the major causal variable of second language acquisition. According to Schumann, the degree to which a learner acculturates to the target language culture determines the degree to which the individual acquires the second language.

[3]Zhang is a fictitious name.

program in International Public Administration, a 2-year M.A. program in public administration and international management.

In Taiwan, Zhang's English language instruction consisted of six years of study, two to four hours a week, in grades 7–12. Required of all Taiwanese secondary school students, these English classes emphasize the study of grammatical rules rather than oral communication and are often taught by a nonnative speaker of English. During his undergraduate years, Zhang's courses were entirely in Chinese, except for one course by an American who taught in English. Before applying to graduate schools in the United States, Zhang attended at least one course at a private language institute to increase his TOEFL score.

Zhang's brother completed an M.A. at the Monterey Institute (MIIS) in 1983 or 1984. He had entered the program with a Test of English as a Foreign Language (TOEFL) score slightly below the required 550 for graduate studies but with very strong quantitative skills. It was understood that during his first year of academic study, he would bring up his TOEFL score to 550, receiving extra tutoring in English if necessary.

With the precedent set by his brother, it was not surprising that Zhang was also admitted conditionally to MIIS for graduate studies in mid-March of 1990. With an initial TOEFL score of 480, Zhang was required to attend ESL classes full-time for eight weeks during the second half of the 1990 spring semester and for eight weeks during that summer. During the summer he also audited a course, Principles of Economics, related to his graduate program, International Public Administration.

After studying ESL intensively for 16 weeks with passing grades, Zhang was eager to begin graduate studies in the fall of 1990. In fact, he expressed the desire to take a heavier course load than normal in order to graduate early, in 1½ years instead of 2. Although he was cautioned against it, Zhang registered for 18 unites (12 is the minimum required for full-time study; courses vary in number of units from 2–4). That fall, Zhang took seven courses, three in English Studies and four, including one mini-course (1 unit), in his graduate program.[4] In spite of his hard work, Zhang's GPA at the end of the semester was 2.6, below the 3.0 minimum required for successful graduate study.

Aware of the stakes involved in improving his GPA, Zhang realized he would have to lighten his course load for the spring. Accordingly, in the spring of 1991, he registered for five courses, totaling 14 credits. Three were

---

[4]English Studies (ES) courses are offered for credit to students who are concurrently completing coursework in degree programs but who need additional work in English language skills. Grades in ES courses count towards the GPA. Most ES courses are designed for nonnative English speakers, although native speakers sometimes elect to take one course, Writing Workshop, which is evaluated pass/fail.

English Studies courses, including a Writing Workshop, and two were graduate courses. By the end of the spring semester, Zhang's GPA had increased to 2.8, an improvement but still short of the required 3.0.

After considerable discussion with his instructors in both his graduate program and in English Studies, the Academic Dean met with Zhang in late May to inform him that he would not be able to continue his graduate studies at MIIS. A few weeks later the Dean was asked what he thought Zhang's specific problems for his academic difficulties were. The Dean responded, "Language," in particular comprehending spoken and written English and writing. The Dean was convinced that Zhang would either struggle all the way or fail to make the grade if he were allowed to continue his graduate studies at MIIS. After a year and a half, the Dean felt Zhang's record was simply not promising enough. He recalled similar problems with Zhang's older brother, who had struggled successfully to complete his M.A. in spite of "language problems." The difference, according to the Dean, was that Zhang's brother was very strong in math while Zhang was not, as indicated by his grade in one course, Financial Accounting.

Of the four English Studies courses for which Zhang received grades in the 1990–1991 academic year, he received Cs in three: English Comprehension: Listening/Reading, Advanced Composition, and American Society and Culture. He also received a C in one major graduate course, Financial Accounting (4 units). His grades in five other graduate program courses that year were A−, B, A−, B, and B+. (Table 1.1 summarizes Zhang's academic record for 1990–1991.) The two courses in which he received A−

TABLE 1.1. Yang's Courses and Grades During the 1990–91 Academic Year

| Course | Number | Description | Units | Grade |
|--------|--------|-------------|-------|-------|
| **Fall Semester 1990** | | | GPA: | 2.63 |
| ES | 320 | Advanced Composition | 3 | C+ |
| ES | 325 | English Comprehension: Listening/Reading | 2 | C |
| ES | 330 | Writing Workshop | 2 | P |
| IM | 531A | Financial Accounting | 4 | C |
| IM | 561B | Managerial Economics (Micro) | 2 | A− |
| PA | 401 | Public Administration Issues | 4 | B |
| PA | 582 | Workshop: International Team Management Skills | 1 | A− |
| **Spring Semester 1991** | | | GPA: | 2.8 |
| ES | 310 | Advanced Oral Grammar/Nonnative Speakers | 2 | B |
| ES | 330 | Writing Workshop | 4 | P |
| ES | 380 | American Society & Culture | 2 | C |
| IM | 532A | Managerial Accounting | 3 | B |
| IM | 420 | Public Budgeting | 3 | B+ |

were both 1- or 2-unit courses, which contributed less to his overall GPA than the other graduate courses. Still, Zhang clearly performed better in his graduate program courses than the English Studies courses, at least as indicated by grades.

It is tempting to attribute Zhang's higher grades in his graduate program courses to differences in the evaluation criteria of faculty from different disciplines. Research has documented departmental differences in evaluation criteria and in tolerance for errors in student writing (Bridgeman & Carlson, 1983; Johns, 1991; Vann, Lorenz, & Meyer, 1991).

For example, Bridgeman and Carlson reported differences in a survey of undergraduate English faculty (UGE) and faculty from six other disciplines (graduate management, civil engineering, electrical engineering, psychology, chemistry, and computer science) in their ranking of 12 criteria for evaluating written work. They also found that the percentage of departments reporting the use of the same standards for evaluating native and nonnative English speakers was lowest for graduate management departments (55%), compared to 75% for UGE departments. Thus, not only do departments differ on evaluation criteria, but they may not apply their criteria equally to all students. As a further caution, Vann, Lorenz, and Meyer (1991) point out that faculty response to surveys on student writing does not always reflect their classroom behavior.

In Zhang's case, differences in evaluation criteria may have contributed to differences in the grades he received in his English Studies and graduate program classes. However, other factors, including actual differences in Zhang's academic performance must also be considered. Johns (1991) addresses the problem of differential performance in writing in her case study of an ESL writer.

Johns sought to understand why her subject, "Luc," a Vietnamese undergraduate student, performed better in one academic writing context than in another. Despite an A− average in his major, biochemistry, Luc had nonetheless failed the freshman-level writing competency test at his university four times. From weekly interviews over a semester, Johns learned that Luc's understanding of writing expectations and his ability to develop effective strategies to meet them in one context—his science courses—did not necessarily transfer to others, namely, the writing competency exam.

The present study also focuses on the characteristics of an individual writer, from his perspective as a graduate student as well as that of some his teachers. Zhang's struggle to improve his academic record and his eventual academic dismissal raise questions about his proficiency in English, his sociolinguistic competence and motivation for studying, and his strategies for learning. In the following section, each of these topics is discussed in turn.

## PROFILE OF A GRADUATE ESL WRITER

### English Language Proficiency

Zhang's TOEFL scores from December 1989 to May 1991 offer a starting point for evaluating his proficiency in English. Table 1.2 summarizes Zhang's TOEFL scores during this period.

The largest increase in Zhang's overall TOEFL score occurred between the December 1989 and September 1990 testing dates, an interval of nearly 10 months. There is no evidence of improvement in the two subsequent TOEFLs, administered in mid-December 1990 and early May 1991, approximately 4½ months apart. Although these two total TOEFL scores and subscores dropped slightly relative to the September TOEFL, the differences between the three sets of scores from September 1990 to May 1991 are not significant.[5] One pattern, however, is the consistently lower subscore for listening, a weakness that Zhang blamed for depressing his total TOEFL scores.

The relatively large gain in TOEFL score required to indicate a true increase in proficiency has not been ignored by researchers. In a study comparing the initial TOEFL scores of 376 foreign graduate students and their subsequent GPA after one semester of study, Light, Xu, and Mossop (1987) found that TOEFL scores did not correlate highly with GPA, their measure of academic success. Although TOEFL scores were not an effective predictor of GPA, Light, Xu, and Mossop found that the scores did correlate significantly with the number of credit hours students earned during the first semester of graduate work ($r = .19$, $p < .01$). In other words, the higher the TOEFL score, the more graduate credits students earned (range: 3–18 credits). With a September 1990 TOEFL score of .537, Zhang's decision to register for 18 credits that fall undoubtedly contributed to his compromised chances for academic success that term.

An important implication of the Light et al. study is that while language proficiency as measured by the TOEFL is an important variable, other variables, such as communicative skills, also contribute to the academic success of foreign students. This conclusion suggests a role for other forms of evaluation that assess how well a nonnative speaker of English actually functions in the classroom.

---

[5]According to the 1990–91 *Bulletin of Information for TOEFL and TWE*, "the standard error of measurement of the total score is approximately 14 scaled score points" (p. 22). This means that there is a 68% chance that an individual's true proficiency falls within a range of 14 points above or below the observed TOEFL score. To be 95% certain that an increase in TOEFL score reflects a true gain and not just random variation, an individual's score would have to increase by at least 23 points.

TABLE 1.2. Summary of TOEFL Scores

| Test Date | Total Score | Listening Comprehension | Structure and Written Expression | Vocabulary and Reading Comprehension |
|---|---|---|---|---|
| Dec. 1989[a] | 480 | — | — | — |
| Sept. 1990[a] | 537 | 51 | 56 | 54 |
| Dec. 1990 | 517 | 47 | 54 | 54 |
| May 1991 | 527 | 50 | 55 | 53 |

[a]Official TOEFL scores. Subscores were not available for the December 1989 TOEFL. The 1989 TOEFL was given in Taiwan; the others in the U.S. The December 1990 and May 1991 scores are unofficial, based on TOEFL exams given at the local institution (MIIS).

Zhang's performance on inhouse diagnostic measures of English proficiency at MIIS in the spring of 1990 correspond closely in level to his TOEFL scores. In a 15-minute interview designed to test for oral proficiency, Zhang received a score of 4 out of a possible 9. On a writing sample holistically evaluated from 1 to 6, Zhang received a 3. These scores placed Zhang firmly in the middle range of English proficiency, indicating the need for continued ESL instruction before beginning graduate studies.

An excerpt from a paper written for his fall 1990 Advanced Composition course provides additional evidence of his proficiency level in writing after 16 weeks of ESL instruction. The excerpt is taken from the first two paragraphs of the final draft, entitled "The Acid Rain and its Harmful Consequences."

> When the earth started its life, our planet has begun its plentifully changeable phases of biological evolution and environmental variation. And the earth has always been adjusted by its self-function when there were some natural variation, like flooding or earthquakes, and man is suitable to his living spaces as well. However, with industrialization human beings have created a lot of things threatened to our earth. At the same time, they also produce harmful stuff to our surrounding environment. Acid rain is one of obvious examples.

At the discourse level, as part of the introduction, Zhang has learned the technique of starting with a broad topic (here, the earth), and gradually narrowing it down to the focus of the paper, acid rain. He has also learned to use transitions to make connections between sentences (*however, at the same time*). But at the sentence level, numerous problems remain, for example, errors in verb tense, word choice, and subject–verb agreement. At this stage, Zhang clearly needs additional work in writing and editing before he can be expected to write acceptable research papers in his graduate courses.

## Sociolinguistic Competence and Motivation for Learning

Canale's notion of sociolinguistic competence (1983) serves as a point of reference for interpreting Zhang's interactions with teachers and classmates. In Canale's words, "Sociolinguistic competence . . . addresses the extent to which utterances are produced and understood *appropriately* in different sociolinguistic contexts depending on contextual factors such as status of participants, purposes of the interaction, and norms or conventions of interaction" (p. 7; emphasis in original). According to Canale, sociolinguistic competence is reflected in all four communication modes (speaking, listening, reading, writing) and contains two dimensions: appropriateness of meaning and appropriateness of form. Appropriateness of meaning refers to the degree that certain communicative functions (e.g., commanding, questioning, informing), attitudes (e.g., politeness and formality level), and ideas are considered acceptable in a particular situation. For example, in an American university classroom, students may be encouraged to ask the instructor questions, but it is normally considered rude to interrupt the instructor in order to ask a question or to make a comment. Appropriateness of form refers to how acceptably, in terms of grammatical form and style, a particular set of words expresses a communicative function. For example, the ESL student who is taught to use the imperative form "Please repeat" to request repetition of information will find it receives an awkward reception in a non-ESL classroom.

Excerpts from interviews with Zhang's teachers provide a partial picture of Zhang's sociolinguistic competence in one academic context, the classroom. In response to the question, "Do you have any possible explanation for Zhang's performance in your course or his difficulties in progressing in English?", one English Studies teacher, Molly Lewis Hulse, who taught the American Society and Culture class, responded as follows:

> Every so often you run across somebody like Zhang. It's so easy to say, "Well, this person has obvious psychological problems, or that person's got a poor educational background. . . ." [But] I don't have anything like that in particular for Zhang. I don't think he's particularly skilled in social graces; I don't think he's particularly attuned to social realities. For example, his speaking out in class at times. He couldn't read the, I don't want to call it censure, but the negative feelings in the class about him. He didn't seem to respond to that. He didn't have any sense of humor about his difficulties. So I see him as a person who's like a horse with blinders, and his blinders go all the way around. He's not real in tune with other people, and so he's not

picking up a lot of cues that [other] people, even though they may [be] at the same level of language . . . are picking up constantly.

The sometimes negative reactions of Zhang's classmates to his ideas were compounded by their difficulty in understanding him. As Hulse recounts,

> All of the students, of course, were nonnative speakers of English. Most of them were European though. And their English was quite good. So I think they resented the time that it took for Zhang to articulate something. And then what I would generally do would be summarize it and paraphrase it. So that I knew everyone would understand what his comment was. . . . Sometimes I'm not sure that I understood. . . . But I tried to take what he was giving us and make it into something that would benefit all of us.

Hulse's attempts at reformulating Zhang's comments into something intelligible not only reflect her respect for students' ideas, but also point to pronunciation and word-choice problems that hampered Zhang's communication with others

This difficulty in understanding Zhang's spoken English was shared by the Coordinator of English Studies at MIIS, Cherry Campbell, who was also his instructor in the course, English Comprehension: Listening and Reading. Campbell attributed Zhang's problems in oral communication mainly to pronunciation and grammar: "Even when he was trying to simplify down to phrases to clarify what he was getting at . . . we would sometimes have trouble. So pronunciation was the first problem. And grammar may have also been a problem, but it was mainly pronunciation."

But when prompted to speculate on possible explanations for Zhang's slow progress in English, Campbell first noted Zhang's general lack of interest in U.S. culture and people, as represented by the academic community at MIIS. As she reported:

> He's not really very integrated into the society here at the Institute, it seems to me, or into any given class' society. I mean, if you think of the classroom as its own little community or whatever. He talked a lot in my class, but during every break he was off by himself. . . . In fact, I always see him coming and going in his car and never really interacting at all with students on campus. So he's probably not getting the kind of general campus collegial community help that you can get that would improve your language learning or your understanding of the society if you're a nonnative speaker on a campus like this.

Hulse, the other English Studies teacher, also noted Zhang's lack of integrative motivation for studying in the United States (Gardner, 1985; Gardner & Lambert, 1972). In her words,

His idea of what he's doing here isn't necessarily related to his interest in American culture, Americans, English as a language. He's not the sort of person who's seeking satisfaction from .contact with this culture and the people in it. . . . For him, it's a very utilitarian, pragmatic attitude towards this school, his training, and the language. He's got somewhere to go. And he needs English, but he only needs English insofar as it gets him where he wants to go.

Both Campbell's and Hulse's comments imply that Zhang's English proficiency and, possibly, academic record, would have benefitted from more informal contact in English with others at MIIS and in the surrounding community. Hulse added, somewhat ruefully, that interest in and curiosity about another culture and its people is something that cannot be taught, only encouraged.

Despite the often assumed advantage of integrative motivation in acquiring another language, it does not appear to be a prerequisite for success. Research on the acquisition of English in a foreign context has shown that learners can be highly successful with stronger instrumental motivation, such as the goal of improving one's career prospects, than integrative motivation (Kachru, 1977; Lukmani, 1972). In a native English-speaking context like the United States, however, it is unclear whether or how much integrative motivation is necessary for success in an academic degree program.

Other researchers have been concerned that the concept of integrative motivation has been defined too broadly. For example, Graham (1984) claims that there is a distinction between integrative and *assimilative* motivation. As reported by Brown (1987), integrative motivation refers to the desire of language learners to learn another language "in order to communicate with, or find out about, members of the second language culture" (p. 117) without necessarily having direct contact with the second language group. In contrast, assimilative motivation has as its goal "the drive to become an indistinguishable member of a speech community," usually after extended contact with the target culture (p. 117). Thus, individuals can be integratively motivated without necessarily losing their identity in the second language culture. A now common example of this more limited sense of integrative motivation occurs within the international community of scientists, which regularly uses English to communicate in journals and at professional meetings worldwide.

Gardner (1985) maintains that the related concepts of motivation for language learning and orientation to language learning have been confused. Orientation refers to one's reasons for learning a second language, which Gardner and others have grouped into the general categories instrumental and integrative. Motivation describes a composite of three characteristics, "attitudes towards learning the language, desire to learn the language and motivational intensity" (p. 54), which may or may not be related to a particular orientation. Integratively oriented learners are typically interested in forming closer links with the second language community. Gardner (1985) notes, however, that while integratively oriented learners may exhibit stronger motivation for language learning than learners with other orientations, "this association isn't guaranteed a priori" (p. 54). That is, individuals may have strong integrative orientations toward learning the second language but may not be highly motivated to do so.

In sum, notions of integrative and instrumental motivation have changed substantially since they were first proposed more than 20 years ago, and with them, easy predictions about the importance of one type of motivation over another. Although there is no conclusive evidence that integrative motivation is necessary for successful language learning in a second language culture, Gardner's extensive review of studies (1985, Ch. 4) indicates a strong relation between integrative motivation and achievement in language learning. Certainly, second language learners inevitably miss out on multiple opportunities for learning if exposure to and use of the target language is limited to the classroom.

In fact, Naomi Fujishima attributed a large part of Zhang's difficulties in his academic program to his limited exposure to English outside of school. Her contact with Zhang as his Writing Workshop instructor in the fall of 1990 and as a private ESL tutor in the early summer of 1991 enabled her to get a sense of Zhang's living situation outside of school. As she reported:

> He's got a whole extended family living with him. And they don't speak a word of English, so he's speaking all Chinese at home, and I don't know about at school. The only exposure he has to English is in the lectures and Writing Workshop and his classes.

Thus, the picture we have of Zhang is that of a highly motivated and disciplined young man intent on learning English in order to complete his graduate program. However, after one semester of graduate study, English continued to be a stumbling block for Zhang, and he was forced to re-evaluate both his approach to studying and his timetable for completing his studies.

## Learning Strategies

Since the mid-1970s, interest in learning strategies has mushroomed. Beginning with Rubin's work (1975) describing the learning strategies of good language learners, other researchers, teachers, and teacher-educators have joined forces to study and promote language learning strategies so that second and foreign language learners can improve and better control their own learning. Rigney (1978) has defined learning strategies in a general way as operations used by learners to aid "the acquisition, retention, and retrieval of information" (p. 170). Focusing on language learners, Scarcella and Oxford (1992) defined learning strategies as "specific actions, behaviors, steps, or techniques—such as seeking out conversation partners, or giving oneself encouragement to tackle a difficult language task—used by students to enhance their own learning" (p. 63).

Recently, Oxford (1990) outlined a framework for describing learning strategies that consists of six categories:

1. *Memory strategies*—for example, grouping, imagery, rhyming, structured reviewing
2. *Cognitive strategies*—for example, analyzing, summarizing, and general practicing
3. *Compensation strategies*—for example, guessing meanings from context, using synonyms or gestures when the precise expression is not known
4. *Metacognitive strategies*—for example, paying attention, planning for language tasks, self-evaluating one's progress
5. *Affective strategies*—for example, anxiety reduction, self-encouragement, self-reward
6. *Social strategies*—for example, asking questions, cooperating with native speakers of the language, becoming culturally aware.

Although these categories sometimes overlap (for example, applying the affective strategy, self-reward, would appear to require self-evaluation, a metacognitive strategy), they identify general distinctions between learning strategies.[6] They will be referred to in the following discussion on Zhang's reported use of learning strategies.

Molly Hulse refers to Zhang's limited strategies as one possible explanation for his low performance in her course. At first, she was impressed with Zhang as "a very dutiful student," "conscientious," and prompt in completing assignments. But later, she realized the shortcomings of simply playing the role of model student. As she says, "That's such a limited strategy. That's only going to get him part of the way. It's this adding on of new and unfamiliar behaviors that I don't see him doing." Interestingly, recent research by Ehrman and Oxford (1989) has shown that when left on

---

[6]In a more recent article, Oxford and Cohen (1992) have revised their framework for describing learning strategies, in response to several conceptual and classificatory problems. They have expanded the number of strategies to seven: forming concepts, testing hypotheses, personalizing, remembering new material, managing your learning, controlling your emotions, and overcoming limitations.

their own, students tend to fall back on learning strategies that mirror their basic learning style. For Zhang, conforming to his expectations of a good student – being punctual, attentive in class, and conscientious in completing assignments – reinforced his image of himself as a successful student. Unfortunately, while these behaviors may contribute to academic success, they do not guarantee it.

After interviewing Hulse, Schneider was curious to learn how much Zhang had been exposed to learning strategies in other English Studies classes. In fact, the term *strategy* comes up repeatedly in Campbell's description of her English Comprehension class, which Zhang took in the fall of 1990. Describing the course content, she refers to "strategies for notetaking in lectures and from reading passages" and "strategies for organizing notes and adding to them" among the many skill- and strategy-building activities in the course.

During the interview with Campbell, Schneider related how she had sat down with Zhang at one of their Writing Workshop sessions in the spring of 1991 to determine how he approached reading a chapter from one of his graduate course textbooks. After learning how long it generally took him to read a chapter, she shared a few tips on how she read textbooks or journal articles. This prompted Campbell to add,

> You know, something else that occurs to me . . . it could be that he doesn't have a strong enough control of the strategies he's being advised about. For example, after you sat with him on the reading and showed him how to annotate and mark margins, little notes, and stuff, do you think he was doing that later?. . . . It was the type of thing we were working on in the class all [fall 1990] semester. And I wonder if he forgets about these strategies, if he doesn't really consistently work them into his own study skills.

Campbell's explanation is reminiscent of Anderson's (1983, 1985) three stages of skill acquisition in adults: cognitive, associative, and autonomous. In the cognitive stage, learners are taught how to complete a task or attempt to figure it out on their own. Performance is quite slow as learners consciously work through the steps required of the task, sometimes verbally prompting themselves along the way. In the second or associative stage, learners begin to detect errors in the original representation of their knowledge and gradually correct them as the connections between the components of the new skill become stronger. Performance begins to speed up as the required steps become internalized. In the third or autonomous stage performance of the skill becomes almost automatic with little demand on working memory or consciousness. Most important for understanding the process of SLA is the recognition that skilled performance develops gradually.

Both Hulse and Campbell reported that Zhang's performance in their courses was the lowest in the class. From Campbell, it was evident that Zhang did not lack opportunities to acquire new strategies, for he was exposed to multiple strategies and skills involved with listening and reading academic English. He also referred to them in his class journal, in which students reflected on the kinds of strategies they used to comprehend reading, lecture, and discussion material in their classes. But his poor class performance did not indicate any sophisticated use of strategies. From this description, it may be that Zhang was mired in the first stage of Anderson's skill acquisition scheme, the cognitive stage.

Zhang also made a few references to learning strategies in his journal for his Spring 1991 Writing Workshop with Schneider. Many workshop sessions focused on sentence-level grammar and word-choice problems in his papers for other courses. The journal, however, was intended to encourage Zhang to reflect more broadly on his other classes and to work on his fluency in writing.

What Schneider discovered was a student faced with seemingly insurmountable problems as he struggled to complete lengthy research papers for his International Public Administration courses. Again and again the problems of narrowing a topic for research and finding an organizing principle for his papers came up. In his March 22, 1991 entry, Zhang mentioned talking to other students about his research, the first time Schneider was aware of his using a cooperative social strategy (Oxford, 1990). (References to strategies are in bold.) **"Sometimes, I discussed with my friends or my classmate about my research.** I think it is better than I do myself, but it still can't give a good solution totally." (Spelling errors have been corrected; otherwise, Zhang's journal entries are reproduced verbatim.)

But the problems of finding an adequate research topic and organizing his ideas continued to plague him, and Zhang searched for other solutions. Reflecting on his past academic writing experiences in the same entry, Zhang noted:

> Although I had done some research papers in my native language, it seems there are many different ways to do. And academic ideas, culture, and attitudes are different. Additionally, the writing skills have a lot of differences. So I should change some attitudes to do my writing.

This excerpt reveals Zhang's awareness of different writing conventions, styles, and formats in academic writing in Chinese and English. Zhang's recognition of these differences is an important first step in modifying his writing to more closely resemble academic standards in the U.S. But at the time, in the middle of the spring 1991 semester, Zhang seemed unable to bridge the gap.

In his next journal entry, dated 4/10/91, Zhang identified three problem areas in his writing and proposed an affective strategy to help overcome them. In his words,

> How can I start to writing properly? How can I organize the content for my research? And how can I write a good essay to let reader understand? I think these three hows always surround me when I want to write an essay or a paper. **Probably, to calm down myself is very important factor when I want to write something.**

Zhang's journal entries continued to reveal the difficulties he faced in completing the reading and writing assignments for his graduate course-work. In his next entry, dated 4/16/91, he described an earlier conversation with his Public Budgeting professor, who had pointed out to him that his research for the course project was too broad in scope. Realizing this, Zhang planned to reorganize his approach to doing the research, a metacognitive strategy, but not without some frustration.

> I discovered I had done wrong ways for my researches because I was used to read a lot articles and input my ideas, but I caught [?] a so widely that I could not focus on a field to research deeply. **I think it is not only to narrow my researches, but also to narrow my ideas and my writing content. And depending on my information, I should have an outline and method to organize my idea and writing content.** . . . In short, I was used to think my writing should arrive a certain level, but why I cannot improve my academic writing skills?

Reading and discussing this entry with Zhang, Schneider found herself vacillating between admiration for his ability to pinpoint his writing problems and frustration at his difficulties in writing intelligibly for his different academic audiences. Soon after the Spring 1991 semester ended, she consulted with his professor for the Public Budgeting course, Gil Gunderson, to get his impressions on Zhang.

Gunderson was both knowledgeable and sympathetic to Zhang's case. During the semester, he said that some of Zhang's questions went right to the heart of the course. However, he felt that Zhang's oral and written English held him back from achieving his full potential. Gunderson gave Zhang a B on his public budgeting paper, stating that he had "overly covered the material" and "strayed from the analytical framework," but that in spite of these problems, it was "basically a good effort." As part of the project, students presented oral summaries to the class. Gunderson reported that Zhang was "very well-prepared, even over-prepared" for his presentation, but that it "got bogged down in detail." In the question-and-answer period following the presentation, Gunderson noted that in response to his classmates' questions, Zhang tended to repeat the same answer rather than try to clarify his original point. This happened often enough that Gunderson wondered if Zhang had a hearing problem. However, this possibility was never pursued.

From oral interviews with his teachers and Zhang's journal entries, it is clear that Zhang relied on behavioral strategies to complete his assignments: behave like a model student, act as if you understand what is going on in class, participate in class regularly, plan carefully before writing, and allow time to rewrite. However, when faced with problems such as negative feedback on his performance, Zhang seemed unable to regroup or show flexibility in his approach to completing a task. His response to obstacles was usually a dogged determination to "work harder." Yet underneath, he felt anxious when faced with the challenging tasks of writing an extended paper, understanding lengthy readings, or writing an essay exam. Without the resources to modify his approach to studying and writing academic discourse, he experienced only limited success in his graduate program.

## CONCLUSIONS AND IMPLICATIONS

Zhang's case is particularly frustrating for those who, consciously or unconsciously, accept the work ethic as a model for academic success. Unfortunately, in his case, practice did not make perfect. As a seemingly able and highly motivated student, Zhang gave early indication that he would ultimately succeed in graduate school. In his graduate courses (although not always his English Studies courses), Zhang demonstrated again and again his willingness to rework his papers and spend extra time researching materials. But he didn't feel confident enough to write extended papers on his own "without writing workshop teacher's direction."

There are no easy answers to explain Zhang's limited academic progress and his ultimate failure to complete his graduate program at MIIS. Looking back on his writing samples, journal entries, interviews with his teachers, and our personal reflections, a few generalizations emerge. First, Zhang's difficulties in his academic program appear to be attributable in part to his proficiency in English, particularly his problems in expressing himself comprehensibly in speech and writing. Second, Zhang's low interest in U.S. culture and his lack of participation in campus life eliminated many opportunities for him to learn from peers outside of class, for example, to refine his English and to better understand his course assignments and graduate school life in general. Third, while some students with similar or lower TOEFL scores are able to circumvent and eventually overcome their weaknesses in other ways, perhaps by using compensatory strategies (Oxford, 1990), Zhang was not.

Other factors may also underlie Zhang's stalled progress. It may be that Zhang's performance was prematurely evaluated. As research by Collier (1987) shows, developing the needed skills and content knowledge to perform at grade-level norms requires many years of study. Additionally, it is possible that Zhang invested substantially more time in his graduate courses, perceiving them to be more important than his English Studies courses, even though he knew that all courses contributed to his GPA. Fujishima also pointed out that Zhang's sense of obligation to his family may have competed with his studies. Living with family members and having a brother who owned a restaurant nearby undoubtedly diverted his attention at times. Finally, as Gunderson suggested, Zhang's progress may have been hindered by an undetected hearing problem, due to his exposure to cannon and other artillery fire during his military service. Such a problem would partially explain his difficulties in listening comprehension.

As with any case study, it is inappropriate to generalize any findings to a larger population, in this case, foreign students experiencing difficulties in their academic programs.[7] What general conclusions this study offers lie in the questions it raises and the implications they have for policy decisions affecting foreign students, communication between academic programs, and course development.

One basic policy that affects foreign students from the start is admissions. If a minimum TOEFL score is required for admission to graduate school, how rigid should that standard be? In addition to recommendation letters and school transcripts, what alternative criteria provide valid indicators of academic success? Once a student is in the system, that is, admitted to an academic program, what responsibilities does the local institution have to assure the student's success?

This last question points to an often missing link in the foreign student equation: communication between ESL programs and the academic programs that their students aspire to or enroll in. From the interview with Gil Gunderson, one of Zhang's graduate course instructors, Fujishima and Schneider were surprised to learn that Gunderson had been unaware of how tenuous Zhang's graduate status was. In his fall 1990 Public Administration Issues course, Gunderson characterized Zhang as "by far the one [foreign student] that had the most difficulty in English." Zhang received a B in that course, which Gunderson acknowledged as generous, but close to what he deserved. That same semester, Zhang received three C's, two in English Studies courses and one in Financial Accounting. Communication that fall between Zhang's English Studies instructors and graduate program instruc-

---

[7]But as Donmoyer (1990) pointed out, single-case studies may be more applicable in applied fields such as education, counseling, and social work, in which individuals and not just sample groups are the focus.

tors could have provided insights into whether Zhang's problems were course-specific or more global, in which case a coordinated effort across programs might have helped Zhang improve his record.

Unfortunately, in most graduate schools, lack of time and lack of established links between academic departments and programs discourage such cross-program communication. As higher level ESL courses are created to meet the specialized needs of graduate students, establishing contacts among faculty in graduate programs becomes critical. These exchanges are useful not only for solving individual crises but also for course development purposes.

It appears, then, that ESL instructors, administrators, and course developers have a responsibility to resist the isolationist tendencies of some academic departments in higher education. By reaching out to members of other departments and programs, they can also learn about the discourse communities their ESL students will soon enter and obtain examples of authentic assignments to use in designing advanced-level ESL courses. Thus, serving the needs of graduate ESL students means more than providing language instruction. It also means developing ties and specialized courses with faculty in these students' future academic programs so that at advanced levels, ESL courses become a springboard for continued academic success.

## REFERENCES

Anderson, J. R. (1983). *The architecture of cognition.* Cambridge, MA: Harvard University Press.

Anderson, J. R. (1985). *Cognitive psychology and its implications* (2nd ed.). New York: Freeman.

Ballard, B. (1984). Improving student writing: An integrated approach to cultural adjustment. In R. Williams, J. Swales, & J. Kirkman (Eds.), *Common ground: Shared interests in ESP and communications studies* (pp. 43–52). Oxford, UK: Pergamon Press.

Bridgeman, B., & Carlson, S. (1983). *Survey of academic writing tasks required of graduate and undergraduate students* (Rep. No. 15). Princeton, NJ: Educational Testing Service.

Brown, H. D. (1987). *Principles of language learning and teaching* (2nd ed.). Englewood Cliffs, NJ: Prentice-Hall.

Canale, M. (1983). From communicative competence to language pedagogy. In J. Richards & R. Schmidt (Eds.), *Language and communication* (pp. 2–25). London: Longman.

Cazden, C., Cancino, H., Rosansky, E., & Schumann, J. (1975). *Second language acquisition sequences in children, adolescents, and adults* (Final report). Washington, DC: U. S. Department of Health, Education, and Welfare.

Collier, V. P. (1987). Age and rate of acquisition of second language for academic purposes. *TESOL Quarterly, 21*, 617–641.

Donmoyer, R. (1990). Generalizability and the single-case study. In E. W. Eisner & A. Peshkin (Eds.), *Qualitative inquiry in education: The continuing debate* (pp. 175–200). New York: Teachers College Press.

Ehrman, M. E., & Oxford, R. L. (1989). Effects of sex differences, career choice, and psychological type on adults' language learning strategies. *Modern Language Journal, 73,* 1-13.

Gardner, R. C. (1985). *Social psychology and second language learning: The role of attitudes and motivation.* London: Edward Arnold.

Gardner, R. C., & Lambert, W. E. (1972). *Attitudes and motivation in second language learning.* Rowley, MA: Newbury House.

Graham, C. R. (1984, March). *Beyond integrative motivation: The development and influence of assimilative motivation.* Paper presented at the 18th TESOL Convention, Houston, TX.

Johns, A. (1988). The discourse communities dilemma: Identifying transferable skills for the academic milieu. *English for Specific Purposes, 7,* 55-59.

Johns, A. (1991). Interpreting an English competency examination. *Written Communication, 8,* 379-401.

Kachru, B. (1977, July). New Englishes and old models. *English Language Forum.*

Kessler, C., & Idar, I. (1979). Acquisition of English by a Vietnamese mother and child. *Working Papers on Bilingualism, 18,* 65-80.

Light, R. L., Xu, M., & Mossop, J. (1987). English proficiency and academic performance of international students. *TESOL Quarterly, 21,* 251-261.

Lukmani, Y. (1972). Motivation to learn and language proficiency. *Language Learning, 22,* 261-274.

Oxford, R. (1990). *Language learning strategies: What every teacher should know.* New York: Newbury House/Harper & Row.

Oxford, R., & Cohen, A. D. (1992). Language learning strategies: Crucial issues of concept and classification. *Applied Language Learning, 3* (1-2), 1-35.

Reid, J. (1989). English as a second language composition in higher education: The expectations of the academic audience. In D. M. Johnson & D. H. Roen (Eds.), *Richness in writing: Empowering ESL students* (pp. 220-234). New York: Longman.

Rigney, J. W. (1978). Learning strategies: A theoretical perspective. In H. F. O'Neill, Jr. (Ed.), *Learning strategies* (pp. 165-205). New York: Academic Press.

Rubin, J. (1975). What the 'good language learner' can teach us. *TESOL Quarterly, 9,* 41-51.

Scarcella, R. C., & Oxford, R. L. (1992). *The tapestry of language learning: The individual in the communicative classroom.* Boston, MA: Heinle & Heinle.

Schmidt, R. (1983). Interaction, acculturation, and the acquisition of communicative competence: A case study of an adult. In N. Wolfson & E. Judd (Eds.), *Sociolinguistics and language acquisition* (pp. 137-174). Rowley, MA: Newbury House.

Schumann, J. (1978). *The pidginization process: A model for second language acquisition.* Rowley, MA: Newbury House.

Shapira, R. G. (1978). The nonlearning of English: Case study of an adult. In E. Hatch (Ed.), *Second language acquisition: A book of readings* (pp. 246-255). Rowley, MA: Newbury House.

Spack, R. (1988). Initiating ESL students into the academic discourse community: How far should we go? *TESOL Quarterly, 22,* 29-51.

Vann, R. J., Lorenz, F. O., & Meyer, D. M. (1991). Error gravity: Faculty response to errors in the written discourse of nonnative speakers of English. In L. Hamp-Lyons (Ed.), *Assessing second language writing in academic contexts* (pp. 181-195). Norwood, NJ: Ablex.

Watkins, B. T. (1992, November 25). Foreign enrollment at U.S. colleges and universities totalled 419,585 in 1991-92, an all-time high. *Chronicle of Higher Education,* pp. A28-A29.

# CHAPTER 2

# Good Writing:
# I Know It When I See It

**Ilona Leki**
*University of Tennessee*

This study examined the criteria used by a group of ESL students, writing teachers, and content area teachers to rank order four essays written by ESL students. Twenty college-level ESL students were asked to rank the essays three times: first, according to the students' preferences; second, according to what the students' thought might be the preferences of their English teachers; and third, according to how the students thought their content area teachers might rank the essays. A total of 29 ESL writing, non-ESL writing, and content area teachers were then asked to rank the same essays. All participants were interviewed on their rankings. The results showed that ESL students were not particularly skilled at predicting the rankings given by the teachers, that the faculty members were not very consistent among themselves, that criteria for rank ordering the essays varied fairly widely, and that even with the same stated criteria, faculty differed in their identification of those criteria in specific essays.

## INTRODUCTION

When we as educators rely on writing assessments as part of the admissions or the graduation process in institutions of higher education, we tacitly assume, as do our institutions, that we have defined good writing and that we can, with confidence, recognize it. Assessments of these kinds invoke a culturally defined and socially transmitted belief in absolute standards of excellence. When we teach freshman writing courses, implicit in the enterprise is the notion that we know what good writing is and that we can teach it to our students within the confines of a non-discipline-specific writing course. We communicate those same assumptions to our students, who expect to learn to write well by taking our courses. This expectation may be especially strong for ESL students since they are likely to have had fewer and less varied occasions to write in English than their native English-speaking (NES) counterparts and therefore are more likely to take our word that what we teach them in our writing classes is how to write well. In these official contexts, writing well becomes almost monolithic, an absolute category of performance apparently readily recognizable to the initiated, in this case, to the members of the academic discourse community. Good writing: I know it when I see it.

Yet as writing instructors we also know that the concept of good writing is context bound, that what is good writing in one instance is not as successful for all circumstances, that different contexts impose different, even contradictory constraints on writers. It is for this reason that Diederich's (1974) often-cited study yielded the results it did. Diederich asked 53 readers to comment on 300 essays and to rank the texts on a scale of 1 to 9. His readers were drawn from many walks of life: lawyers, teachers, artists. Every text he used received every ranking between 1 and 9; 94% of the essays received more than 7 different scores and none received less than 5 different grades. In other words, there was very little consistency among the raters, no universally agreed upon objective standards for rating these texts. Such results are not completely surprising since, given that they had different professions, these readers were certainly reading with different purposes in mind. They constituted several quite different discourse communities, each with its own standards and expectations.

What of our academic discourse community? That we share standards and expectations of "good writing" is implicit in our teaching and assessment of writing. But the problem with these standards and expectations is that we cannot be certain if, or to what degree, our assumptions are shared by other constituents of our community. Investigations such as McCarthy's (1987) case study of a native English-speaking student and Johns's (1991) study of an ESL student in fact imply a wide disjuncture between writing expectations within a particular discipline (where, for example, Johns's student Luc was considered a successful writer) and expectations of a university-wide writing competency exam, which Luc repeatedly failed. Bridgeman and Carlson (1983) and Hamp-Lyons (1990) document differences between text evaluation criteria used by English department faculty and faculty from other disciplines. Conklin (1982) cites students in her study as reporting that writing for English classes is different from writing for any other course.

The study reported in this chapter attempts to extend the findings cited above through text-based, open-ended interviews of ESL students, ESL writing instructors, writing instructors of native English speaking students, and faculty members from other content areas across the disciplines. The following general questions guided the investigation: How much do our students know about our assumptions about good writing? What assumptions do we share across disciplines about "good writing"? In particular, what kinds of criteria do writing teachers (native speaker and ESL teachers) and our content area colleagues share?

## METHODS

In order to collect information on one academic community's assumptions about student writing, I asked the participants in this study to read, rank order, and then talk about their reactions to four ESL student essays. I hoped that by rank ordering and explaining their rankings of these essays, the faculty and students would articulate their expectations for good writing and that categories of good writing qualities would emerge. In other words, rather than focusing on qualities arguably present in the texts, this study focused on the readers and their criteria for excellence. (See Witte & Faigley, 1981, for a discussion of native speaker research on textual qualities and overall evaluations; Mallonèe & Breihan, 1985, and Schwartz, 1984, for faculty responses to student writing.)

Twenty ESL university students from ESL freshman English courses volunteered for the study. (Geographical areas represented: Latin America, 3; the Middle East, 3; East Asia, 6; Southeast Asia, 4; West Africa, 1; Indian subcontinent, 2; Europe, 1.) The faculty group consisted of 8 ESL writing teachers, 7 teachers of writing for native speakers, and 14 content area teachers from a variety of disciplines: agriculture, architecture, business, biological sciences, engineering, humanities, physical sciences, and social sciences. This group was chosen because each of these teachers had either expressed a particular interest in student writing or had numbers of nonnative speakers in their classes.

The essays, of approximately 400–500 words each, were selected from among essays written by ESL students as part of their course work in ESL freshman composition classes and had all received good evaluations there. Since the intention of this study was to elicit general criteria for evaluating writing, no effort was made to control for essay content. The authors were two males and two females representing four different countries of origin (Sweden, Lebanon, Singapore, and Venezuela). Essay 1 was about the pros and cons of nuclear power; Essay 2 was on the differences between the United States and Sweden in their ideas on welfare programs; Essay 3 was on dreams and dream interpretation; and Essay 4 was about how Muslim women were resisting traditional notions about how they should behave.

Since several published studies already discuss faculty reaction to error in ESL student writing, and since I hoped to get reactions focused on more macro features of the texts, all obvious errors in spelling, punctuation, word choice, and grammar were corrected, but otherwise the writing was left intact to permit the flavor of the original to show through as much as possible. (See Vann, Meyer, & Lorenz, 1984, for faculty perception of error gravity; Santos, 1988, for reaction to content as well as to errors; Lee, 1977, and Johns, 1981, for faculty expectations for student language skills; and Eskey, 1983, for a discussion of the importance of grammatical accuracy.)

Each of the 20 students was asked to take the four essays home, read them at their leisure, and rank them three separate times. The first ranking would reflect their own preferences. For the second ranking, they were asked to predict how their English teachers would rank the same four essays. In the third ranking they were asked to think of a particular content area teacher they had at that time and to predict how that teacher would rank the essays. The students were then interviewed on the reasons for their rankings.

Each of the 29 teachers was simply asked to rank order these essays according to the criteria they might apply in looking for good student writing. They too were then interviewed.

While the actual rankings of the four essays were interesting, the primary intention of this study was to uncover some general categories of criteria which students assumed teachers would use to evaluate writing and criteria teachers actually describe themselves as using. The comments of these groups of people raise important issues about evaluating writing and about assumptions members of the academic community hold and have transmitted to ESL students about excellence in writing.

## RESULTS: STUDENTS' EVALUATIONS

One of the questions guiding this study was intended to explore students' ability to predict how their teachers would rank writing and why. The results showed little evidence that students are in fact able to predict their English and content area teachers' rankings. Of the 20 students in the study, 12 predicted that English teachers would rank Essay 2 on Sweden and the United States as the best essay, while only 4 of 15 English teachers selected that one as the best. On the other hand, 8 of 15 English teachers selected Essay 4 on Muslim women as the best one, while only 3 of 20 students were able to predict that outcome. As for the worst essay, student predictions were almost evenly spread among Essays 1, 3, and 4, whereas 7 of 15 English teachers considered Essay 1 on nuclear power the weakest.

TABLE 2.1. Student Prediction of Rankings by English Teachers

|  | Best | Second Best | Third Best | Worst |
|---|---|---|---|---|
| Essay 1 | 0 | 9 | 4 | 7 |
| Essay 2 | 12 | 2 | 5 | 1 |
| Essay 3 | 5 | 3 | 7 | 5 |
| Essay 4 | 3 | 6 | 4 | 7 |
| $N = 20$ | | | | |

TABLE 2.2. Rankings by ESL Teachers

|  | Best | Second Best | Third Best | Worst |
|---|---|---|---|---|
| Essay 1 | 2 | 1 | 3 | 2 |
| Essay 2 | 2 | 5 | 0 | 1 |
| Essay 3 | 1 | 0 | 3 | 4 |
| Essay 4 | 3 | 2 | 2 | 1 |
| $N = 8$ | | | | |

TABLE 2.3. Rankings by Teachers of Composition to Native Speakers

|  | Best | Second Best | Third Best | Worst |
|---|---|---|---|---|
| Essay 1 | 0 | 1 | 1 | 5 |
| Essay 2 | 2 | 3 | 1 | 1 |
| Essay 3 | 0 | 1 | 5 | 1 |
| Essay 4 | 5 | 2 | 0 | 0 |
| $N = 7$ | | | | |

Students' predictions of the rankings made by their content area teachers were not much better. Students predicted a much wider range of rankings for both the best and the worst of the essays than the content area teachers actually produced. The highest rankings were predicted about evenly for Essays 2, 3, and 4, yet half the content area teachers selected Essay 4 (on Muslim women) as the best essay. Students predicted that content area teachers would dislike Essay 1 (on nuclear power), which was the case, but also that an equal number would rate Essay 4 (on Muslim women) the lowest, whereas Essay 4 was, in fact, the favorite among content area faculty.

In the rankings which reflected students' own preferences, their divergence from assignments made by faculty is also apparent.

During the interviews students were asked to explain the reasons for each of their three separate rankings. For themselves students preferred essays that they perceived as excelling in three areas: generating interest, displaying quality information, and conforming to rhetorical expectations. To be interesting, the essay had to be "entertaining," "not boring." It had to give

TABLE 2.4. Student Prediction of Rankings by Content Area Teachers

|  | Best | Second Best | Third Best | Worst |
|---|---|---|---|---|
| Essay 1 | 3 | 4 | 6 | 6 |
| Essay 2 | 6 | 8 | 2 | 3 |
| Essay 3 | 5 | 4 | 6 | 4 |
| Essay 4 | 5 | 3 | 5 | 6 |
| $N = 20$ | | | | |

TABLE 2.5. Rankings by Content Area Teachers

|  | Best | Second Best | Third Best | Worst |
|---|---|---|---|---|
| Essay 1 | 0 | 2 | 3 | 9 |
| Essay 2 | 3 | 3 | 5 | 3 |
| Essay 3 | 4 | 4 | 5 | 1 |
| Essay 4 | 7 | 5 | 1 | 1 |
| $N = 14$ | | | | |

TABLE 2.6. Student Ranking According to Their Own Preferences

|  | Best | Second Best | Third Best | Worst |
|---|---|---|---|---|
| Essay 1 | 2 | 4 | 2 | 12 |
| Essay 2 | 4 | 8 | 5 | 3 |
| Essay 3 | 11 | 1 | 6 | 2 |
| Essay 4 | 3 | 7 | 7 | 3 |
| $N = 20$ | | | | |

TABLE 2.7. Rankings of All Teachers Combined

|  | Best | Second Best | Third Best | Worst |
|---|---|---|---|---|
| Essay 1 | 2 | 4 | 7 | 16 |
| Essay 2 | 7 | 11 | 6 | 5 |
| Essay 3 | 5 | 5 | 13 | 6 |
| Essay 4 | 15 | 9 | 3 | 2 |
| $N = 29$ | | | | |

good specific examples. The subject had to be "uncommon" yet on a topic the students "could relate to." To please these students a piece of writing also had to have a substantial amount of high-quality information. A good essay "talks about a lot of things" and gives information that is, like the topic, "not common"; statistics, facts, and references impressed the students.

Possibly because the students had most frequently heard teachers discuss this area, the longest and most precise list of descriptors for the writing that these students preferred reflected rhetorical concerns. Good essays "get to the point," are easy to follow, concrete, precise, and short. Several students mentioned not liking the essays that they considered too long, too detailed, or too full of information. (Such reactions may well reflect the effort even these university-level ESL students still need to make to read these pieces.) Students liked good introductions and several gave as an example Essay 3 on dreams, which began with a set of questions: "What is a dream or makes up a dream? Is dreaming a necessary part of sleep? Are there different interpretations of dreams in different countries?" They liked what they saw as support for points and good conclusions. They appreciated "good diction," large vocabularies, and a "scientific sound," or what some students called "sophisticated English." Several students mentioned good grammar as one of the criteria for good writing and, despite the fact that the obvious grammar errors had been eliminated from these essays, found fault with the grammar of some of the essays.

## RESULTS: WHAT STUDENTS THINK FACULTY WANT

The ESL students interviewed for this study had definite ideas about what English teachers and content area teachers expect from student writing. When asked what they felt their English teachers looked for in their papers, the ESL students most frequently mentioned organizational concerns (e.g., introduction, body, conclusion, good thesis, clearly divided), good grammar, sophisticated language, and interesting topics.[1] In an amusing example of their sensitivity to audience, more than one student mentioned that they thought the English teachers would rank Essay 4 especially highly because of its subject, which deals with Islamic women. They said English teachers "go for cultural topics," and, furthermore, most of their English teachers are women and prefer topics related to women!

My English teacher is a woman. So she would like to read about this subject.

These students said they felt that English teachers focused on structure and did not emphasize content as much as "style" and that in writing for English classes "your facts don't have to be very accurate." One student lamented this focus and then proceeded to reassure himself that despite the

---

[1]All the students in this study were currently in ESL classes and were referring to their ESL writing teachers in their discussion. It is unlikely that they had any experience with teachers of writing to NES students.

English teachers' skewed view of writing, true quality would ultimately triumph over more pedestrian concerns.

> Unfortunately, it seems to me that an English teacher is ready to just look at the structure and grammar of an essay or at what he or she is teaching right at that time. However, an English teacher usually is a good evaluator and will give a really excellent essay a good credit.

In general, the students talked about the criteria used by English teachers as though those criteria were disconnected from the real world and only applied in the English class. For example, during the interview one student complained that the assignment in one of her English classes had been to write an autobiographical statement as though applying for a scholarship. She only received a B + on this assignment from the English teacher. This upset her because using that same autobiographical statement, she actually applied for and won the scholarship. The contradiction between winning the scholarship and her English teacher's evaluation of her essay proved to her that the English teacher was unfair and was using criteria to judge her writing which were not universally accepted.

Certainly, this is not the first-time English teachers have heard the complaint that grading is arbitrary. But this student's comment reminds us that the illusion of universal acceptability flourishes among students. This student expected to be judged by universally accepted criteria; if a paper is good, it is good for all time, in all places. (And do we not encourage those very illusions when we say that the writing of Shakespeare, for example, or anyone else in the literary canon, is universal and timeless?) Her paper was meeting expectations set by the scholarship office but not those set by the English class. The student may view this anomaly in one of two ways: either, whoever rates her writing highest is using the universally accepted criteria, while the other reader is being arbitrary; or, universal or not, the criteria used in the real world, not in the English class, are the only authentic ones, the only ones that matter, potentially making the English class irrelevant for this student and others, merely another hoop to jump through in order to graduate. Low evaluations of writing in English classes are not only unfair but also irrelevant to anything outside the English class.

In discussing what they felt their content area teachers looked for in their writing, the students mentioned most frequently that the subject of the writing should be interesting to the teacher and that teachers were attracted to subjects related to their own areas of expertise and were, therefore, likely to rank highly essays that, in effect, flattered them by focusing on those areas. In predicting that content area teachers, like English teachers, want to read about what they are personally interested in, several students expressed a certain cynicism. One student mentioned that it was his impression that content area teachers do not like to read about problems in the United States, particularly not in writing done by "foreigners." The idea that teachers let personal preferences interfere with their evaluation seemed to trouble several students. Perhaps the students feel that if teachers rank highly what they are interested in reading about, they are violating an unspoken covenant of objectivity. They are once again ranking arbitrarily and not according to some kind of universally accepted criteria. In other words, these students seem to say teachers should not act as real readers reading for interest or information. Ideally, they should control themselves and behave like teachers. But lamentably, in the real world, teachers do not give good grades to papers on subjects they do not personally like.

Students also felt that content area teachers appreciate writing that shows the result of research by including a great deal of information, accurate facts, "technical information and formulas," data, and statistics. These content area teachers do not rank highly student work that relates old news or contains no current information, that is "shallow," "impractical," or "too abstract," or that is "not scientific." In other words, unlike English teachers, these teachers are seen as holding students to high standards of quality in content and as able to disregard the kind of formalist, strictly rhetorical features of writing perceived as being dear to English teachers.

The earlier student who commented about "a really excellent essay" and the student who felt frustrated by her English teacher's failure to see the excellence in her autobiography exemplify a contradictory attitude that underlies the comments of many of these students. On one hand, the students are able to see that criteria used by English teachers are not the same as those used by content area teachers; on the other hand, they also seem to feel that "a really excellent essay" is really excellent no matter who is reading it and are frustrated when confronted with evidence that teachers' evaluations are not consistent. The implication seems to be that when evaluating real essays, teachers are obliged to read objectively and should ignore their own personal reactions and preferences. Only in so doing can all be assured that the teachers will recognize "a really excellent essay."

The students' criteria for ranking according to their own preferences combine elements of their descriptions of the main concerns of their English teachers and of their content area teachers. Like their content area teachers, these students were impressed by interesting, informative writing, but like their English teachers they felt good writing exhibited rhetorical skill, such as the ability to organize clearly, to write striking introductions, and to use "good diction," or appropriate vocabulary. Nevertheless, the students did not agree on which essays exhibited these criteria; their rankings of the essays differed fairly widely (see Tables 2.6 and 2.7). In other words, agreeing upon the criteria does not entail agreeing upon which examples meet those expectations. The disparity in their rankings points to the inevitably implicit nature even of explicit criteria. Hidden behind the criteria these students advanced for evaluating writing lay individual and disparate understandings of those criteria. Students' not being able to agree on which introduction is "good" perhaps does not surprise us. But it does recall Walvoord and McCarthy's (1990) finding that even nonevaluative terms like *thesis statement* may be understood differently in different disciplines across the curriculum.

## RESULTS: TEACHERS' EVALUATIONS

ESL students are perhaps unaccustomed both to evaluating writing and to articulating, in English, the standards they might apply in their evaluations. English and content area faculty are accustomed to both, and they too were interviewed on their responses to these student essays.

First, in general terms and contrary to what students predicted, the more the faculty knew about the subject matter of the essays, the more critical they were. Thus, the ESL faculty may have found Essay 4 on Islam interesting but they were quite critical of it; the economics and history professors were especially disparaging of Essay 2 on poverty in Sweden and the U.S.; the engineers found fault particularly with Essay 1 on nuclear power. As the faculty discussed the arguments that the students had made in the essays, it became clear that the difference between legitimately arguing a point and simply arguing by assertion is not only a factor of how much evidence is shown in the essay but, even more so of how likely a given reader is to believe and be swayed by that evidence, which in turn is governed by that reader's knowledge of the topic.

As the students had predicted, the faculty (content area as well as English) were concerned with issues of organization, but not quite as the students anticipated. The concerns were not formalist but rather content driven. For example, several faculty members pointed out that the students sometimes seemed to be making contradictory remarks in their writing because they did not develop their ideas fully enough. This comment was made especially in reference to Essay 1 on nuclear power, in which the student seemed to be both arguing against nuclear power because it is dangerous and arguing for nuclear power because it is helpful, but seemed to be unaware of the contradiction. Ostensibly an organization problem, the contradiction in this student's writing arose, according to one faculty member, from a failure to pursue an idea to its logical implications.

Similarly, many faculty members mentioned the overriding importance of an introduction. These readers clearly wanted to be oriented to the essay topic and informed of where the paper was going as early as possible, and they rated highly those papers in which they saw such planning (but see

Scarcella, 1984, for a discussion of *excessive* orientation in the writing of nonnatives). One NES writing teacher put the importance of introductions squarely into the realities of university life:

> I teach four courses a semester so here's something I always tell my students is that . . . the thing that's going to be read, obviously . . . most closely by a teacher is the introduction and if you can, in a nutshell give me a kind of summary, I mean, an outline of what you're going to talk about, where you're going with it, kind of a thesis, and then a focus about how you're going to go about it, then it's going to be easier reading for the reader. It can be a very good paper in the body, but if you've lost, just rhetorically speaking, if you've lost your audience right there, and you force them to work in the body, then, I mean, whether it's fair or not that's going to be kind of a realistic consideration in the final grade.

It is possible that what the students view as formalist requirements for writing introductions are actually concerns related to content, to the readers' need to be oriented to the topic, or to altogether different, more practical issues.

Prompted by discussion of these essays, several faculty volunteered that they generally find students, not *only* nonnative speakers but definitely *also* nonnative speakers, especially from certain cultural backgrounds, reluctant to draw conclusions from their own discussions and that this reluctance detracts from the quality of their written work. One faculty member stated that when challenged about their failure to write appropriate conclusions, students are likely to respond either that the facts can speak for themselves or that readers are entitled to draw whatever conclusion they like from the discussion.[2] While students may interpret the requirement for a conclusion as arbitrary and formalistic, the faculty appears to value conclusions not as an organizational ploy, but as evidence of intellectual engagement with the essay's ideas.

More generally on this question of drawing a conclusion, students seemed to be under the impression (taught in English classes perhaps?) that good writing, what some students called "scientific" writing, should not express a personal point of view although many of the content teachers said that they want students to show the kind of engagement or involvement with their topics that comes with taking a particular point of view. Several of the faculty members interviewed stressed that they tell their students to defend

---

[2]An equally plausible reason for their reluctance may of course arise from the students' feeling that drawing a conclusion themselves from their discussion is risky; the reader may find the conclusion wrong or unwarranted or naive. Thus, students may be unwilling to go out on a limb and take the stand that their paper suggests. On the other hand, it is also possible that students are simply unable to see what their discussion suggests as a conclusion.

or develop their point of view by explaining the facts that persuaded them to take that point of view, but the students seem to be hearing something different. In talking about what they thought content area teachers wanted, students had mentioned that writing should be what they called "scientific" and should not express a personal point of view but just "tell the facts." But one history professor describes her attempts to get students to engage their topics by explaining that she looks for "an argument and detail:"

> I try to remember to say to them that there's a difference between judgment and opinion. If you state this is what I believe about this material you should be able to back that up very carefully, and so I want them to stick their necks out and say something about how they're evaluating it but on the other hand, cautiously.

Or as a sociology professor points out:

> It really turns me on if . . . I ask them to make it clear that they have done some critical thinking about this, that they have turned these things over in their mind and thought about it longer than it took them to write the paper. . . . Realistically, I realize that these are 18-year-olds and haven't thought seriously about too many things, so I'm not shocked when I don't see it, but I do tell them unless I ask for them, I don't want personal opinions.

The difference between judgment and critical thinking on the one hand, and personal opinion on the other hand may simply elude these students, and this confusion may result in their failure, which the faculty noted, to draw a conclusion from their own discussion, despite the students' awareness of the faculty's wish for this formal structural feature called a conclusion. The students seem to hear not that they should defend their stand but that they should avoid taking a stand.

In sum, then, although the students were moderately successful in predicting several of the criteria their teachers use to evaluate writing, they also seemed to misinterpret some of their teachers' concerns. Where the students may see a strictly formalist concern for rhetorical matters, the teachers' real focus may, in fact, be on content *mediated* through directives to develop ideas, to write good introductions, to come to conclusions. This misinterpretation might account for the students' relative lack of success in predicting rankings despite their more accurate descriptions of teachers' criteria. The issue of the disparity between the students' and the teachers' interpretation of evaluation criteria seems particularly urgent with ESL students, who may have had little formal training in writing in English before their experiences in U.S. colleges and, therefore, have little on which to base their anticipation of their academic audience's needs.

## THE ACADEMIC DISCOURSE COMMUNITY SPEAKS

During the interviews with the faculty, it became increasingly clear that some of the most interesting findings of this study were related to the diversity of perspectives which the faculty bring to bear in reading and evaluating student writing. As the faculty described their criteria for ranking these essays and for evaluating writing in their classes, only the most general kind of consistency of criteria emerged. Certainly, everyone agreed that organization, logic, development, and everything else writing teachers presumably emphasize are important elements in good writing, but for individual teachers quite different aspects of writing appeared as most salient in their evaluations. While some stressed the students' commitment to the writing, others stressed what they called good "flow" of the language; while some pored over the introductions of these student essays looking for evidence of organization, others looked especially for evidence of risk taking.[3]

Lack of consensus also emerged among the faculty as to when various criteria were being met. While the faculty might agree on the importance of logic, development of ideas, or organized presentation of argument, in specific essays, there were many discrepancies between the criteria cited and the recognition of those criteria in a given essay. For example, two of the teachers said they valued the use of data to argue a point, but one teacher cited Essay 1 as an instance where the student had successfully argued a point, and another criticized the same essay for having no argument, for being "just a book report."

From the many hours of commentary resulting from the faculty interviews, I have selected some of the more provocative comments the faculty made about the four student essays.

## On Organization

While many faculty members commented on the importance of clear organization, several said they did not like or encourage formulaic writing. Several saw Essay 1 on the pros and cons of nuclear power and Essay 2 comparing Swedish and U.S. attitudes toward welfare as examples of formulaic writing or as examples of the kind of "perfunctory organizational patterns that high school students write." Others saw Essay 1 on nuclear

---

[3]There is no claim made here that the criteria the faculty discussed in their evaluations of the four sample essays are the same criteria that they would use in evaluating writing in their own courses. Obviously, the nature of the assignment in an actual course brings with it additional or different tacit or explicit evaluation criteria. Nevertheless, the criteria these faculty mentioned clearly play some role in their general sense of quality in writing.

power as not organized at all. Commenting on Essay 2 on Sweden and the United States, where some saw an example of formulaic writing, others regarded Essay 2 as the model of a well-organized essay.

## On Introductions

Both content area and writing faculty stressed that strong introductions predispose them to react positively to a piece of writing. But whether or not a particular introduction was strong was open to debate. The use of questions, for example, in the introduction of Essay 3 on dreams was alternately described as:

> "A clever, novel idea" which "got my attention" and which "clearly set up the organization of the paper" because each paragraph answered one question.

and

> "Sophomoric," "silly," and "typical of what undergraduates naively think is striking."

## On Conclusions

The conclusion of Essay 2 on Sweden and the U.S. was described in turn as "reasonable and balanced," as "not possible given the discussion," that is, as arbitrary, and as "a cowardly middle-of-the-road cop out." One professor criticized the conclusions of Essay 2 as conventional and another praised them as clearly organized and showing real insight.

## On Language

For one faculty member the language of Essay 1 was "better" than the language of Essay 2 because it was more formal; another said that the language of Essay 1 was less formal than all the rest and more native sounding. Another said Essay 4 was the most native sounding.

The same paper, Essay 4 on Islamic women, was described as exhibiting some sophistication in the use of English, because the student attempted more than just subject/verb/object sentences, and as suffering from lack of clarity, because the sentences were too complex. The professor who found this essay unclear mentioned that the graduate students in his department are instructed to analyze any piece of writing they do by using a commercially available computer program which will warn the writers when their sentences go over 20 words in length; to be clear, sentences must be short and direct.

Several professors mentioned the importance of "flow" in good writing and said they rated highly writing which exhibited good flow. But it was difficult to pin down more precisely the nature of "flow."

## On the Use of References

The student who wrote Essay 2 on attitudes in the United States and Sweden toward welfare programs used a short quote from *Collier's Encyclopedia*, which elicited the following comments:

It was "gracefully done."

"*Collier's* is not a good source for a serious paper."

References showed student was "involved in the writing, taking it seriously, and trying to get away from generalities."

References showed student was "uncommitted to the writing"; references were just "slapped on."

References showed student was trying to "snow" the teacher; quoting any encyclopedia is not acceptable.

Documentation is needed for paragraph 2 of Essay 3.

Documentation is not appropriate for any of these essays because they are all too short.

## On Essay #4 on Muslim Women

This essay generated the largest volume of commentary. The main idea of this essay is obvious, according to one faculty member; according to another, however, there is no main idea. Some felt the essay shows "maturity of thought"; others characterized it as "nothing but a hodgepodge of facts."

Several thought the essay had been written by a woman and raised the ranking when they learned it was written by a man. These raters assumed that such an essay would have been more difficult for a man to write, that a man would have had to think a great deal to come up with such an essay. A woman, on the other hand, was assumed to have already thought over the matters discussed in the essay and so was given less credit for perceptiveness or maturity of thought.

Some faculty rated this essay highly because the student seemed to be bringing personal experience (probably assuming it was written by a woman) and a personal commitment to the essay; others criticized it precisely because the personal experience seemed to be so evident: The student had an axe to grind and was excessively vehement, a sign of immaturity in writing.

(As it turns out, unbeknownst to me, or apparently to this student's writing teacher, much of this essay was lifted from a popular ESL reading text. Yet another hazard of teaching writing!)

## The Odd Angle

One surprise in the faculty's interviews was their free admission of a kind of idiosyncrasy or arbitrariness that went into judging these essays and extends into evaluating writing done for their own courses. Several faculty members, for example, reported that they enjoyed, rated highly, and encouraged their students to produce writing that is different from the things the faculty had read over the years, essays that take "the odd angle" or a creative perspective. This interest in the odd angle, or "being entertained," as one put it, points to a problem for young or inexperienced students, including students writing outside their majors, and most especially ESL students, who may have had few occasions to write essays or reports in English or even in their L1s and are unlikely to have developed much sense of what kinds of arguments or angles are cliches. How are students to determine what kinds of essays individual members of the faculty have read over the years in order to find an angle that is odd for that particular faculty member? Just as one example of the problem, the series of questions which begin Essay 3 on dreams charmed some faculty, who called it "fresh," and annoyed others, one of whom dismissed it as "freshman-y," that is, as indicative of a predictable and low-level stage of development. Thus, even if students do try to surprise faculty, do take stylistic and substantive risks in their writing, lack of disciplinary or writing experience may cause students to hit upon approaches that are novel for some faculty and tedious for others and so to evoke opposite responses.

Also troubling to hear was the certainty many of these professors exhibited in ranking the essays and in discussing the characteristics of good writing. Several faculty members, both English and content area, perhaps jokingly but with some conviction behind the joke, remarked that the rankings were obvious and that they were quite sure that everyone else would come up with the same rankings as they had.

## Differences between English and Content Area Faculty

Whether or not English faculty and content area faculty agreed on rankings, a striking difference between these two groups was the focus of their commentaries. While all these faculty members were equally likely to bring up rhetorical issues such as the need for introductions, theses, development, and so on, most of the English faculty went no further, while the content area faculty frequently also focused their evaluative commentary, as students had predicted, on quality of information or argument. An engineering professor, for example, criticized Essay 2 for the assertion that the 30% middle-class income tax paid in Sweden is high:

> I look for technical accuracy. It talks about 30% income tax is high; that's just plain wrong.

The following excerpts, also in reference to Essay 2, are typical of the difference in focus between English and content area faculty. A writing teacher says:

> This writer has a sense of the pattern of organization of comparison/contrast; it's rather mechanical but at least this person knows that you balance points and so forth and . . . at least in the last sentence he or she was getting at a main point, that there needs to be this moderation, but it never really was developed in the essay itself, but yet there was an attempt to present something. . . . It really isn't developed very much but the organizational pattern and the sense of purpose in the organization is there.

By contrast here is how one of the history teachers talked about the same essay:

> [Reading from essay] "Most Americans feel they should be responsible for themselves." I'm not sure about that. In living through a welfare state system in my own lifetime, I have to think, no; the response to people in poverty is they rely on the state, not themselves. . . . There's implied in those earlier statements an acceptance of the idea that the poor will always be with us or that gaps in wealth are a natural result of whether it's competitive urges, you know, part of our characters, or the system that we live in.

Nowhere in any of the commentary made by writing faculty was there evidence of this kind of engagement with ideas expressed in the essays.

While ESL and NES writing teachers made similar kinds of comments, as is clear from Tables 2.2, 2.3, and 2.5, the NES writing teachers' ratings were closer to those of the content area teachers than were the ratings assigned by the ESL faculty. Although numbers this small can only be suggestive, a trend showing ESL writing teachers as out of line even with other writing faculty would be potentially disturbing.


## IMPLICATIONS

As a result of what I learned from my interviews with these students and faculty, as an ESL writing teacher, I am faced with the question of how I can help my students better represent to themselves the expectations of content area faculty in particular. The enterprise is not an easy one given what I read as the disparity of opinions and judgments expressed by the faculty. Yet the philosophical justification underlying the very existence of ESL freshman English classes and writing exams is that, at least within the university, there is agreement on standards for writing beyond sentence-level concerns. But how is a student to interpret opposite comments about the same piece of writing, comments like "this piece of writing is a hodgepodge of facts" vs. this same piece of writing "shows maturity of thought"?

The student and faculty commentary on these essays makes it evident that, although these groups may well be able to agree on certain criteria for "good writing" and may even use the same words to describe those criteria, behind explicit standards of clear organization, appropriate vocabulary, effective introductions, and strong conclusions lie implicit understandings of those terms. This implicitness and perhaps undefinability of these standards precludes the possibility of simply agreeing on a definition of good writing and teaching it once and for all, as we might follow a cake recipe. We have an obligation to our students to make our standards as explicit as possible, while realizing at the same time that even with explicit criteria for good writing, there is much that will remain implicit and, therefore, difficult for our students to comprehend and respond to.

Walvoord and McCarthy (1990) point out, for example, that in the business class they observed a "thesis" is expected to develop from definitions articulated and arguments made; in the history class, however, the "thesis" initiates the argument. They warn that even terms like thesis are instantiated in essentially different ways across disciplines. Recent studies of task representation expose similar mismatches. Nelson (1990) examines differing interpretations of a particular assignment as intended by a professor and as interpreted by an NES student. The professor describes the assignment this way:

> This assignment should be challenging. I purposely made it difficult. Students have to boil down the information from the lectures and reading and present a concise argument. . . . I believe conciseness forces students to take a stand, to weigh the value of every word.

And here's how the student describes this same assignment:

> This was an easy assignment. All you had to do was reiterate what you'd read. I picked lots of names and cited important-sounding incidents . . . essentially I paraphrased the reports I read. I think this assignment was another case of

the instructor trying to have us learn through reiteration of read[ing] material. In my opinion, it didn't work and was a waste of class time.

The teacher expected a synthesis and the student provided a regurgitation.
  Implicitness also creates problems outside of the classroom, for writing evaluators. Many institutions have writing entrance and exit exams for which faculty are trained to do holistic evaluations, not only writing faculty but, in order to involve the whole academic community, content area faculty as well. It is obvious that holistic raters must be carefully trained and their readings frequently normed or adjusted to a stable standard. But anecdotal evidence suggests that the following scenario is not unheard of: A group of faculty members have been trained to evaluate a set of writing samples; the criteria for the evaluation are clear and familiar. Yet someone evaluates a paper as a failure because of the many comma splices, a category of error not even mentioned in the criteria. Readers for Educational Testing Services' Test of Written English for international students are familiar with the experience of hearing other readers voice justifications for their rankings that have nothing to do with the criteria in the rating guidelines, despite the careful, extensive training that ETS does of TWE readers. Hamp-Lyons (1991) describes the British Council's English Language Testing Service writing exam for international students. The exam had disciplinary modules allowing, for example, engineering students to write on topics presumably appropriate for applied science disciplines. Unfortunately, the raters were all English teachers and, in their comments on their ratings of the essay exams, criticized essays for the very qualities usually expected and admired by professors in those disciplines.
  The results of this study also point to the question of how writing can be judged outside of a specific rhetorical context. "Good writing," in fact, is shown to mean writing that meets particular requirements set for a particular readership at a particular time and place. The student who won the scholarship with the autobiographical sketch which was not rated as A work in her English class experienced the frustration that comes with the belief that absolute quality exists regardless of context. Presumably, the self-assuredness the faculty expressed about their own responses to the essays is also a product of that same belief, the belief that abstract standards of quality in writing exist context free. And yet, consensus among the faculty on which essays exhibited those abstract qualities was not great, and, more importantly, is unlikely to occur outside of a specifically defined context.
  The importance of context has long been recognized in other domains. Reading theory, for example, emphasizes the role of the reader collaborating in the creation of textual meaning. The excellence of good writing

resides only partially in the text. Some of what is perceived as excellent in a text is produced by individual readers' construction of the text's very meaning. Such views of reading also help us understand the potential difficulty in reaching consensus simply on the meaning of a text, not to mention the quality of a text.

The diversity of faculty reaction to the student essays also points to the many discourse communities subsumed under the term *academic*, each community with its own set of expectations for student, and certainly also professional, texts. Yet, to return to the question raised at the beginning of this discussion about the legitimacy of non-discipline-specific writing courses, as we teach writing we implicitly pose as representatives of others in the academic community for whom our students will be writing. Content area faculty and students alike assume that writing teachers represent the rest of the academic discourse communities at our institutions. This is the assumption that justifies requiring students to take writing courses; clearly, we do not teach writing so that students will be able to write for us alone, for a single member of one segment of the academic community.

Within the academic discourse communities, categories of stylistic preferences certainly exist. Some disciplines are likely to value writing that communicates a sense of personal commitment on the part of the student to the positions taken in the essays. Others are less likely to demand commitment but might be more concerned that a piece of writing include an exhaustive review of material pertinent to the topic discussed. While members of some disciplines represented in this study seemed comfortable with a variety of organizational styles, others looked for more predictable patterns of presentation of ideas.

In the last 10 years or so there has been increased interest in analyzing professional writing in various disciplines (Bazerman, 1985; Myers, 1985, 1990) and even more recently in examining the expectations for the writing of college students across the curriculum (Chiseri-Strater, 1991; Flower et al., 1990; Herrington, 1985; Walvoord & McCarthy, 1990). All of these studies are of NES writers, but it seems especially important to communicate those expectations to ESL students, who may have extremely limited experience in anticipating expectations of English-speaking academic audiences.

Some ESL writing professionals have raised the question of just how far we as writing teachers can expect to be able to go in terms of meeting the demands of the various discourse subcommunities within academia, suggesting that writing teachers cannot and should not be expected to know the standards and expectations of each of those individual communities (Spack, 1988). Others have maintained the contrary, that the focus, particularly of ESL writing instruction, should be on English for Academic or Specific

Purposes (EAP or ESP); that is, rather than analyzing writers and their processes, we should be analyzing the readers of ESL students' writing and the academic communities in which that writing takes place (Hamp-Lyons, 1986; Horowitz, 1986a, 1986b; Johns & Connor, 1989). If we follow those who argue that we should abandon attempts to develop a clearer sense of standards and expectations of diverse academic subcommunities, we must ask ourselves what discourse community we as ESL writing teachers represent. ESL writing teachers are arguably even less justified than NES teachers might be in maintaining a "noncareerist" focus in their writing classes since many ESL students have a strictly utilitarian purpose in learning to write in English.[4] And yet, at least in their rankings in this study, ESL writing teachers, who might be most justified in trying to represent faculty expectations across the curriculum, appeared to be less in line with content area faculty than were teachers of NES students.

Whether or not ESL writing classes take an EAP/ESP focus, such a focus does not mean that writing teachers need to learn or teach formats for writing biology lab reports or case studies in economics, although ESL students sometimes request this very training (Carson & Leki, 1992), but rather that writing teachers be sure to emphasize, especially to ESL students, the socially determined nature of writing options, preferences, and conventions and to discourage in our students the belief in absolute standards, which they might assume they can learn to meet in our writing classes.

The results of this study suggest the ESL writing teachers have an obligation to examine our collective conscience about teaching: Again, whose discourse community do we represent as we read our students'

---

[4]In speaking of goals for their classes, several NES teachers in this study mentioned the importance of students' developing critical thinking skills. While manifestation of those skills for monolingual NES students is only possible in written or spoken English, obviously ESL students may write and speak poor English and still think quite critically, logically, and profoundly in their own languages. Thus, we need to at least consider the possibility that an assumption that ESL students do not have and must be taught critical thinking skills may be altogether presumptuous.

I would also like to note that an important issue that might be raised here is the question of the writing class as the locus not for inculcating students into an established dominating system (the university, for example) but rather for challenging that system. Unfortunately, this issue is beyond the scope of this discussion. While writing teachers may construe their roles in a variety of ways, my objective here is the exploration of the role of the writing teacher as, in some way, the representative of the academic community. This focus is justified by the fact that many in that community, and many students, assume that the purpose of required freshman writing classes is to prepare students for their lives as writers within that community and perhaps beyond. For an interesting exchange on the issue of writing classes which might train students to specifically resist the domination of the established order, see Canagarajah's comments and Raimes' reply in the TESOL Quarterly Forum (1993).

writing? Whose standards are we using to evaluate our students' writing and why those? What is the relationship between what happens in our writing classes and our students' future writing (and thinking) requirements?

In the meantime we may also need to teach ESL students a variety of stances to take when confronting writing projects beyond the writing classroom. We can, for example, help them to become conscious of the existence of different writing contexts so that they automatically ask what the purpose of a writing task is and who the audience will be. In our ESL writing courses we can also help students develop a critical attitude not only toward information they gather but toward their own arguments as well. However, if we are to be credible in our representations of what our students will face in their writing assignments across the curriculum, we may also need to recognize and admit to our students that, despite implicit and explicit claims made in many freshman writing classes, lower division students are often asked only to display knowledge (particularly on essay exams), not to analyze or synthesize. In her study of essay exams across the curriculum, Conklin (1982) points out that lower division students may need to "acquire knowledge before they can be expected to do anything with it — but this purpose for giving examinations needs to be made public" (p. 160). Because of all that is not made public, and since we require nearly all college-level students to take writing courses, we need to train and encourage ESL students to take control in all their classes, as far as they are able, of the varying contexts in which they write by seeking an explicit explanation and clarification to their own satisfaction of all criteria which will be used to evaluate any writing they might be required to do. In our own classes, that might mean including students' input in setting the criteria for writing quality. If nothing else, such a policy might help to undermine the belief in the existence of universally accepted, absolute standards of "good writing."

One point of consensus in the comments made by students and faculty alike in the study reported here was the acknowledgment that the participants were interested in and therefore favorably impressed by essays which taught them something they did not already know. ESL students benefit from knowledge of at least two cultures. We need to encourage them to take advantage whenever possible in their writing of their own unique, diverse experiences.

One of the faculty members I interviewed asked me what I had found during this study, and when I told her of the diversity of views I had heard, she remarked, attempting to account for that diversity, that some of the faculty themselves were not very good writers. Yet, however well or badly professors may write — or read and comment on students' writing — they are the final arbiters in evaluating writing in their classes. It seems we should take care not to lull students into a false sense of security that if they are writing what *we* like, they are also writing what other professors necessarily value. The issue of gauging faculty reaction to the writing of nonnative speakers is one of particular importance to ESL writing instructors since, for ESL students, unlike their NES comrades, it is quite possible that the only audiences they will ever have for their writing in English are their college professors in the United States. Yet these college and university faculty inhabit not a unified intellectual or academic community but rather, as anthropologist Geertz (1983, p. 161) described academic disciplines, "intellectual villages." complete with local and sometimes parochial standards and values tenaciously adhered to. In order to foster genuine interaction between our village, the ESL writing class, and the diverse intellectual villages our students will enter, perhaps we need to follow Geertz' suggestions: "The first step is surely to accept the depth of the differences; the second to understand what these differences are; and the third to construct some sort of vocabulary in which they can be publicly formulated" (p. 161).

Because we require nearly all students to take writing courses, English departments are uniquely obligated to learn more about the many academic discourse villages around us, to develop awareness of what other faculty on our campuses are assuming about writing, and to use our expertise to support our colleagues' conscious examination of their diverse criteria for high-quality writing.

## REFERENCES

Bazerman, C. (1985). Physicists reading physics: Schema-laden purposes and purpose-laden schema. *Written Communication, 2*, 3–24.

Bridgeman, B., & Carlson, S. (1983). *Survey of academic writing tasks required of graduate and undergraduate foreign students*. Princeton, NJ: Educational Testing Service.

Canagarajah, A. S. (1993). Comments on Ann Raimes's "Out of the woods: Emerging traditions in the teaching of writing. Up the garden path: Second language writing approaches, local knowledge, and pluralism. *TESOL Quarterly, 27*, 301–306.

Carson, J., & Leki, I. (1992, October). *ESL writing instruction and content course requirements: A pilot investigation*. Paper presented at Southeast Regional TESOL, Biloxi, MS.

Chiseri-Strater, E. (1991). *Academic literacies*. Portsmouth, NH: Boynton/Cook.

Conklin, E. L. (1982). *Writing answers to essay questions: A naturalistic study of the writing process*. Unpublished doctoral dissertation, Indiana University of Pennsylvania, Indiana, PA.

Diederich, P. B. (1974). *Measuring growth in English*. Urbana, IL: National Council of Teaching Educators.

Eskey, D. E. (1983). Meanwhile, back in the real world . . .: Accuracy and fluency in second language teaching. *TESOL Quarterly, 17*, 315–323.

Flower, L., Stein, V., Ackerman, J., Kantz, M., McCormick, K., & Peck, W. (1990). *Reading to write: Exploring a cognitive and social process*. New York: Oxford University Press.

Geertz, C. (1983). *Local knowledge: Further essays in interpretative anthropology*. New York: Basic Books.

Hamp-Lyons, L. (1986). No new lamps for old yet, please. *TESOL Quarterly 20*, 790–796.

Hamp-Lyons, L. (1990). Second language writing: Assessment issues. In B. Kroll (Ed.), *Second language writing* (pp. 69–87). New York: Cambridge University Press.

Hamp-Lyons, L. (1991). Reconstructing "academic writing proficiency." In L. Hamp-Lyons (Ed.), *Assessing ESL writing in academic contexts* (pp. 127–153). Norwood, NJ: Ablex.

Herrington, A. (1985). Writing in academic settings: A study of the contexts for writing in two college chemistry engineering courses. *Research in the Teaching of English, 19*, 331–359.

Horowitz, D. (1986a). Process, not product: Less than meets the eye. *TESOL Quarterly, 20*, 141–144.

Horowitz, D. (1986b). What professors actually require: Academic tasks for the ESL classroom. *TESOL Quarterly, 20*, 445–462.

Johns, A. (1981). Necessary English: A faculty survey. *TESOL Quarterly, 15*, 51–57.

Johns, A. (1991). Interpreting an English competency examination: The frustrations of an ESL science student. *Written Communication, 8*, 379–401.

Johns, A., & Connor, U. (1989, March). *Introducing ESL students into academic discourse communities: Differences do exist*. Paper presented at TESOL Conference, San Antonio, TX.

Lee, N. (1977). *The competency in English needed by international students at an American state university*. Paper presented at NAFSA Conference, Boston, MA.

Mallonèe, B., & Breihan, J. (1985). Responding to students' drafts: Interdisciplinary consensus. *College Composition and Communication, 36*, 213–231.

McCarthy, L. (1987). A stranger in strange lands: A college student writing across the curriculum. *Research in the Teaching of English, 21*, 223–265.

Myers, G. (1985). The social construction of two biologists' proposals. *Written Communication, 2*, 219–245.

Myers, G. (1990). *Writing Biology: Texts in the social construction of scientific knowledge*. Madison: University of Wisconsin Press.

Nelson, J. (1990). *"This was an easy assignment": Examining how students interpret academic writing tasks* (Center for the Study of Writing Tech. Rep. 43). Berkeley, CA: University of California.

Raimes, A. (1993). The author responds . . . *TESOL Quarterly, 27*, 306–310.

Santos, T. (1988). Professors' reactions to the academic writing of nonnative-speaking students. *TESOL Quarterly, 22*, 69–90.

Scarcella, R. (1984). How writers orient their readers in expository essays: A comparative study of native and nonnative English writers. *TESOL Quarterly, 18*, 671–688.

Schwartz, M. (1984). Response to writing. A college-wide perspective. *College English, 46*, 55–62.

Spack, R. (1988). Initiating ESL students into the academic discourse community: How far should we go? *TESOL Quarterly, 22*, 29–52.

Vann, R., Meyer, D., & Lorenz, F. (1984). Error gravity: A study of faculty opinion of ESL errors. *TESOL Quarterly, 18*, 427–440.

Walvoord, B., & McCarthy, L. (1990). *Thinking and writing in college*. Urbana, IL: National Council of Teaching Educators.

Witte, S., & Faigley, L. (1981). Coherence, cohesion, and writing quality. *College Composition and Communication, 32*, 189–204.

# CHAPTER 3

# Redefining the Task: An Ethnographic Examination of Writing and Response in Graduate Seminars

**Paul Prior**
*University of Illinois at Urbana-Champaign*

This chapter explores EAP needs analysis for academic writing tasks. Reflecting on a series of qualitative studies of students' writing and professors' responses in graduate seminars, Prior traces the evolution of his research methodology toward increasingly detailed ethnographic designs and of his theoretical understanding toward sociohistoric perspectives on discourse and knowledge. Examining how academic writing tasks were cued, produced, read, and evaluated by particular participants over time, Prior finds that tasks are complexly shaped by the multiple histories, activities, and goals that participants bring to and create within seminars. Prior's depiction of the situated processes professors and students engage in as they dialogically construct academic genres raises key issues in EAP theory and pedagogy.

A fundamental step in special-purpose language teaching and research is needs analysis; the first step of which is determining what situations the learner will need to function in, what tasks she will need to undertake, what language forms are typically used for those tasks in those situations, and how that language is functionally employed. Needs analysis does not automatically determine curriculum and pedagogy (Hutchinson & Waters, 1987). However, if explicit needs analyses are not undertaken to inform teaching, then teaching will be guided by the implicit theories held by teachers and embedded in curricula. If we are undertaking a needs analysis for international airline pilots, the data, while difficult to get, seem relatively straightforward. The language comes from a fairly fixed, fairly limited, and relatively predictable domain. If, however, we are seeking a needs analysis for "the academic writing of university students," our inquiry gets rather more complicated.

Research on the academic writing needs of nonnative speakers of English (NNSE) in university settings has so far relied on several approaches: intuitive/anecdotal analysis of cultural and linguistic contrasts (e.g., Ballard, 1984; Houghton, 1980; James, 1984; Kaplan, 1966), surveys or interviews of students and professors (e.g., Bridgeman & Carlson, 1983; Johns, 1981; Ostler, 1983), textual analysis of classroom writing prompts (e.g., Braine, 1989; Horowitz, 1986a, 1986b), textual analysis of professional and school genres (e.g., Dudley-Evans, 1986; Howe, 1990; Lackstrom, 1981; Oster, 1981; Swales, 1990a, 1990b; Swales & Najjar, 1987), and professor judgments of manipulated student essays (e.g., Santos, 1988). Several studies have employed multiple methodologies. For example, Tarone, Dwyer, Gillette, and Icke (1981) combined analysis of professional texts with subject–specialist interviews. Belcher (1989), seeking a triangulated perspective on how disciplinary professors socialize graduate student NNSE into departmental and disciplinary writing practices, combined a survey of students with case studies that involved interviewing selected students and examining professors' responses to their writing. Swales (1990a) developed several case studies of graduate NNSE, combining interviews, questionnaires, analysis of subjects' writing from ESL and disciplinary settings, and comments elicited from subjects' professors. English-for-Academic-Purposes (EAP) composition specialists can also look to a comparable body of literature in first language studies of specialized discourse and rhetoric (e.g., Bazerman, 1988; Edmondson, 1984; Hunter, 1990; Landau, 1991; McCloskey, 1985; Myers, 1989, 1990; Nelson, Megill, & McCloskey, 1987; Rose, 1983; Williamson, 1988).

EAP approaches to needs analysis have primarily generated valuable data on professor and student perceptions of academic writing and on formal features of academic texts (often professional rather than student texts — evidently on the assumption that school and professional genres are essentially the same). However, these approaches have rarely examined how academic writing tasks are realized as concrete historical activities situated in the classroom and institutional contexts of the disciplines and in the personal and social lives of the participants. Composition researchers have only recently begun to report situated studies of disciplinary writing in university settings.[1] Taken as a whole, these situated studies have suggested

---

[1]For examples of situated and partially situated studies of academic writing, see. Belcher (1989), Berkenkotter, Huckin, & Ackerman (1988, 1991), Blakeslee (1992), Casanave (1990), Chiseri-Strater (1991), Clark & Doheny-Farina (1990), Doheny-Farina (1989), Herrington

that writing tasks in disciplinary classrooms are cued, produced, and evaluated through complex, largely tacit, social and intellectual processes. Studies indicate that different disciplines (Faigley & Hansen, 1985; Walvoord & McCarthy, 1990), different classes within a discipline (Herrington, 1985), and even a single professor responding to different students or tasks (Prior, 1991) may have different expectations, reflected in varying criteria for evaluating student work.

While situated research has greatly enhanced our understanding of the diversity and complexity of writing in the university, it remains limited in several important ways. A relatively small number of cases have been studied, and sampling has been fairly concentrated (e.g., mostly English courses or WAC-influenced courses in other disciplines, mostly undergraduate, mostly NSE). Designs have rarely been comparative or longitudinal. Finally, these studies have struggled with difficult issues in the collection, analysis, and representation of the complex array of contextual and textual data potentially available to the researcher, a struggle often resolved by a reductive emphasis on the characteristics of students' texts rather than a fuller examination of the literate processes involved in academic work. Thus, limited attention has been paid to the complex interplay between students' texts and such factors as:

biographic, interpersonal, institutional and sociocultural contexts
the literate processes students engage in as episodes of reading and writing, listening and talking, sensing and acting contribute to production of specific texts
professors' situated reading, response and evaluation practices and
the strategic work that participants bring to bear in accomplishing and interpreting interactions within and outside the classroom.

The central argument of this chapter is that a triangulated, ethnographic examination of how academic writing tasks are cued, produced, and received by particular people in particular settings provides a very different perspective on such tasks than that inferred from texts and perceptions alone.

## EXPLORING ACADEMIC NEEDS:
## AN EVOLVING METHODOLOGY

One way to formulate the question of academic needs for writing is to examine the nature of academic writing tasks. Doyle (1983) defined

---

(1985, 1988), McCarthy (1987), Nelson (1990), Prior (1991, 1992), Rymer (1988), Sternglass (1988), Swales (1990a), Walvoord & McCarthy (1990).

academic tasks in terms of three elements: the products students produce, the operations students undertake, and the resources available to students for accomplishing their work. He went on, however, to say that academic tasks are fundamentally altered when they are placed within the social organization and history of the classroom. To explore how academic writing tasks are accomplished within such specific sociohistoric contexts, I have conducted three qualitative studies of writing and response in graduate seminars at a major midwestern university. Over the course of these three studies, my understanding of both academic writing tasks and my own task as a researcher has altered fundamentally.

As I planned the first of these studies, I hoped that a close examination of professor response might provide some key insights missed by earlier approaches that looked at what professors assigned and what students wrote, but not at how professors read and evaluated student writing. I was motivated by a felt sense that, as Doyle (1983) pointed out, "The answers a teacher actually accepts and rewards define the real tasks in classrooms" (p. 182). While I have since come to question the absolute privileging of the professor's perspective implied by such a bottom-line approach, I believe that determining what gets accepted and rewarded is crucial to understanding the academic writing task, particularly as ethnographic and qualitative accounts of both classroom and disciplinary practices have routinely revealed wide gaps between *stated* goals, values, and practices and *in-use* goals, values, and practices (e.g., Bloome, Puro, & Theodrou, 1989; Collins, 1985; Gilbert & Mulkay, 1984; Inghilleri, 1989; Knorr-Cetina, 1981; Latour & Woolgar, 1986; McNeil, 1986; Ulichny & Watson-Gegeo, 1989).

In my first study, of a curriculum seminar in education, I sought "the task" (assuming that there was *one*) by examining the professor's written response. Specifically, I collected students' final drafts with the professor's comments and grades on them, conducted semistructured interviews with the professor about his goals and expectations for the seminar and the papers, and distributed questionnaires asking students about their backgrounds and their perceptions of tasks in the seminar. To analyze the professor's written response to students' papers, I developed a provisional system of response classifications and counted the number of words in each category for each paper. Influenced by discourse analyses of interviews (e.g., Gilbert & Mulkay, 1984; Potter & Wetherell, 1987), I viewed the professor's comments as interested accounts and was prepared to find multiple, even contradictory accounts of goals and practices.

As I attempted to integrate quantitative and categorical data on response with the professor's accounts of his goals and practices, I became puzzled by what appeared to be anomalous responses to several students' work. For example, the professor had indicated that substantive response was critical, and content-oriented comments generally peppered the margins of his students' papers. However, one A paper had *no* written response to content until the final summary comment. I could see no explanations within the student's text for this unusually limited response. Fortunately, I had received a questionnaire from the student author of that paper. Using that very limited contextual data, I began to reconsider the professor's response. Asked what the writing assignment for the seminar required, the student had written beyond the space provided, adding a two-page essay in which she argued that the professor's emphasis on the personal and his ambiguous descriptions of writing tasks amounted to an unethical form of psychological experimentation. I suspected that the professor's reserved response to this student's writing reflected the general tenor of the interpersonal relationship that had been established between them through classroom interactions.

As I attempted to understand the data, I began to connect these "anomalies" to theories of reading and social cognition as constructive acts (e.g., van Dijk & Kintsch, 1983; Fish, 1980; Fiske & Taylor, 1984; Schank & Abelson, 1977). I speculated that the professor's responses to his students' writing, Doyle's bottom lines of acceptance and reward, were shaped by his appraisal of the students themselves, based primarily on classroom interactions.[2] Reviewing other situated studies of writing, I noted that Herrington (1988) and Doheny-Farina (1989) had both suggested that the substance and style of professors' classroom interactions were reflected in the form, topics, and argumentation found in students' writing. Thus, my central methodological conclusion from the first study was that I needed a more ethnographic, more contextualized research design to explore how the intellectual and social history of classroom interactions played out in both the students' writing and the professor's response.

With these goals in mind, I revised the methodology for my second study, expanding the scope of data collection to include:

classroom observation
collection of class documents (the syllabus, student texts, handouts)
questionnaires about personal and academic backgrounds and disciplinary interest
semistructured interviews with students about their writing for the seminar

---

[2]Hull, Rose, Fraser, and Castellano (1991) document this process in a case study of a bilingual/bicultural student in a freshman composition course. They describe how the student's teacher read cultural differences in classroom behavior as signs of confused thinking and dubbed the student "the Queen of Non Sequiturs." Although the student's essays were reasonably good and showed improvement, the teacher discounted them (suggesting she must have had outside help) and evaluated her writing as weak.

semistructured interviews with the professor about his goals and expectations

collection of students' final texts with the professor's written responses/ grades and

text-based interviews with the professor.[3]

Observation would allow me to examine how classroom contexts influenced students' writing and the professor's response. The text-based interviews with the professor would allow me to explore reasons behind written responses, particularly to test if the professor was reading and responding to students as well as texts. Finally, the addition of student interviews would provide more information on the contexts and intentions behind their texts, data that I thought would be helpful in understanding the professor's response.

Following the same professor into a graduate seminar on second languages education, I began this second study (Prior, 1991) with the intention once again of discovering and describing *the* academic writing tasks of the seminar through careful examination of the professor's response and evaluation. However, the data soon led me to question that goal. My notion of "the writing task" evaporated as I was repeatedly confronted with the complex and multiple images of the seminar's writing tasks offered by participants in various contexts and at various times. The focus of my research began to shift as I attempted to categorize this multiplicity of task representation.

I began to see that the task the professor assigned was not the same as the task the students understood.[4] As I reviewed student interviews and examined their written texts, it also became clear that students' representations of the assigned writing tasks drew on many sources other than the professor's statements of those tasks: students made inferences based on their prior school experience, the models offered in the assigned readings,

---

[3]Two types of text-based interviews were conducted. The first was a stimulated elicitation in which I asked the professor to look over students' papers briefly and to comment on whatever seemed most salient about their content, their history, or the writer. The second followed a modified version of the discourse-based interview procedure Odell, Goswami, and Herrington (1983) describe. In discourse-based interviews, the researcher brackets selected passages from the text and then crosses them out to propose a deletion or writes in some alternate text to propose a change or addition. The writer is then asked to decide whether she would agree to the proposed changes or not and to explain the reasons. The modification to this procedure was that the professor was interviewed about the students' texts and asked to respond to proposed changes both in the students' writing and in his own comments.

[4]In her study of how students in a composition course represented a summary writing task, Flower (1990) suggests that if there are 14 students in a class, then there will be 14 task representations. Studies of task representation in writing assessment (e.g., Ruth & Murphy, 1988; Tedick, Bernhardt, & De Ville, 1991) also have found multiple task interpretations.

and their perceptions of the professor's personality and intellectual biases. In fact, identifying the "assigned tasks" was itself difficult as the professor frequently restated or alluded to them in ways that suggested subtle and not-so-subtle differences and as students frequently initiated implicit and explicit negotiations over the tasks. Nor did the students' task representations, arising out of this complex, situated history of statement, restatement, inference, and negotiation, translate directly into the students' active undertaking of tasks. Rather than attempting to passively match the professor's expectations (as I had implicitly assumed they would), the students acted to achieve personal, departmental, and career goals as well as to meet course requirements.

When I began analyzing the professor's written comments and text-based interviews, I found his response even more complex than I had imagined in the first study. A large number of factors appeared to influence not only his evaluation of students' papers, but also his basic construction of their meaning. The meaning of students' final written texts seemed to have been constructed in particular readings, readings in which the professor's personal goals, contexts, knowledge, and affect mixed with the multiple contexts evoked by the texts, the students, and the history of the class. The evaluations arising out of these situated readings represented not so much textual judgments of discourse conventionality as inferences about students' effort, thought, and knowledge. It was also evident that the responses represented not just evaluations, but also goal-oriented actions: helping students develop their research ideas, facilitating their personal and professional growth, and achieving the procedural display necessary to fulfill basic role obligations.

Finally, I began to see that my expanded series of task categories (*stated, restated, inferred, understood, negotiated, undertaken, read,* and *responded to*) were each in turn multiple, varying with time, person, and setting. Given the multiplicity of interpretations, the situated nature of participants' goals, and the multidimensional intersections of private and public histories in this seminar, I concluded that its academic writing tasks were indeterminate historical moments in human relationships, which, like all such moments, combined elements of order, convention, and continuity with elements of chance, anomaly, and rupture.[5]

Results from the second languages seminar (Prior, 1991), particularly the varied forms of task multiplicity, led to further methodological revisions as

---

[5]I do not believe that this conclusion is limited to graduate seminars. Nelson's (1990) excellent examination of how freshmen in disciplinary classes came to understand and produce their writing assignments suggests that these processes also occur in large, undergraduate lectures and are not limited to the smaller more interactive setting of a graduate seminar. Her wonderfully ironic and cautionary tale of an introductory sociology assignment gone awry is particularly rich in its implications.

I designed a third study. First, to see how students interpreted and acted on professor response, I planned to do selected text-based interviews with students after they received responses from the professor and particularly to examine any revisions or other consequences of that response. Second, to more fully understand students' literate processes, goals, and representations of context, I planned to collect drafts and process logs (see Nelson, 1990) if possible and to expand the depth of student interviews. Finally, I decided to capture the details of critical classroom interactions by audio-taping seminar sessions whenever possible. Seven questions guided my third study:

1. What are the disciplinary and institutional contexts for this class?
2. What are the professor's goals and rationales for the writing tasks in this class?
3. How does the professor communicate expectations for form and content?
4. How do students interpret writing tasks?
5. How do students undertake writing tasks?
6. How does the professor evaluate and respond to the students' final written texts?
7. How do the students interpret and act on the professor's written response?[6]

As this research design was implemented, my plan to investigate "another seminar" serendipitously turned into a study of four seminars in quite different disciplinary/departmental settings (geography, American studies, agricultural economics, and sociology). Before turning to discussion of this final study, I should summarize the value of an ethnographic approach for needs analysis of academic writing tasks. Such an approach allows a close examination of how Doyle's (1983) task elements (operations, resources, and products) are realized in a local history of participants' situated actions. While no report can provide more than a very partial portrait of the lived experience implicated in classroom events, the particularity of that lived experience is fundamental. Attempting to reify the five professors whose classes I have investigated into a prototypic image of "American professors" or to construct the unfolding events of their seminars as transparent man-

---

[6]I would suggest that variations and elaborations on these seven questions might be a useful tool for EAP students as well as EAP researchers. Having students engage in ethnographic investigations of their own disciplinary settings represents a powerful and potentially empowering pedagogic tool (e.g., Johns, 1990). Not incidentally, Sternglass (1988) and Flower (1991) point to the pedagogical potential of introspective and retrospective protocols to make students more aware of how their interpretive and productive actions can contribute to or limit their academic work.

ifestations of disciplinary cultures would be radically reductive, as would ignoring the diversity among the 64 students (including 17 NNSE) enrolled in them. Each seminar occurred in particular institutional circumstances and involved particular students, professors, and tasks; the seminars emerged as a local micro history of events embedded within other micro- and macro histories. Traditional approaches to needs analysis would have us seek the typical dimensions of these seminars, transforming them into abstract, anonymous structures occurring anytime anywhere; what ethnographic analysis can do is ask us to see the complex particularity and situatedness of each seminar *as* a typical dimension that should not be ignored.

## CONSTRUCTING ACADEMIC GENRES:
## RECONCEPTUALIZING THE TASK

Data from the four seminars of the third study reinforced and expanded on earlier findings, documenting the power of classroom and other contexts in shaping what and how students wrote, how professors read and responded to students' texts, and how students took professors' responses. As I analyzed these data, I became increasingly aware of the need to find theoretical tools that respected the multiplicity and historicity I was uncovering, theories that conceptualized discourse as an event (cf. Phelps, 1988, 1990). Sociohistoric approaches to discourse and knowledge (e.g., Bakhtin, 1981, 1986; Becker, 1988; Tannen, 1989; Vygotsky, 1978; Wertsch, 1991) offered an array of valuable analytic tools strongly oriented to both multiplicity and history.

Bakhtin's (1986) notion of speech genres offered a particularly useful perspective on the seminars. In some ways, Bakhtin's understanding of genres is similar to current, socially oriented approaches (e.g., Miller, 1984; Swales, 1990a). Miller and Swales have both argued for the need to relate texts to social action, for the view that genres are constituted not only through textual forms, but, more fundamentally, through the relatively stable goals of social actors in typically recurring social situations. Swales (1990a) further grounds generic discourse in the regulatory influences of discourse communities.[7] Bakhtin (1986) also relates genres to relatively stable spheres of social activity; however, his notion of speech genres differs along four basic dimensions. First, it suggests that the goals structuring generic activity need to be viewed as multiple rather than unified, varying with time, place, and participants. Second, it suggests that generic activity should be grounded not only in the goals of discourse, but in the processes

---

[7]Swales (1992) has begun to revise his theories of both genre and discourse community to incorporate some Bakhtinian notions.

anization of the discourse as well. And again, it views social organizations as multiple and concrete rather than abstract. Third, it places content and the negotiation of he center of genre and insists that meaning be seen as multiple, and historically situated. Finally, it emphasizes the view that the stab.. of a society are dynamic achievements emerging from the constant multileveled operation of centripetal (unifying) and centrifugal (disunifying) forces. As a corollary of the situated multiplicity of all discourse, Bakhtin (1986) particularly stresses the flexibility of speech genres and their extreme heterogeneity.

Bakhtin's (1981, 1986) sociohistoric approach to language is grounded in *utterance,* the words spoken or written by a particular person in a living context, rather than in the anonymous sentence diagrammed on the page, reversing Saussure's (1959) privileging of the system of language over the actuality of speech. For Bakhtin, a key notion is that utterance is dialogic. Dialogism operates at all levels of discourse, from the global level of languages across historical epochs to the single word uttered in a specific instance. The dialogic nature of utterance emerges from the interaction of the *centripetal* forces that seek to unify language and the *centrifugal* forces that stratify it. At global levels, centripetal forces are seen in government policies favoring or repressing particular dialects, in the construction of grammars and dictionaries, in the canonization and dissemination of ideological works (in art, science, commerce, civic life, religion), in the socializing influence of common schooling, and so on. However, these centripetal forces can never succeed in creating a unified language. They are met by centrifugal forces of stratification: the overlapping, nested socio-ideological languages of groups constituted by class, gender, occupation, organization, religion, politics, intellectual theory, generation, the socio-historic moment, and even particular individual influence. At local levels of interpersonal (and even intrapersonal) communication, centripetal and centrifugal forces operate as well.

> In each epoch, in each social circle, in each small world of family, friends, acquaintances, and comrades in which a human being grows and lives, there are always authoritative utterances that set the tone—artistic, scientific, and journalistic works on which one relies, to which one refers, which are cited, imitated, and followed . . . Our speech, that is, all our utterances (including creative works), is filled with others' words, varying degrees of otherness or varying degrees of "our-own-ness," varying degrees of awareness and detachment. These words of others carry with them their own expression, their own evaluative tone, which we assimilate, rework, and re-accentuate. (Bakhtin, 1986, pp. 88–89)

What is important to recognize is that what is centripetal at one level of social organization may be centrifugal in relation to a higher level. For example, strongly religious parents may, to a certain extent, unify the socio-ideological language of their children around fundamental Christianity, functioning as a centripetal force in the family and the local religious community, but as a centrifugal force in the context of a much more secular city. It follows from this perspective that what Bakhtin called social languages, the languages of professions and disciplines, are not unified either. What we have taken as an object to uncover, the language and conventions of a discourse community, are seen instead as an evolving, multivoiced force, a complex field generated by the multidirectional operation of internal and external forces of centralization and stratification.

Bakhtin sees the dialogic nature of utterances as defined by the intersection of three types of response. First, an utterance responds to past utterances, forming a "link in the chain of speech communication" in which "each utterance refutes, affirms, supplements, and relies on the others, presupposes them to be known, and somehow takes them into account" (Bakhtin, 1986, p. 91). It is crucial to keep in mind that response to utterances is not linguistic intertextuality alone; utterances, as the actual speech (text) of individuals in specific situations, index social and personal contexts as well as intellectual concepts and are charged with affective and evaluative overtones as well as semantic meanings. Linked to referential, social, and individual worlds by a complex web of associations and feelings, utterances are not neutral significations in a semiotic system. Second, utterances are understood as well as said, and that understanding is active: "It assimilates the word to be understood into its own conceptual system filled with specific objects and emotional expressions, and is indissolubly merged with the response, with a motivated agreement or disagreement" (Bakhtin, 1981, p. 282). While cognitive psychologists acknowledge responsive understanding, they usually conceptualize that understanding as strictly linguistic and propositional (e.g., the relationship between a representation of a written text as an ordered set of semantic propositions and a similar representation of a recall protocol by a reader). Bakhtin embodies response, describing it as emotional and evaluative as well as semantic, as reactive as well as interpretive. Third, utterances are addressed, responding to the future as well as the past: "Every word is directed toward an *answer* and cannot escape the profound influence of the answering word that it anticipates" (Bakhtin, 1981, p. 280). Utterances anticipate answers: the active response of listeners (or readers), future utterances by the speaker herself or others, and future events in the world.

In discussing "speech genres," Bakhtin (1986) is referring to genres of concrete *utterance*, not of systematic language forms alone.

All the diverse areas of human activity involve the use of language. . . . Language is realized in the form of individual concrete utterances (oral and written) by participants in the various areas of human activity. These utterances reflect the specific conditions and goals of each such area not only through their content (thematic) and linguistic style, that is the selection of lexical, phraseological, and grammatical resources of the language, but above all through their compositional structure. All three of these aspects—thematic content, style, and compositional structure—are inseparably linked to the whole of the utterance and are equally determined by the specific nature of the particular sphere of communication. Each separate utterance is individual, of course, but each sphere in which language is used develops its own relatively stable types of these utterances. These we may call speech genres. The wealth and diversity of speech genres are boundless because the various possibilities of human activity are inexhaustible, and because each sphere of activity contains an entire repertoire of speech genres that differentiate and grow as the particular sphere develops and becomes more complex. Special emphasis should be placed on the extreme heterogeneity of speech genres (oral and written). (Bakhtin, 1986, p. 60)

Bakhtin's (1986) connection of spheres of activity to the form, content, and concrete circumstances of communication suggests seeing genres as patterns of situated activity. To translate his ideas into more familiar terms, I would say that speech genres are constituted by the content (particularly its intertextual status), the literate processes undertaken (including reading and writing, talking and listening, sensing and acting; including use of tools and resources both social and material), linguistic and discursive forms (their style and construction), contexts (personal, interpersonal, institutional, and sociocultural), and the kinds of responses and outcomes anticipated and actually occurring. Genres may represent relatively stable configurations in the ways texts are produced and received, but genres are also dynamic—multivoiced, multigoaled phenomena generated by the complexly orchestrated interaction of centripetal and centrifugal forces in the unfolding micro- and macro-histories of the world. Genres in this view emerge as considerably more complex than typical notions of genre, but this specification also offers a principled way to explore how genres are employed, reconfigured, and reaccentuated as situations vary.

As I began to analyze data from the third study through the sociohistoric lens of speech genres, I found rich insights into how writing and response were accomplished in these seminars, yet I faced a dilemma. Attempting to classify what speech genre each seminar represented seemed to freeze and reify the dynamic activities I was tracing. Finally, I realized that I was continuing to assume that genres must implicate some kind of template, a fixed structure that stood behind the texts. I began to wonder if a different approach to knowledge might not apply and recognized in this question echoes of similar dilemmas in sociology and psychology.

As a sociologist interested in social order and interaction, Garfinkel (1967), like Bakhtin, decided to focus on the situated interaction of people and saw that the meaning of those interactions was radically indexed in the local, historical presuppositions of the participants. However, Garfinkel also argued that social order is *interactionally achieved* through the artful practices of group members. Criticizing the passive model of the person in sociology and psychology, Garfinkel (1967) argued that norms and conventions should not be seen as the hidden agents of social interaction, that instead sociologists and psychologists should focus their attention on the interpretive and interactional *work* being done by participants that creates a sense of norm-ality or convention-ality.

> A favored solution [of psychologists and sociologists] is to portray what the member's actions will have come to by using the stable structures — i.e., what they came to — as a point of theoretical departure from which to portray the necessary character of the pathways whereby the end result is assembled. Hierarchies of need dispositions, and common culture as enforced rules of action, are favored devices for bringing the problem of necessary inference to terms, although at the cost of making out the person-in-society to be a judgmental dope. (Garfinkel, 1967, p. 68)

Garfinkel's analyses echo some recent thinking about the representation of knowledge in cognitive psychology. Early versions of schema theories from the 1970s, versions that saw schemata as stable structures governing interpretation and action, were fundamentally revised in the early 1980s by some of their principal architects. Schank, for example, still cited for his and Abelson's 1977 theory of scripts, radically revised his theories, stressing the importance of particular, episodic experience:

> Part of the justification for this modification of our old view of scripts is that it really is not possible to say *exactly* what is and what is not part of any script. Particular experiences invade our attempts to make generalizations. To put this another way, we do not believe in the script as a kind of semantic memory data structure, apart from living breathing episodic memories. What we know of restaurants is compiled from a multitude of experiences with them and these experiences are stored with what we have compiled. (Schank, 1982, p. 23)

After proposing mechanistic theories of interpretation by semantic structures in the 1970s, van Dijk and Kintsch (1983) revised their theories of discourse comprehension to emphasize the centrality of episodic memory, the importance of on-line situational models, and the need for strategic processes that are complex, open, and variable rather than rules that are closed and fixed. Applying this episodic, strategic, situational perspective to the still popular notion of scripts, Kintsch and Mannes (1987) note that theories of scripts as stable mental structures are not tenable, suggesting instead that scripts are "generated from an unorganized associative net in response to a specific task demand in a specific context" (p. 62). They argue that situated script generation (as opposed to instantiation) is needed to account for the flexibility and context sensitivity people demonstrate in their cognitive functioning.

The four seminars of the third study pointed to the power of cultural spheres to shape participants' activities and texts. Seminars grounded in the institutional contexts of the classroom displayed activities centered on the exchange of performances for grades, while those more grounded in the institutional contexts of departmental programs or disciplinary forums displayed quite different patterns of activity. The institutional and disciplinary positioning of a seminar, its processes of participant selection, and its particular unfolding history, all of these factors appeared to shape the work students and professors performed in fairly powerful ways. For example, none of the papers from any one of these seminars would have been read without surprise and confusion if handed in in another seminar. Topical analyses (Miller & Selzer, 1985; Prior, 1991, in press) particularly pointed to relations, complex and unstable, but relations nonetheless, between classroom contexts, students' texts, and professors' responses. However, variation appeared within as well as between seminars. In all four seminars, particular personal, interpersonal, and social contexts shaped individual students' work and professors' evaluations. Each professor read markedly different texts (implicating different work) and evaluated them as appropriate, sufficient, and even commendable. This variability in students' work and professors' evaluation, a variability that went almost unnoticed by participants, is a key finding. The complex patterns of activity seen in the four seminars of my third study highlighted the situated plasticity of speech genres and suggest that speech genres, like scripts, are best understood not as instantiated canonical templates governing interpretation and action, but rather as strategically generated interactional achievements.

To illustrate the kinds of data that led me to explore sociohistoric approaches to discourse and knowledge, I will present in the next two sections some examples taken from two seminars selected to represent the range of spheres of activity found in the study. *Geography* best illustrated patterns of activity centered in the institutional contexts of a seminar, while *Sociology* was so tied to other institutional and disciplinary contexts that its status as a seminar was almost fictional.

## CONSTRUCTING SPEECH GENRES: GEOGRAPHY

In *Geography as a Discipline*, Arthur Kohl, a senior professor, was teaching a prose seminar (three were required for graduate students) in the area of geographic thought and philosophy (one of seven designated areas).[8] In class, Kohl seemed open and iconoclastic, a teller of academic tales, but his informality mixed uneasily with instruction delivered primarily through lecture. Six students enrolled in *Geography*, but two dropped after the first meeting. Three of the four who remained had completed their written work when my data collection ended: John, an MA student interested in cartography; Liz, an MA/PhD student interested in culture and global development; and Betty, an MA/PhD student interested in urban economics from the Republic of China (the only NNSE in the seminar).

*Geography* displayed a pattern of activity centered in the seminar and the exchange of performance for grades. Kohl cued a variety of disciplinary and institutional topics in relation to the single writing task for the quarter. Figure 3.1 traces the varied ways the task was explicitly cued at several key junctures in the seminar. Introduced as a "final" and referred to as three "blue book essays," the writing task received limited attention during the quarter. Noting that prose seminars offered broad surveys, Kohl had indicated that one essay of the final would call for a survey. Discussing the in-depth topical essay, Kohl advised students to consider topics that they could develop for master's or PhD work. As the date approached, students sought to clarify the task (e.g., whether it was in-class or take-home), but it was not finalized until the last class session. Even then, Kohl's cueing was not particularly detailed; the fact that the final version included two essays instead of three was not even mentioned.

The content of the course provided other cues for the writing task. The overall organization of the course was chronological, beginning with the roots of geography in ancient Greece and ending with a focus on critical and postmodern theories in 20th-century geography. The syllabus gave a "catchy" title for each session (e.g., *Old World, New Ideas: Antipodal Utopias; Hettner to Hartshorne to Chance: Triple-Play*; and *Post-everything*). Kohl emphasized relations between philosophy and geography. Highlighting debate in the discipline, Kohl repeatedly modeled critique of received opinion, contesting the typical origin story of geography, deconstructing landscape classifications such as the Great Plains, and sharply criticizing the transfer of scientific concepts and quantitative methods to human geography. This diverse topical content represented a basic resource for students in producing their texts.

In response to these cues, John, Liz, and Betty produced fairly different texts (see Figure 3.2 for extracts from the three texts). John filled one blue book (handwritten) on the in-depth topic and four pages of a second blue book in critiquing the course. For his topical essay on the history of cartographic representation, he wrote short paragraphs and referred to few sources. Except for a few short quotations, his final product, thus,

---

[8]All names of participants and their institutions are pseudonyms.

**Task description from syllabus handed out in session one.**
Final: Critique
- Value of the Seminar
- Topics: as a whole
- Topic: one, in depth

**Research interview week 8. Liz is asked to describe the tasks of the seminar.**

Liz:   Uh, do the reading every week, um think about a topic that particularly interests you, 'think about it' whatever that means, and then um write about it at the end of the quarter

Paul:  How do you, what form do you have to write about it in?

Liz:   Well I think he said he'll distribute a blue book, um, essay form, I think we'll just write an essay

Paul:  Ok, and the topics?

Liz:   And the topics, I'm not clear about the topics, I assume he means the topics on the syllabus although uh eeerr, I don't think I'm actually going to do the task that way, I mean um,

Paul:  What

Liz:   I'm uh, I'm interested in the French school of geography, and that doesn't appear actually per se on the syllabus, as a-as an entity in itself, but I'm sort of picking up strands that I think are related to it, from each of the sessions that we've had

**Seminar exchange at end of session in week 8.**

Liz:   Do we- are we going to meet and write that in class?

Kohl:  No.

Liz:   Oh [laughter]

Kohl:  On the tenth week, the last meeting we have, I'll just say uh, by the end of finals week turn in something, and I'd like three sort of comments, one on the way in which we did this, the sequence of readings and so on, did they make sense, or how did it flow through the - should we have done something different, started with the modern and go back to the roots rather than picking up a thread, ( ), secondly, I want you to pick out some particular theme you want to comment on, that you're interested in, I suspect it has to do with methodology of your own particular research, and I'd like some critical comment of whatever you've been reading outside, that is, common readings have led you to do more work in something else, or in some other class you're doing something for your masters papers or your Ph.D. thesis, in other words contributed [pause] ok, so next time

**Description of task written on chalkboard at beginning of final session (Week 10).**
Take-Home Final—end of Finals Week
2 Questions—Two Blue Books maximum in length
1. Critique of seminar—Organization, Readings, Sequence, etc.
   (only limitation—keep in mind this was designated as a Pro-seminar by the department.)
2. Your choice—one topic in depth or a comparison of two or more readings.

*(continued)*

**Figure 3.1.**   Images of a writing task from *Geography*

**Seminar exchange at beginning of final session (Week 10).**

**Kohl:** I'm not asking you to write in a blue book if you have a computer or you type or something like that, that's fine with me, but I don't particularly want a long paper

**Liz:** About how long would you suppose a blue book is if you typed it double spaced, do you have any i—I mean, do I have to write the thing in here first and then type [laughter]

**Kohl:** No, just estimate how many words you've got to a page

**Liz:** Oh, ( )

**Kohl:** The point is that uh, you could write forever on any topic you choose, it's basically how you organize this second question that is the criteria I would use evaluating what you said, because I think that if you get the questions (straight) and see a buildup of those questions and some kind of a conclusion that's really the key to a good answer, I don't know that there's any right answer to any of this, did you all get copies of the papers?

**Figure 3.1.** *(continued)*

resembled an in-class essay. Betty, on the other hand, produced texts on a letter quality printer—a page and a half for the course evaluation and five pages on the topic. Discussing Kohl's place in debates over the role of science in geography, her in-depth essay resembled a short term paper, including a 10-item bibliography, standard citation, and paragraph-length quotes from sources. Liz struck an intermediate note, writing a little over two pages (letter-quality print) in response to each prompt. In her topical essay on French School geography, she referred to sources regularly, but maintained a fairly informal style.

Kohl read the essays, commenting briefly on each, and graded them. He responded to the content of John and Liz's essays and to the content and language of Betty's. Kohl's evaluations were not harsh, but he did use grades to differentiate student performance, A's to reward work he appreciated and B's to mildly censure work he did not. Analysis of the cases suggests that the meaning of each text emerged out of personal and interpersonal as well as institutional contexts and histories.

Presenting an overview of map making from ancient Greece to the modern era, John's essay (see extract in Figure 3.2) blended prominent seminar topics (representations of the world; the chronological development of geography as a discipline) with a topic that John was personally interested in and knowledgeable about, cartography. In his critique of the course, John indicated that the early survey was quite useful, but that the modern topics, particularly critical theory, raised issues that he neither understood nor was interested in. In an unusual example of evaluation being explicitly topicalized in writing, John, whose participation in the seminar had been nil, concluded his critique with a plea: "I hope you can see your way clear not to fail me." While Kohl acknowledged the accuracy and

**John on maps**

Meanwhile, an idea fundamental to the evolution of geography (and of cartography), a spherical earth, gained widespread acceptance and led to attempts to determine the earth's circumference. Using his knowledge of geometry, Eratosthenes succeeded in calculating the size of the earth with a remarkable degree of accuracy (given the limits of geographic knowledge at the time).

Logically, this brought about the development of globes and depictions of a spherical world on flat surfaces based upon the concept of projection. Hipparchus of Nicaea, an astronomer and follower of Eratosthenes, contributed much to modern cartography, including the Stereographic and Orthographic projections, and a refined rectangular system or (graticule) of parallels and meridians. He also insisted on the accurate location of places according to latitude and longitude, as determined by astronomical observation.

Indeed, it was astronomy which provided the first three lines of reference for early cartographers: the Equator and the Tropics of Cancer and Capricorn. . . .

**Liz on *genre de vie***

As interesting as the roots of culture in nature is Durkheim's concern for social morphology: structures of society. Buttimer asserts that, with the concept of *genre de vie*, Vidal uses Durkheim's idea of the livelihood group as the unit of cultural and geographical analysis. By combining the society-milieu relationships suggested by Ratzel with the livelihood group as organizing unit, *genre de vie* offers a principle for rich evocations of culture. While description is the strength of the French School, explanation has been perceived as its weakness. Vidal's critics disparaged a lack of methodological rigor in his holistic approach to understanding cultures and places. Buttimer acknowledges that Vidal was better at characterizing cultures than at analyzing the actual mechanisms which shape culture. (She does imply that Vidal had outlined specific ways in which *genre de vie* could inform empirical studies of particular regions; but these ideas were never satisfactorily carried out). Even the concept of contingency, which alleviates concern over the determinism issue, leaves analysis somewhat uncertain. Contingency has proved the stumbling block in structuralist research, as well as in Vidal's. The claim that there are causal mechanisms underlying society, each of which may result in a variety of seemingly contradictory events, defies empirical testing of one's theory.

In addition to the criticism that *genre de vie* lacked explanatory value, Buttimer points out that Vidal's ecological and holistic studies were viewed as helpful only when applied to "traditional" societies. They seemed inadequate to explain and describe complex "modern" societies. Today, cultural ecologists are also burdened by this charge. I think the feeling is that, the farther people stray from the land (in terms of its direct role in their subsistence), the less rooted they are in the local environment, and the less relevance the local environment has for maintaining culture, save as history.

I do not dispute these criticisms; indeed, it seems to me that such charges are applicable to all of the geographies I find most appealing. However, I think there is a place for these works which preserve the adventure of geographic discovery. . . .

*(continued)*

**Figure 3.2** Extracts from second *Geography* essay

**Betty on scientific method**

Geographical and historical methods are based on Kant's classification of knowledge. Although Kantian time-space limits our imagination in multi-dimensional space, yet it is basically the way we look at this phenomenal world. For example, we can study a place by knowing its location, size, shape, history and population, and so on. Then we should know the cultural groups of this place, and try to understand their behavior patterns such as their traditions, customs, heritage, preferences and habits. After collecting these facts, we should record the data on the map, and describe the place as a whole in a well-organized form of writing.

However, one problem remains unsolved between the processes of data-collecting and description of spatial phenomena. How can we conceptualize the physical world? It seems there is no clear answer for this question. The most common way is by characters, that is, the process of conceptualization relies on good writing. However, the inconsistency and misinterpretation of terminology causes problems in communication. Also, sometime scholars use very technical and complicated word to describe the empirical world, which isolates the studies away from the public. Eventually, geographical inquiry remains distant from the reality. Thus, looking for a way to improve conceptualization of spatial phenomena is needed.

Since we talk a lot about the scientific method in social sciences, we have to ask a question: can geography become scientific? It depends. If we try very hard to quantify the studies of geography into mathematical regulations, the answer is no. Not every issue of geography can be quantified.

**Figure 3.2.**  (*continued*)

detail of John's first essay, he was not particularly impressed with it. Map making clearly was a disciplinary topic and the historical overview did match the chronological organization Kohl employed; however, John presented an unproblematized, textbook history, whereas Kohl had emphasized philosophical reflection and critical evaluation. Kohl's strongest reaction in the interview was to John's critique, which he felt signalled an anti-intellectual attitude. Kohl explained in the interview that John's blue book grade, a B, was based both on John's essays and his limited participation in the seminar.

Liz's topical essay took a historical topic (French School geography) that she was interested in (see Figure 3.1 interview) and wrote about it in ways that were personal, philosophical, and problematizing (see extract in Figure 3.2). In the seminar, Kohl had distributed an article he had written on French geographic thought, particularly that of Vidal. In a text-based interview, Kohl indicated strong approval of Liz's performance in class and her essays:

Yeah, I thought that she was the best student by far in there. . . . and obviously I had some attachment to her particular interest in the French School, since I've been doing work on that, published papers on that, I think that um, she's probably as good a student as I've had in that kind of a seminar[9]

Liz received the only A in the seminar; however, her own perceptions of her topical essay were far less laudatory. In an interview almost four months after the quarter, Liz recounted one pattern of activity that the seminar evoked.

> Um, I wrote it, I wrote it in a hurry it's- it's difficult for me to write and I didn't really allow very much time, maybe I allowed enough time for somebody else, but not for me, you know I did it, I think I did it, um the day before I had to leave town, um yeah, and I do remember being very disappointed in this paper, although um, um it seemed to me that I prepared all along in the class, I didn't actually know what I was going to write, but I knew what I was interested in from the very beginning of the quarter, which was the French geographers, and um so I paid particular attention to them when we did some of that reading, and when we had the discussion about them, I was a little more tuned in, and I did some reading on my own, just sort of over the course of the quarter, but I still, up until the very day I was supposed to write this essay, I didn't really know what I wanted to say, so uh, it was kind of a tough one to write

Liz later indicated that she had not expected an A when she turned in her essays. Her comments suggest she undertook the writing for this seminar in a serious but limited fashion. Another indication of how she took the task came later in the interview. Finding that she had not picked up the essays, I asked if she eventually would have:

**Liz:**   No, no [emphatic, laughing]
**Paul:**   You just would have
**Liz:**   I just, it's done, you know, [laughing] and it's over with, ok?

Liz's lack of interest in Kohl's response reinforces the conclusion that her activity was centered in the institutional demands of the seminar. There was no question of revision here; the exchange was completed in filing grades with the registrar. In a text-based interview, I asked Liz to comment on Kohl's responses. One of his final summary comments read: "As you may

---

[9]In the interest of space, I have deleted my backchannel responses (e.g., "umhm") from transcripts. A hyphen "-" indicates an abrupt stop. Ellipses have their usual meaning. Empty parentheses indicate an unintelligible segment; parentheses around text indicate uncertain transcriptions. Punctuation and line divisions are used to improve the readability of the transcript; they do not reflect an analysis of breath groups or intonation contours, though they may sometimes relate to such features.

have guessed I find the French School more original in its thinking and not a big borrower of ideas from Ratzel and Durkheim." I asked Liz if she had guessed this:

> Um, never thought about it, I mean I know that he loves the French school, I mean that came across in the seminar, but um, more original in its thinking and not just borrowers from Ratzel and Durkheim, hm, no I hadn't guessed that, I mean, I didn't know very much about it so uh, you know, tracing the antecedents of something like the French School of geography is a total mystery, I mean if somebody tells me that uh Ratzel and Durkheim had, you know, sort of contributed to this line of thought, then, sounds good, you know what I mean? [laughing] 'cause — what do I know? ok

Asked how useful Kohl's comments were, Liz answered "not very" and then went on to discuss how she often found a gap between professors' responses and her own sense of her knowledge.

> I mean I'm sure he can't know that I was very uncertain about all of these terms I was using, *genre de vie*, you know, was I using it the right-? well he knows what it is exactly, and um so he may- he just glossed over reading it, whereas I had to really kind of struggle with it and, and I'm not sure if I did get it in the end, you know? But he might read more into it than is there, I guess

The gap between Kohl's evaluation of Liz's work and Liz's own evaluation raises interesting questions. Such gaps point to the need to look beyond the surface of words to determine how meaning and knowledge are being negotiated. Liz's suggestion that Kohl read more meaning and knowledge into her words than she had put into them seemed plausible; other data from the third study pointed to just such a process. (For a more detailed exploration, see Prior, 1992.) This process of *reading into* might help create a sense of coherence among diverse written products; it might also contribute to disciplinary enculturation, facilitating a sustained interaction between people whose knowledge of the field is quite asymmetrical (cf. Ochs, 1991). In other words, Kohl might not only be reading more meaning into Liz's use of terms like *genre de vie*; he might also be reading more disciplinarity into Liz's text, as these terms evoked intertextual connections to his own knowledge of geography. I would also suggest, however, that Kohl's positive evaluations arose not just from Liz's use of specialized terms, but also from her evocation of central topical themes that Kohl had emphasized in the classroom, both substantive (philosophy, critique, and history) and task-related (personal interests, outside readings). That they shared an interest in French geography may also have contributed. Betty's essay examined Kohl's own place in modern geographic debates. It opened by quoting from and discussing several articles Kohl had written about the translation of concepts from the physical sciences into human geography. The extract in Figure 3.2 comes from near the conclusion of Betty's five-page essay. Betty's text seemed to respond quite directly to the topics of the seminar. She focused on Kohl's own work in geographic thought, a topic Kohl had raised both in class discussion and through distribution of his own articles to students. She appeared to be addressing geography from the kind of philosophical and problematized perspective he stressed. However, Kohl edited Betty's language at a number of points and indicated his dissatisfaction in his summary comment at the end of her essay:

> You are on the right track, I believe, but your vocabulary and syntax aren't quite up to communicating your thoughts. I sympathize with what your ideas are — and, therefore, I think I know what you are saying — but I can't prove it by what you actually write. Good straight-forward writing is difficult — and takes time, and practice.

In an interview, Kohl pointed to an interpersonal context (an unfinished, year-old independent study) that shed further light on both Betty's essay and his response:

> Betty's a problem, she can't write, so I've had her in every two weeks for an hour or two, and what she's trying to do outside of this particular class and the reason she sat in the class was essentially to figure out what my particular role in the last 30 years has been in geographic thought, I don't usually encourage students to do that, but since she's a foreigner, and she's had a very traditional geographic education in Taiwan, it seemed to me to be a good time for- to introduce this, because she'd been interested in (a) thesis topic and in our- her other courses, in what's essentially economic urban geography, in what's going to happen to urban types and sites and locations and relationships in the Far East, but she can't write, yet in exchanges with her, every two weeks for an hour or so, it's very clear that she has ideas, and she vigorously defends her ideas, I accuse her of uh trying to make geography into a mathematical science and so on, and uh she uh falls back on what to me is an excuse, that she can't express herself [he laughs] you know in English

As our interview continued, Kohl moved back and forth between Betty's problems writing in English and her conflicting philosophical orientation to geography. When asked what specific problems in Betty's writing led him to say that she couldn't write, Kohl replied:

One of the problems with Far Eastern students and to a certain extent some European students who come here is they have trouble with prepositions, and they leave them out, so you don't know essentially what the referent is, so you think you're on the right track halfway through the sentence and then the predicate comes and you begin to wonder, "Is that what they really meant?" they haven't specified *this*, *that*, *the*, *an*, *a*, so you're not exactly sure that the thought is carried through, my only help was, tell her to keep on writing, write and write and write and write some more, seems to me there is, she's not dumb, she's got plenty of ideas, but she uh has sort of a basement level that she doesn't get beneath in order to converse, so a lot of the problems are basically writing and speaking carried through, when she's here and we're speaking, then I can correct her, when I get a paper, all I can do is, make a note, then I get tired of making so many notes on a page, and then we talk about it, and uh, we finally begin to communicate better, find out what she's really trying to say, I think I'm getting educated to her speech [I laugh, he laughs] so when I say "I think you're on the right track," I wouldn't have said that probably six months ago, because I wouldn't know whether she was on the right track or not I- it's- it's the syntax mostly, she knows all the words, but they don't come together properly, and it isn't that it's uh poor English, it's funny English, I have American students who write worse than she does, but somehow the structure of the sentence, the syntax, the grammatical argument is clear, even with poor American students, they at least are thinking in English, every now and then I begin to think I'm trying too hard, maybe I shouldn't try to understand her, in the sense of putting things in there, let her flounder around, but then she gets so goddamned discouraged that she's not making progress, and I think she has a tendency to put things off and switch from one course to another, she's had about three advisors in the department since she came, sort of gravitated to me because I'll listen to her, I-, is my impression,

**Paul:** are you her advisor now?
**Kohl:** yeah I was suddenly assigned that, I didn't ask for it, (she) didn't ask for this (), I don't think she can get a degree basically unless she has vast improvement

Kohl concluded his comments by telling of another Chinese student who perplexed his professors by treating "land use map" and "land map use" as synonymous. Kohl's two accounts of Betty's problem, language difficulties and theoretical conflicts, may reflect alternative schemes in an interpretive repertoire rather than something that could be resolved into a single "true" interpretation (cf. Gilbert & Mulkay, 1984). His remarks in this transcript suggest how interpersonal and social contexts may merge with evaluation. When Kohl reads Betty's text, he sees Betty through both categorical and particular lenses. Categorically, she is an advisee, a Chinese foreign student, a nonnative speaker of English, and the product of a traditional education. Particularly, Betty is the student who has been in his office a number of times, who argues with him about the role of science in geography, who puts things off, who has had three advisors, and who may fail because of language problems.

The gap between Kohl's and Liz's evaluation of her work, the complex interpersonal history implicated in Kohl's evaluation of Betty, and Kohl's indication that his grade on John's essay related to classroom participation as well as the text at hand, all point to complexly situated processes of evaluation and response, but not necessarily terribly engaged processes. To produce their texts, the students could apply routine strategies: considering the varied topical content cued by the seminar, reviewing other intertextual resources (e.g., disciplinary knowledge at hand; familiar textual forms), employing routine textual production activities, and interrogating their own goals. Drawing on these resources, students produced varied texts. Of course, as a dialogic phenomenon, speech genres are constituted in acts of reading as well as writing. Kohl read the three very different texts as "the essays" he asked for, regardless of their differences in format and print, topics and language, length and citation. The writing task in *Geography* appeared to occur primarily within the institutional sphere of the class-room, to evoke performances for grades. That Betty's essay may have been addressing her relationship with Kohl as well or that Liz may have been pursuing personal interests, not just course demands, does not alter that basic judgment of the sphere of activity. It may, however, suggest another point: a speech genre may represent a particular balance of centripetal and centrifugal forces. Kohl's task cueing in this seminar left considerable topical space underdetermined; thus, the diversity that emerged in the final texts may reflect the relatively centrifugal nature of the task itself.

## CONSTRUCTING SPEECH GENRES: SOCIOLOGY

*Sociology*, a seminar organized by Professor Elaine West, was a topical offering without a title. It counted toward a departmental requirement for advanced research, but was only offered pass/fail. The most salient institutional context, in fact, was not the seminar. The seven PhD students in the seminar were all employed as research assistants in Adolescence Study (the Study), a longitudinal survey of local high school students and their parents. Professor West was the principal investigator of the Study, and Professors Lynch and Harris, who sat in, were coinvestigators. Five of the seven students were West's advisees and at least four had decided to use the Study's data for their dissertations, so the departmental program was another strong context in the seminar. Three students had already (when the quarter began) been listed as coauthors on one or more of the 15 conference papers or journal articles generated from the Study; thus, disciplinary contexts were also salient. One measure of the centrality of these other contexts was the fact that West, Lynch, Harris, and five of the students had met biweekly as an unofficial seminar the previous two quarters.

The generic activity in *Sociology* was centered in three spheres: the work contexts of the Study; the departmental contexts of preliminary examinations, dissertation prospectuses, and advising; and the disciplinary contexts of refereed publication in journals and presentation at professional conferences. The seminar provided a forum for the students to present and get responses to their individual projects related to the Study. As an intact research team with an established agenda, the seminar opened with West suggesting that students should produce more developed versions of the work they had started the previous two quarters and reviewing what students planned to present. After this first meeting, most sessions were devoted to discussion of one student's written work and research. Discussions focused on substantive issues of theory and research design as well as the texts themselves.

In *Sociology*, the content of students' writing was strongly influenced by the topics embedded in the design of the Study. Regardless of their individual interests, the students were working with a study that West had planned, a study that presented longitudinal (rather than cross-sectional) data on adolescents and their parents; that sampled a particular set of demographic, biographic, attitudinal, and psychological items; that assumed a four-part contextual scheme (family, school, peer group, and work); and that embodied a quantitative approach and a disciplinary location (sociological social psychology). Students might graft other schemes and other questions onto this design, seek other disciplinary locations, but they could not ignore it. Once they decided to use the data set, they had to fit their interests to the data that had been collected.

The activities that students undertook reflected their positions and histories in the Study and the status of their academic programs. The five students who had been involved with the Study and the informal seminars of previous quarters presented a near-final draft of a conference proposal (Moira), a near-final draft of a dissertation prospectus (Sean), rough drafts of preliminary examinations (Lee and Linda), and a draft of a coauthored article for a journal (Thomas with Harris). Two students who were new to the Study/seminar presented work they were assigned to do for the Study: initial drafts of sections (the literature review and statistical tables) for a technical report The institutional and programmatic differences between students emerged more clearly as I solicited "drafts related to the seminar." I received texts dated as much as eight months before and four months after the seminar (the latter representing when I stopped data collection). Sean provided eight drafts of his preliminary examination, six of his dissertation prospectus, and seven of a coauthored article for a journal. (About half of these drafts had been responded to by West or another professor.) From Moira, I received four drafts of her preliminary examination (three with written responses from West) and seven drafts of a conference paper (five with written responses from West). In both cases, revisions closely followed the written responses from West. At points, response and revision were very intense indeed. For example, in responding to one three-paragraph section of the fifth draft of Moira's conference paper, West edited the text extensively (17 responses that added 106 words and deleted 83). In the sixth draft, written within a week of the fifth, Moira had acted on all 17 responses, inserting 105 of the 106 words and deleting all 83 from the three paragraphs. This deep engagement contrasts very sharply with Liz's engagement in *Geography,* where she did not even pick up her essays. However, not every student in *Sociology* was so engaged, as we will see particularly in Park's case.

To illustrate how contextual effects mediated task production and reception, I will focus on the writing tasks two students, Park and Lee, undertook for the seminar. Park and Lee were both NNSE from Korea who had obtained master's degrees in sociology at U.S. universities and then transferred to Midwest University to obtain PhD degrees. Both planned to return to Korea to seek faculty positions. In the seminar sessions, Park and Lee generally participated little, though Lee participated more often than Park and seemed more fluent. Park and Lee both received satisfactory grades for the seminar. However, Park was new to the Study, while Lee had worked in a key position for almost two years. In spite of their similarities, the differences between the products they produced, the processes those products emerged from, and the consequences of those products were so sharp that they raise the issue of whether their patterns of activity in *Sociology* were even roughly comparable. The way West treats this difference also points to how contexts may shape situated evaluation.

West had assigned Park and the other new research assistant to work on sections of a technical report. Park's task was to run some statistical analyses and produce tables to accompany the report; the other student was asked to do a related literature review. Park and the other student presented their work in an early session. The other student presented the literature review, which was found conceptually problematic, first, and then Park's turn came. Park had a great deal of trouble communicating orally and was very uncertain about his analyses. Later in that session, West, after noting how little time these presenters had had, indicated that Park had provided more data, rawer data, and data that did not illustrate some of the central trends she had been concerned with (e.g., gender differences).

In text-based interviews, West discussed the copresentation with Park:

Right, well, in their case, they had newly come onto the project so I did not feel that they would have- you know—that they shouldn't be subject to the same requirement of producing a finished paper, because they were at, you know, great disadvantage given that the other students had had two quarters to develop their ideas, so instead what we decided was that they would each do part of a paper that we would continue to work on during the summer, and that this would be you know coauthored with me as well, and uh so I think that, whereas the two parts did not turn out to be very well integrated, that it- both of them kind of learned what it meant to integrate some empirical work with some theoretical considerations, and so we're continuing to do this. . . . [West discusses the other presenter's work] So you see this is a very different kind of academic exercise, I mean to have, you know, such different expectations and products from the various students, but I view this all in the spirit of the, you know, of professional training, that you have to kind of get at the student where they are at in their particular development, and then try to help them from that point, so that's why I didn't want to be grading the students on a you know grade basis, that they'd either satisfactorily completed or not, and I feel that all of them did learn something, that they were able to you know make progress, now Park I think will be working on the [Study] for his dissertation. . . . [West discusses the other presenter briefly], and in the case of Park, I really don't have a sense of his you know writing capacity as of this point

Park's comments in an interview three months after his presentation suggest how limited his engagement with this task was.

**Paul:** How did you choose the presentation that you did this spring?
**Park:** Well, I didn't choose, I don't know how it was choose but the profess, um professor asked us to do that, especially for me and [the other "new" student], but the other students different, continue the true work

**Paul:** Could you kind of summarize what happened in the presentation, and what were the outcomes, what followed from it, are you still working on this basically?
**Park:** Uh no, not exactly
**Paul:** Did you do anything else on this after the presentation

**Park:** No
**Paul:** It was done, ok, so can you summarize sort of what was the discussion about this
**Park:** Well [he laughs] I cannot remember () discuss at that time

**Paul:** Did you ever get written feedback on this?
**Park:** No. . . . but the uh, there were some mistakes in my presentation of the tables so, professor gave me some kind of directions about how to correct, I corrected it and uh I just gave it to her.

Both Park's and West's comments suggest a quite limited task. West saw Park's tables as problematic, but pardonable given Park's short tenure in the Study. Park evidently saw the task as a difficult work assignment that was finished, contrasting it with other students' "true work." In the first session, as West was reviewing what work students would do, Park asked if it was possible to change from his assigned task. West said they could talk about that later.

While Park had just entered the Study and the seminar, Lee had been working in the Study for two years. As a data analyst, Lee was well positioned in the Study in terms of authorship. Lee had third or fourth authorship on six articles or presentations, placing him only below West (14), Sean (10), and Lynch (7). However, Lee's inclusion in authorship came strictly from database management and data analysis; he had done no writing on any of those six papers. Given his history in the Study, Lee, like Sean, might have been expected to complete a preliminary exam and perhaps even a prospectus in the final quarter of the seminar. Instead, he only produced a rough draft of a prelim, as was signalled by the memo he attached to it when he distributed it:

> This is the very, very first draft of my prelim paper. I could write something down in a meaningful (?) way only in the first two chapters. After that, I basically laid out what I am going to do for finishing this paper. I am not still confident about the way things are presented in this paper. I would very much appreciate your constructive criticism and suggestions.

The draft that Lee produced was an 8-page review of the literature on status attainment (bibliography not included) and a very sketchy 4-page outline of his extension of the model. One section of that outline, for example, consisted of the following paragraph.

4. Mobility Table Analysis
   The tradition of mobility table analysis has been carried through with the advancement of statistical procedures analyzing contingency tables. Even

though my thesis is not going to rely on this procedure, I will briefly review the development of this camp in the study of intergenerational mobility.

While some sections were more developed than this one, it does suggest the rough quality of Lee's draft. Moreover, when I interviewed Lee about his prelim 4 months later, it was clear that he had not revised it or even carefully examined West's responses.

In a text-based interview, West reflected on Lee's performance in the seminar.

**West:** Ok, Lee, you know, Lee does have difficulty expressing his ideas, I think he's improved quite a bit, since he started here, I had him in a social psychology class a few years ago when he initially entered the program and, you know, I've noticed he's gotten a lot better in his writing, I feel that Lee is not as motivated to, you know, finish very quickly, he's interested in returning to Korea and having a lot of expertise in methodological things and, you know, especially related to computers and special programs and so on and statistical analysis, and so he's taking a lot of course work while he's doing this, and he's not as intensively focused and, you know, interested in moving along through, so I think that his progress has been slower, but I-I believe too that he has quite a lot of promise and that, you know, with time his writing will continue to improve, and he has-he is extremely smart, and he's very good at his computer work, which is, you know, really important to develop those research skills as well, you can see on this page I say, "Unclear, rewrite it, you need two sentences here, one explains this and the other explains," you know, to kind of help him to to organize it, [looking at the paper], and he did not do as thorough a literature review as some of the other students and I had given him, you know, titles, but he didn't incorporate all of them, and he just kind of very much skimmed this toward you know the end so

**Paul:** In a meeting before you had given some titles of things to take into

**West:** Yeah, right, in fact I gave him a long list in writing of the things that he should consider, I think that it's just not, you know, it's not along his time schedule to, you know, move this this quickly, but I considered Lee kind of a special case, in that this is supposed to be a research seminar and demonstrate, in our department, I don't know if you're familiar- the department's research requirement, the students are supposed to take one seminar that involves hands-on research experience

**Paul:** Yeah

**West:** And this is a newly instituted requirement, it went into effect I
think a couple of years ago, and so students have to fulfill their
research requirement by taking a seminar like this, and either
working with a faculty member on a paper or developing their
own paper, and he's done a tremendous amount of that through,
you know, all of the other papers that we've worked on, you've
seen the list, so I thought that he definitely satisfied the, you
know, the research requirement, so he received an S on the course
as well, although I would have liked to have seen a more complete, you know, prelim than he was able to develop by this time

West's responses to Lee and Park illustrate the influence in *Sociology* of
the interpersonal and institutional histories the Study had established. West
accounts for the very different work they produced in terms of their
different histories in the Study and the informal seminars that preceded this
official seminar. It is interesting that West felt the need to justify giving Lee
credit for a research seminar when his work was somewhat less than what
might be expected, but did not bring up this issue for Park, whose work was
presumably far below what would be expected. It is also clear that neither
Park nor Lee was involved in the kind of intense disciplinary work that
Moira and Sean, in close collaboration with West, displayed. Clearly,
literate activity in *Sociology*, both students' writing and West's response,
was dominated by the Study, the departmental program, and disciplinary
forums.

## CONCLUSION

Examining academic writing tasks as they are produced and read in context
and over time reveals such tasks as fundamentally situated and multiple (cf.
Nelson, 1990; Nespor, 1987). The historical continuity of tasks and the
influence of multiple contexts on tasks also suggests that we need to look
beyond single-classroom studies. Nespor (1987) argues that individual
classrooms should be seen only "as partial settings of the 'academic careers'
that students create as they move through complex sets of classroom
environments" (pp. 227–228). Swales' (1990a) case studies of graduate
NNSE raise the issue of what needs we should be addressing. Finding out
what students need for success in classes may not represent what they need
for institutional progress, which in turn may not represent their needs in
professional work after they graduate. When we locate academic writing
and response within the histories and contexts of students and teachers, we
also need to reexamine what our tasks are as researchers and practitioners

of English for Academic Purposes. If academic discourse and academic environments are complex, constructed and unfolding events and not closed systems susceptible to taxonomic and rule-oriented description, then we cannot simply specify and teach "academic writing tasks." Are needs analyses then of any use? My answer is that they certainly are. The various approaches taken by EAP researchers so far have increased our understanding of the linguistic and rhetorical composition of academic texts, of some of the problems students face in academic environments, and of the ways that students and professors name and account for aspects of academic performance. Ethnographic, sociohistoric approaches to needs analysis can add to this accumulating knowledge by enhancing our awareness of the situated processes and resources students use in producing writing and professors use in responding to it.

Discussing the restricted transfer of learning from well-structured lessons to naturally occurring complex settings, Spiro, Vispoel, Schmitz, Samarapungavan, and Boerger (1987) suggest that knowledge representations for students should have the following features: "multiple interconnectedness between different aspects of domain knowledge, multidimensional or multiperspectival representation of examples/cases, and allowance for various forms of naturally occurring complexity and irregularity" (p. 178). Thus, they argue, what is needed is "cognitive flexibility." Perhaps it is time for EAP to direct less attention to static conceptualizations of communicative competence that lead us into well-structured knowledge representations and more attention to considering how we can facilitate students' development of the communicative flexibility needed to achieve communication in dynamic, situated interaction. When we view EAP pedagogy through this lens, we will find many valuable practices already in place, practices that employ authentic materials, language, and tasks; that create opportunities for experiential learning (e.g., ethnography, adjunct courses, observation and interview projects); that allow for self-initiated expression and dialogue (e.g., dialogue journals); and that emphasize self-directed inquiry. We may also find that the simple rules and systems we have sometimes offered are still of use when re-presented as heuristic strategies rather than universal facts. What a sociohistoric perspective can add is a clearer sense of the complexities and uncertainties we are preparing students for and an alternate way to account for language acquisition and use.

Examining academic writing tasks as speech genres, that is, as they unfold in concrete situations at specific times with particular participants, we begin to encounter the dialogic forces shaping academic activity and discourse, to see the situated interpretive and interactional work that generates meanings and texts, and to sense how that work is socially mediated or socially impeded. Taking this perspective will not provide a new technology for EAP pedagogy. It will not make our work as teachers, curriculum designers, testers, or researchers easier; in fact, in some ways, it will complicate it. However, it surely matters if we perceive our students as full subjects working to achieve their social, intellectual, and affective goals within complex, emergent streams of situated activity rather than as "academic dopes" endlessly re-encoding the abstract rules and conventions of monologic discourses.

# REFERENCES

Bakhtin, M. (1981) *The dialogic imagination: Four essays by M. M. Bakhtin* (C. Emerson & M. Holquist, Trans.; M. Holquist, Ed.). Austin: University of Texas Press.

Bakhtin, M. (1986). *Speech genres and other late essays* (V. W McGee, Trans; C. Emerson & M. Holquist, Eds.). Austin: University of Texas Press.

Ballard, B. (1984). Improving student writing: An integrated approach to cultural adjustment. In R. Williams, J. M. Swales, & J. Kirkman (Eds.), *Common ground: Shared interests in ESP and communication studies* (pp. 43–53). (ELT Document No. 117). Oxford, UK: The British Council and Pergamon Press.

Bazerman, C. (1988). *Shaping written knowledge: The genre and activity of the experimental article in science.* Madison: University of Wisconsin Press.

Becker, A. L. (1988). Language in particular: A lecture. In D. Tannen (Ed.), *Linguistics in context: Connecting observation and understanding* (pp. 17–35). Norwood, NJ: Ablex.

Belcher, D. (1989). How professors initiate nonnative speakers into their disciplinary discourse communities. *Texas Papers in Foreign Language Education, 1,* 207–225.

Berkenkotter, C., Huckin, T. N., & Ackerman, J. (1988). Conventions, conversations, and the writer: Case study of a student in a rhetoric Ph.D. program. *Research in the Teaching of English, 22,* 9–44.

Berkenkotter, C., Huckin, T. N., & Ackerman, J. (1991). Social context and socially constructed texts: The initiation of a graduate student into a writing research community. In C. Bazerman & J. Paradis (Eds.), *Textual dynamics of the professions* (pp. 191–215). Madison: University of Wisconsin Press.

Blakeslee, A. (1992). *Inventing scientific discourse: Dimensions of rhetorical knowledge in physics.* Unpublished doctoral dissertation, Carnegie Mellon University, Pittsburgh, PA.

Bloome, D., Puro, P., & Theodorou, E. (1989). Procedural display and classroom lessons. *Curriculum Inquiry, 19,* 265–291.

Braine, G. (1989). Writing in science and technology: An analysis of assignments from ten undergraduate courses. *English for Specific Purposes, 8,* 3–15.

Bridgeman, B., & Carlson, S. (1983). *Survey of academic writing tasks required of graduate and undergraduate foreign students* (Report No. 83–18). Princeton, NJ: Educational Testing Service.

Casanave, C. P. (1990). *The role of writing in socializing graduate students into an academic discipline in the social sciences.* Unpublished doctoral dissertation, Stanford University, Stanford, CA.

Chiseri-Strater, E. (1991). *Academic literacies: The public and private discourse of university students.* Portsmouth, NH: Boynton/Cook.

Clark, G., & Doheny-Farina, S. (1990). Public discourse and personal expression: A case study of theory-building. *Written Communication, 7,* 456–481.

Collins, H. M. (1985). *Changing order: Replication and induction in scientific practice.* London: Sage.

van Dijk, T. A., & Kintsch, W. (1983). *Strategies of discourse comprehension.* New York: Academic.

Doheny-Farina, S. (1989). A case study of one adult writing in academic and nonacademic discourse communities. In C. B. Matalene (Ed.), *Worlds of writing: Teaching and learning in discourse communities of work* (pp. 17–42). New York: Random House.

Doyle, W. (1983). Academic work. *Review of Educational Research, 53,* 159–199.

Dudley-Evans, T. (1986). Genre analysis: An investigation of the introduction and discussion sections of M.Sc. dissertations. In M. Coulthard (Ed.), *Talking about text* (pp. 128–145). Birmingham, UK: English Language Research, University of Birmingham.

Edmondson, R. (1984). *Rhetoric in sociology.* London: The MacMillian Press.

Faigley, L., & Hansen, K. (1985). Learning to write in the social sciences. *College Composition and Communication, 36,* 140–149.

Fish, S. (1980). *Is there a text in this class? The authority of interpretive communities.* Cambridge, MA: Harvard University Press.

Fiske, S. T., & Taylor, S. E. (1984). *Social cognition.* New York: Random House.

Flower, L. (1990). Introduction: Studying cognition in context. In L. Flower, V. Stein, J. Ackerman, M. Kantz, K. McCormick, & W. Peck *Reading-to-write: Exploring a cognitive and social process* (pp. 3–32). New York: Oxford University Press.

Garfinkel, H. (1967). *Studies in ethnomethodology.* Englewood Cliffs, NJ: Prentice-Hall.

Gilbert, G. N., & Mulkay, M. (1984). *Opening Pandora's box: A sociological analysis of scientists' discourse.* Cambridge, UK: Cambridge University Press.

Herrington, A. J. (1988). Teaching, writing and learning: A naturalistic study of writing in an undergraduate literature course. In D. A. Jolliffe (Ed.), *Advances in writing research Vol. 2: Writing in academic disciplines* (pp. 133–166). Norwood, NJ: Ablex Publishing.

Herrington, A. J. (1985). Writing in academic settings: A study of the contexts for writing in two college chemical engineering courses. *Research in the Teaching of English, 19,* 331–359.

Horowitz, D. (1986a). What professors actually require: Academic tasks for the ESL classroom. *TESOL Quarterly, 20,* 445–462.

Horowitz, D. (1986b). Essay examination prompts and the teaching of academic writing. *English for Specific Purposes, 5,* 107–120.

Houghton, D. (1980). Writing problems of Iranian students. In G. M. Greenall & J. E. Price (Eds.), *Study modes and academic development of overseas students* (pp. 79–90) (ELT Document No. 109). London: The British Council.

Howe, P. M. (1990). The problem of the problem question in English for academic legal purposes. *English for Specific Purposes, 9,* 215–236.

Hull, G., Rose, M., Fraser, K. L., & Castellano, O. (1991). Remediation as social construct: Perspectives from analysis of classroom discourse. *College Composition and Communication, 42,* 299–329.

Hunter, A. (Ed.). (1990). *The rhetoric of social research: Understood and believed.* New Brunswick, NJ: Rutgers University Press.

Hutchinson, T., & Waters, A. (1987). *English for specific purposes: A learning-centered approach.* Cambridge, UK: Cambridge University Press.

James, K. (1984). The writing of theses by speakers of English as a foreign language: The results of a case study. In R. Williams, J. M. Swales, & J. Kirkman (Eds.), *Common ground: Shared interests in ESP and communication studies* (pp. 99–113; ELT Document No. 117). Oxford, UK: The British Council and Pergamon Press.

Johns, A. M. (1990). Coherence as a cultural phenomenon: Employing ethnographic principles in the academic milieu. In U. Connor & A. M. Johns (Eds.), *Coherence in writing: Research and pedagogical perspectives* (pp. 209–226). Alexandria, VA: Teachers of English to Speakers of Other Languages.

Johns, A. M. (1981). Necessary English. *TESOL Quarterly, 15,* 51–57.

Inghilleri, M. (1989). Learning to mean as a symbolic and social process: The story of ESL writers. *Discourse Processes, 12,* 391-411.

Kaplan, R (1966). Cultural thought patterns in intercultural education. *Language Learning, 16,* 1-20.

Kintsch, W., & Mannes, S. M. (1987). Generating scripts from memory. In E. van der Meer & J. Hoffman (Eds.), *Knowledge aided information processing* (pp. 61-80). North Holland: Elsevier Sieman.

Knorr-Cetina, K. D. (1981). *The manufacture of knowledge.* Oxford, UK: Pergamon.

Lackstrom, J. E. (1981). Logical argumentation: The answer to the discussion-problem in EST. In L. Selinker, E. Tarone, & V. Hanzeli (Eds.), *English for academic and technical purposes: Studies in honor of Louis Trimble* (pp. 12-22). Rowley, MA: Newbury House.

Landau, M. (1991). *Narratives of human evolution.* New Haven, CT: Yale University Press.

Latour, B., & Woolgar, S. (1986). *Laboratory life: The social construction of scientific facts.* Princeton, NJ: Princeton University Press.

McCarthy, L. P. (1987). A stranger in strange lands: A college student writing across the curriculum. *Research in the Teaching of English, 21,* 233-265.

McCloskey, D. N. (1985). *The rhetoric of economics.* Madison: University of Wisconsin Press.

McNeil, L. M. (1986). *Contradictions of control: School structure and school knowledge.* New York: Routledge & Kegan Paul.

Miller, C. R. (1984). Genre as social action. *Quarterly Journal of Speech, 70,* 151-167.

Miller, C. R., & Selzer, J. (1985). Special topics of argument in engineering reports. In L. Odell & D Goswami (Eds.), *Writing in nonacademic settings* (pp. 309-341). New York: Guilford.

Myers, G. (1990). *Writing biology: Texts in the social construction of scientific knowledge.* Madison: University of Wisconsin Press.

Myers, G. (1989). The pragmatics of politeness in scientific articles. *Applied Linguistics, 10,* 1-35.

Nelson, J. (1990). This was an easy assignment: Examining how students interpret academic writing tasks. *Research in the Teaching of English, 24,* 362-396.

Nelson, J. S., Megill, A., & McCloskey, D. N. (Eds.). (1987). *The rhetoric of the human sciences: Language and argument in scholarship and public affairs.* Madison: University of Wisconsin Press.

Nespor, J. (1987). Academic tasks in a high school English class. *Curriculum Inquiry, 17,* 203-228.

Ochs, E. (1991). Misunderstanding children. In N. Coupland, H. Giles, & J. Wieman (Eds.), *"Miscommunication" and problematic talk* (pp. 44-60). Newbury Park, CA: Sage.

Odell, L., Goswami, D., & Herrington, A. (1983). The discourse-based interview: A procedure for exploring the tacit knowledge of writers in non-academic settings. In P. Mosenthal, L. Tamor, & S. Walmsley (Eds.), *Research on writing* (pp. 221-236). New York: Longman.

Oster, S. (1981). The use of tenses in 'reporting past literature' in EST. In L. Selinker, E. Tarone, & V. Hanzeli (Eds.), *English for academic and technical purposes: Studies in honor of Louis Trimble* (pp. 76-90). Rowley, MA: Newbury House.

Ostler, S. E. (1980). A survey of academic needs for advanced ESL. *TESOL Quarterly, 14,* 489-502.

Phelps, L. W. (1988). *Composition as a human science: Contributions to self-understanding of a discipline.* New York: Oxford University Press.

Phelps, L. W. (1990). Audience and authorship: The disappearing boundary. In G. Kirsch & D. H. Roen (Eds.), *A sense of audience in written communication* (pp. 153-174). Newbury Park, CA: Sage.

Potter, J., & Wetherell, M. (1987). *Discourse and social psychology: Beyond attitudes and behaviour.* London: Sage.

Prior, P. (in press). Girl talk tales, causal models, and the dissertation: Tracing the topical contours of context in sociology talk and text. *Journal of Language and Learning Across the Disciplines.*

Prior, P. (1992). *Contextualizing writing and response in graduate seminars: A sociohistoric perspective on academic literacies.* Unpublished doctoral dissertation, University of Minnesota.

Prior, P. (1991). Contextualizing writing and response in a graduate seminar. *Written Communication, 8,* 267–310.

Rose, M. (1983). Remedial writing courses: A critique and proposal. *College English, 45,* 109–128.

Ruth, L., & Murphy, S. (1988). *Designing writing tasks for the assessment of writing.* Norwood, NJ: Ablex.

Rymer, J. (1988). Scientific composing processes: How eminent scientists write journal articles. In D. A. Jolliffe (Ed.), *Advances in writing research, Vol. 2: Writing in academic disciplines* (pp. 211–250). Norwood, NJ: Ablex.

Santos, T. (1988). Professors' reactions to the academic writing of nonnative-speaking students. *TESOL Quarterly, 22,* 69–90.

de Saussure, F. (1959). *Course in general linguistics.* (W. Baskin, Trans.; C. Bally & A. Sechehaye, Eds.). New York: McGraw-Hill.

Schank, R. (1982). *Dynamic memory.* London: Cambridge University Press.

Schank, R., & Abelson, R. (1977). *Scripts, plans, goals, and understanding: An inquiry into human knowledge structures.* Hillsdale, NJ: Erlbaum.

Spiro, R., Vispoel, W., Schmitz, J., Samarapungavan, A., & Boerger, A. E. (1987). Knowledge acquisition for application: Cognitive flexibility and transfer in complex domains. In B. Britton & S. Glynn (Eds.), *Executive control processes in reading* (pp. 174–194). Hillsdale, NJ: Erlbaum.

Sternglass, M. S. (1988). *The presences of thought: Introspective accounts of reading and writing.* Norwood, NJ: Ablex.

Swales, J. M. (1992, April). *Re-thinking genre: Another look at discourse community effects.* Paper presented at the Genre Seminar, Ottawa, Canada.

Swales, J. M. (1990a). *Genre analysis: English in academic and research settings.* Cambridge, UK: Cambridge University Press.

Swales, J. M. (1990b). Nonnative speaker graduate engineering students and their introductions: Global coherence and local management. In U. Connor & A. M. Johns (Eds.), *Coherence in writing: Research and pedagogical perspectives* (pp. 187–207). Alexandria, VA: Teachers of English to Speakers of Other Languages.

Swales, J., & Najjar, H. (1987). The writing of research article introductions. *Written Communication, 4,* 175–191.

Tannen, D. (1989). *Talking voices: Repetition, dialogue, and imagery in conversational discourse.* Cambridge, UK: Cambridge University Press.

Tarone, E., Dwyer, S., Gillette, S., & Icke, E. (1981). On the use of the passive in two astrophysics journal papers. *The ESP Journal, 1,* 123–140.

Tedick, D., Bernhardt, E., & DeVille, C. (1991). Interpreting essay examination topics used for assessing content knowledge: Differences among test makers, test raters, and test takers. *Journal of College Reading and Learning, 24,* 63–80.

Ulichny, P., & Watson-Gegeo, K. (1989). Interactions and authority: The dominant interpretive framework in writing conferences. *Discourse Processes, 12,* 309–328.

Vygotsky, L. (1978). *Mind in society: The development of higher psychological processes.* (M. Cole, V. John-Steiner, S. Scribner, & E. Souberman, Eds.), Cambridge, MA: Harvard University Press.

Walvoord, B. E., & McCarthy, L. P. (1990). *Thinking and writing in college: A naturalistic study of students in four disciplines.* Urbana, IL: National Council of Teachers of English.

Watt, J. (1980). Performance of overseas postgraduate students: A management teacher's view. In G. M. Greenall & J. E. Price (Eds.), *Study modes and academic development of overseas students* (pp. 38–43), (ELT Document No. 109). London: The British Council.

Wertsch, J. V. (1991). *Voices of the mind: A sociocultural approach to mediated action.* Cambridge, MA: Harvard University Press.

Williamson, M. M. (1988). A model for investigating the functions of written language in different disciplines In D. A. Jolliffe (Ed.), *Advances in writing research, Vol. 2: Writing in academic disciplines* (pp. 89–132). Norwood, NJ: Ablex.

# CHAPTER 4

# Local Interactions: Constructing Contexts for Composing in a Graduate Sociology Program

**Christine Pearson Casanave**
*Keio University, Japan*

This chapter adds to the growing body of research on academic writing that suggests that the notion of contexts for composing is eminently local, historical, and interactive. Evidence from an 18-month-long ethnographic study of a culturally diverse group of first-year doctoral students learning to write and think like sociologists indicates that students constructed contexts for writing predominantly from sources that touched their lives directly— people in the immediate environment (with their differing personal histories, value systems, interests, and definitions of the field), the system of training embodied in a set of required core courses, and the specific writing tasks in each of those core courses.

Without rejecting the disciplinary community metaphor altogether, the study emphasizes its limited usefulness in characterizing what happens as students learn to write in particular academic settings (one of the points being that there are no abstract academic settings). I argue that a more meaningful approach to understanding the constructed nature of writing contexts is one that considers the immediate, local, and interactive factors that impinge upon individual students as they write in these settings. It is this local aspect of the writing context that helps explain why students do not seem to be socialized into disciplinary communities, particularly in the social sciences, in more uniform and predictable ways.

---

*I would like to thank the National Council of Teachers of English for a small grant that helped fund the original research project reported here. My thanks also go to Elaine Chin for her valuable feedback on an earlier version of this chapter.

*"I am concerned about the way in which the particular values and particular languages of academic discourse exclude students who come from back-grounds other than young, white, middle-class America."*

—Marilyn Cooper (Cooper & Holzman, 1989, p. 205)

## INTRODUCTION

On a clear fall California day, a classroom at a private research university began to fill up with students who had signed up for a graduate sociology course in theory analysis. Among those students were 12 who had been accepted in the university's doctoral program in sociology. This was the first class of the first day of their first year—the beginning of a demanding 5-course core requirement in sociological theory and methods that would extend into their second year.

By any standards, this first-year group was about as diverse as they come. There was a French-Canadian, two mainland Chinese, a Korean, a Japanese-American, two students from Puerto Rican backgrounds, a Mexican-American, and only four "mainstream" white Americans. There were five males and seven females. Their backgrounds varied greatly—only a few had Bachelor's or Master's degrees in sociology.

They were beginning a graduate program that had a 30-year, primarily white male history, and that had distinguished itself over the years for its rigorous quantitative studies in social-psychological research. One of the founders had been teaching the theory analysis course for most of those years, and as he strode into class on this day, tall and straight-shouldered, balding, chin jutted out, the atmosphere in the classroom hummed with a quiet tension. He arranged meticulously handwritten but well-used notes into tidy piles on the desk, and after some introductions to the requirements of the course, began a two-session overview of the course, focusing heavily on European traditions of sociological theory and the philosophy of science. At the conclusion of the overview lectures, Adams had listed 25 terms and names on the chalkboard, and had mentioned 25 others, the specialized meanings of which the majority of students had never encountered.[1] At the end of the first session, the Chinese woman, looking pained and tired, turned off her tape recorder and approached the professor from her front row seat to query him about numerous gaps in her notes. The woman from a Brooklyn Puerto Rican family sighed and closed her notebook in which she had written some terms and drawn some flowers.

---

[1]For example: dissolubility, general law, diffusion, metatheory, theoretical research program, theoretical strategies, hermeneutics, "covering law" thesis, Hempel/Oppenheim/Popper paradigm of explanation, *verstehen*.

The Chinese man, shaggy, sullen and silent, left the room having taken no notes at all. A couple of the white Americans, serious and unsmiling, consulted each other quietly and then left class together.

So began the required core course sequence, which included 16 writing assignments in the four courses given in the first year. The sequence was ostensibly designed to bring a diverse group of students to more or less the same conceptual and methodological place within the next year and a half, and to some extent it did. But at the end of the first year, the individual students were simply not behaving in the way that the traditional view of disciplinary socialization predicts they should. True, they were passing with As and Bs, and nine of them would in fact continue for the PhD. But the students continued to differ as much in their interests, choices, and directions as they did in their cultural and linguistic backgrounds. For example:

- The Japanese-American woman, who stayed in the program, did much of her subsequent course work in the East Asian Studies department.
- The Chinese woman began to specialize in statistics and to wonder why she had chosen sociology as a major. The Chinese man, an eccentric even in the eyes of his own compatriots, disappeared at the end of the first year.
- The Mexican-American woman took her second year in the Law School, committing at the end of that year to a double major in sociology and law.
- The bilingual woman from a Puerto Rican family in Brooklyn left the program after a year and eventually shifted to a Master's program on the East Coast in family social work.
- Three of the white Americans figured out the system rather quickly and made pragmatic decisions to conform to the extent they could without compromising their ideals excessively. A fourth left the program.

Meanwhile, in spite of these differences, all students were doing the same kind of writing as part of their core course requirements. In part through this writing, they were beginning to understand how certain values and practices from science had influenced the kind of sociology they were learning, to develop a feeling for what theory was and its role in sociological research, and to learn skills they would need in the profession (statistics, how to write journal articles, how to present written work, and critique the work of others in a public forum). They were also developing a language that allowed them to communicate, if not with all sociologists, at least with certain subcommunities of them.

While writing was certainly not the only factor influencing how individual students in this study developed in relation to the discipline of sociology, I am considering it a powerful lens through which we can better understand this development in the graduate school context. Moreover, discipline-based writing tasks help shape the development itself. By writing discipline-specific documents, students are learning to speak like members of the discipline (whether or not they eventually adopt the language, practices, and values of the discipline for themselves), and to represent in conventional ways what the field does. In this way, through their writing students are able to test what it feels like to commit to an intellectual tradition. Writing can thus function to introduce novice community members to discipline-specific issues that lie buried in jargon and research activities — issues that ultimately have to do with what it means to identify oneself as a member of a discipline or profession. As Reither (1985) noted, "writing is . . . one of those processes which, in its use, *creates* and *constitutes* its own contexts" (p. 621). By looking at how individual students construct different contexts for composing from the same writing assignments, we can better understand the diverse responses of a multicultural, multilinguistic graduate student population to the socialization experience.

In this chapter, I first discuss aspects of the disciplinary community metaphor and some of its global and local contextual dimensions. I then use the core course writing tasks as a tool to explore some of the local factors that helped shape individual writing contexts created by several of the students in this first-year doctoral program. These local factors undercut the compelling but sometimes overly simplified notion of disciplinary socialization and contribute to a view of disciplinary writing and socialization as highly complex, interactive, and locally situated, and therefore not fully predictable.

## CHARACTERIZING DISCIPLINARY COMMUNITIES

It has been fashionable for some time to portray student writers in colleges and universities as novices or apprentices immersed in academic knowledge and discourse communities (Bartholomae, 1985; Bizzell, 1982; Bruffee, 1983; Doheny-Farina, 1989: Schwegler & Shamoon, 1991; Slevin, 1988). The main idea behind this portrayal is that only by learning the discourse conventions of a community can students participate as members of that community. Through these discourse conventions, the argument goes, novices are introduced to the specific values and practices of the community, and are thus able to "enter the conversations" of that community (Berkenkotter, Huckin, & Ackerman, 1991). The notion of this broad social context into which writers are immersed has been characterized by various "community" metaphors (discourse, academic, speech, interpretive, disciplinary), and has been used to help explain how people come to be identified as insiders to particular groups.

## Context at the Community Level

The "community" metaphor so widely used in writing research was adopted by social scientists in part as a result of the interest generated by the work of Thomas Kuhn (1970), who himself was profoundly influenced by microbiologist Ludwig Fleck's (1935/1979) writings on "thought collectives." Even if we reject the primarily one-way characterization of context and community that this view implies, there are still aspects of it that help us understand why members of different so-called communities perceive the same phenomena in different ways and why writers within those communities share certain values and visions.

Kuhn characterized the scientific community as consisting of the practitioners of a scientific specialty who share language, beliefs, and practices. Members are able to practice the same specialty by virtue of the fact that they have "similar educations and professional initiations," that they have "absorbed the same technical literature and drawn many of the same lessons from it," that they share goals and professional judgments, and that their communication is "full" (Kuhn, 1970, p. 176).

Of particular interest to studies of students learning to write in academic settings is the idea that scientists inhabiting the same community share "educations and professional initiations." Kuhn does not elaborate on what he means here, but we can guess he is referring to graduate programs and early work experiences. This aspect of a novice's training was depicted by Toulmin (1972) as "enculturation," a notion adopted by Jolliffe (1984/1985; Jolliffe & Brier, 1988) as "disciplinary enculturation." Toulmin, like Kuhn, describes enculturation as predominantly a one-way process—namely, the process whereby the senior generation of scientists passes knowledge to junior apprentices (p. 159). The term is now applied broadly to the kinds of changes the students undergo as they are socialized into various academic disciplines—changes, as Kuhn suggested, that alter one's way of seeing and understanding. These different ways of seeing and understanding the world are also revealed in the texts that different disciplinary communities produce, which reflect deep epistemological differences about the nature of knowledge and how it can be known (Bazerman, 1981; Hansen, 1987).

It is claimed that such disciplinary differences pose problems for both undergraduate and graduate students learning to write and think in a variety of disciplines. For example, studies have documented the difficulties that students have in locating themselves within different disciplinary contexts as they try to write texts that fit each discipline's preferred forms and ways of thinking (Berkenkotter, Huckin, & Ackerman, 1988; Casanave, 1992; Chiseri-Strater, 1991; Faigley & Hansen, 1985; Herrington, 1985; McCarthy, 1987; Williamson, 1988). These studies show that conflicts arise across disciplinary boundaries as well as between disciplinary constraints and school-task constraints. Neither the disciplinary nor the school contexts demand much in the way of personal contributions of students' own knowledge and interests, which tend to get repressed as conflicts arise (Chiseri-Strater, 1991). Indeed, as Perelman (1986) notes, "the penalty for adhering to some sort of personal self at the expense of the institutional self is often severe" (p. 475).

Characterizing disciplinary communities with this broadly conceived metaphor has helped writing scholars understand the legitimately different ways that academicians conceptualize and talk about their worlds. Nevertheless, it has met with limited success in terms of being adequate for helping us understand individual writers in specific settings. Once applied to specific settings, the compelling "disciplinary community" metaphor tends to break down, as the meaningful units get smaller and smaller. We find subcommunities within communities, and multiple embeddings of microsocieties within subcommunities, and finally a great diversity of a small number of individuals in the innermost circle. This dilemma helps explain the interest in case studies of people learning to write in particular settings, most of which underscore the powerful influence of local constraints and interactions. It is at the personal level—the level of the individual—that all conceptualizations of context and community become instantiated in the lives of real people engaged in real writing tasks. Without rejecting the larger notions of context and community, we can focus on more local characterizations as a way to understand the complex and interactive nature of context as it is constructed by individual writers.

## Context at the Local, Historical, and Interactive Levels

The writing context has been characterized in many ways: as the cognitive, social, and cultural environment of the writing activity (Piazza, 1987), as a shared and unfolding social reality (Brandt, 1986), as involving the functions of production and (eventual) use (Nystrand, 1986), as depending on societal, historical, and local factors (Ackerman, 1989), and as a multisymbolic, collaborative, and situated forum for meaning making (Witte, 1992). For my purposes in this chapter, I would like to make a case for the importance of the local, historical, and interactive aspects of the contexts that writers in academic settings construct for themselves. These local factors reside both outside the writer (people, settings, assignments) and inside the writer (intentions, intellectual histories, interests). As Cooper (1982) noted some years ago,

> [m]ost texts come richly provided with contexts. The student's paper [is] produced at a particular time . . . at a particular place . . . in a particular course . . . in a particular school . . . in a particular society . . . in response to a particular teacher's particular assignment with particular intentions on the student's part . . . (p. 111)

This local and historical perspective has been described by scholars from a variety of fields. Geertz (1983), for example, emphasizes the importance of personal relations among faculty in his descriptions of the "intellectual villages" of academe, pointing out that personal (and other "nonintellectual") factors must be invoked as a way to understand the ingrown and local nature of academic communities. He states that the relations among the inhabitants of these intellectual villages "are typically not merely intellectual, but political, moral, and broadly personal (these days, increasingly marital) as well" (p. 157).

Personal factors of other kinds help build the contexts in which academics work and write. One is the relative status of the academic (e.g., newcomer or old guard) and another is the very direct (hence personal) relation between a writer and his or her "impersonal" reviewer. As Myers (1985) showed in his study of two biologists revising grant proposals in response to reviewers' comments, the interactions differed for the younger and more well-established biologists. The result was that they created different rhetorical contexts for themselves and made different rhetorical choices.

Not only faculty colleagues, but students, too, are influenced heavily by those people and experiences in the immediate surroundings. In a fascinating but infrequently cited study of how medical students develop a professional self-image, Huntington (1957) discovered that students' self-images shifted according to the social context and to types of experiences with people around them. Faculty, nurses, classmates, and patients influenced them in different ways according to the varying expectations they held for students. For example, when around faculty, the students behaved like students; when around nurses and patients, they took on an air of authority. In other words, when the actors in an interaction shifted, the students' shifting definitions of themselves helped create a new context in which to learn about the field of medicine.

The personal histories of students themselves also help them define contexts in which to write. In the area of academic writing, sometimes these personal histories facilitate writing and sometimes they hinder it. Hare and Fitzsimmons (1991) found that students who had backgrounds in teaching and learning communities could more easily simulate academic discourse than could students who had little such experience. Anna and Nick, on the other hand, the undergraduate students studied by Chiseri-Strater (1991), found few ways they could draw on their personal experiences and interests to good advantage in their college courses. The gap was too great between their personal histories and the constrained ways of knowing in the academic world. Other evidence of the powerful influence of very personal, local aspects of learning to write in academic settings (e.g., the influence of particular teachers and the guidelines they provide) has been documented at the secondary and undergraduate levels (e.g., Anson & Forsberg, 1990; Applebee, 1984; Herrington, 1985, 1988; Nelson, 1990; Nelson & Hayes, 1988).

The few studies of graduate students learning to write within disciplines also point to the local, personal, and interactive nature of context building. Berkenkotter, Huckin, and Ackerman (1988) described how the informal writing style of a new PhD student in rhetoric clashed with the more formal discourse conventions required in specific classes in his program. Feedback from professors caused him discomfort until he was able to make some compromises over time that resulted in a more flexible discourse style (Berkenkotter, Huckin, & Ackerman, 1991). Casanave (1990) documented the same phenomenon with "Richard," a first-year student in a doctoral program in sociology (who appears as a character in the present study). Richard, like Nate, brought with him to his doctoral program a strong sense of personal voice learned in previous English classes that clashed with the voice expected by his core course professors. Chin (1991) discovered that first-year journalism students drew from local influences in their environments, including physical surroundings and a particular departmental history, in the process of learning what the concept of "story" meant to them within the culture of journalism. Prior (1991) also highlighted the local, historical, and interactive influences on graduate students learning to write in "disciplinary microsocieties." In his study of 15 students in an education program (including eight nonnative speakers of English) he not only demonstrated the influence of students' previous interests and experiences and of the assignment parameters on the research proposals the students wrote. He also showed how the students "interpreted" the professor (e.g., his personality). Of particular interest to this chapter is Prior's evidence of how an ethnically and culturally diverse group of students struggled to make sense out of a series of very locally situated writing assignments.

In short, writers in academic settings (including faculty themselves) construct contexts for writing according to a complex interaction of many local and personal factors, including their own intellectual histories (Ackerman, 1989) and the particular histories of departments at particular schools. This is not to deny the importance of broader factors, such as norms for reading, writing, and schooling in society and in academic discourse communities. It is, rather, to stress the importance of understanding how individual writers draw on resources from within and around themselves as they gradually learn to identify themselves as writers for particular communities or to recognize that they do not want to belong.

## WRITING IN A SOCIOLOGY DOCTORAL PROGRAM

In this section I'd like to return to some of the first-year doctoral students in sociology who were introduced at the beginning of this chapter. In particular, I'm interested in how they constructed contexts for writing and thinking like sociologists out of a somewhat tension-ridden set of local sources consisting of professors, a teaching assistant, peers, texts, and specific classes and writing tasks.

In the 1987–1988 academic year, I acted as an observer-participant in two core courses on sociological theory, audiotaping all class sessions, and as a periodic observer in one of two methods (statistics) classes. For 18 months, I interviewed students and faculty participants, and collected handouts and several open-ended questionnaires as well as the papers that students wrote. The focus of the inquiry was predominantly how the writing tasks contributed to the students' evolving sense of how (or whether) they fit into this community of sociologists.

### The Setting and the Key Players

As mentioned in the introduction to the chapter, the study took place in a small graduate sociology department (about 60 students) that had been established over 30 years earlier by a handful of professors committed to a particular kind of social-psychological research. Several of the "old guard" founding faculty were still around, and two of them taught the two theory courses that were part of this study. The broad disciplinary community, if there was one, might be described as one influenced by the values and practices of science.

In their first year, all students were required to take two core courses in theory and three in methods (statistics) in their first year and into their second year (see Figure 4.1). (The majority of data for this study comes from the two theory courses and the second of the three methods courses.)

During this year, the 12 students shared office space in a large room partitioned by carrells. Chinese, Japanese, Korean, Hispanic, Caucasian: all interacted with each other regularly, even if minimally, as a result of this office arrangement. The teaching assistant that year for Theory Analysis

| FALL | WINTER | SPRING |
|---|---|---|
| Theory Analysis (Prof. Adams) | Theory Construction (Prof. Bernstein) Methods 1 (Prof. Cavanaugh) | Methods 2 (Prof. Davison) |

Figure 4.1.   First year required core courses in the doctoral program

and both methods classes was a third-year student from Germany who attended and participated in all class sessions and held regular office hours in another location to help students with their writing assignments.

Dr. Adams,[2] who we met earlier in this chapter on the first day of his Theory Analysis class, was chair of the department at the time. He had a reputation with some for seeming arrogant in his mannerisms and language. Dr. Bernstein, who had taught the Theory Construction class for many years, was viewed by the students as a less powerful person than Adams. The first-year students learned quickly by word of mouth of his reputation as a rather narrow-minded perfectionist and idealist. Previous groups had protested his requirement that students apply strict principles of science and logical analysis to sociological research.

While the majority of my time was spent in the theory classes, the methods professors, too, played a role in this project. Dr. Cavanaugh was a pale, precise young woman who had graduated from the same program and stayed on to teach the first methods class. She introduced students in as gentle a way as possible to the world of statistical analysis and to the writing of "research article" papers modeled on quantitative-style journal articles in the field. Dr. Davison, also young and well liked, continued the journal article assignments in his more advanced statistics course. As a newcomer to the department, he shared some of the "culture shock" that the first-year students experienced as they struggled with the jargon and concepts used in the department.

Among the students, three worked closely with me for a year and a half. Richard, 28, clean-cut and confident, came from a middle-class white family in California. He had a Master's degree in sociology, and because he was married, wanted to get through the program as quickly as possible so as to get settled into a job. Virginia, at 22, was one of the youngest in the group, whose oldest member was 40. From a Brooklyn, New York family of Puerto Rican ancestry, she had studied sociology as an undergraduate and entered this doctoral program in the hope of taking some of her newly

---

[2]All names used in this chapter are pseudonyms.

acquired expertise back to the working-class minority communities in New York. English was her dominant language but she was also competent in Spanish. Pretty and quiet, she rarely spoke in any of the core classes. Lu-Yun, a Chinese woman of 36, had left her husband and child in the People's Republic of China to study in an interdisciplinary Master's program on the East Coast and then to complete a doctoral program in sociology. From a family of university educators, she nevertheless had struggled to educate herself during the Cultural Revolution, when she was obligated to "herd sheep" in the country, as Dr. Adams put it. As a result of the university's English test for foreign students, she was required to take an advanced writing course.

In short, the professors and students in this program formed a diverse group, each needing to create a context for writing, thinking, and researching that defined him or herself in relation to ambiguities, tensions, and multiple ways of knowing that characterized the broader field of sociology. As they interacted with each other, with the demands of particular classes within the core course system of training, and with specific writing tasks, each created a unique context to some extent, even when language and values overlapped. The contexts that the students created, in particular, cannot easily be characterized by a predominantly one-way process of enculturation. The notion of disciplinary enculturation (Jolliffe, 1984/1985; Toulmin, 1972) as a metaphor to guide our understanding of the social construction of contexts for composing in disciplines seems inadequate in this light, except in the broadest of senses.

## Local Interactions

In their first-year core courses, students wrote a total of nine major papers and seven shorter exercises or working papers. The major papers were all modeled on existing discourse styles in the academic world: in the theory classes, the literature review and the dissertation proposal; in the methods classes, the formal research article (three each quarter). The short papers in the theory classes were considered skill builders that prepared students for the kinds of thinking and writing they would need to do on a larger scale later.

Let us look at some specific examples of how students created contexts for themselves, not simply by taking on the values and practices of a larger community, but by pushing and pulling their way through a maze of different local ways of knowing and of practicing sociology. On the surface, much of the writing that students did reflected these tensions poorly in the sense that even the foreign students adopted a rather uniform impersonal academic style, for the most part, beginning quite early in the semester.[3] The tensions and complexities of the interactions involving people, the system of training, and the writing assignments are revealed, however, in interviews, open class discussions, and questionnaire responses.

*Interacting with the people.*    The people with whom first-year graduate students come into direct contact help them define the field and determine whether and how they fit in. Likewise, students, by their reactions (resistance, rebellion, cooperation, suggestions) help professors shift and adapt their courses to changing times and changing needs. Ultimately, these mutual influences presumably help define the broader field and change it over time. Regardless of the extent of these influences, the effect of the human interactions in a particular academic program cannot be predicted easily, since it depends on the personalities and backgrounds of the key players and their responses to each other.

In this sociology doctoral program, some of the first-year students found Dr. Adams to be arrogant, distant, and elitist in the way he displayed his vast knowledge of a field that he defined in primarily white male European and American terms. His lectures were peppered with esoteric terminology and German names that students could not pronounce. Moreover, they were delivered with encyclopedic precision that could easily intimidate those who did not share his intellectual history. Virginia, whose Puerto Rican working-class background had sensitized her firsthand to many minority issues, determined from her personal discomfort with Adams that his kind of sociology was alien to her world. Lu-Yun also found Adams distant and incomprehensible. After lectures, she often claimed not to know what he had been talking about, and eventually came to wonder what "the use of sociology" was. Several of the white Americans, while overwhelmed at first, came to admire his renaissance-style knowledgeability.

Bernstein struck students as less elitist but as more narrow-minded and intransigent in his views of what good sociology consisted of. He insisted that students adhere to basic values and practices of science and of formal logic in their Theory Construction course. Most students did not share his idealism, though Richard, for one, came to appreciate it more in his second and third years in the program. Few students felt comfortable consulting either of these "old guard" professors about individual problems; Lu-Yun went to Adams often in the first month of the term to check the meanings of terminology *in spite of* her discomfort.

In the cases of Adams and Bernstein, then, personal qualities of the professors appeared to influence how students felt about the value of

---

[3]As Geisler (1990) noted, the account of personal interactions that are part of how every piece of writing is produced gets repressed in the published text.

formal, precise, analytical approaches to theory. For students like Virginia and Lu-Yun, the writing tasks designed by these professors felt distant and impersonal, more like formal school exercises than like personally meaningful explorations. On the other hand, Richard came to admire Adams' vast knowledge and Bernstein's focused way of thinking, in spite of the fact that he suffered in writing his first theory exercises for both professors. He found over time that Adams and Bernstein espoused values that he could toy with, think about, and selectively adopt for his own. Richard thus resisted the writing tasks assigned by these professors less than did Virginia and Lu-Yun and engaged with them at a more personal intellectual level.

The students influenced these two professors in a variety of ways, too. Adams recognized that with the increasing number of Asian and minority students in the program, his formal lectures on "lineages" in European and American sociology were probably falling on uncomprehending ears. It was unclear whether this knowledge would eventually lead to any changes in his syllabus, but the motivating factor and the awareness were there. Bernstein had changed his Theory Construction course in a number of small ways over the years in response to student protests, and this year was team teaching it with Adams in an attempt to placate students further. The changes in this year's course primarily affected the system of evaluation. In previous years, students had been evaluated exclusively by examinations. This year, Bernstein had reluctantly agreed with Adams' suggestion to forego all exams. Instead, students wrote. The writing tasks were devised as a series of short working papers leading to a final research proposal-style paper.

Both of the younger methods professors were viewed as warm and supportive individuals who seemed especially interested in making sure that the intimidating world of statistics did not alienate students. Partly as a result of the accessibility of these professors, and partly because the statistics papers were more straightforward than the conceptually dense theory papers, few students rejected the quantitative approach to sociology outright. Some commented on the mechanical, uncreative nature of such an approach, or, like Lu-Yun, found it surprising at first that numerical analyses could be manipulated to shift the researchers' results in the desired directions. Most, however, appreciated the fact that they were learning a "received" form and method of doing sociology that would help them get published later. Virginia had lamented the lack of more qualitative, descriptive work in this program. Nevertheless, she found that her comfortable personal relationship with these professors helped her find value in a quantitative exploration of sociological issues and in basic statistical skills.

Interactions among the students also influenced each student's experience of socialization. Relations among the students in this first-year cohort were, according to all accounts, closer than most. Many of them socialized together and discussed and complained about their core courses together. When it came to their writing tasks, the students "learned from each others' mistakes," as one student phrased it. Richard, for one, consulted with one of his classmates regularly about the writing assignments, perhaps coincidentally with the one whose office carrel was closest to his. Physical proximity, in other words, facilitated certain combinations of peer interactions over others. On the other hand, Lu-Yun and Virginia also had adjacent carrells, but rarely consulted each other when they were confused by a writing task. They also were less sociable than Richard and his office partner, and did not speak out voluntarily in class. Virginia tended to make decisions by herself, or occasionally to go to Lona, the other Hispanic woman in the group, for advice. When Lu-Yun had difficulties with her writing tasks in the theory classes, she tended to consult several upper-year colleagues from Korea and China, who had written some of the same kinds of papers in previous years.

Students also interacted often with the German teaching assistant in their theory and methods classes. He not only helped them with assignments but gave written feedback on some of their papers. The teaching assistant paid particular attention to the foreign students' initial struggle with theoretical issues and jargon in Adams's and Bernstein's theory classes and spent many hours consulting with them on written work. A foreigner himself, he, too, had suffered greatly in his first year in the program and had considered dropping out.

Additionally, in some of the contentious discussions in the theory classes, the students showed political, philosophical, feminist, and idealist-humanist leanings that added diversity and richness to the human interactions in the class. More assertive students, such as Lona, with her Mexican-American background and interest in law, helped keep the group aware of what they called the real world of real people in sociological study, especially when discussions of theory had, in their minds, become absurdly abstract and esoteric. This diversity, and the relative closeness of the group members, helped give some students confidence to question and critique what they were learning, and to make choices about what to take for themselves from the training they were receiving.

In short, the first-year core course writing tasks were inextricably connected to a world of people. It was the people with whom the students came into regular contact who shaped the socialization experience from the first day. These people, whether professors, other members of the cohort, or upper-year students, contributed in very real ways to the students' developing sense of what the field was like and of their own place in it. Students were pushed and pulled, confused and questioned, challenged and supported by those around them. It was in this peopled environment that they undertook their writing assignments. It was people who helped students interpret, evaluate, and shape these assignments for themselves.

It was not only students' interactions with people around them that helped determine what their experiences were like in the program. These students also had strong feelings about the program's system of training, as did the professors who had designed it.

## Interacting with the System of Training

The requirement of core courses in sociological theory and methods for all beginning doctoral students had been instituted many years before. Hence, there was a well-established framework in place for this system of training, built out of tradition. Broadly, the system can be described, as Adams (one of the originators) phrased it, as an apprenticeship, where it was believed that students needed to *do*, not just know about, sociology. For example, in spite of the fact that Dr. Adams gave students a thick course reader for the Theory Analysis course, few students read many more than the first several articles. The main requirement in the course was not that students read and remember, but that they think and write. The same philosophy character- ized the other core courses as well. Throughout all the core courses ran a deep respect for science, numbers, analytical thinking, and formal discourse conventions.

*The professors' views.*  Each professor brought his or her own per- sonal intellectual history to the program. Stemming from these differences, each professor's attitudes toward the system of training differed somewhat, even though there seemed to be broad agreement that some kind of rigorous skills training was essential. We can look at the system of training, then, through the eyes of the four professors according to the extent to which they adhered to formal theory and "scientific" quantitative methods in their own work and according to the messages they sent to students in class discus- sions and in guidelines for written work. While the broad similarities can perhaps be explained by the "community" metaphor, it is the differences that help explain some of the tensions that students experienced as they wrote their papers during the core course sequence.

The most idealistic and formalist-oriented of the four professors was Bernstein, whose own high ideals, he claimed, prevented him from pub- lishing as much as others who were more "flashy." "To be flashy," he said, "and have people talk about you, is not the same as doing solid scholarly work. And I believe in doing solid scholarly work." And this was an ideal he wished to pass on to students during the core course sequence. Adams said about Bernstein: "He prefers students with no background in sociology because we don't have to unteach them so much." But Bernstein was finding it increasingly difficult over the years to maintain tight control over the "solid, scholarly training" he offered his students, given students' resistance to what they felt were narrow and overly formal and prescriptive requirements. The first-year group in this study, for example, had already been thoroughly prepared for Bernstein by the upper-year students; hence, Bernstein spent a number of class sessions on the defensive as students pushed for a less formal, more "human" sociology. However, his commitment to the study of formal logic as part of students' training seemed unshakable. Bernstein, in short, believed that creativity could occur only with the framwork of a clear structure, and that that framework, along with the logic of its components, should be learned first.

Adams, on the other hand, seemed less concerned about formalities, and more about independent thinking. "I like to encourage anybody who has an imaginative idea," he stated. "Imagination is more important than only analysis at this stage of the game as far as I'm concerned." Nevertheless, his authoritative manner, meticulously prepared lecture notes, generally flawless delivery, and relatively highly structured writing assignments suggested that he believed that students needed a great deal of structure and guidance in their initial training.

In the methods classes, professors Cavanaugh and Davison understood the value of theory in doing sociology, but admitted that in their own work and in the training they provided in their classes they did not treat theory formally at all. As for the German teaching assistant, he himself was still developing his views about what appropriate graduate training should consist of. He liked discussions of theory, but found to his frustration that American scholars, unlike those from his European training, avoided dealing with questions of "truth." He also had mixed feelings about the value of structuring students' training too tightly. It may be helpful, he claimed, since sociology is an ambiguous field, but it also "promotes ritualism, rule following, one-dimensionality, noncritical sociology." He referred to American students as "sheep," willing to take in whatever their professors had to say. His own critical and assertive attitude was frequently observed by students during discussions in the first theory class, where he challenged some of Adams' ideas in ways that clearly broke Adams' stride. His stride broken, Adams revealed himself to the first-year students as less articulate and authoritative than was apparent from his well-rehearsed lectures.

In spite of these differences, all four professors, and to some extent the teaching assistant, believed strongly that the primary goal of the training they offered was to prepare students for the life of a professional sociologist. Sociologists write, they all said, and often in prescribed formats; they present papers at conferences and have their worked critiqued publicly; they add to a body of knowledge. (None mentioned that sociologists also teach.) Students therefore should write a lot, and (as they did in the two theory classes) learn to conduct public oral critiques of each others' work. The training in the core courses, revolving around analytical writing, reflected a common commitment to this view of what one does as a professional sociologist.

Conspicuously absent from the professors' views was specific mention of the relevance of the department's system of training for a multicultural, multilingual group of students. Rather, implied in the views of both theory professors were two notions that suggested that cultural and linguistic differences mattered little at this level of training.

First, analyzing and constructing theory were thought to be relatively culture neutral, in the sense that they involved abstract and logical modes of thinking. This view is contrary to current views of how thinking and writing get done within disciplines. Nevertheless, it apparently still underlies much science-oriented work in the social sciences. As Bernstein noted, science can never be value- (or culture-) free, but researchers are obliged to remove as much "bias" as possible by following principled procedures. It was thought that learning such principles had a sort of universal value, then, in the sense that abstract principles could be applied later to a wide range of contexts and sociological problems.

Second, the professors believed that they were preparing students to compete in the world of sociology that they (the professors) knew. It was expected that students would be writing for the discipline's most prestigious journals, presenting papers in the discipline's conferences, and teaching in universities where this kind of training would help them do high quality research. In the case of students from China, it was presumed they would return to the PRC and help found the relatively new discipline of sociology according to the principles they had learned. In short, the system of training, from the eyes of the professors, had a certain universal appeal. The principles and skills that students learned as part of their writing were meant to apply across cultures and languages.

*The students' views.*   The students saw their training in several ways: as a type of "indoctrination" into a certain kind of sociology, as socialization into the department (learning to be a student again, developing a common language, "surviving Adams"), and as preparation to do a dissertation according to department expectations. Many students expressed early reactions to the training in terms of resistance to what they saw as the values and practices of science, as embodied in specific beliefs and practices espoused by the professors in the training experiences. Nevertheless, at the beginning, their views were more diverse than those of the faculty, some shifting over time to become more compatible with one or more people in the department and some shifting even further away from the kinds of sociology practiced there.

The uncomfortable tensions created as the students interacted with specific aspects of their training are revealed in a number of ways: in skeptical questioning during class discussions, in sincere but frustrating efforts to understand the rationale behind the core course sequence, in attempts to integrate the values being explicitly and implicitly taught into their existing value systems, and in resistance to specific issues and practices arising in the training. Out of these tensions, the students had to construct contexts for themselves in which to complete specific writing assignments but also in which to define themselves, over time, as sociologists. This was difficult for the mainstream white American students, but particularly confusing for students from nonmainstream cultural backgrounds.

Virginia had problems with the system of training from the outset. She noted early in the academic year that she was "learning not to view certain types of works as sociological" (e.g., descriptive works) because they did not follow certain norms of scientific research. Other students expressed irritation at the presumption that sociology could or should be done according to values and practices from the natural sciences. In the spring of her first year, Lu-Yun (who had been slow to express opinions, believing herself "too empty") commented that techniques they were learning from the sciences "won't suit social science that much." She expressed her reservations about the skills she was learning as follows: "Maybe that's good for natural science. Social science is not precise itself. So I don't think we can apply very precise methods to unprecise science."

Lu-Yun maintained some skepticism over the next year, but continued in the program in the belief that she would find it all making sense once she had enough background knowledge in "five or six years." But several years later, her confusion about the question of "precision" in sociology had lingered, while her commitment to the value of statistics for a broad variety of other purposes had expanded.

Richard, whose background had prepared him fairly well for this kind of program, noted that when he began it, he knew he would be studying a social *science*, but didn't know "they had their own little school of theory." "THIS place," he said, "is a lot more experimental than any other place I've been or was exposed to. I think that's just probably a function of the fact that they're more scientized than other people." He emphatically stated that he did not like experimental research methods, and so felt uncomfortable with "the party line here," which he referred to as "positivistic scientism." But at the conclusion of two more core courses and a great deal of writing, Richard expressed a shift in attitude, toward acceptance of the type of world he was being trained to enter: "I mean, I'll let them play their game, and you know, I might even step into that ring once in a while and play along because . . . you know, there's the rules of the game. You have to get published, you have to do research, be scientific, whatever." In the spring of his second year, looking back on the core course experience, Richard reluctantly conceded that the training he got in Bernstein's theory class (which he had originally disliked intensely) had provided him with "a useful way of looking at things." It was the dogmatism, he claimed, that had "turned [him] off."

Lona, the Hispanic student interested in law, also expressed skepticism of the scientific training they were receiving. In response to values and practices underlying the writing tasks in Bernstein's Theory Construction course, she said:

> You sort of get a preview of that in the first theory course, but it's not really pounded into your head until Bernstein's course. You know, we're scientists, and we're gonna have our hypotheses, and we're gonna test our hypotheses, and we're gonna-you know. Just this whole idea. I don't know. It just seems very uncreative in some ways. And I think I was skeptical to begin with, but the course made me more skeptical. I just kind of have rebelled against it.

Virginia found that her methods courses taught her some valuable skills that she might be able to use in the future. But the theory courses were another matter. After finishing the final papers in her Theory Analysis class, she expressed her skepticism about the system of training that both Adams and Bernstein were committed to. Trying to explain her lack of a sense of satisfaction or accomplishment, she said, "I guess it had to do with the fact that I couldn't see any relevance of the course to my personal life. Or to my career. So I felt like I was, you know, doing time."

Virginia's personal life, and her future career, were worlds filled with people, not abstractions. Many of the people were poor, of different colors and cultural backgrounds. They were struggling to make a life for themselves in the inner city of New York. She left the program after a year, making a decision not to abandon these people in favor of learning how to do formal logical analyses of theoretical knowledge claims.

The reactions expressed by Lu-Yun, Richard, Lona, and Virginia encapsulate some of the different ways that students interacted with the training they received in their core courses. In certain areas, there came to be broader agreement, such as on the need to impose some order on a chaotic social world and on the value of theory of some kind in guiding all thinking about sociological matters. But in general, during the first-year core course sequence itself, this small cohort of doctoral students lived unavoidably in a world characterized by tensions, ambiguities, and uncertainties created out of the interactions between their own evolving belief systems and those embodied in the core course training. It was in this atmosphere of tension and evolving beliefs that students had to write nine major papers and seven shorter working papers over the academic year.

## Interacting with the Writing Tasks

The writing assignments of the core course professors understandably reflected their particular views of what sociology was, what students needed to learn to become sociologists, and how they should best learn it (see Casanave, 1990, for the full text of all the theory paper assignments and two examples of the methods paper assignments). Ideally, the professors' and students' assessments of the function and value of these tasks coincide. But such was not the case in the first-year core courses, particularly in the two theory classes taught by Adams and Bernstein.

In Adams' Theory Analysis class, the students were supposed to begin the kind of analytical thinking and writing they would need to do to prepare a dissertation proposal, and later, to frame their own research. They analyzed several rather ambiguous theories, read in the original (by Merton and others), by writing three short ungraded "exercises" according to prescriptive guidelines for how to do this. Students' understanding of the guidelines themselves depended on their understanding of some rather esoteric terminology that was conceptually difficult (e.g., *domain of a theory, underived premise, scope of a theory, basic assumptions of a theory*). Later in the quarter, Adams' two major papers required that students synthesize a small body of literature (given out as bibliographies in the case of Paper 1) in order to analyze the development of a theory over time and to identify an "unsolved problem." In these papers, Adams seemed pleased if students came up with something he had not himself thought about before. Nevertheless, in small group conferences designed to help students prepare for an oral presentation based on Paper 1, Adams guided students through their theoretically dense issues to his preferred interpretations. Few questioned this authority, since they knew it stemmed from over 30 years in the field, from personal acquaintance of many of the key personalities being discussed, and from the fact that he knew intimately each of the readings on the bibliographies that he had prepared for students.

In his Theory Construction class, Bernstein designed his writing tasks with input from Adams. They consisted of four working papers on a theoretical issue of students' choosing, each building on the other and leading up to a major paper in which the writers proposed and evaluated a "theoretically interesting question." The paper was to include the four working papers in some form, as a statement of a problem, hypotheses ("knowledge claims"), competing hypotheses, suggestions for how the problem could be investigated with quantitative "indicators," and formal logical analysis of the competing knowledge claims. By learning a specialized kind of analytical thinking in their core course writing tasks, Bernstein reasoned, students would be prepared to write a theoretically sound dissertation proposal. But from his perspective, students needed to be compelled to interact with writing tasks in ways that fit his goals; they would not or could not do this on their own.

In the methods classes, students had to write three journal article-style papers each quarter from models supplied by Cavanaugh and Davison from professional journals. Students chose their own topics from existing databases and practiced three different kinds of statistical analyses on the data. Close adherence to the standard quantitative journal article format was required, and feedback addressed deviations from this format as well as the statistical aspects of the papers. Dr. Cavanaugh, the first methods teacher, said that when she read students' papers she tried to "think about giving them feedback that would help bring these papers up to publishable quality." The German teaching assistant, on the other hand, disapproved of the journal article requirement, which he found resulted in "poor language style" when students imitated the style in the field's journals.

The students reacted in different ways to the explicit and implicit values that were embodied in these assignments. In the two theory courses, for example, most students were overwhelmed by the maze of terminology they had to get through simply to understand the oral and written descriptions of the writing tasks. Native English speakers as well as nonnative English speakers like Lu-Yun struggled to assimilate this new conceptual world created by the terminology and to use it, if not overtly, at least indirectly, in their interpretations of the assignments.

Lu-Yun's interactions with the early writing assignments are particularly interesting because of the perceptions she had of herself. She considered herself a sort of blank slate—a person with no knowledge, no background, and no ideas—and so "took for granted" what the theory professors told her. She claimed to need input from outside to complete her writing tasks (consultations with Adams, the teaching assistant, upper-year students) as well as repeated reviews of handouts containing key definitions and concepts. For the early writing tasks she spent hours copying sentences from the source texts on the backs of discarded library reference cards, rereading them along with her class notes and handouts, and asking Adams to explain key concepts. She also read the old papers written by her Korean and Chinese upper-class colleagues. In short, in composing her theory papers, Lu-Yun interacted not only with the original source text she was analyzing. She also interacted with at least six local sources: her own notes, class handouts and paper guidelines, the professors and teaching assistant, upper-class colleagues, the written work of upper-class colleagues, and her own drafts.

Virginia, also somewhat lost at first with regard to key concepts, terminology, and expectations in the theory classes, used some local resources less frequently than did Lu-Yun in creating a context in which to compose. She felt herself to be less of a *tabula rasa*, and so tended to rely more on internal resources – private interpretations stemming from her particular background and experience. She was also shy and a bit reclusive, lacking confidence to share her work with classmates who she felt could handle "the strange language" in this sociology program better than she could. As for local external resources, she reread source texts and notes, but less intensely than did Lu-Yun, and revised little once she had produced a draft. She relied heavily on the teaching assistant for help on the papers for the first theory class and on a minority professor outside the core course sequence for help revising an unsatisfactory paper in the second (Bernstein's) theory class and for help on her methods papers. She found Adams "elitist" and Bernstein unhelpful, so avoided them. Additionally, to some extent, she helped create a context for her writing by imagining how she would explain certain ideas to her mother. Though her mother was not part of her real audience, Virginia used her as an imagined audience. This seemed to be a device for managing her writing style and ensuring that her writing and thinking were clear. But by the end of the first quarter, she explained, this had become impossible because of the abstract nature of the language and concepts.

In a sense, Virginia's interactions with the writing tasks, particularly in the theory classes, were always superficial attempts at completing the tasks according to expectations she did not fully understand or approve of. As a bilingual, bicultural woman, she felt alienated from the monocultural, male-oriented models for "doing theory." For example, of the written work in the second theory class she said, "I felt like I was always writing for Bernstein, using Bernstein's language and the stuff from Bernstein's lectures." Virginia, in other words, felt no ownership over her writing. Moreover, she recognized clearly that the "context of use" (Nystrand, 1986) involved no readers beyond her theory professors, even in her imagination. Her real and imagined audience for the methods papers, on the other hand, consisted of professors and a hypothetical journal-reading public.

In contrast, Lona, also a bilingual, bicultural woman, tried to take ownership of her final paper for Bernstein and as a result received an incomplete for "not following the term paper guidelines." She was one of the few students in the cohort who regularly tested the boundaries of assignments and expectations – who pushed back in the face of constraints:

> He gave us the little list, and I knew I hadn't done some things on the list [because the guidelines] are stupid. Really dumb and useless. What I left out

was the logical derivations. I was just pushing the idea of how much was this
little list he gave us a kind of formula, and how much was it guidelines.

Her revision followed Bernstein's guidelines, but she had made her point, as
well as come to understand the game.

Richard, on the other hand, eventually found value in the writing tasks,
which seemed to help him interact with his own evolving ideas in productive
ways. He tried on the persona of the sociologist in ways that Lu-Yun and
Virginia did not. He wrestled with issues of writing style (his had been
judged too informal), of methodology (about which he was pulled in
conflicting directions), and of admittedly fuzzy thinking. He interacted a
great deal, in other words, with himself and his drafts as he wrote,
particularly in conjunction with the theory papers. In drafts of some of the
more difficult working papers, he sometimes asked himself questions, such
as "What am I trying to do here?" and then proceeded to write his way
through the confusions.

In another aspect of their interactions with the specific writing tasks,
some students were put off by the prescriptive guidelines given for much of
the written work in the core courses, particularly in the theory classes. They
referred to the assignment instructions as "recipes" or "cookbooks." But
students simultaneously found the guidelines comforting crutches for
actually getting the writing done. For example, Richard was one of those
who eventually admitted that the tight structure of the assignments had
been valuable. On a questionnaire about the writing tasks in one of the
theory classes, he wrote that the "structure added focus and limits for me.
It was tight enough to insure that we got it done." He explained that this was
"important for grad school and professional work because you're judged on
completed projects, not just ideas."

Lu-Yun and Virginia also appreciated the tight guidelines, but for more
pragmatic than deeply personal reasons. They noted that the guidelines
helped them know what the professors expected and helped them compensate for lack of background knowledge, thus making the papers easier to
write. Professing ignorance about how other sociologists did sociology,
Lu-Yun just "followed the steps" that formed the foundation of each
course's writing assignments. In Bernstein's Theory Construction class, for
example, she understood her writing tasks as fitting the following prescrip-
tion for how to do sociological research: "you find the observation
phenomenon, then you form hypothesis. Maybe I think hypothesis is a
knowledge claim. Then you test that, and limit it with scope conditions.
After you test it, you see whether the findings agree with your hypothesis. . . . I think this is what I got."

Bernstein would probably be pleased with Lu-Yun's description. Nevertheless, Lu-Yun continued to proclaim throughout the entire first year and well into the second that she had little idea how this information could be applied to her personally or even to research on human beings within the field of sociology.

Virginia appreciated the guidelines, too, noting that they helped her know what the professors wanted so that she would not be "fishing in the dark." It was in this way that she learned several of the conventions for writing a research proposal, such as the need to provide empirical evidence and to start a project with a research question. Without the guidelines, she said, "I wouldn't have thought of starting the first working papers [in Bernstein's class] with a question. You know? Maybe at the end I would've, or somewhere in the middle." But she also felt that the strict guidelines might inhibit creativity. They served primarily a pragmatic, school-oriented function for her: "You just follow the list, check it off, and then get it done."

Both Lu-Yun and Virginia, then, used the prescribed structures of the writing tasks as part of course survival strategies that allowed them to compensate for lack of background knowledge and experience. But they did not interact with the writing tasks, particularly those in the theory classes, in ways that were personally meaningful to them.

Regarding the methods papers, even though some students described these papers as "cookbook recipes" (as they also had for Bernstein's papers) that elicited no creativity from the writers, all students found them valuable in the sense that they gave them practice at a style and system of analysis that they believed would open doors for them later. There was much less concern for theoretical foundations in these papers than in the papers for the theory classes. One student commented that the writing was "much more of a professional training mechanism. You're gonna write papers your whole life," he continued, "and this is how you do it."

In sum, in interacting with the core course writing tasks, the students in this first-year cohort learned as much about individual professors and peers and about course survival strategies as they did about the larger community of sociology as a social science discipline.[4] Because individual professors differed somewhat in their beliefs about and orientations to sociology (e.g., greater or lesser interest in and reliance on theory, logic, or numbers), students learned how to write for each one as a survival strategy. As part of the survival strategy, each student learned to construct his or her own contexts for composing from specific local interactions among the writer, the writing tasks, and a variety of local resources—human and material, internal and external. The contexts that were created thus differed from

---

[4]Sociology has been described as a diverse discipline, perhaps characterized more by fragmentation than by an identifiable "community" character (Becker, 1986).

student to student. Some students, such as Richard, found a way to make the local interactions work for him in personally meaningful ways. But Lu-Yun and Virginia, perhaps coincidentally a foreign student and a minority student, each seemed to find it difficult to create contexts for writing from these local interactions that were more than pragmatic solutions to a school-based writing problem.

## THE COMPLEX LOCAL NATURE OF CONTEXT: IMPLICATIONS FOR EMERGING SCHOLARS WITHIN A DISCIPLINE

We have seen in this study some of the many ways that the professors, teaching assistant, and students interacted with each other, with the system of training, and with the writing tasks in the core course sequence. A great deal of diversity is evident, as is the power and complexity of the local and concrete influences on the writing contexts that students were forging for themselves in this environment. The students in this first-year cohort did not all evolve into "scientific" sociologists in the next couple of years, a fact pointed out by the "epilogue" describing individual students in the introduction to this chapter. The sociology program's rigorous disciplinary training, revolving around highly structured writing tasks in a demanding core course series, apparently could not guarantee that the "apprentices" would carry on the hallowed traditions.

The processes by which students construct contexts in which to write cannot therefore be captured satisfactorily by the "disciplinary community/ enculturation" metaphor. Rather than being immersed in communities of unidirectional contextual influences, student writers use a multiplicity of local resources to respond to their training in diverse ways. They not only take in established aspects of the system, but they push back in response to other aspects and reject others altogether.

But some students in this study did not recognize they had the power to influence the system, to help shape the writing context, and to define with confidence and flexibility (if not with full understanding) the professional self-images they were developing. They did not realize, in other words, that the necessarily interactive nature of their socialization experiences could help them "own" these experiences. Those students who actively participated in the shaping of their experiences (e.g., Richard and Lona) struggled with, but were not in any sense crushed or trapped by, the sometimes overwhelming demands of their first-year core course sequence. Virginia took charge of her own professional development only when she left the program and eventually entered another that fit her better than this one had. Perhaps Lu-Yun did the same: after four years, she was continuing to develop her expertise in statistics rather than committing to a dissertation topic in what she still felt was the fuzzy field of sociology.

In general, perhaps an early awareness of both the interactive and "game-like" nature of learning to write in a graduate program can help students construct contexts for composing that both get the job done and contribute to their own understanding of what it means to participate in a discipline at the professional level. As a fourth-year student from China put it, and as Richard had discovered, the trick was in discovering the power of flexible thinking and writing — in learning how to play the game and step in and out of it as necessary. Such awareness may be particularly important for foreign and minority students who find themselves in a social science program that does not emphasize cultural diversity in subject matter or research methods. Students who recognize the multidirectional and local nature of socialization can thus try on different disciplinary personae without having to commit to them. In this view, they will always perceive themselves as having power to resist, push back, toy, experiment, and, if necessary, continue looking.

Cooper (Cooper & Holzman, 1989) has suggested the "discourse community" metaphor hides complexity, because it no longer feels like a metaphor, but seems to be "a natural, unavoidable way to think about discourse in its social contexts" (p. 204). If we keep the "community" metaphor, we need, first, to remember that it is only a metaphor. With this in mind, we then need to imbue it with a more viable interactive dimension, one that captures some of the complexity faced by writers as they compose in real situations, as has been suggested by Witte (1992), Prior (1991), Ackerman (1989), and others. Much of this complexity involves the many local factors at work as students write. In discussing how people construct meaningful utterances, Bakhtin noted that it is the "nearest social situation" that determines an utterance's meaning. "Verbal communication," he argued, "will never be understood or explained outside of this link to the concrete situation" (Todorov, 1984, p. 43). The same can be said of the writing that students do as part of their disciplinary socialization.

## REFERENCES

Ackerman, J. (1989). Translating context into action (Tech. Rep. No. 27). Pittsburgh: Center for the Study of Writing, Berkeley and Carnegie Mellon.

Anson, C. N., & Forsberg, L. L. (1990). Moving beyond the academic community: Transitional stages in professional writing. *Written Communication, 7,* 200–231.

Applebee, A. N. (1984). *Contexts for learning to write: Studies of secondary school instruction.* Norwood, NJ: Ablex.

Bartholomae, D. (1985). Inventing the university. In M. Rose (Ed.), *When a writer can't write: Studies in writer's block and other compositing problems* (pp. 134–165). New York: Guilford Press.

Bazerman, C. (1981). What written knowledge does: Three examples of academic discourse. *Philosophy of the Social Sciences, 11,* 361–387.

Becker, H. S. (1986). *Doing things together: Selected papers.* Evanston, IL: Northwestern University Press.

Berkenkotter, C., Huckin, T. N., & Ackerman, J. (1988). Conventions, conversations, and the writer: Case study of a student in a rhetoric Ph.D. program. *Research in the Teaching of English, 22,* 9–45.

Berkenkotter, C., Huckin, T. N., & Ackerman, J. (1991). Social context and socially constructed texts: The initiation of a graduate student into a writing research community. In C. Bazerman & J. Paradis (Eds.), *Textual dynamics of the professions: Historical and contemporary studies of writing in professional communities* (pp. 191–215). Madison WI: University of Wisconsin Press.

Bizzell, P. (1982). College composition: Initiation into the academic discourse community. *Curriculum Inquiry, 12,* 191–207.

Brandt, D. (1986). Toward an understanding of context in composition. *Written Communication, 3,* 139–157.

Bruffee, K. A. (1983). Writing and reading as collaborative or social acts. In J. N. Hays, P. A. Roth, J. R. Ramsey, & R. D. Foulke (Eds.), *The writer's mind: Writing as a mode of thinking* (pp. 159–169). Urbana, IL: National Council of Teachers of English.

Casanave, C. P. (1992). Cultural diversity and socialization: A case study of a Hispanic woman in a doctoral program in sociology. In D. E. Murray (Ed.), *Diversity as resource: Redefining cultural literacy* (pp. 148–182). Alexandria, VA: Teachers of English to Speakers of Other Languages.

Casanave, C. P. (1990). *The role of writing in socializing graduate students into an academic discipline in the social sciences.* Unpublished doctoral dissertation, Stanford University, Stanford, CA.

Chin, E. (1991). *Learning to write the news.* Unpublished doctoral dissertation, Stanford University, Stanford, CA.

Chiseri-Strater, E. (1991). *Academic literacies: The public and private discourse of university students.* Portsmouth, NH: Boynton/Cook.

Cooper, M. (1982). Context as vehicle: Implications in writing. In M. Nystrand (Ed.), *What writers know: The language, process, and structure of written discourse.* New York: Academic Press.

Cooper, M., & Holzman, M. (1989). *Writing as social action.* Portsmouth, NH: Boynton/Cook.

Doheny-Farina, S. (1989). A case study of one adult writing in academic and nonacademic discourse communities. In C. B. Matalene (Ed.), *Worlds of writing: Teaching and learning in discourse communities of work* (pp. 17–42). New York: Random House.

Faigley, L., & Hansen, K. (1985). Learning to write in the social sciences. *College English, 34,* 140–149.

Fleck, L. (1935/1979). *Genesis and development of a scientific fact* (F. Bradley & T. J. Trenn, Trans.; T. J. Trenn & R. K. Merton, Eds.). Chicago: University of Chicago Press.

Geertz, C. (1983). *Local knowledge: Further essays in interpretive anthropology.* New York: Basic Books.

Geisler, C. (1990, April). *The nature of expertise in writing.* Paper presented at the Annual Meeting of the American Educational Research Association, Boston, MA.

Hansen, K. (1987). *Rhetoric and epistemology in texts from the social sciences: An analysis of three disciplines' discourse about modern American blacks.* Unpublished doctoral dissertation, University of Texas at Austin.

Hare, V. C., & Fitzsimmons, D. A. (1991). The influence of interpretive communities on use of content and procedural knowledge in a writing task. *Written Communication, 8,* 348–378.

Herrington, A. J. (1988). Teaching, writing, and learning: A naturalistic study of writing in an undergraduate literature course. In D. A. Jolliffe (Ed.), *Writing in academic disciplines* (pp. 133–166). Norwood, NJ: Ablex.

Herrington, A. J. (1985). Writing in academic settings: A study of the contexts for writing in two college chemical engineering courses. *Research in the Teaching of English, 19,* 331–361.

Huntington, M. J. (1957). The development of a professional self-image. In R. K. Merton, G. G. Reader, & P. L. Kendall (Eds.), *The student-physician* (pp. 179–187). Cambridge, MA: Harvard University Press.

Jolliffe, D. A. (1984/1985). *Audience, subject, form, and ways of speaking: Writers' knowledge in the disciplines.* Unpublished doctoral dissertation, University of Texas at Austin.

Jolliffe D. A., & Brier, E. M. (1988). Studying writers' knowledge in academic disciplines. In D. A. Jolliffe (Ed.), *Writing in academic disciplines* (pp 35–87). Norwood, NJ: Ablex.

Kuhn, T. S. (1970). *The structure of scientific revolutions* (2nd ed.). Chicago: University of Chicago Press.

McCarthy, L. P. (1987). A stranger in strange lands: A college student writing across the curriculum. *Research in the Teaching of English, 21,* 233–265.

Myers, G. (1985). The social construction of two biologists' proposals. *Written Communication, 2,* 219–245.

Nelson, J. (1990). This was an easy assignment: Examining how students interpret academic writing tasks. *Research in the Teaching of English, 24,* 362–396.

Nelson, J., & Hayes, J. R. (1988). *How the writing context shapes college students' strategies for writing from sources* (Tech. Rep. No. 16). Pittsburgh: Center for the Study of Writing, Berkeley and Carnegie Mellon.

Nystrand, M. (1986). *The structure of written communication: Studies in reciprocity between writers and readers.* New York: Academic Press.

Perelman, L. (1986). The context of classroom writing. *College English, 48,* 471–479.

Piazza, C. L. (1987). Identifying context variables in research on writing: A review and suggested directions. *Written Communication, 4,* 107–137.

Prior, P. (1991). Contextualizing writing and response in a graduate seminar. *Written Communication, 8,* 267–310.

Reither, J. A. (1985). Writing and knowing: Toward redefining the writing process. *College English, 47,* 620–628.

Schwegler, R. A., & Shamoon, L. K. (1991). Meaning attribution in ambiguous texts in sociology. In C. Bazerman & J. Paradis (Eds.), *Textual dynamics of the professions: Historical and contemporary studies of writing in professional communities* (pp. 216–233). Madison: University of Wisconsin Press.

Slevin, J. F. (1988). Genre theory, academic discourse, and writing within disciplines. In L. Z. Smith (Ed.), *Audits of meaning: A festschrift in honor of Ann E. Berthoff* (pp. 3–16). Portsmouth, NH: Boynton/Cook.

Todorov, T. (1984). *Mikhail Bakhtin: The dialogic principle* (W. Godzich, Trans.). Minneapolis: University of Minnesota Press.

Toulmin, S. (1972). *Human understanding.* Princeton, NJ: Princeton University Press.

Williamson, M. M. (1988). A model for investigating the functions of written language in different disciplines. In D. A. Jolliffe (Ed.), *Writing in academic disciplines* (pp. 89–132). Norwood, NJ: Ablex.

Witte, S. P. (1992). Context, text, and intertext: Toward a constructivist semiotic of writing. *Written Communication, 9,* 237–308.

# PART II

# Research

CHAPTER 5

# Writing in the Natural Sciences and Engineering

**George Braine**
*University of South Alabama*

This study analyzed and classified writing assignments from upper-division courses in the natural sciences and engineering, disciplines which attract a significant percentage of foreign students. The sample, which consisted of 80 assignments collected from 17 courses at The University of Texas at Austin, was classified into five writing genres: Summary/Reaction, Experimental Report (Lab), Experimental Report (Design), Case Study, and Research Paper. Nearly 75% of the sample belonged to the two experimental report genres. An analysis of experimental reports from six subject areas revealed that paraphrase and summary were the dominant writing skills required in writing these reports. The following pedagogical implications of the study are also discussed: (a) formulating academic writing courses for undergraduate foreign students majoring in the natural sciences and engineering, (b) teaching the genres and underlying writing activities, (c) individualizing the curriculum, and (d) deemphasizing the library research paper.

Over the years, researchers from English departments have made numerous attempts to determine the nature of writing in other disciplines. They have analyzed assignments, surveyed teachers and students, and analyzed student essays and teacher responses to these essays. The basis of this research is the awareness that English teachers should have a better understanding of academic writing in order to teach it.

Although initial research into academic writing covered many disciplines

113

in a single study, later research has focused on single disciplines such as business and the social sciences. This shift in focus is based on the assumption that separate disciplines are singular discourse communities with their own writing conventions.

The focus of this study is writing in the natural sciences and engineering (NS & E), which appears to have received little attention in previous research. In the case of ESL writing courses, these disciplines are significant because they attract a large number of foreign students. Although statistics from the Institute of International Education (IIE) indicate that more than 35% of the foreign undergraduates enrolled at American universities major in the natural sciences and engineering (Zikopoulos, 1989), the percentage appears to be higher at research institutions. For instance, at The University of Texas at Austin, which has the third highest enrollment of foreign students in the nation, 54% of the undergraduate foreign students registered during the 1990–91 academic year were enrolled in the College of Natural Sciences and the College of Engineering (*Statistical Handbook*, 1990–91).

The disciplines considered for this study, the natural sciences and engineering, share sufficient characteristics to be considered a single discourse community. In both disciplines, reports resulting from laboratory experiments conducted under controlled conditions appear to be the most frequent writing genre. Further, students of both areas share a basic knowledge of mathematics and science. Accordingly, this study has significant relevance for ESL writing courses: (a) the presence of a large population of foreign undergraduates who major in the NS & E, (b) the compatibility of the two disciplinary areas in terms of discourse conventions, and (c) university regulations which require these students to take composition courses, at least at the lower-division level.

## PREVIOUS SURVEYS OF ACADEMIC WRITING

A significant number of surveys have attempted to determine the nature of academic writing. Questionnaires, used by Behrens (1978), Kroll (1979), Ostler (1980), Eblen (1983), Bridgeman and Carlson (1984), and Wallace (1985), are the most frequently used data gathering instrument in survey research. If a questionnaire is to serve its intended purpose, the data gathered must be accurate and reliable. An often used technique to ensure the accuracy and reliability of incoming data is to pretest the questionnaire on a sample of respondents, which enables the researcher to eliminate areas of ambiguity before the final version of the questionnaire is administered. However, of the surveys listed above, only Bridgeman and Carlson mention the use of pretest strategies in the formulation of the questionnaire.

Other than Bridgeman and Carlson, the researchers who developed and used questionnaires were associated with mainstream English departments or with English as a second/foreign language programs. When such researchers question students and faculty from other disciplines, the researchers tend to use terminology that they are familiar with to identify writing genres, which may not be identical with the terminology used by the students and faculty being queried. As Swales (1986) has shown, those who "routinely or professionally operate within a genre are more likely to possess an overt knowledge of the conventions of a genre" (p. 4) than those who become involved in it only occasionally.

A listing of some terms used by researchers to taxonomize academic writing illustrates this problem.

Behrens (1978)   reports, themes or essays, research papers
Kroll (1979)     papers integrating mathematical or statistical data with a report, reports of lab experiments in continuous discourse, term papers
Ostler (1980)    lab experiments, book reviews, research proposals, research papers
Eblen (1983)     lab reports, article summaries, research papers
Bridgeman &      lab reports, article summaries, research papers, expository/
Carlson (1984)   critical writing, group writing, case studies
Wallace (1985)   article summaries, article abstracts, group writing tasks, case studies, analysis papers, comparison/contrast papers, documented research papers, lab reports

A closer examination of one genre, the lab report, illustrates the confusion which could result from the use of questionnaires. The writing of a lab report requires a complex mixture of writing skills such as summary, paraphrase, seriation, description, comparison and contrast, cause and effect, interpretation of data, analysis, and the integration of mathematical and scientific data into a text. Thus, researchers who list papers which integrate mathematical or statistical data (Kroll), or analytical papers (Eblen), or analysis papers and comparison/contrast papers (Wallace) as separate from lab reports would not only be applying multiple terms to describe what is essentially a single genre, but would also confuse the respondents to their questionnaires—faculty and students from other disciplines. The use of multiple terms suggests theoreticians' speculations of how academic discourse should be taxonomized, since not even book reviews and article summaries are self-explanatory terms.

While questionnaire designers appear to have used multiple terms to identify essentially similar genres, faculty from separate disciplines sometimes use different terms to identify what is essentially the same genre. The ubiquitous lab report, assigned by instructors throughout the range of NS & E disciplines, best illustrates this phenomenon. A lab report may also be known as a standard experiment in chemical engineering, a final report in aerospace and petroleum engineering, a technical report in mechanical engineering, and a memorandum in electrical engineering (Braine, 1989). Thus, the use of a variety of terms not only by the researchers but also by faculty members could only increase the inaccuracy of the data.

Some researchers have admitted the shortcomings of their surveys. For instance, Behrens (1978) acknowledged that surveys like his "might be a more accurate measure of what people think . . . than what they actually do" (p. 60), whereas Eblen (1983) admitted that "self-reports may blend respondents beliefs and intentions with actual practice" (p. 347). Horowitz (1986) criticized some of the surveys mentioned above for beginning with a "set of preconceived classifications" of writing tasks (p. 448), compelling the respondents to use the particular terminology used in each survey. To Horowitz, the logical approach was to analyze the writing tasks before classifying them.

Two researchers, Rose (1983) and Horowitz (1986) did not use questionnaires. Instead, they collected actual assignments from university instructors and created writing genres after examining the data. Rose's sample consisted of 445 quizzes, examinations, reports, and papers from 17 academic departments at UCLA. Horowitz examined 54 writing assignments from 17 academic departments at Western Illinois University.

Rose's often quoted study and its applications to curriculum design display at least two shortcomings. First, the sample of writing assignments consisted of quizzes and examinations as well as take-home (nonexamination) assignments. Because answers to quizzes and examinations are written under time pressure to a specific audience (usually course instructors) already familiar with the subject matter, masses of information can be regurgitated, often in a rambling and disorganized manner. Course instructors may only care for content, paying little attention to organization and style. On the other hand, take-home assignments are usually of a highly controlled nature: Teachers provide the topic, detailed instructions on procedural sequence and content organization, and in some courses, manuals which explain the writing task in greater detail. Extensive data and background information and reference articles and/or books for further reading are also frequently provided (Braine, 1989; Horowitz, 1986).

Unlike quizzes and examinations, a significant percentage of take-home assignments are designated for a real or hypothetical audience beyond the classroom (Braine, 1989). Thus, students not only follow prescribed formats as described earlier, but are often required to adapt their writing styles to suit a specific audience. Engineering majors, for instance, may be required to write reports to a nontechnical manager, and microbiology majors may be assigned to write magazine articles explaining the results of their research to a lay audience. Therefore, the mere regurgitation of information acceptable in examinations will not be permitted in take-home assignments. Rose's decision to place these two types of writing under one category may therefore be open to question.

The second shortcoming in Rose's study is the classification of the assignments into schemata or modes. These schemata, such as seriation, classification, analysis, and so on, are only contributory skills to a broader writing task. For instance, even a "book/article review" assignment requires summary, paraphrase, evaluation, and comparison/contrast skills. Hence, the classification of academic writing according to contributory skills could only fragment and thereby misrepresent the writing process.

Horowitz's (1986) analysis of assignments had a number of advantages over that of Rose. First, the sample consisted only of take-home assignments. Second, the academic departments and courses from which the sample was collected were specified. Finally, the classification of assignments was not according to modes as Rose had done, but according to the overall task of each assignment. Horowitz's classification yielded seven task categories, which not only captured the essential difference between tasks, but also caught the similarities between tasks which initially appeared different. A closer look at one category illustrates the basis for Horowitz's classification.

> **Report on a specified participatory experience** . . . none of the data needed to be obtained from a reading . . . students were assigned a specific "scene," either to observe passively or to participate in . . . They were also armed with a list of things to look for in that scene and a framework within which to interpret what they observed. The writing task itself usually involved reporting details of the experience . . . and then coming to some kind of conclusion about . . . the experience. This conclusion was also typically an answer to an explicit question. (p. 450)

The lab report genre belongs to the above category. However, unlike *lab report*, a term which may evoke different scenarios in varying contexts, Horowitz's category explicitly describes the activities that are required to perform the tasks, as well as the framework within which the task must be performed.

Accordingly, of the studies discussed so far, Horowitz's appears to be the only one which created a reliable classification after analyzing the assignments. However, his sample consisted of assignments from academic disciplines as diverse as marketing and biology, thereby ignoring an important conceptual basis for academic writing mentioned earlier in this chapter: Each discipline is a separate discourse community with its own writing conventions. The inclusion of assignments from the humanities, the social sciences, business, and science in a single sample is contradictory to the above concept, thereby limiting the study's usefulness to academic writing curriculum design.

To sum up, this discussion of previous surveys of academic writing has revealed the inadequacies of questionnaires as data gathering instruments; analyses of assignments was shown to provide more accurate data. The need to separate examination papers from take-home assignments before writing genres are formulated was also shown. Finally, this discussion has highlighted the need to narrow studies of academic writing to disciplines which have common discourse conventions.

## THE PRESENT STUDY

In order to discover what papers are assigned in undergraduate courses in the NS & E, assignment handouts were collected from instructors at the College of Natural Sciences and the College of Engineering at The University of Texas at Austin. The sample consisted of 80 assignment handouts obtained from 17 courses in 12 academic departments. Table 5.1 shows the distribution of the sample by academic departments.

TABLE 5.1. Distribution of Assignments by Academic Departments

| Department | Course Title | Number of Assignments |
|---|---|---|
| *Natural Sciences* | | |
| Botany | Lab Methods in Cell Biology | 10 |
| Chemistry | Advanced Analytical Chemistry | 02 |
| | Physical Methods for Biochemistry | 02 |
| Home Economics | Intro. to Home Economics Education | 05 |
| Microbiology | Microbiology | 03 |
| Physics | Quantum Phenomena | 05 |
| Geology | Mineral Resources | 02 |
| | | |
| *Engineering* | | |
| Aerospace | Design & Testing of Aero. Structure | 02 |
| Chemical | Che. Eng. Fundamentals Lab | 09 |
| | Process & Projects Lab | 05 |
| Civil | Eng. Economy & Construction Management | 03 |
| | Professional Engineering Management | 03 |
| | Contracts & Specifications | 01 |
| Mechanical | Mechanical Measurements | 06 |
| Petroleum | Petrophysics & Fluid Flow | 10 |
| | Petroleum Engineering Design | 06 |
| Electrical | Electrical Eng. Projects Lab | 06 |
| | Total | 80 |

Table 5.2 shows the distribution of the sample according to the terms used by course instructors.

Following Horowitz's approach described earlier, the assignments were analyzed and classified into genres based on their instructional specifications, required task(s), and organization. Almost 95% of the assignments in the sample fitted into five genres. The distribution of assignments according to the genres is shown in Figure 5.1. Sample assignments from Summary/ Reaction, Experimental Report (Design), Case Study, and Research Paper are given in Appendices A–D.

The five genres were defined as follows:

- *Summary/Reaction* requires the writing of a summary and/or a critique of a prescribed article. An evaluation of the value and/or relevancy of the article to a student project may also be required.

TABLE 5.2. Distribution of Assignments According to Type*

| Type | Number of Assignments |
| --- | --- |
| Article Review | 01 |
| Article Summary | 01 |
| Case Study | 01 |
| Commodity Profile | 01 |
| Description | 01 |
| Design | 01 |
| Essay | 02 |
| Executive Summary | 01 |
| Final Report | 02 |
| Lab Experiment Writeup | 02 |
| Lab Report | 34 |
| Memorandum | 04 |
| Memo Report | 04 |
| Progress Report | 06 |
| Proposal | 01 |
| Reading Report | 03 |
| Report | 03 |
| Research Article | 01 |
| Research Paper | 03 |
| Standard Experiment | 05 |
| Technical Report | 02 |
| Topic Review | 01 |
| Total | 80 |

*Terms used by course instructors to label assignments.

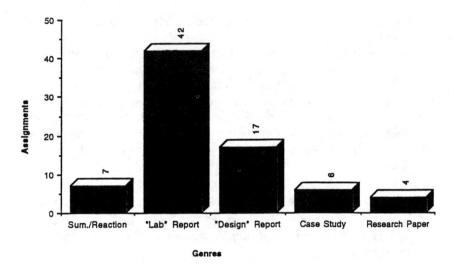

**Figure 5.1.** Distribution of assignments according to genres

- *Experimental Report (Lab)* requires the students to participate in a prescribed experiment in a laboratory in order to investigate a process. The students are often provided with sequential instructions for the conduct of the experiment. The data for the written report must be obtained from the experiment, and often, a series of questions guide the students in reporting results. The reports are usually sequenced as abstract, introduction, theory, apparatus and procedure, results, and conclusion.

- *Experimental Report (Design)* requires the students to participate in a laboratory experiment in order to improve a process, or the design of a piece of equipment. The process or the equipment is prescribed by the course instructor. The data has to be obtained from the experiment. When the experiment is a semester-long project, weekly reports, mid-semesterly progress reports, and a final report are usually required. The final report is usually sequenced as abstract, introduction, apparatus and procedure, results, conclusions, and recommendations.

- *Case Study* requires the students to use knowledge or a theory to solve a hypothetical problem. The scenario (of the problem) and all data are usually prescribed. Based on an analysis of the problem, the students are required to either propose a solution, or to choose one from a given list. The students are also required to justify the solution they have proposed or chosen.

- *Research Paper* requires the students to combine information from a number of sources. The topic for the paper is either specified or must be selected from a list. Occasionally, the organization of the paper is also indicated through a list of issues to be covered. Often, students are required to write a proposal or an abstract for approval by the course instructor before the research paper is written.

The writing genres formulated for this study show a number of advantages over taxonomies developed for previous studies. For instance, instead of using terms such as lab reports, term papers, critiques, research papers, expository/critical writing, group writing, brief research papers, themes or essays, documented reports, analysis papers, and so on (Behrens, 1978; Bridgeman & Carlson, 1984; Eblen, 1983; Kroll, 1979; Ostler, 1980; Wallace, 1985) without definition, the genres in this study use traditional terms supported by extended definitions. Further, by using traditional terms, this approach avoids the creation of yet another taxonomy, such as Horowitz's (1986).

Because almost 75% of the sample consisted of experimental reports, six experimental reports included in lab manuals from botany, aerospace engineering, chemical engineering, mechanical engineering, petroleum engineering, and electrical engineering were analyzed in order to determine the underlying writing skills.

## Analysis of Experimental Reports

One assumption which formed the basis of this study is that NS & E are compatible disciplines in terms of common discourse conventions. In fact, as this study has shown, the writing in these disciplines appears to fall neatly into just five genres. Further, the experimental report appears to be the most dominant genre in these disciplines.

As Herrington (1985a) has shown, experimental reports are of two types, lab and design. In lab experiments, the conceptual issue is scientific/technical, and the experiments usually involve the investigation of a process. In design projects, the issue is more deliberative since the purpose is the design of a process or product that is technically feasible and economically expedient. Despite this fundamental difference, Herrington (1985b) observes that the transition from lab courses (which students take up to their senior year) to a design course (taken in the senior year) was difficult for many students. In fact, some students she observed "made claims more appropriate to the lab course (i.e., 'scientific' rather than 'deliberative') in their first design reports" (p. 407). An examination of sample experimental reports from both lab and design courses contained in lab manuals provided in some courses considered for this study showed that although the two reports were conceptually different, the differences were reflected minimally in the report formats. Hence, in the analysis of experimental reports for this study, lab and design reports are considered together.

As noted earlier, the writing of experimental reports appears to require a complex mixture of skills such as summary, paraphrase, seriation, description, comparison and contrast, cause and effect, interpretation of data, analysis, and the integration of mathematical and scientific data with a text. Because experimental reports appear to be the dominant genre in the NS & E courses, an analysis of the reports may explain the reasons for the large increase of plagiarism noted in the technical writing of foreign students.

However, since the sample for this study did not include experimental reports written by students, sections of experimental reports contained in the *Laboratory Report Guide* for the Chemical Engineering Fundamentals Lab course and instructions contained in lab manuals provided to students in other courses were used for the analysis.

Whether referred to as a lab report, a final report, a progress report, a technical report, a standard experiment, or a memorandum, the aim of all lab or experimental reports is to present in a logical and organized form the results of a scientific or engineering experiment. Bazerman (1985) has noted four features common to scientific experiments: personal factors are minimized, precise measurements are made, extraneous factors are controlled, and often, a theory is tested. In addition, the conduct of the experiment and the writing of the report are carefully controlled by course instructors. For instance, in almost every lab or design assignment considered for this study, the instructors specified the topic of the experiment and the sequence in which the experiment was to be performed, and in most assignments, outlined the sequence in which the experiment was to be reported. When such detailed information was not provided within the assignment itself, students were either given additional lab notes which contained such information or were referred to appropriate textbooks.

This analysis begins with a comparison of the experimental report formats provided by instructors in botany in the natural sciences, and aerospace, chemical, mechanical, petroleum, and electrical engineering. The formats are compared in Table 5.3.

Three formats required the writing of abstracts, all six formats an introduction or its equivalent, three formats a section titled *Theory*, five formats a section dealing with apparatus and procedure, all six formats a section titled *Results*, and four formats required conclusions. Accordingly, a typical experimental report could be sequenced as abstract, introduction,

TABLE 5.3. Experimental Report Formats from Botany and Five
Engineering Courses

| Botany | Aerospace | Chemical | Mechanical | Petroleum | Electrical |
|--------|-----------|----------|------------|-----------|------------|
| Introduction | Abstract | Abstract | Objective & Summary | Introduction | Abstract |
| Materials & Methods | Introduction | Introduction | Facilities & Instrumentation | Apparatus | Introduction |
| Results | Theory | Theory | Experimental Procedures | Procedures | Theory |
| Discussion | Apparatus & Procedure | Apparatus & Procedure | Results | Hazards | Solution |
| References | Results Conclusions | Results Recommend- ations | Discussion Conclusions | Results Conclusions | Results Conclusions |

theory, apparatus and procedure, results, and conclusions. The analysis of a section common to all six formats, the introduction, will now be described.

All six formats required an introduction. In the botany course, students were required to "examine and explain the background of the experiment [and] describe the objectives and provide a summary of the necessary theory to understand and interpret the results of the observations" (*Botany 323L Syllabus, Spring 1988*, p. 5). In the aerospace and chemical engineering lab manuals, the introduction was described as "supplying the reader with sufficient background information to understand the present study and evaluate its results" (*Technical Writing Manual*, p. 13). In writing the introduction, students were advised to state the nature and scope of the problem investigated, review the pertinent literature, and state the method of investigation. This included a rationale for choosing a particular method of investigation.

In the guidelines for experimental reports provided in the mechanical engineering course, the objective and summary section (equivalent to the introduction section in other formats) is required to consist of a statement of the purpose of the experiment, a description of how the purpose was accomplished, and a statement of the results and their significance.

In the petroleum engineering course, the introduction section must cover the following areas: the purpose of the experiment, the scope of the experiment, relevant background to the experiment, if any, and the plan of outline of the report.

In the Electrical Engineering *Senior Lab Course Notes*, students are advised to "get right to the point" (p. 13) without general introductory comments. In order to ensure the coherence of the report, the introduction must be tied in with the conclusion by the use of the same wording, and restating the question that was answered in the conclusion. Thus, the abstract, the introduction, and the conclusion will be similar in content.

The Laboratory Report Guide to the Chemical Engineering Fundamentals Laboratory course provides the following sample Introduction:

1. Introduction
The purpose of this experiment was to measure the pressure drop in packed beds in which water was flowing counter currently to air. The air flow was measured with a critical orifice apparatus, the water flow was measured with a turbine meter, and the pressure drop was measured using a Validyne DP cell. Calibration curves for the turbine meter and the Validyne cell were given to directly measure liquid flow rates from pps, and pressure drops from millivolts (mv) respectively. Two packed towers were used in this experiment, one with Raschig ring packing, and the other with spherical granular packing. The pressure drops were determined in inches of water per foot-depth, and the velocities in pounds per feet square. The Leva plot allowed for correlations for the pressure drops and the fluid velocities (flooding velocity) at flooding points. All data concerning experimental pressure drop curves less than flooding were compared to the Leva correlation. (p. 9)

The above Introduction was written in partial response to the following assignment.

Ch. E. 253M
Experiment No. 9
PRESSURE DROP IN IRRIGATED PACKED BEDS
The objective of this experiment is to measure the pressure drop in packed beds in which water is flowing counter currently to air. The flooding point is to be determined along with the necessary characteristics of the packings. The experimental data are then compared to empirical correlations in the literature. . . . In this experiment, a Validyne DP cell will be used to measure pressure drops, a turbine meter to measure liquid mass velocities, and a critical orifice assembly to measure gas mass velocities. . . . Your report will deal only with the Raschig rings. Compare your data with the Leva correlation and the Ergun equation described in Experiment 8. . . . Your report will deal only with the spherical packing. Compare your data with the Leva correlation and the Ergun equation described in Equation 8 (pp. 1–17)

Thus, in writing the introduction of the experimental report, students are required to state the purpose of the experiment, review the theory, summarize the experimental procedures, and state the results. Except for the brief summary of results, the introduction consists of information obtained from the assignment handout or a reading. In transferring this information to the report, the most frequently used writing activities are paraphrase and summary.

Table 5.4 summarizes the results of the analysis of sample experimental

TABLE 5.4. Structure of Typical Experimental Report Showing Corresponding Writing Activities

| Section of Report | Writing Activities |
| --- | --- |
| Abstract | Summary of entire report |
| | Activity: Summary |
| Introduction | Transfer of information from assignment |
| | Activities: Paraphrase, Summary |
| Theory | Transfer of information from assignment or from readings |
| | Activities: Paraphrase, Summary |
| Apparatus & Procedure | Transfer of information from assignment or from readings |
| | Activities: Paraphrase, summary |
| Results | Presentation of data |
| Conclusions | Analysis and interpretation of data |

reports and assignment handouts, indicating the writing activities which are required in each section of a typical experimental report.


## PEDAGOGICAL IMPLICATIONS

The statistics quoted earlier have shown that a high percentage of under-graduate foreign students appear to major in NS & E, which raises the possibility of forming separate composition courses for these students. The analysis of the structure of the experimental report genre, which forms the bulk of the sample of assignments in the study, has indicated that a substantial amount of information has to be transferred from other sources (lab notes and textbooks) to experimental reports. Accordingly, summary and paraphrase were found to be vital writing skills.

Within the context of these findings, the feasibility of forming lower division academic writing courses for foreign students majoring in NS & E will now be discussed. Later, the academic writing curriculum within such courses will be explored.

### Writing Classes for Natural Sciences and Engineering Majors

Perhaps the most significant pedagogical implication of this study is that the writing tasks of the NS & E possess sufficient generality to be placed within a smaller number of genres. In addition, students in these disciplines share a knowledge of mathematics and basic scientific concepts. Accordingly, separate writing classes for such students is both justifiable and feasible.

In the United States, academic writing courses for foreign students, where writing instruction is integrated with the study of an academic subject, has been structured in two ways: as English for Specific Purposes (ESP) courses, and as adjunct courses to designated subject courses. In this volume, Jacoby, Leech, and Holten describe a course at the University of California, Los Angeles (UCLA), which introduces the fundamentals of the experimental report to science majors. The adjunct courses are best illustrated by the course described by Johns (this volume) and by the Freshman Summer Program at UCLA, in which English courses are linked with content area courses. During a 7-week period, students may be concurrently enrolled in English and Introductory Psychology, the two courses complementing each other through coordinated assignments (Snow & Brinton, 1988).

Despite the existence of such courses, the majority of lower division writing programs conducted by the English departments do not consider the students' majors during the structuring of classes. Although the needs of foreign students have occasionally led to the formation of separate freshman English classes (Dehghanpisheh, 1987), such classes still consist of students from diverse academic disciplines. What is necessary, and justifiable in the context of the large number of foreign students who major in NS & E, is the formation of classes according to the students' academic disciplines.

Since each discipline could be considered a separate discourse community, academic writing courses should, ideally, focus only on one discipline. That is, separate courses (such as "Writing in Electrical Engineering," "Writing in Chemistry," etc.) would be needed for students from the respective disciplines. However, for logistical reasons such as lack of teachers, such narrowly focused courses are not usually feasible. Instead, composition courses which deal with broader areas like the natural sciences, engineering, business, and the social sciences are feasible. Such courses are best formed at the lower division level, because students often need academic writing skills from their freshman year itself.

## Teaching the Genres and Writing Skills

Of the five genres formulated in this study, most English teachers can be expected to be familiar with (and able to teach) summary/reaction, case studies, and research papers. The experimental report, however, is probably the genre that is farthest from the domain of most English teachers. Nevertheless, a general discussion of the structure and function of each section of experimental reports in the academic writing class is possible. This will be discussed later under Individualizing the Curriculum.

What the English teacher can teach with confidence are the writing skills that are crucial to experimental reports. Paraphrase and summary appear to be the overwhelmingly dominant skills required in the writing of these reports. In two other genres, summary/reaction and research paper, paraphrase and summary were the most important writing skills.

Research has highlighted the high degree of plagiarism in the technical writing of foreign students. Abraham's (1987) study, which focused on the technical writing of foreign undergraduate students, revealed that of the 64 papers examined, 36 contained clear instances of plagiarism. According to Abraham, several students who did not plagiarize did so

> at a terrible price, producing paraphrases that obscured or altered the meaning of their sources. At least one student created a paraphrase that expressed the exact opposite of what his source had said. Other students created paraphrases that were utterly incomprehensible. . . . Only a fraction of the twenty-eight papers displaying acceptable documentation also contained competent organization, content, grammar, and mechanics. (p. 54)

Brogan and Brogan (1982), noting the high incidence of plagiarism in foreign students' technical writing, explain that the students may find it "far easier to copy someone else's apparently fluent interpretation than to devise their own halting, cumbersome prose" (p. 2) and suggest that paraphrase and summary writing should receive emphasis in composition classes. Johns (1981) has also recommended that paraphrase and summary be taught to ESL students.

A crucial issue in teaching paraphrase and summary relates to the nature of scientific and engineering writing. The analysis of experimental reports revealed that, to a large extent, information had to be transferred from the assignment handout or a reading to the report. However, this information has to be transferred in the same sequence as in the original, a practice not usually required in most summary writing. For instance, in the typical composition class, the rearrangement of information is not only allowed, but may even be encouraged for stylistic purposes. Such rearrangement of information would not be acceptable in the writing of experimental reports.

## Individualizing the Curriculum

As stated earlier, students who major in NS & E appear to belong to a single discourse community. However, the specific disciplines (such as chemistry, physics, chemical engineering) of these students display distinctive variations in the performance of similar tasks, such as in the writing of experimental reports. For instance, no two formats of the experimental reports listed in Table 5.4 are structured in the same sequence. Thus, even with a seemingly homogeneous group of students, teachers may be once again faced with the problem of adapting the curriculum to meet the needs of individual students.

Individualization has been defined as "the process of finding a way to create a set of general assignments that can be used by each of the students in a given class in respect to their individual needs" (Trimble, 1985, p. 23). This technique can be usefully applied in an academic writing class for NS & E students in the following manner. When learning the experimental report format, for instance, students can be asked to bring assignments from their academic majors. While the overall format of the task (such as abstract, introduction, theory, apparatus and procedure, results, discussion, etc.) could be discussed in general, students could write a report based on the actual assignments they have brought to class. Such assignments could be collected by the teacher and used as curriculum material in subsequent semesters. In this context, the English teacher is the language expert, and each student an informant from his or her discipline, a form of collaborative learning that will enable the teacher to manage with only a basic knowledge of the students' disciplines. Peer critiquing of the reports (or memos or proposals) by students of the same discipline will ensure the accuracy of the contents.

## Deemphasizing the Research Paper Assignment

In most freshman English courses, the types of writing taught include narration, exposition, description, evaluation, and argumentation. The research paper, which is usually the final writing assignment, receives greater emphasis than other assignments not only because it reinforces the types of writing taught earlier, but also because it is assumed to be the nearest approximation of academic writing attempted in the freshman English course.

However, only 5% of the assignments considered for this study were classified as research papers. This suggests that, at least in academic writing courses meant for NS & E students, the research paper should receive less emphasis than it does in freshman English classes.

# SUGGESTIONS FOR FURTHER RESEARCH

The rationale for the formation of "centralized" academic writing courses for natural sciences and engineering majors was the high percentage of undergraduate foreign students who major in these disciplines. Another area which attracts a significant percentage of foreign students in prebusiness, which in turn justifies the formation of academic writing classes which focus on business writing. For these reasons, research into the nature of business writing appears to be justified.

## REFERENCES

Abraham, J. E. (1987). *Preventing and detecting plagiarism in the technical reports of foreign students.* Unpublished masters thesis, University of Texas at Austin.

Bazerman, C. (1985). *The informed writer: Using sources in the disciplines* (2nd ed.). Boston: Houghton Mifflin.

Behrens, L. (1978). Writing, reading, and the rest of the faculty: A survey. *English Journal, 67,* 54–60.

*Botany 323C Syllabus.* (1988, Spring). Department of Botany, The University of Texas at Austin.

Braine, G. S. (1989). Writing in science and technology: An analysis of assignments from ten undergraduate courses. *English for Specific Purposes Journal, 8,* 3–16.

Bridgeman, C., & Carlson, S. (1984). Survey of academic writing tasks. *Written Communication, 1,* 247–280.

Brogan, K. M., & Brogan, J. D. (1982, April). *Yet another ethical problem in technical writing.* Paper presented at the 13th Annual Meeting of the College English Association, Houston, TX.

*Course Syllabus, CHE 253, Chemical Engineering Fundamentals Lab.* (1988, Spring). Department of Chemical Engineering, The University of Texas at Austin.

Dehghanpisheh, E. (1987). An overview of undergraduate ESL program models: A comparison of administrative policies for international students. *TESOL Quarterly, 21,* 570–577.

Eblen, C. (1983). Writing across the curriculum: A survey of university faculty views and classroom practices. *Research in the Teaching of English, 17,* 343–348.

Herrington, A. J. (1985a). Writing in academic settings: A study of the contexts for writing in two college chemical engineering courses. *Research in the Teaching of English, 19,* 331–359.

Herrington, A. J. (1985b). Reasoning and writing. *College Composition and Communication, 36,* 404–413.

Horowitz, D. (1986). What professors actually require: Academic tasks for the ESL classroom. *TESOL Quarterly, 20,* 445–462.

Johns, A. M. (1981). Necessary English: A faculty survey. *TESOL Quarterly, 15,* 51–57.

Johns, A. M. (1987). Our students, ethnography, and the university culture. *TexTESOL III Newsletter, 8,* 1–4.

Kroll, B. (1979). A survey of the writing needs of foreign and American college freshmen. *ELT Journal, 33,* 219–227.

*Laboratory Report Guide. Chemical Engineering Fundamentals Laboratory.* (1988, Spring). Department of Chemical Engineering, The University of Texas at Austin.

Ostler, S. E. (1980). A survey of the academic needs for advanced ESL. *TESOL Quarterly, 14,* 489–502.

Rose, M. (1983). Remedial writing courses: A critique and a proposal. *College English, 45,* 109–126.

*Senior Lab Course Notes.* (1988, Summer). Department of Electrical and Computer Engineering, The University of Texas at Austin.

Snow, M. A., & Brinton, D. M. (1988). Content-based language instruction: Investigating the effectiveness of the adjunct model. *TESOL Quarterly, 22,* 553–576.

*Statistical Handbook, 1990–91.* (1990). Office of Institutional Studies, The University of Texas at Austin.

Swales, J. (1986, April). *A genre based approach to language across the curriculum*. Paper presented at the RELC Seminar, Singapore.

Trimble, L. (1985). *English for science and technology*. Cambridge, UK: Cambridge University Press.

Wallace, R. (1985). *English for specific purposes in ESL undergraduate composition classes: Rationale*. Unpublished doctoral dissertation, Illinois State University, Normal, IL.

Zikopoulos, M. (1989). *Open Doors: 1987–88*. New York: Institute of International Education.

## APPENDIX A

Sample Assignment from *Summary/Reaction* Genre

**Subject:** Microbiology
**Course Title:** Microbiology 361
**Assignment 1**

Choose one of the following topics, or see me regarding alternative topics. Select a research article appropriate to your topic and write a review of the article. The paper should be approximately 4–5 pages, typed, double-spaced, and should include the following: What was the purpose of the study, how was the study done, what were the results, and what conclusions can be drawn. (Your conclusions may not be identical with the author's. If you disagree, state why.) A copy of the article is to be turned in with your review. Suggested sources for articles:

Infection and Immunity
Journal of Bacteriology
Journal of Virology
Journal of Infectious Diseases
Applied and Environmental
Microbiology
Journal of General Microbiology

Index Medicus and Current Contents are useful for locating articles.

Grading will be based on content of the review, which may be influenced by the choice of articles, and on writing style, clarity, and grammar.

**Suggested Topics:** Focus on virulence, pathogenicity, or host–microbe interactions. Let me know when you have selected a topic. No more than two people will write on a single topic. Choose carefully since the paper will form the basis of the third writing assignment.

adhesins
antigenic variation in Neisseria
hemolysis
hemaglutinis
cytotoxins
enterotoxins
motility
capsules
surface layers
proteases
siderophores (e.g., aerobactin)
Costridium difficile
Yersinia enterocolitica or
  pseudotuberculosis Vobrio
parahaemolytica
influenza virus

Campylobacter
Legionella pneumophilia
Klebsiella
Haemophilus
Mycobacterium leprae
Pseudomonas aeruginosa
Streptococcus pyogenes
Salmonella enteriditis
Mycoplasma
Plasmodium
Bacillus thurengiensis
hepatitis
HIV

## APPENDIX B

Sample Assignment from the *Experimental Report (Design)* Genre

**Subject:** Chemical Engineering
**Course Title:** Process and Projects Lab
DEVELOPMENT DEPARTMENT
UNITEX ENGINEERING CORPORATION
Austin, Texas
**TO:** Development Group Members          **Date:** Jan. 18, 1988
**FROM:** Chief Engineer
**Subject:** CSTR Reactor Study

You are to conduct a feasibility study. We wish to convert 4, 4, 4-tris-dimethyl-amino-triphenyl-carbilnol (crystal violet dye) to its sodium salt by reaction with sodium hydroxide, with a minimum of 95% conversion. The raw dye is available as an aqueous solution at a concentration of $4.8 \times 10-5$ gmol/liter and the sodium hydroxide is in aqueous solution at 0.0079 gmol/liter.

We have 2 CSTR reactor trains, consisting of 2 reactors each. All reactors are 4000 gallons apiece. We need the following information from you to determine the feasibility of the project:

1. Amount of crystal violet dye (in pounds) which can be processed in one day (24 hour operation).
2. When starting up, how much time will be required to reach steady state in the first and second reactors in each train?*
3. Supply the flow rates of all the streams. Assume that the sodium hydroxide and dye inlet streams will be at the same flow rate.
4. Devise a better reactor configuration which will provide more product at the required specification. Recommend your configuration and report your conclusions.

*Theoretically, the transient CSTR will never reach a true steady state. Define steady state as the time at which the concentration of dye in the effluent, as given by the transient CSTR equation, is within 1% of the concentration given by the steady state CSTR design equation.

## APPENDIX C

Sample Assignment from the *Case Study* Genre

**Subject:** Civil Engineering
**Course Title:** Engineering Economy & Construction Management

Report to Corporate Management (These managers have a strong technical background.) Basis for Preliminary Authorization You are the new manager of the Capital Project Evaluation group in the Bevo Company. You have been requested to prepare a request and analysis for preliminary authorization for a new Portland cement plant. Your report should consist of (a) a maximum 1-page executive summary, (b) an analysis report with appropriate graphs and/or tables to support your recommendations, and (c) any appendices that are necessary to further support the analysis.
Complete economic analysis covering:
Capital investment (cost) Operation and Maintenance: $10 million per year
Money value (interest) Depreciation—20-year 150% declining balance
Sales income?        Sensitivity analysis
                  Taxes
Raw materials $50 million per year
Salvage value at the end of per year lifetime—$0

BASIS FOR PAPER - "Bevo Company"
Portland Cement Plant
Capital Investment = $100.000.000
Life = 20 years
Raw materials cost = $50,000,000/year (90% production level)

Sales and sales management costs = 5% of sales
Operations, labor and maintenance costs = 10% of capital costs
Taxes = 35% of taxable income
IRS depreciation allowed in 20 years = 150% of declining balance
Plant is forecast to run at 90% capacity (avg.)
Sales bad debt average 2% per year Sales are uncertain, but use $16.5
  million as the basis for plant running at 90% capacity

## APPENDIX D

Sample Assignment from the *Research Paper* Genre

**Subject:** Geology
**Course Title:** Geology 341 (Mineral Resources)
GEO 341 THIRD WRITING ASSIGNMENT
This assignment is intended to provide you with a writing experience of a
more geologic nature than the first/second assignment. You should choose
you topic carefully to represent a subject about which you have some
scientific insight and one that has a significant amount of recent literature.
It is also important that you select a topic that is manageable within the
page limitations of the text. See a current issue of *Economic Geology* for
recommended form of reference, bibliography, tables, and so on. Be
*succinct*; use tables, charts, figures, etc. to summarize information. All
illustrations should be placed in a separate section following the reference
section.

*SUGGESTED FORMAT* — will not apply to all topics
Text (not to exceed 8 double-spaced typewritten pages)
Introduction - statement of problem, location, brief history, discovery,
  mining, production, etc.
Regional Geology - stratigraphy, structure, igneous activity, tectonic devel-
  opment, etc.
District (or Mine) Geology - discussion of host rocks, form and nature of
  the ore bodies, mineralogy or ore and gangue, alteration, factors
  controlling location of ore bodies, etc.
Origin of the Deposits - metallogenic setting, timing, timing of mineraliza-
  tion, mechanism for transport and precipitation, etc.
Conclusions - *your* major findings
References
Illustrations

*Some Suggested Research Topics*

Geology of an ore deposit in a mafic complex

Geology of an alkalic complex ore deposit

Geology of a porphyry Cu or porphyry Mo deposit

Geology of massive sulfide deposit

Geology of a lode Au deposit Geology of a laterite deposit

Geology of a sedimentary iron or manganese

Tectonic setting of a major ore deposit or district site

Mineral resources of an appropriate Petrogenetic affinities of a major ore deposit site county in Texas

Geology of a paleoplacer Au-U deposit or district

Geology of a nonmetallic mineral deposit Stratigraphic setting of a major ore deposit site or district


A brief research proposal must be submitted for approval. You will make a brief oral presentation of your investigation to the class.

# CHAPTER 6

# Writing Critically Across the Curriculum

Diane Belcher
*Ohio State University*

This chapter first provides a rationale for teaching critical writing, or evaluative readings of texts, to ESL students, especially at the graduate level. It is argued that critical writing will help students begin to see themselves as experts-in-training, to overcome their reluctance to challenge established authority, and to understand the social dynamics, or the ongoing dialectic, of their fields of study. Following the rationale, this chapter suggests a means of teaching critical writing through analysis of the common features of book reviews and article comments from disciplines across the curriculum: the common text structures, evaluative criteria, and politeness strategies which can be found in fields as disparate as Chinese literature and medicinal chemistry. Numerous examples of these cross-disciplinary commonalities are presented and their likely pedagogical value discussed.

My teacher's intuition has long told me that critical writing, or responding in an evaluative, analytical way to texts, is good for students. The "good" that I have been confident that critical writing assignments would do for my ESL students, who have been mainly first-year graduate students, was that these tasks would force my students to think critically about the domain-specific knowledge they were immersed in. While some teachers in the disciplines seem to think that students are likely to become critical when they reach a certain "subject saturation" point (Engeldinger, 1988, p. 196), it has struck me (Belcher, 1988), as it has others (e.g., Flower, 1989), that student writers, whether native or nonnative speakers, are not automatically made critical through subject-area reading. In addition to encouraging my students to approach disciplinary texts critically, I have also hoped that critical review assignments would help my students make the leap from "knowledge telling" to "knowledge transforming" (Bereiter & Scardamalia, 1987; Cumming, this volume). I have envisioned my students not just summarizing what they have read, but entering into dialogue with their subject-area reading (see Flower, 1990), mentally placing it in the context of all that they had previously read and experienced in their fields of study, if not in life, and both discovering and assessing their own thoughts on various disciplinary topics (Durst, 1987).[1]

Many of my students, however, have been less than enthusiastic about the benefits of critical writing. Invariably, when I ask students to write a critical review of a published research article or a book chapter, there are objections to the project as pointless and well nigh impossible to accomplish, given who they, my students, are and what they know. In fact, whether or not students can or should write critically about disciplinary texts is a matter of contention among composition specialists, some of whose arguments might well be seen as lending support to the objections typically raised by my reluctant critical writers.

## A RATIONALE FOR TEACHING CRITICAL WRITING

One line of argument that I have often heard advanced by ESL students is that as relative novices in their fields, they do not know enough to be critical. Disciplinary discourse researchers such as Becher (1989) would likely agree that one needs a certain amount of subject matter knowledge and understanding of how claims are usually established in a field in order to criticize works in that field. Mulkay (1977) has even argued that *only* those with the same level of knowledge and experience in a specialty are able to be competent reviewers. Of course, these scholars and my students are right: A high level of domain expertise is needed to authoritatively and persuasively critique works in a specific discipline. However, the creation of definitive, professionally suasive critiques is not my goal when I assign critical writing. Jolliffe and Brier (1988) have observed that there is an advantage to attempting to write like an expert even before one actually is an expert. They feel that "to acquire the kinds of writer's knowledge that experienced participants in a discipline have, a novice must write about the discipline's subjects, using its genres and its preferred styles" (p. 54). In

---

[1] I don't intend to imply, though, that summarizing is a trivial, easily accomplished task for nonnative speakers. Johns and Mayes (1990) as well as Kirkland and Saunders (1991) have shown us how linguistically and cognitively demanding summarizing can be for ESL students.

other words, a student must begin to act like an expert in order to become one. In their study of writing in an anthropology class, Herrington and Cadman (1991) found that even as undergraduates, students were expected to write like experts-in-training, that is, less like "receivers and demonstrators of knowledge" and more like people capable of "shaping their own thinking and writing" (Herrington & Cadman, 1991, p. 196.)

Sometimes, however, my students are reluctant to critique not just because they feel relatively ignorant of their disciplines, but because they are intimidated by the authority of any established knowledge in their fields of study. This can be especially true for ESL students who come from cultural and educational backgrounds in which, as Ballard (1984) and Matalene (1985) note, there is much reverence for scholars and scholarly work, where the students have been trained to absorb knowledge dispensed by their teachers and to memorize and imitate, not dissect, scholarly texts. Grabe (1991) has pointed out that students from countries where there is limited access to printed materials may just not be aware of how common counterarguments are in countries where multiple sources of information are readily available. Cultural pluralists, such as Land and Whitley (1989), argue that as teachers of ESL students, we should be tolerant and accepting of other rhetorical traditions, that we should broaden the canon rather than shape students into the likeness of our Western academic selves. However, if the students' traditional view is uncritical of established expert knowledge, should we benevolently preserve it? One of my (and I'm sure others') objectives when asking students to write critically is that they will begin to put themselves on an equal footing with experts. Olson and Torrance (1983) have remarked that writing, especially about reading, has the ability to teach students that texts "are authoritative not by virtue of the status of the writer or speaker but because they stand up to criticism within a peer group" (p. 40). In his overview of the development of scientific argumentation in the West, Back (1991) has observed that argument by authority, that is, using the testimony of authorities, is no longer the primary academic rhetorical strategy. Teaching critical writing is one way of familiarizing students with a type of argumentation which challenges, rather than depends on, textual authority.

The final kind of student resistance to critical writing that I want to mention has to do with disciplinary differences. Students in the natural sciences, engineering, and mathematics, areas that ESL students often major in (Braine, this volume), frequently claim that professionals in their fields never argue. Rather than criticize each other, these professionals build on each others' work. Indeed, many disciplinary discourse specialists, for example, Bazerman (1981) and Zuckerman and Merton (1971), have noted that knowledge in these sciences is advanced in a more consensual and cumulative way than in the social sciences and humanities. When

Bridgeman and Carlson (1983) surveyed faculty in the natural sciences and engineering, the professors indicated that students in their fields had little need to learn to argue. However, as Johns (1990) and McCarthy (1987) have remarked, faculty may have only tacit knowledge of what they actually do in their texts. While the goal of research writing in the natural sciences is certainly consensus building, or as Gross (1991) put it, to have one's assertions accepted as facts, the means of achieving that goal is rhetorical. Beneath an apparently nonargumentative and uncritical research report may lie a quite contentious subtext. Swales (1990) has shown us that a common rhetorical move in research article introductions is exposure of a gap, or shortcoming, in existing knowledge in a field, hence an implicit, sometimes explicit, critique of prior texts. Myers (1989) has uncovered numerous subtle face-threatening speech acts in scientific articles. Jolliffe and Brier (1988) as well as Myers (1989) pointed out that students, especially undergraduates, are likely to be oblivious to the amount of social interaction in the disciplines — that is, finding fault with, rejecting, ignoring others' knowledge claims — because all that the students have usually read in their fields of study is textbooks. If we do not encourage students to read and react to texts that experts write for their peers, certainly there is little reason to expect students to be aware of the role that criticism plays in the natural sciences, or in any other disciplines.

## READING TO WRITE CRITICALLY:
## WHAT EXEMPLAR TEXTS CAN TEACH US

One way to demonstrate to students that critical writing is common across the curriculum as well as to enable the acquisition of the procedural knowledge of form (Smagorinsky, 1992) that will help students take on the role of expert and begin to challenge authority in their fields is to expose them to the explicit criticism that exists in most, if not all, disciplines. A trip to their college libraries will quickly show students that there are book and article reviews in their own and other fields, although, as Becher (1989) mentioned, in some fields book reviews are more common; in others article reviews, usually referred to as "comments," are more frequent.[2] The teacher who takes on the role of ethnographer with her students (see Johns, 1990) will discover that in fact there are a surprising number of cross-disciplinary commonalities in this literature — common text structures, common evalu-

---

[2]Another critical review genre, the literature review, or "thematic surveys of particular topics" (Becher, 1989, p. 83), often provides a type of criticism too subtle for students to easily see, since it is expressed in the selection, emphasis, and juxtaposition of research findings.

ative criteria, common politeness strategies — and that these commonalities can serve as a heuristic for critical writers-in-training.

Of course, there are differences as well as similarities across disciplines in critical writing. Bazerman (1981), Becher (1989), MacDonald (1987), Zuckerman and Merton (1971), among others, have shown us how epistemologically disparate disciplines can be. Nevertheless, there are also generic commonalities in the explicit critical writing in diverse fields. In order to illustrate this I have chosen book reviews and article comments from recent issues (1990–1991) of journals in 14 different fields or subfields, which, in turn, fall into 7 broad areas of study: (a) Business: Business Economics and Marketing, (b) Education: Physical Education and TESL; (c) Engineering: Electrical and Mechanical Engineering; (d) Humanities: Chinese Literature and Fine Arts; (e) Mathematics: Applied and Theoretical Mathematics; (f) Natural Sciences: Medicinal Chemistry and Physics; and (g) Social Sciences: Anthropology and Sociology. Obviously, I cannot generalize about the rhetorical strategies of critical writing in any of these fields on the basis of the samples I have collected. After all, I have selected reviews or comments from one issue of one journal per field. I can only say that in this small but wide-ranging sample I can find cross-disciplinary commonalities, and that these, in turn, may serve as broad indications of how expert academic writers, no matter what their field, approach reading and writing critically.

## TEXT STRUCTURE: SOME COMMON AND UNCOMMON RHETORICAL STRATEGIES

Responding to a perceived overemphasis on the formal features of text types to the exclusion or neglect of content or function, ESL composition specialists have advised against direct teaching of textual form (for overviews of the evolution of ESL composition see Raimes, 1991, and Silva, 1990). Yet recent research on composing processes indicates that genre appropriateness is part of an array of very basic considerations that writers attend to when they begin composing (Bereiter & Scardamalia, 1987). It has also been observed that academic writing assignments outside of composition classes seldom fail to specify a genre (see Braine, Johns, and Prior, all in this volume), that the formal features of some genres may not be obvious to NNS (nonnative speaker) readers (Carrell, 1984), and that knowledge of the formal schemata of written texts seems to help NNS students produce texts that are likely to strike NS readers as coherent and well formed (Scollon, in press). In addition, Jolliffe and Brier (1988) have observed that "knowledge of organization, arrangement, form, and genre" can systematically lead to knowledge of subject matter (p. 46).

If we look at the book reviews and article comments I have chosen in terms of the arrangement of summary and critique, we can find two basic types of text structure, awareness of which I think should enable students to understand what expert writers in the disciplines generally feel obliged to provide in their reviews. Awareness of the structural elements should also help the students appreciate the vital informative and evaluative roles played by reviews, the time-saving sorting out that the disciplines, with their ever-increasing influx of new publications, always require.

This service function of reviews is conspicuous in two of the most easily recognizable and popular types of critical review text structure: the discrete summary/critique review, that is, introduction, summary, critique (see Arnaudet & Barrett, 1984) and the "cycling" summary/critique review (term borrowed from Swales, 1990, who uses it for a different purpose), that is, introduction, summary, critique, summary, critique, summary, critique, and so on. The discrete type of review may consist primarily of summary and conclude with a final evaluative overview which states the reviewer's position in clear, straightforward terms, as in the following:

> This book provides about the best treatment possible of the metal-cutting process for the case of homogeneous steady-state strain from the continuum mechanics point of view. It should be studied by all serious researchers in this field for the insight it provides into the intricacies of the process. It should be noted that the author clearly indicates in the preface that the material science (structural) aspects of material behavior are not considered in his treatment. As long as this limitation is recognized and kept in mind, this is a useful contribution. However, to ensure that this important point not be overlooked, it is unfortunate that the title did not read "Continuum Mechanics of Metal Cutting." (The actual title: "Mechanics of Machining: An Analytical Approach to Assessing Machinability") (*Journal of Applied Mechanics*, 253)

Other discrete reviews may have very brief summaries, followed by lengthy critiques, which also conclude with a very transparent summative-evaluative statement. This latter, primarily judgmental type of discrete review appears to be a very common format for article comments, in which the authors can assume audience familiarity with the work under review since the original article and the review are published in the same journal. Pointing out the fact that book reviews often contain more summary than do article comments can bring home to students the extent to which the form of texts in their fields is driven by the expert writers' awareness of audience needs.

Cycling reviews, which offer an efficient way to review an extremely long text, can also conclude as discrete reviews do, with clear, very reader-friendly summative evaluations, but sporadic commentary on specific sections of the text under review will have preceded the final evaluation. Here is a typical example of the cycling format:

Chapter 3 continues to use this material, where numerous level 2 and level 3 variants of Gaussian elimination are presented. Again, there are no specific recommendations of which variant to use on which machine. Chapters 4, 5, 7, and 8 present level 2 and level 3 versions of Cholesky. . . .

Chapter 6 is the main chapter on parallel algorithms. It is limited to Cholesky and QR decomposition, because pivoting has no elegant implementation on many architectures. Distributed memory and shared memory algorithms are presented. Issues of asynchronicity versus synchronicity . . . are discussed along with simple models to predict performance. This chapter has a strong architecture/software/operating systems flavor. (*SIAM Review*, 690)

The introductions of both the discrete and cycling types of reviews also appear to be keyed to audience needs. Many of these introductions serve their disciplinary audiences as very expedient guides to the latest literature by concisely and immediately orienting the reader, either by opening with an explicit statement of the reviewer's overall estimate of the work reviewed or with a one- or two-sentence summary of the contents of the entire work (or a combination of the two), as in the following:

Paul Krugman has written a brilliant gem of a briefing book on economic policy issues for the 1990's. . . . (*Business Economics,* 66)

This well written and organized monograph presents a very thorough continuum mechanics approach to steady-state metal cutting where the chips produced are in the form of continuous ribbons. (*Journal of Applied Mechanics,* 253)

Prof. Atta-ur-Rahman . . . has embarked on an ambitious project involving the systematic tabulation of all known natural products, together with information on their sources, molecular formulas, melting points, and spectral characteristics. (*Journal of Medicinal Chemistry,* 471)

The unmarried elderly become so through a variety of paths . . . but all share certain "practical issues of living" without a spouse. How their marital status and gender interact in dealing with life situations is the focus of *The Unmarried in Later Life.* (*American Journal of Sociology,* 1586–1587)

There is another type of critical review, however, which seems, at least at first sight, far from reader-based (Flower, 1979). The introductory component in this type of review is so extensively developed, so far removed from the immediate business at hand (reviewing a specific new work), that it hardly seems to qualify as the deductive type of text structure that Hinds (1990) and others (e.g., Kaplan, 1966) feel to be typical of English L1 texts. Indeed, one can easily imagine diligent composition teachers marking the margins of such reviews with "Where is your thesis statement?" or "Do you really need all this background information?" This third type of review may, in fact, devote a third to a half of the entire review to scene setting, before launching into the review proper. In my samples with this text structure (both book reviews and article comments), their seemingly excessive and indirect introductions prefaced either extremely negative or extremely positive critiques.[3] The segue in an anthropology book review of this type, which begins with an overview of several decades of literature in the social studies of science, explicitly reveals this reviewer's rationale for such a top-heavy structure: "Read against these current questions, Charlesworth et al.'s *Life among the Scientists* seems oddly out of date" (*Current Anthropology*, p. 79). The rationale for such a superstructure is far less explicit in a similarly organized book review in mathematics, although the implied purpose is easily enough discerned: to heighten the reader's appreciation of the value of the text reviewed. After spending 5 out of the 12 pages in his review on a highly personalized account of the development of the study of dynamics, this reviewer moves on to the actual review with:

> One can read some discussion of these issues in *The Mathematical Intelligencer* and hopefully we will read more, even in the *Bulletin*. But I will not play Zuckerman in *The Facts* to David Ruelle's Philip Roth. First of all I am not a fictional character, secondly I wasn't asked to. Ruelle does not distinguish the high from the low-quality chaos literature, which was for me the only (slightly) disappointing aspect of this enjoyable book. Ruelle has written an excellent introduction to dynamical systems and bifurcation theory. . . . What are the main features of the theory? (*Bulletin of the American Mathematical Society*, 204–205)

I should note that this surprisingly belletristic review, which reads like a 19-century personal essay, stands in marked contrast with another review that appears in the same issue of the *Bulletin*. That review wastes no time at all, beginning immediately with: "Let G be a finite group. Let p be a prime, . . . (*Bulletin*, 195).

For student-readers of reviews, the moral of a lesson informed by the types of text structure I have just described should be loud and clear: that there is a great deal of diversity within the critical review genre, within each

---

[3]Another likely reason for lengthy introductions is that reviewers can't assume reader familiarity with the literature of every specialized research area in any discipline. Myers (1990), in a discussion of research articles in biology, suggests still another reason for a more discursive than usual style. Myers remarks that unconventional formats may be especially appealing to writers who want to emphasize the significance of their topic. They may feel a need "to retell a whole narrative from the beginning, rather than dealing with just one incident within the narrative given by the scientific literature. In these terms, each deviation from what the editors expect may be . . . an assertion of the status of the claim, of its originality" (p. 81).

field, and even within single issues of a journal, and that while there appear to be formal constraints on the genre, the form is malleable enough to serve the individual critical writer's sense of purpose and audience.

## EVALUATIVE CRITERIA: READABILITY AND CREDIBILITY

The most common evaluative criteria in the book reviews I examined have audience as their focal point. In reviews across the disciplines one can easily find statements identifying the appropriate or intended audience for the work under review and evaluating that work with respect to its ability to reach and hence benefit its implied audience. The fact that such statements are often given prominent placement, in introductions and conclusions, suggests that audience appropriateness may be one of the most decisive factors in reviewers' judgments of the value of a work. The following excerpts from book review introductions and conclusions will give some indication of the extent to which consideration of audience unites reviewers across the curriculum:

*Introductions*
Keith McMahon's new book . . . is worthy of the attention of all who are interested in traditional Chinese fiction and in the comparative study of narrative. (*Chinese Literature*, 147)

The book . . . is meant both for teachers of any foreign language and for English-speaking adult learners of foreign languages with an interest in the "how" (or "how best") aspects of their task. (*ELT Journal*, 78)

In my review of the first edition of this book . . . I said it was an admirable attempt at addressing three audiences: students, scientists who need to compute, and numerical analysts. In particular, the rapid growth in theory and practice made it quite challenging to address a diverse audience. (*SIAM Review*, 690)

A Professor of Economics at the Massachusetts Institute of Technology specializing in international trade and finance, Krugman is a scholar who can translate his impressive knowledge on a wide range of economic topics into lively, readable prose for a general audience that remains intellectually balanced and rigorous. (*Business Economics*, 66)

*Conclusions*
The result is a highly readable piece of prose. . . . Yes, this account does "demystify" science, but only in the limited sense that the practice and institution of science are shown to be *associated with* a whole series of "non-scientific" events and circumstances. I suspect that those natives for

whom this book is intended would readily concede this much; it is, perhaps, something they already "know." (*Current Anthropology*, 80)

Beginners will like the fact that the proofs are clear, easy to follow, and preceded by an account of the intuition they are based on. Experts will find a scattering of new results, as well as treatments of recent results that are considerable improvements of the original papers. In short, the book is a delight for the young and old, so buy it. (*SIAM Review*, 693)

In short, I suspect that *The Power of Images* has itself the power to effect dramatic revisions in both art history and aesthetics. This is an expression not only of admiration, but of hope; *The Power of Images* seems to me a corrective for both the reticence of art historians and the arrogance of aestheticians. (*The Journal of Aesthetics and Art Criticism*, 86)

The volume would be a valuable reference to any medicinal chemist, molecular pharmacologist, or student who has an interest in drugs acting at receptors. However, the unavailability of this volume separately from the entire set will probably place it beyond the reach of many who could most use it. (*Journal of Medicinal Chemistry*, 473)

Apparently, the ability to effectively address a wide audience, even extending beyond the author's field, is valued by reviewers in a number of disciplines.

In article comments, audience considerations are less prominent. Since comments are usually responses to reports on new research findings, their evaluative criteria are primarily concerned with determination of the validity of the new knowledge claim, focusing on the theoretical framework, methodology, data analysis, and the reasonableness and significance of the conclusions in the research article. The point of the comment is thus usually to express an opinion as to whether or not the authors have really made a new and useful contribution to their field, as we can see in the following excerpt:

Our conclusion is that the approach by Pegg and Barnett is incorrect. The limiting procedure they proposed neither gives a well-defined Hermitian phase operator in Hilbert space nor provides a satisfactory description of the phase properties of the quantized electromagnetic field in an alternative way. (*Physical Review A*, 2577)

Frequently those who feel motivated to write a comment are precisely those whose own knowledge claims or stances are most closely related to the just-published research findings. These commentators, with their intimate knowledge of the research topic, are not only in an ideal position to critique their fellow professionals' work, but are also the ones most likely to be challenged by the latest findings. The following excerpt from another physics comment illustrates the challenges felt (and advanced) by commentators:

> The main reason for the discrepancy between the results of Ramos, Pyper, and Malli's calculations and our earlier calculations is that Ramos, Pyper, and Malli ignored electron-correlation effects completely, while for these molecules an intermediate coupling scheme that takes into account both spin-orbit and electron-correlation effects is essential. Since electron-correlation effects are substantial for molecules such as . . . , Ramos, Pyper, and Malli's claim that they obtain a reasonable description of bonding and good dipole moments is not justified. To the contrary, our works have shown that the nature of bonding in these molecules is substantially altered both by electron-correlation and spin-orbit effects. (*Physical Review A*, 2581–2582)

While the evaluative criteria in comments seldom seem to directly address such audience-centered concerns as readability and potential range of readers, commentators do concern themselves with the persuasiveness of new research articles, and may comment very pointedly on the degree to which the authors make their case clear enough to be comprehended and accepted by their colleagues in the field:

> As computation of determinants is one of the most fundamental problems in matrix analysis and we can only speculate on the eigenvalue algorithm, it would certainly be extremely interesting and very helpful if the authors would explain in detail which numerical method was actually used in their computations. . . . (*IEEE Transactions on Microwave Theory and Techniques*, 1761)

> Although Cauraugh's . . . hypotheses are specific, the rationales for the predictions are not developed adequately. No case is made for why the response-preference manipulation would be expected to interact with the other variables. (*Research Quarterly for Education and Sport,* 119)

> Pardoe has done Pacific Basin bioarchaeology a real service by introducing and ably demonstrating that yet another model from population genetics can be applied to the complex problems of this vast region. The model provides a powerful means for predicting expected results given certain assumptions. My chief concern is that Pardoe seems to have been a bit hasty in dismissing findings contrary to his own. I strongly suspect that he can marshal a vast body of facts to deal with this concern and readily dismiss my speculations. (*Current Anthropology*, 17)

The advantages of calling students' attention to the evaluative criteria in the book review/article comment literature seem to me severalfold. Students are likely to develop a stronger sense of the types of criteria employed in their field to judge new knowledge claims. Additionally, they will see that ability to reach and persuade one's intended audience is valued by professionals across the curriculum. Of course, many composition courses already routinely stress the importance of audience, yet international students, especially if they are in graduate school, may feel that they will not need to worry about audience so much when they write exclusively for readers in their own fields, who share essentially the same background knowledge. And international students who come from cultures that may have a tradition of preferring more reader-responsible texts (texts that put a heavy decoding burden on the reader), as Hinds (1987) has suggested the Japanese do, may be especially wary of making their English texts too accessible and thus insulting to readers. The prominence and frequency of audience considerations in the evaluative criteria of reviews written by experts in the very fields that our students are themselves pursuing degrees in should help persuade them that accessibility is a virtue much to be desired even by professionals.

## THE POLITENESS STRATEGIES OF EVALUATIVE LANGUAGE: FRIENDLY PERSUASION?

Becher (1987, 1989) has pointed out some fascinating varieties of terms used to encode evaluative statements in different disciplines. For historians, for example, high praise is likely to be expressed by way of modifiers such as "scholarly" and "original," while sociologists prefer to laud studies as "stimulating" and "rigorous," and physicists opt for "elegant," "productive," and "economical" (Becher, 1987, p. 264). Becher observes that these preferred evaluative terms correlate with the particular meaning-making systems of each field. Helping students familiarize themselves with this field-specific evaluative terminology should provide them with a valuable shorthand for communicating with others in their fields.

My reading of critical texts across the disciplines, however, has made me more aware of a commonality in the evaluative language, especially of book reviews, a commonality that could help embolden students who are reluctant challengers of authority in their fields. I have noticed a great deal of cautious indirectness in the expression of negative criticism in a number of disciplines.[4] There appears to be an almost obligatory prefacing of

---

[4]I am certainly not the first to point out the cautiousness of criticism in the disciplines. Becher (1989) has remarked that there is "a fair amount of evidence to suggest a deliberate avoidance or damping-down of critical comment in contemporary academic writing" (p. 99). And North (1992) notes of book reviews in the field of rhetoric and composition: "Shoved onstage alone to make a 1500- to 2500-word pronouncement on a book someone has taken years to write to an audience lost behind the footlights . . . most of us chart a cautious course" (p. 358).

negative commentary with positive commentary, or use of what Pomerantz (1984) in reference to spoken assessments calls "agreement prefaces" (p. 72). This indirectness may seem especially surprising to some nonnative speakers who have generalized that native English speakers, especially Americans, are very direct in writing and speech. Beebe and Takahashi (1989), however, have observed that in some situations Americans may actually be more indirect than Japanese speakers, who are often assumed to be extremely indirect. Beebe and Takahashi discovered that Americans in their sample were more likely than Japanese to soften face-threatening speech acts (FTAs) with positive opening remarks. Similarly, Johnson and Roen (1992) found in their analysis of peer reviews written by American graduate students in TESL that a "good news/bad news pairing strategy" was commonly used to redress specific FTAs (p. 45). At the global, or whole text, level, the writers in Johnson and Roen's study frequently framed their reviews with opening and closing compliments. I have found similar global and local discourse strategies in published reviews across the curriculum.

The following, an introductory paragraph in a book review, is a typical example of an agreement preface, or the "good news first" approach, in a published review:

> The authors tackle several ambitious tasks. They review the complete history of marketing thought and address such questions as marketing's relationship to society, marketing's stature in the scientific community . . . and the formulation of a general theory of marketing. Because of the number and magnitude of these objectives, some are accomplished better than others. (*Journal of Macromarketing*, 38)

It appears, in fact, that the more damning the intended criticism, the more extravagant the prefatory praise will be, as can be seen in another opening paragraph in a book review:

> Gregory Currie's *An Ontology of Art* is one of the most imaginative, probing, lucid, and sophisticated treatments of the ontology of works of art to appear in recent years. Though its two main theses are, in my judgment, mistaken. . . . (*Journal of Aesthetics and Art Criticism*, 79)

At the local level, in specific comments in the body of book reviews, the same softening strategy can easily be found:

> In McMahon's favor it can of course be conceded that the stories examined at length are picked because they are useful heuristically . . . and no attempt is made to present a complete interpretation of each. Be that as it may, I think most readers will, here again, feel somewhat cheated by McMahon's failure to

make cumulative use of the paradigms proposed by the author over the book as a whole. (*Chinese Literature*, 149)

A number of reviewers in various disciplines also appear to feel obliged to conclude the entire review on a positive note even when their review has been primarily negative. After a long catalogue of complaints, the *Chinese Literature* reviewer cited above concludes with these kind words:

> There is much food for thought in these pages, and I think we can look forward in the future to more important monographs from Professor McMahon. (*Chinese Literature*, 150)

In one of the most scathing reviews in my sample, which criticized the editor of a work for failing to critically assess the literature on his topic, ignoring the latest developments, and relying on inexperienced assistants who were all "devoid of doctoral degrees," there was still a diplomatic, though qualified, closing:

> It should be added, however, that the project is worthwhile and deserves to be continued, provided that much greater dedication to high standards is applied. (*Journal of Medicinal Chemistry*, 471)

Clearly such positive closing comments do not transform negative overall estimates of a work into positive estimates. The diplomatic closings seem to be made more in an effort to, in Galtung's (1981) words, "mop up the blood and put wounded egos together" (p. 825).[5]

Writers of article comments may feel less obligated to soften the blow through indirectness. A few initial lukewarm words of praise may be followed by a direct attack:

> This is an intuitively attractive theory. It apparently bridges interpretive and institutional approaches to the sociology of culture. . . . Griswold's model has the appearance and promise of being a complete, holistic theory that is at once novel and traditional.
>
> Griswold's model suffers from the following problems. (*American Journal of Sociology*, 1577–1578)

---

[5]Galtung (1981) gives the following example of what he refers to as the "Saxonic" intellectual style, which, he feels, fosters debate and discourse: "The first discussant will open his/her speech with the usual comment to the effect that: 'I greatly enjoyed listening to Mr. X's presentation, admiring his mastery of the facts . . . as well as his way of marshalling the facts together, but. . . .' The 'but' clause may then become quite extensive, with lots of cutting edges and biting points, but more likely than not there will be a complimentary, congratulatory point at the end" (p. 824).

Comment conclusions can be very direct in their negative final judgments, as in the earlier cited "Our conclusion is that the approach by Pegg and Barnett is incorrect" (*Physical Review A*, 2577). Perhaps because authors often have an opportunity to respond to comments, and generally do, commentators feel there is less need to counterbalance their negative remarks.[6]

Reluctant critical writers could benefit from attending to the evaluative language of critical reviews in several ways. They will see that professionals in their field, even if it is one of the natural sciences, do indeed engage in disputation and openly criticize each other. Of course, in research articles, as MacRoberts and MacRoberts (1984), Myers (1989), and Swales (1990) have found, the criticism of prior texts can be much more subtle and implicit, and students need to recognize the situatedness of different critical styles. What the evaluative language of critical reviews can give students (as suggested earlier) is a window on the dynamics of their discipline that they may not otherwise have. It can show them that colleagues can (and usually are expected to) remain respectful even as they challenge each others' findings.

## CONCLUSION

One of my student critical writers stands out in my mind both for the strength of his initial objections to being forced to write critically about a text in his field of study and for the eagerness with which he eventually took advantage of the opportunity to critique his own advisor's work. In practically the same breath this student had insisted that criticism in his field, an applied natural science, did not exist, and revealed that he was troubled by his advisor's published attack on recent attempts to apply statistical analysis to an area in which it had not previously been used. After discovering how common criticism of scholars was in his and the fields of everyone else in his class and that he could voice criticism respectfully, my

---

[6]Rose's (1992) response to a review of one of his books, *Perspectives on Literacy*, reveals how unrestrained even book reviews can be in their criticism. It is obvious that Rose does not feel that being able to respond in print to the review lessens the pain and damage: "The author of a critical review has the right to take issue with the books under consideration and to offer perspectives that differ with those held by the book's authors, but Sandra Stotsky's review . . . of an anthology on literacy I edited with Eugene Kintgen and Barry Kroll . . . went beyond criticism to broadside and personal denunciation. Stotsky characterizes the work we did with words like: 'incoherence,' 'puzzling,' 'incredible,' 'mystifying,' 'unforgivable,' 'cynical,' 'intellectual incest.' Such talk hurts and baffles. I do not want to go at Stotsky's accusations point by point — that would quickly become odious and defensive — but I do think it necessary to go on record against charges that cut to the heart of my, Kintgen, and Kroll's professional lives" (p. 81).

student wrote a very carefully balanced yet, in his own eyes, enormously bold review of one of his advisor's publications. The sample reviews that he and his classmates analyzed had not only provided him with linguistic and rhetorical strategies with which to express his critical thoughts but also encouraged him to acknowledge and develop those thoughts.

How do I know that the student I've just described or any other student will continue to write critically after leaving the relatively safe haven of an ESL classroom? I do not. However, as Coe (1987) has noted, pointing to feminist assertiveness training as a prime example, "providing appropriate forms is one of the most important techniques for enabling a new kind of communication" (p. 25). Some of my students may not feel entirely comfortable writing critically about disciplinary texts until they are more confident in their subject-area expertise, but all of my students will leave my class knowing that they can (both in the deontic and the epistemic sense) write critically about what they read in their fields of study, and that they should.[7]

## REFERENCES

Arnaudet, M., & Barrett, M. (1984). *Approaches to academic reading and writing*. Englewood Cliffs, NJ: Prentice-Hall.

Back, K. (1991, September). *Numbers as rhetoric in social science: The founding of political economy*. Paper presented at the 8th Meeting of the International Society for the History of Rhetoric, Baltimore, MD.

Ballard, B. (1984). Improving student writing: An integrated approach to cultural adjustment. In R. Williams, J. Swales, & J. Kirkman (Eds.), *Common ground: Shared interests in ESP and communication studies*. Oxford, UK: The British Council and Pergamon Press.

Bazerman, C. (1981). What written knowledge does: Three examples of academic discourse. *Philosophy of the Social Sciences, 11*, 361–387.

Becher, T. (1987). Disciplinary discourse. *Studies in Higher Education, 12*, 261–274.

Becher, T. (1989). *Academic tribes and territories: Intellectual enquiry and the cultures of disciplines*. Milton Keynes, UK: The Society for Research into Higher Education and Open University Press.

Beebe, L. M., & Takahashi, T. (1989). Sociolinguistic variation in face-threatening speech acts: Chastisement and disagreement. In M. R. Eisenstein (Ed.), *The dynamic interlanguage: Empirical studies in second language variation* (pp. 199–218). New York: Plenum.

Belcher, D. (1988, March). *Critical writing and the Chinese ESL student*. Paper presented at the 23rd Annual TESOL Convention, San Antonio, TX.

Bereiter, C., & Scardamalia, M. (1987). *The psychology of written composition*. Hillsdale, NJ: Erlbaum.

Bridgeman, B., & Carlson, S. (1983). *Survey of academic writing tasks required of graduate and undergraduate foreign students*. Princeton, NJ: Educational Testing Service.

---

[7]Braine (personal communication) has pointed out that book reviews and article comments are often the first opportunities that ESL graduate students have for publication in their fields. North (1992) similarly observes that reviews "represent a good way of breaking in and staying active" (p. 352).

Carrell, P. (1984). The effects of rhetorical organization on ESL readers. *TESOL Quarterly, 18*, 441–469.

Coe, R. (1987). An apology for form: Or, who took the form out of the process? *College English, 49*, 13–28.

Durst, R. K. (1987). Cognitive and linguistic demands of analytic writing. *Research in the Teaching of English, 21*, 347–376.

Engeldinger, E. (1988). Bibliographic instruction and critical thinking: The contribution of the annotated bibliography. *RQ (Reference Quarterly), 28*, 195–202.

Flower, L. (1979). Writer-based prose: A cognitive basis for problems in writing. *College English, 41*, 19–37.

Flower, L. (1989). Cognition, context, and theory building. *College Composition and Communication, 40*, 282–311.

Flower, L. (1990). Negotiating academic discourse. In L. Flower, V. Stein, J. Ackerman, M. Kantz, K. McCormick, & W. Peck (Eds.), *Reading-to-write: Exploring a cognitive and social process* (pp. 221–252). New York: Oxford University Press.

Galtung, J. (1981). Structural, cultural, and intellectual style: An essay comparing saxonic, teutonic and nipponic approaches. *Social Science Information, 20*, 817–856.

Grabe, W. (1991). Current developments in second language reading research. *TESOL Quarterly, 25*, 375–406.

Gross, A. (1991). Does rhetoric of science matter? The case of the floppy-eared rabbits. *College English, 53*, 933–943.

Herrington, A., & Cadman, D. (1991). Peer review and revising in an anthropology course: Lessons for learning. *College Compositions and Communication, 42*, 184–199.

Hinds, J. (1987). Reader versus writer responsibility: A new typology. In U. Connor & R. Kaplan (Eds.), *Writing across languages: Analysis of L2 Text* (pp. 141–152). Reading, MA: Addison-Wesley.

Hinds, J. (1990). Inductive, deductive, quasi-inductive: Expository writing in Japanese, Korean, Chinese, and Thai. In U. Connor & A. Johns (Eds.), *Coherence in writing: Research and pedagogical perspectives* (pp. 87–109). Alexandria, VA: TESOL.

Johns, A. (1990). Coherence as a cultural phenomenon: Employing ethnographic principles in the academic milieu. In U. Connor & A. Johns (Eds.), *Coherence in writing: Research and pedagogical perspectives* (pp. 209–226). Alexandria, VA: TESOL.

Johns, A., & Mayes, P. (1990). An analysis of summary protocols of university ESL students. *Applied Linguistics, 11*, 253–271.

Johnson, D. M., & Roen, D. H. (1992). Complimenting and involvement in peer reviews: Gender variation. *Language in Society, 21*, 27–57.

Jolliffe, D. A., & Brier, E. M. (1988). Studying writers' knowledge in academic disciplines. In D. A. Jolliffe (Ed.). *Advances in writing research, vol. II: Writing in academic disciplines* (pp. 35–87). Norwood, NJ: Ablex.

Kaplan, R. (1966). Cultural thought patterns in intercultural education. *Language Learning, 16*, 1–20.

Kirkland, M., & Saunders, M. (1991). Maximizing student performance in summary writing: Managing the cognitive load. *TESOL Quarterly, 25*, 105–121.

Land, R., & Whitley, C. (1989). Evaluating second language essays in regular composition classes: Toward a pluralistic U.S. rhetoric. In D. Johnson & D. Roen (Eds.), *Richness in writing: Empowering ESL students* (pp. 284–293). New York: Longman.

McCarthy, L. (1987). A stranger in strange lands: A college student writing across the curriculum. *Research in the Teaching of English, 21*, 233–265.

MacDonald, S. P. (1987). Problem definition in academic writing. *College English, 49*, 315–331.

MacRoberts, M., & MacRoberts, B. (1984). The negational reference: Or the art of dissembling. *Social Studies of Science, 14*, 91–94.

Matalene, C. (1985). Contrastive rhetoric: An American writing teacher in China. *College English, 47*, 789–808.

Mulkay, M. J. (1977). Sociology of the scientific research community. In I. Spiegel-Rosing & D. de Solla Price (Eds.), *Science, technology and society: A cross-disciplinary perspective* (pp. 93–148). London: Sage.

Myers, G. (1989). The pragmatics of politeness in scientific articles. *Applied Linguistics, 10*, 1–35.

Myers, G. (1990). *Writing biology: Texts in the social construction of scientific knowledge.* Madison: University of Wisconsin Press.

North, S. (1992). On book reviews in rhetoric and composition. *Rhetoric Review, 10*, 348–363.

Olson, D. R., & Torrance, N. (1983). Writing and criticizing texts. In B. M. Kroll & G. Wells (Eds.), *Explorations in the development of writing* (pp. 31–42). New York: Wiley.

Pomerantz, A. (1984). Agreeing and disagreeing with assessments: Some features of preferred and dispreferred turn shapes. In M. Atkinson & J. Heritage (Eds.), *Structures of social action: Studies in conversation analysis* (pp. 57–101). Cambridge, UK: Cambridge University Press.

Raimes, A. (1991). Out of the woods: Emerging traditions in the teaching of writing. *TESOL Quarterly, 25*, 407–430.

Rose, M. (1992). A comment on (Sandra Stotsky's) "On literacy anthologies and adult education: A critical perspective." *College English, 54*, 81–83.

Scollon, R. (in press). Eight legs and one Elbow: Stance and structure in Chinese English compositions. In *Launching the literacy decade: Proceedings of the Second North American Conference on Adult and Adolescent Literacy.*

Silva, T. (1990). Second language composition instruction: Developments, issues, and directions in ESL. In B. Kroll (Ed.), *Second language writing: Research insights for the classroom* (pp. 11–23). Cambridge, UK: Cambridge University Press.

Smagorinsky, P. (1992). How reading model essays affects writers. In J. Irwin & M. A. Doyle (Eds.), *Reading-writing connections.* Newark, DE: International Reading Association.

Swales, J. (1990). *Genre analysis: English in academic and research settings.* Cambridge, UK: Cambridge University Press.

Zuckerman, H., & Merton, R. K. (1971). Patterns of evaluation in science: Institutionalization, structure and functions of the referee system. *Minerva: Review of Science, Learning and Policy, 9*, 66–100.

# APPENDIX A: DATA SOURCES

## Business

### Business Economics

Barnett, W. S. (1991). Review of *The age of diminished expectations: U.S. economic policy in the 1990's*, by P. R. Krugman. *Business Economics, 26*, 66–67.

### Marketing

Johnson, J. (1990). Review of *Marketing theory: Evolution and evaluation*, by J. Sheth, D. Gardner, & D. Garrett. *Journal of Macromarketing, 10*, 38–40.

## Education

### Physical Education

Reeve, T. G., & Proctor, R. W. (1991). Comment on "Speed accuracy tradeoff during response preparation," by J. Cauraugh. *Research Quarterly for Exercise and Sport, 62*, 118–120.

## TESL

Kerr, J. (1991). Review of *Success with foreign languages: Seven who achieved it and what worked for them*, by E. Stevick. *ELT (English Language Teaching) Journal, 45*, 78–79.

## Engineering

### Electrical Engineering

Mrozowski, M., & Okoniewski, M. (1990). Comment on "Computation of cutoff wavenumbers of TE and TM modes in waveguides of arbitrary cross sections using a surface integral formulation," by M. Swaminathan, E. Arvas, T. K. Sarkar, & A. R. Djordjevic. *IEEE Transactions on Microwave Theory and Techniques, 38*, 1761–1762.

### Mechanical Engineering

Shaw, M. (1990). Review of *Mechanics of machining: An analytical approach to assessing machinability*, by P. Oxley. *Journal of Applied Mechanics, 57*, 253.

## Humanities

### Chinese Literature

Rolston, D. (1990). Review of *Causality and containment in seventeenth-century Chinese fiction*, by K. McMahon. *Chinese Literature: Essays, Articles, Reviews, 12*, 147–150.

### Fine Arts

Sartwell, C. (1991). Review of *The power of images: Studies in the history and theory of response*, by D. Freedberg. *Journal of Aesthetics and Art Criticism, 49*. 85–86.
Wolterstorff, N. (1991). Review of *An ontology of art*, by G. Currie. *Journal of Aesthetics and Art Criticism, 49*, 79–81.

## Mathematics

### Applied Mathematics

Demmel, J. (1990). Review of *Matrix computations* (2nd ed.), by G. Golub & C. Van Loan. *SIAM (Society for Industrial and Applied Mathematics) Review, 32*, 690–691.
Durrett, R. (1990). Review of *Percolation*, by G. Grimmett. *SIAM Review, 32*, 693.

### Theoretical and Applied Mathematics

Feit, W. (1991). Review of *Brauer trees of sporadic groups*, by G. Hiss & K. Lux. *Bulletin of the American Mathematical Society, 24*, 195–199.
Shub, M. (1991). Review of *Elements of differential dynamics and bifurcation theory*, by D. Ruelle. *Bulletin of the American Mathematical Society, 24*, 199–211.

## Natural Sciences

### Medicinal Chemistry

Shamma, M. (1991). Review of *Handbook of natural products data, Vol. I: Diterpenoid and steroidal alkaloids*, edited by A. Rahman. *Journal of Medicinal Chemistry, 34*, 471.

Stubbins, J. (1991). Review of *Comprehensive medicinal chemistry: The rational design, mechanistic study and therapeutic applications of chemical compounds, Vol. 3: Membranes and receptors*, edited by J. Emmett. *Journal of Medicinal Chemistry, 34*, 473.

### Physics

Balasubramanian, K., Christiansen, P., & Pitzer, K. (1991). Comment on "Relativistic effects in bonding and dipole moments for the diatomic hydrides of the sixth-row heavy elements," by A. Ramos, N. Pyper, & G. Malli. *Physical Review A, 43*, 2581–2582.

Ma, X., & Rhodes, W. (1991). Comment on "Phase properties of the quantized single-mode electromagnetic field," by D. Pegg & S. Barnett. *Physical Review A, 43*, 2576–2577.

## Social Sciences

### Anthropology

Turner, C. (1991). Comment on "Isolation and evolution in Tasmania," by C. Pardoe. *Current Anthropology, 32*, 16–17.

Woolgar, S. (1991). What is "anthropological" about the anthropology of science? (Review of *Life among the scientists: An anthropological study of an Australian scientific community*, by M. Charlesworth, L. Farrall, T. Stokes, & D. Turnbull). *Current Anthropology, 32*, 79–81.

### Sociology

Denzin, N. (1990). Reading cultural texts: Comment on Griswold ("The fabrication of meaning: Literary interpretation in the United States, Great Britain, and the West Indies," by W. Griswold). *American Journal of Sociology, 95*, 1577–1580.

Spitze, G. (1990). Review of *The unmarried in later life*, by P. Keith. *American Journal of Sociology, 95*, 1586–1588.

# CHAPTER 7

# Writing From Sources:
# Case Studies of Graduate Students
# in Business Management

**Ulla M. Connor**
*Indiana University/Purdue University at Indianapolis*

**Melinda G. Kramer**
*Prince George's Community College*

The chapter reports a research study that was designed to examine reading/writing relationships of ESL students in a graduate business writing class. Investigations of students—three ESL and two U.S. students—were conducted to examine problems, strategies, and skills in reading to write (writing from sources) among students reading a business case and writing a case report based on it.

The first goal of the study was to compare strategies of reading comprehension and processes of writing and problem solving (i.e., task representation) among the students. The second goal was to find out whether task representation differed among ESL learners depending on their language skills and previous professional training and experience. Written products of students and transcribed retrospective interviews served as the data.

The results showed that two of the ESL students lacked the strategies of a successful report writer throughout the task representation, from the first reading of the case to the final version of the report. Language proficiency may have affected the ESL students' performance. In addition, professional training and background was found to affect both the ESL and the American students' task representation.

The authors make recommendations for improved ESL reading and writing instruction that emphasize longer texts for reading with increased opportunities for critical thinking and creative problem solving.

## INTRODUCTION

Few studies have examined ESL students in business courses with the exception of Canseco and Byrd (1989). They analyzed a total of 55 course syllabi from 48 different business courses. Based on the analyses of the written syllabi, the researchers came up with several observations, such as that the production of written work is a major part of the requirements and that group work is an important feature of many courses in business. Canseco and Byrd concluded by saying that the "exact nature of these different responsibilities to different types of students needs further research and discussion" (pp. 315).

Whereas Canseco and Byrd's research focused on identifying tasks, the research reported in this chapter explored strategies and processes students used in their reading and writing. This emphasis on processes reflects the shift in ESP literature toward exploring processes of learning tasks in specific situations rather than merely identifying target tasks (Johns, 1991; Mohan & Oszust, 1991). Mohan and Oszust suggest that the switch in emphasis from the study of target tasks to the study of learning tasks is consistent with the current theories of ESP. These current theories consider ESL learning not only the acquisition of language but also the socialization in language in a specific community, context, or genre (Johns, 1991; Swales, 1990).

The concern about examining learning as a socialization process parallels the changing focus in the research on L1 composition. Composition research is moving from an emphasis on cognition to an emphasis on the social construction of meaning. Although writing is still considered a cognitive activity (Flower & Hayes, 1981; Flower et al., 1990), it is also considered a situationally determined activity, a social activity (Ackerman, 1990).

Ackerman's account of students' writing behavior, although developed for L1 writers, is relevant here. Interested in students' performance in reading-to-write assignments at the college level, Ackerman argues that writing behavior is socially structured. Topics, rhetorical means, and linguistic conventions echo previous literate practice as well as the literate practices of discourse communities (p. 173). According to Ackerman, there is an "interplay between a literate heritage, the immediate social or rhetorical situation, and a writer's ability to affect change within a discourse community" (p. 174).

The most comprehensive research dealing with the act of the interpretation of an assignment by L1 student writers has been conducted by Linda Flower and her colleagues at Carnegie Mellon University. Flower (1987; Flower et al., 1990) discusses the interpretation of an assignment by college students and describes task representation as "an interpretative process which translates the rhetorical situation—as the writer reads it—into the act of composing" (1987, p. 7).

Flower found that "a dominant feature of every writer's vision of a task is the organizing plan used to structure what is being read and to structure the writer's text" (p. 43). The organizing plan guides the processes of reading and writing but also helps the writer decide on the actual organization of the text. The organizing plan determines whether students summarize, synthesize, or interpret information.

Flower's research on college-level writers shows that students use different plans and subsequently different strategies when they write. In her studies some students skimmed the text to review and comment on it. Still others saw their task as organizing information under a controlling, synthesizing concept. (Flower defines "synthesizing" operationally as having a synthesizing concept, a substantive idea that not only appears in the produced text but also controls the selection of information and the organization of the text.) Finally, some students went beyond "synthesizing" and "interpreted for a purpose of one's own" to organize a discussion around a unique, rhetorical purpose.

According to Flower, we need to look at the task representation not as a single, simple decision, but as an extended interpretative process that extends throughout the composing process. Writers faced with a writing assignment need to define the problem, the goals of their argument, and the strategies they use in building the arguments. Students need to define the problem and construct a task for themselves by considering all possible operations and strategies they have to accomplish a goal. Figure 7.1 lists the key features in the students' task representations based on Flower's research. These key features include major sources of information (e.g., text, previous concepts), format of text (e.g., school theme, persuasive essay), organizing plan (e.g., summarize, synthesize), and strategies and goals used (e.g., cover key points, learn, influence the reader).

There is indeed growing recognition of the need to investigate how ESL learners handle long readings from a variety of sources for the purpose of writing. Yet, in-depth analyses of reading/writing relationships of international graduate students in specific disciplines are lacking. Business management is one such discipline even though—along with engineering—it attracts the highest percentage of international students in the United States.

International students entering graduate programs in business typically have a good command of the English language; a score of 600 on the TOEFL test is an admission requirement in many business schools. Few schools, however, require a separate score of writing proficiency. The curriculum in American graduate business programs is challenging for international students because it relies heavily on Anglo-American business

---

MAJOR SOURCE OF
INFORMATION

- Text
- Text + My Comments
- What I Already Knew
- Previous Concepts + Text

---

TEXT FORMAT
AND FEATURES

- Notes / Summary ¶
- Summary + Opinion ¶
- Standard School Theme
- Persuasive Essay

---

ORGANIZING PLAN FOR WRITING

To Summarize the Readings

To Respond to the Topic

To Review and Comment

To Synthesize with a Controlling Concept

To Interpret for a Purpose of My Own

---

STRATEGIES

- Gist and List
- Gist and List and Comment
- Read as a Springboard
- Tell It in My Own Words
- Skim & Respond
- Dig Out an Organizing Idea
- Divide into Camps
- Choose for Audience Needs
- Choose for My Own Purpose

---

OTHER GOALS

- Demonstrate Understanding
- Get a Good Idea or Two
- Present What I Learned
- Come Up with Something Interesting
- Do the Minimum and Do It Quickly
- Fulfill the Page Requirement
- Test My Own Experience
- Cover All the Key Points
- Be Original or Creative
- Learn Something for Myself
- Influence the Reader
- Test Something I Already Knew

---

**FIGURE 7.1.**   Key features of students' task representations (Flower, 1987, p. 7)

practice. A central feature of many master's programs is the "case study" approach following the Harvard Business School's model of over 70 years ago. Case study is the analysis of business policy cases that describe business situations. Normally written by business school professors about real companies, these narratives reflect the way problems actually arise in business. The goals of case study are (a) to learn to identify business problems, (b) analyze their causes, and (c) to propose viable solutions. The implicit question posed in every case is "What would *you* do?"

International students have little direct experience with case studies and find them difficult. On the one hand, business cases give students a wealth of information to filter. Students need to plough through a lot of data. On the other hand, necessary information is sometimes missing. The method is intended to invite participation and challenge; students need to defend assertions and opinions and make decisions. Charles (1984), in discussing the teaching of case studies in the classroom, comments on the challenge for ESL students and writes: "If we want to practice evaluative reading, here it is!" Swales (1990) maintains that case studies constitute data overload, present reading problems, and create additional problems for ESL students because they assign groups of students to develop a particular position.

Uber Grosse (1988) evaluated the benefits of using case studies as materials in ESL classes and concludes that they are useful because they present authentic materials and provide content-area concepts and cultural information. They also emphasize a learner-centered, integrated skills approach by emphasizing group discussions, role plays, and simulations. She notes, however, that case studies lack exercises and activities designed for ESL/EFL students and require knowledge of general Anglo-American business concepts.

The present research was designed to examine reading-writing relationships of ESL students in a graduate business school. Investigations of five student writers—three ESL and two U.S. students—were conducted to demonstrate problems, strategies, and skills in reading-to-write among students in a graduate-level business writing class where a business case approach was used. The purpose of the study was to determine both the strategies of reading comprehension and the processes of writing and problem solving among the students. Level of language proficiency as well as writing experience of the students were the independent variables whose effects were considered. This chapter first summarizes previous research in a related area, namely task representations and interpretations among L1 writers in academic settings. Secondly, this paper describes the design of the study, the analysis of the data, and the findings. The last section discusses the implications of the findings for "writing-from-sources" in ESL.

## THE STUDY

### Goals and Design

The goals of the study were threefold. First, we wanted to learn whether the task representation of ESL writers, as reflected both in process and in product, was similar to that of native speakers. Second, the study examined whether the task representation was different among ESL learners depending on their language proficiency level. Our third goal was to determine whether the task representations of the students in the study were dependent on professional training and background.

This study took place in Fall 1989 at a "Big Ten" midwestern university's graduate school of management. Five student volunteers in the graduate-level managerial policy reports course were selected, and each went through the following procedures:

1. Reading a business case and writing a subsequent policy report as part of a classroom task; and
2. Participating in three tape-recorded, structured interviews with one of the researchers present, the first one after the students had read the case, the second one after the students had written a rough draft, and the third one after final drafting. The written report and all accompanying written work were analyzed by the two researchers, and the interviews were transcribed and analyzed.[1]

## Setting

All first-year master's students in the university's graduate management programs are required to take the graduate-level managerial policy reports course in their first semester. The enrollment during the semester when this study was conducted was 117 students; 11 were international students. Four instructors taught the course and graded the reports.

The course has two types of class settings: (a) a large lecture-discussion class (focused on the content of the assigned business case) attended by all students simultaneously, and (b) a smaller lecture-discussion section (focusing on rhetoric and writing issues) involving each instructor and only his or her own students. At the beginning of the semester, all students purchase a "case packet" containing all the cases they will read and write about during the semester, along with a document called the "General Instructions" that details the components of a managerial policy report. The General Instructions define each section of the report, explain what it should contain, and list common report pitfalls and remedies. The instructions emphasize

---

[1]We used retrospective interviews instead of "thinking aloud" protocols because we did not want composing aloud to interfer with the reading and writing processes. Instead of turning the reading and writing into timed tasks, typical of "thinking aloud" studies, we tried to keep the reading and writing situation as natural as possible. It could be argued that using "thinking aloud" protocols we could have gained a closer, more detailed look at the reading and writing processes. Yet, comparisons of "thinking aloud" with other methods such as retrospectives interviewing show that results are very similar (Durst, 1992).

format, specifically a prescribed organizational pattern. Students' reports must follow the format order: Problem Statement, Issues, Alternatives, Recommendation, and Plan of Action.

The case assigned in this study totaled 20 pages, including exhibits. The task in this study required students to read the assigned case, which explained a proposal to expand an educational company to include franchised day care centers. The assigned case also included observations at a board meeting where the proposal was discussed. The students were to assume the role of the consultant who had written the proposal, consider the board members' reactions, and make a final proposal addressed to the board. (Appendix A includes instructions given to students concerning the format of reports as well as a copy of the first page of the assigned case.)

## Subjects

The five subjects in the study included three nonnative speakers of English and two native English speakers. The profiles of the five subjects are given in Figure 7.2 (the names of the subjects are fictitious). We chose international students who represented different cultures and L1 educational

---

*Nonnative Speakers*

(1) Chung—Korean
   asst. bank manager
   10+ years work experience
   some on-the-job writing in Korean
   undergrad internat'l trade major
   590 TOEFL score

(2) Bernard—Belgian
   sales & supervision engineer
   5+ years work experience
   some on-the-job writing in French
   undergrad engineering major
   573 TOEFL score

(3) Pablo—Bolivian
   consultant, Big-8 firm
   3+ years work experience
   extensive on-the-job writing,
      mainly in Spanish
   undergrad engineering major
   637 TOEFL score

*Native Speakers*

(1) Dan—American
   automotive engineer
   5+ years work experience
   some on-th-job writing
   undergrad engineering major

(2) Carolyn—American
   technical writer
   5+ years work experience
   extensive on-the-job writing
   undergrad fine arts major

---

**FIGURE 7.2.**  Subject profiles

systems—Belgium, Bolivia, and Korea. The three international students and the male U.S. student had quantitative backgrounds (engineering, science, business). The international students' TOEFL scores were 573 for the Belgian student, 590 for the Korean student, and 637 for the Bolivian student. We chose our female subject, Carolyn, precisely because as a professional writer with a fine arts degree she offered quite a different background. We were interested in seeing if her task representation—case analysis and writing process—would differ significantly from those of her technically trained peers.

## Data Collection

Data collection for this third case study began after the students had received grades and instructors' feedback on the second report assignment of the semester but before the third report was submitted. Consequently, they had two opportunities to master the format and, between the managerial policy reports and their marketing classes, more than a dozen opportunities to perform case analysis.

With one of the researchers present, the students' instructors asked them a series of preplanned questions on three separate occasions that were timed to correspond roughly to different stages in the students' reading and writing process. The first interview took place while or just after the students had read the case about which they would write their report. The goal was to learn what these students did when they read a business case. The second interview took place before the final draft was written. The goal was to discover what students did as they generated a first (rough) draft. The third interview occurred shortly after the report had been submitted. The goal was to learn what students did when they reviewed or generated the finished draft. (The goals of the interviews, which guided the interviewer's questions, appear in Appendix B.)

Although these interviews were intended to take no more than 15 minutes, most of them ran longer as students sometimes gave more detailed responses. All interviews were tape recorded and then transcribed. We also collected all written artifacts the students could provide: the cases with any marginal notes, underlining, or highlighting; handwritten or computer-generated notes, outlines, and drafts, and so forth.

## Data Analysis

To analyze the data, we examined both the student interview transcripts and all written material produced by the students for the managerial report. Both researchers first read all transcripts and written materials for general impression.

The analyses had two purposes: (a) to describe the process of reading and writing for each student, and (b) to describe the effectiveness and persuasiveness of the problem solving by analyzing the produced managerial report and its relationship with the case itself, the task representation.

To accomplish the first purpose, after the initial readings we analyzed the transcripts in detail and drew flow charts to describe the process of reading and writing for each student. In the charts, we had four columns, as Figure 7.3 — a sample chart for Chung, the Korean student — indicates. The left column shows the processes of reading and writing. In the Korean student's case, he read the case five times, drew an outline after the third reading, wrote a draft after the fourth reading, and wrote a second and final draft after the fifth reading. (Appendix C contains all the versions of the "Issues" section of Chung's report: outline, first draft, second draft, and the final product, a typed version of the second draft.) The other columns were labeled "getting facts," "analyzing issues," and "revising." The Korean student underlined text after the second reading, took notes after the third reading, and transferred facts and phrases from the case text to his report after the fourth and fifth readings of the case. The "analysis" column identifies our judgments concerning the chronology of the determination of the major issues by the student. The final column, "revision," outlines revisions made by the student in the drafts of the report.

| Chronology of Process | | Getting Facts | Analysis | Revision |
|---|---|---|---|---|
| Reading | Writing | | | |
| 1 | | | | |
| 2 | Underlining Text | Underlining Text | | |
| 3 | Outline | Notetaking 2 facts transferred from case text | Major issues/ alternatives determined and ordered | |
| 4 | Draft 1 | 14 facts/phrases transferred from text to rough draft | No change in or addition to initial analysis | Outline filled in to form rough draft. Major language revisions made |
| 5 | Draft 2 | No new facts introduced into paper | Unchanged Goals/strategies outline introduced | Minor language adjustments from Draft 1 6 new sentences added 11 grammatical/ language revisions 2 sentences from Draft 2 discarded |

**FIGURE 7.3.** Summary of Chung's reading and writing processes

For the second part of the data analysis, we conducted a close textual analysis of each student's final version of the managerial report. We examined the content of the report to determine whether the student had identified a problem and how well the student had backed up the claim. We were also interested in whether the expression of the claim and supporting evidence were original or whether they were mere restatements from the case. As an aid, we drew flow charts of the argumentative structure of each student's report.

## RESULTS

Examining the reading and writing process of the subjects and analyzing their written products provided data bearing on the research issues of reading-to-write and task representation among L1 and L2 graduate business students. The following sections first explain the individual students' reading and writing processes, then analyze the task representations through written products, and, finally, summarize the results in relation to the three goals of the study.

### Chung

*Reading/writing process.*    Chung, a Korean with more than 10 years of experience in banking and a TOEFL score of 590, emerges as a writer whose organizing plan is merely to summarize the reading (see Figure 7.3 for a summary of his reading/writing process). A careful analysis of his underlining of the case text shows a need to understand or remember specifics in context rather than a scheme for using the underlined text as preparation for composing a sound argument. The analysis and structuring of issues and questions are set down in the roughest outline form and remain unchanged throughout the writing process. Chung's use of other components of the writing process is largely restricted to surface structure editing (11 grammatical changes made between the second draft and the final draft). The notations and drafts do not reveal a process in which ideas are dynamically used and tested in a series of revisions. (To demonstrate the lack of substantive changes from one version to the other, Appendix C includes all four versions of section "Issues" of Chung's report.)

Chung conjoined the reading and writing processes, as evidenced in the occurrences of facts/phrases being taken directly from the text. In fact, among Chung's prevalent strategies was his reliance on the case text for English language word choice and phrasing (14 instances in the the first draft). This finding is consistent with Raimes's (1985) research, which suggests that lower level L2 students who are insecure in vocabulary choice resort to the strategy of directly borrowing words and phrases.

*Task representation.*  The reading/writing process Chung employed parallels his apparent task representation as evidenced in the content of his report. Instead of identifying a strategic management problem, he restates the situation described in the case: "attempt to establish a nationwide chain of franchised preschools. . . ." Primarily summarizing case ideas, he offers few challenges to the conclusions drawn by the characters in the text. Chung's alternatives are variations of the "go" proposal offered in the case, either with or without "some adjustments." The arguments mounted in favor of these alternatives are largely unsupported or rely on newly introduced evidence: that is, they lack the integrated, cohesive structure of argumentative chains and clusters required for a successful managerial policy report.

Chung's understanding of his assigned task, then, apparently does not go beyond summary and some tentative analysis. The paper's lack of coherence and lack of argumentative structure and devices suggest that the full-scale synthesis and interpretation that would transform the text information into useful management decisions are not part of Chung's task representation.

## Bernard

*Reading/writing process.*  A Belgian with more than five years in engineering and sales (TOEFL score 573), Bernard, like Chung, emerges as a writer who did not have a guiding rhetorical principle for writing in mind when he read the case. Instead, he read for content and summarized the case in his initial outline, importing the case headings for outline headings. The difference between Bernard and Chung is that Bernard is non-text bound, supplementing his original outline with ideas from fellow students in his study group. Unlike Chung, he did not coordinate the reading and writing process but was much more influenced by information that came from outside the case.

Waiting until 3 days before the report was due to attend a study group meeting, Bernard recorded each student's ideas and afterward wrote a second outline in which he reorganized and analyzed ideas from the group. His first draft is a section-by-section elaboration of this most recent outline, completed without rereading the case for evidence—as verified by a lack of support for many of the conclusions offered in this and subsequent drafts. The second draft is a typed version of the first draft, with minor revisions (such as dropping part of a paragraph); the third and final draft includes just a few editorial changes. Instead of transferring language directly from the text, Bernard generated his own prose, occasionally coining phrases that could confuse or mislead the reader, at least the American reader. Sentences such as "financial and human resource investments are not profitable to the company as required by the basic goals" sometimes reduce paragraphs to word salad.

*Task representation.* Bernard identified an acceptable management problem, "to verify project's feasibility in accordance with basic objectives of company," but this potential organizing idea governs the report only sporadically. Whole sections of the report seem analysis-driven and appear to be headed somewhere. However, the many conclusions offered in the report are drawn with only passing references to facts available in the text. The second half of the report, where the issues should be drawn together and arguments for or against various alternatives should be weighed, lacks transitional bridges from the first half. There is very little weighing of evidence or assembling of previous conclusions into argumentative structures. This lack of coherence and cohesiveness forces readers into great leaps of logic. What tightness of thought and presentation that existed in the first half of the report is largely absent from the second half.

Thus, it is reasonable to say that Bernard saw his task as evaluating the merits of the consultant's day care proposal—to agree or disagree. The bulk of his report is an interpretation of case information in light of this analysis. His fundamental reading/writing strategy, to skim and respond, has been carried over into the content of the report as a set of largely unsupported conclusions about the case situation. His shift from text-as-information-source to study-group-as-information-source part of the way through the task very likely has something to do with the lack of supporting evidence in his report. Business students' study group discussions, especially among inexperienced first-year students, tend to focus on drawing conclusions rather than on rigorous validation of them.

The actual analysis underlying Bernard's interpretation of text information remains hidden from his audience: Constructing a valid argument to support his evaluation was either outside Bernard's definition of the task or beyond the amount of time he allowed for writing the report. His report repeatedly assumes the truth of conclusions unproven by evidence from the case text.

## Pablo

*Reading/writing process.* Pablo, a Bolivian student with an engineering background and 3 years' experience as a consultant at a major international accounting/consulting firm (TOEFL score 637), emerges as a writer with a clear organizing plan for "synthesizing around a controlling concept" (Flower, 1987). His self-report of his first text reading mentions that he "takes notes in head and asks questions." During the second reading, which followed immediately, he underlined with various marker colors. At this stage, he "relates ideas to each other" and "thinks of goals" but "hasn't thought about a central problem." Two days later, after the class discussion, Pablo developed an outline in which the central ideas and problem identification focused on the company objectives in the case. He elaborated this outline through seven subsequent drafts in which the central ideas remained constant but the language expanded. A meticulous and skilled writer, Pablo paid close attention to supporting details and transitions as well as grammar and syntax, refining and strengthening these in each draft of his report.

The language with which he describes his reading and writing processes indicates that Pablo views summarizing as a subgoal subordinated to synthesizing, and that he uses synthesis ("relates ideas to each other") as a means for achieving another rhetorical purpose. Questioning the information and assumptions that underlay the day care proposal and comparing the proposal to the company's goals — analytical and interpretive acts — reveal the main goals of Pablo's reading and writing processes. From the beginning, his reading and writing activities are geared toward analyzing the information he finds in the text and interpreting its meaning so that he can render a management decision supportable with case evidence.

*Task representation.* Pablo's report carries out his task representation by weighing the evidence for and against the day care proposal. He analyzes and evaluates the text information, presenting the pros and cons of the expansion plan and bringing in relevant data on each side. In the second half of the report, where the pros and cons must be assessed and a decision rendered, Pablo integrates the conclusions presented in the report's first half, weighs their advantages against their disadvantages, and presents his preferred decision with a quick summary of its merits. The organizing idea which emerged during the reading-writing process maintains its control throughout the report. His aim throughout has been to transform the case material into a sound management decision.

While one can quarrel with points in his interpretation — with his evaluation of the evidence — one cannot quarrel with his argumentative structure or the way he carries out his rhetorical aims. In fact, Pablo's task representation is firm enough that he goes to considerable lengths to anticipate audience needs; for example, he uses bold-faced type and underlining to stress transition links between portions of his argument. ("*However, the situation is changing. First,* people are beginning to realize the importance of early childhood education.").

## Dan

*Reading/writing process.* An American student with more than 5 years of work experience as an engineer in the automotive industry, Dan read the case a total of three times. His self-report and text underlining show that he began to analyze and interpret the case material almost immediately. His first reading was quite purposeful, a search for company goals against which he could measure the proposal described in the case. His underlining and note taking during the second reading suggest an analytical purpose: a search for evidence, characterized by occasional evaluative comments challenging a point of view expressed in the case. His text notes also typically indicated the section of his report in which particular case material might be used: a statement of company objectives bracketed and labeled "intro paragraph for issues section"; a sentence circled and marked "Basic Problem Statement."

Dan compressed outlining and writing a first draft into one step, highly coordinating his reading and writing processes. By the third reading, his examinations of the case were primarily to retrieve already identified evidence for his argumentative claims. Even so, he transported very little original case phrasing into the report outline. With the exception of his problem statement, which borrows heavily from case wording, nearly everything else in the outline and subsequent report is in Dan's language and style. This lack of language transfer further supports the premise that he had identified his primary task to be analyzing, synthesizing, and reinterpreting case data.

Dan's second, partial outline shows the nature of his writing process: first to prepare an outline with all the first-level and many of the second and third-level headings filled in; then to begin "elaborating" the outline by writing paragraphs under the headings. The developed and evolved outline served as the rough draft. The final draft for this assignment was an edited, polished version of the evolved outline.

The economy with which he handled the writing process is noteworthy. From the first reading to the final draft, he was goal directed, wasting no time with aimless reading or undirected note taking. His initial notations show that he was already fitting case facts into the managerial policy report's organizational framework; they also show that analysis and interpretation began to take place almost at once. Dan's compression of outlining and drafting also illustrates his goal directedness. He wanted to maximize output while minimizing time, something graduate business students must learn to do if they are to succeed in the program. Nevertheless, he was willing to revise when newly interpreted facts would not support his previous conclusions.

Although he did not discuss the case with a study group before writing his report, Dan used the case's financial exhibits to test his initial assumptions, much as some students might use their peers to test their ideas. At the case lecture/discussion class, the instructor had warned students that they might find discrepancies or faulty assumptions in the numbers. And, in fact, during the interviews Dan reported having to rework his solution. He said he had to "rethink" his solution "in a completely different light." Between outlines and final draft, some changes occurred in the order of issue subtopics and also in the amount of space and detail devoted to subtopics. The equivalent of content changes, these show that Dan was aware of the need for deep revision as well as sentence-level editing.

*Task representation.*    Clearly, Dan brought to the report writing assignment some rather sophisticated strategies for representing the task and managing his writing process. He understood that he was to solve a problem on paper, using a well-supported argument. In fact, to a degree unusual in the first half of the managerial policy reports course, Dan's paper contains almost no "case rehash"—almost no straight summary of case situations or events. His report is concerned primarily with interpreting old information to draw new conclusions. Dan's typical argumentative pattern is to raise an issue suggested in the case (such as financial risks and returns), present an analysis of case evidence, and finish with conclusions derived from his evaluation of the evidence. He constantly pushes the argument forward with cause-and-effect language (since, because, therefore).

As he indicated during interviews and references in the report itself, the need to respond to the secondary audience, especially case character Vice President Miltag, was part of Dan's task representation. In fact, he uses Miltag's objections to the initial proposal as the organizational focus in the second half of the report.

## Carolyn

*Reading/writing process.*    An American student with over 5 years of work experience as a free-lance technical writer, Carolyn presented quite a contrast to Dan. Although she was equally aware of the assignment's criteria, Carolyn's approach to the task was much more discovery oriented. Her writing process and expectations about what might occur during the process were not necessarily less goal oriented than Dan's, but they were less structured, as her artifacts and interviews revealed.

Whereas Dan's notes tended to be related to points he wanted to make in his paper, and therefore represented interpretations of the data, Carolyn's notes taken during the second of three readings were much more like "think aloud" or conversations with herself: for example, "what is profile of franchisee? is it an investor, is it a retired school teacher (like Miltag suggests)? who?"; "compare franchise operation to company-owned?"; "could land be financed?" These are the comments of a student searching for a way into the case, of someone who had not yet isolated a business problem or even sorted out identifiable issues.

However, Carolyn's note taking did serve an analytical purpose. By posing the questions and trying to group data, she was attempting to move toward viable conclusions and closer to a problem statement. Although she ended up with few hard conclusions and much interior monologue about case facts, she was employing an analytical strategy that went beyond simply summarizing case information. She used both reading and writing to try to jump-start analysis—reading the case and producing handwritten and computer notes recognizable to composition specialists as free writing. Her computer notes also show that she included audience considerations in her task representation, particularly the reader-writer relationship and her assigned role as "Peter Collins," the consultant mentioned in the case.

Shortly after producing the computer notes, Carolyn gave up trying to draft the report and started writing a transmittal letter that was also part of the assignment. By the time she quit for the night she "had summarized what the paper was going to be about," and the next day used the letter as the basis for her first complete draft of the report. Clearly the analytical breakthrough came with the letter which served as both a prompt for and a rough draft of the report. In Carolyn's case, writing was the means by which she was able to discover what she thought; being able to "tell" it in the letter was crucial to being able to continue with the report.

Once she had used the letter to break through her mental block, she ceased to call upon the case text as a stimulus or resource, except to check names and recheck such things as company goals and affiliates. She did not transfer phraseology or organization of information from the case to her paper. Further analysis led her to some conclusions different from those in the original transmittal letter. Thus Carolyn had to revise the content not only in the report but also in the letter.

*Task representation.* Although her task representation and composing strategies ultimately worked, in that she produced a paper that interpreted information and gave it meaning, Carolyn's self-reports show that she lacked the business knowledge to identify or manipulate the hard evidence from the case that would have enabled her to construct a strong argument. Many of the claims in the report are unsupported or weakly supported. Her assertions were often sound, as were the qualitative judgments she provided: The company was in no position to enter the preschool education market with franchises. However, Carolyn did not know how to generate the quantitative data that would have proved her point of view conclusively and allowed her to supply the missing links in the argumentative chain. It's a fairly safe conjecture that this lack of knowledge lies behind much of Carolyn's early frustration with the case, the questions that often appeared in her notes, and the accompanying drafting difficulties. She knew Peter Collins had supplied bad numbers and faulty analysis, but she did not yet have the business tools to rectify what he had left behind. Accurate task representation and resourceful reading/writing strategies do not necessarily ensure sound analysis.

## Summary of Findings

We found that the task representation of the ESL students did indeed differ from that of the native speakers, but not uniformly. The evidence suggests that the Korean student saw his task as one of summarizing the text information and responding to it by endorsing (or slightly adjusting) the proposal put forth in the case. Chung did not create an evidence-supported argument, nor did he seem to see his task as one of challenging and interpreting case information. The Belgian student, likewise, read for content and without apparent rhetorical purpose. Although Bernard tried to be creative and come up with original solutions, his rejection of the text in favor of conclusions relayed during the study group meeting indicates that he did not understand that his rhetorical purpose must include arguing for alternatives by using evidence from the case. Pablo's task representation, however, resembled the task representation of Dan, the American student, rather closely. Pablo saw analysis, evaluation, and arguing an original point of view to be his task from the beginning.

The second goal of the study was to find out whether the task representation was different among ESL learners depending on their language proficiency. The results show that language proficiency indeed may have affected the students' performance. Chung's and Bernard's English language skills—as measured by the TOEFL test—were much lower than Pablo's. Both Chung's and Bernard's reading and writing processes seemed hampered by their difficulties with English vocabulary, grammar, syntax, and discourse-level reading and writing strategies.

The third goal of the study was to ascertain whether the students' professional training and background affected their task representations. The findings suggest that this was the case in the study. Pablo and Dan—both with extensive previous experience in management problem solving—exhibited purposeful reading: At an early stage in their reading they focused on problem solving and challenging the value of the case evidence. They clearly had evaluative and interpretive goals as they read, goals that corresponded to the writing task of identifying the company's management problem and arguing for a solution their report proposed.

## Discussion of Results

The findings suggest that when differences in task representation exist between L1 and L2 writers, the source of these differences may be cultural and educational as well as language-oriented. All five of our subjects had received the same oral and written instructions and had the benefit of the same classroom experience prior to writing their reports. All had been told and been shown through class lecture that their task was to analyze the case information and propose a solution to the case evidence. Two of the five — one ESL student and one native English speaker — were successful in drawing up persuasive arguments, although three of the five (and possibly four of the five, if we are generous in interpreting Bernard's motives) understood their rhetorical task to be an argumentative one.

We are inclined to infer from Dan's educational and employment background in engineering that he brought special tools to the report writing task. Although his writing experience was not extensive, he already possessed a frame of mind trained in problem solving applicable to business cases. Similarly, Pablo's engineering education and his work experience at a management consulting firm had prepared him to represent the task appropriately and to carry it out. His English fluency allowed him to devote time to elaborating his ideas and paying careful attention to expression.

Bernard's educational background in engineering suggests that he might share Dan's and Pablo's approach to problem solving. Why he did not, still puzzles us; other Belgian students with similar backgrounds who had passed through the program in the past tended to be quite good at this type of thinking. Still, Bernard exhibited a certain lack of maturity in his approach to problem solving throughout his first semester in business school. He was quick to offer conclusions in class discussion, or suggest things to do, but when questioned was likely to offer gut-level reactions rather than evidence-derived analysis.

Although she wanted very much to provide the analytical argument that would solve the case problem, Carolyn was the most handicapped by her lack of analytical background. From her comments, it is clear she knew what she wanted to do, but she did not know how to accomplish it. However, Carolyn's experience using written language — and the array of strategies in her writing process — allowed her to represent the task appropriately and move in the right direction.

Chung's task representation is consistent with previous observations of other Asian students, particularly Chinese and other Korean students, enrolled in the graduate management program. When queried as to why their reports repeated case facts but offered few if any conclusions or recommendations, these students often stated that their job as subordinates in a company was not to recommend to their superiors what to do. Rather it was to present the facts as completely as possible so that those higher up could make "good decisions" based on full information. Like his compatriots, Chung seemed to construe his task in the same way. In spite of what he had been told by his instructors, cultural inhibitors may have caused him to exclude interpretation from his rhetorical task. Little wonder, then, that his report failed as an argument: He may have deemed it inappropriate to present one.

## CONCLUSION

This study was planned to explore task representations of ESL and native English-speaking graduate business students while they read a lengthy business case and wrote reports about it. Our goal was to examine how these international students filter a wealth of information and write a persuasive argument. We found that two of these students in the study lacked processes and strategies of a successful report writer. The lack of successful strategies was evident in the extended process of task representation from the first reading of the case to the final written report.

Even though our study was exploratory and our numbers were small, we venture to suggest some implications for teaching. It is obvious from the study that ESL learners need more practice with reading long texts. Most ESL reading textbooks include fairly short readings with intensive comprehension exercises following the reading. ESL teachers need to provide opportunities for students to dig for information in books, magazines, newspapers, and other materials.

The study also indicates that some ESL students may need extra instruction in building arguments from evidence. Reading skills for summarizing and synthesizing are not enough. Because there is no "right" answer to a business problem, no one "textbook solution" for the case, to write an acceptable report students must develop "original" arguments that they support with analyses of case information. Being unable to rely on the "truth" of information presented in case texts is especially difficult for many Asian students, who are taught to respect written texts, not criticize them (Matalene, 1985).

Teaching students to disagree with texts and develop their own points of view is outside of the domain of many ESL reading classes. Charles (1983) suggested that it is best done in genre-specific classes, such as the business course in this study. We think that teaching students to read texts critically should be done in all language classes, genre-specific and general. Study groups, according to Charles—if guided correctly—serve a useful purpose in allowing ESL students to learn to express disagreement, challenge, competition, and collusion. Study groups could also be guided so that they will give students opportunities to practice polite disagreement, for example, through the use of models ("I would suggest," "you can disagree"). We think that any collaborative group work in ESL writing classes could serve this purpose (see Allaei & Connor, 1990, for example, for the use of collaborative groups in ESL writing classrooms).

# REFERENCES

Allaei, S. K., & Connor, U. M. (1990 Fall). Exploring the dynamics of cross-cultural collaboration in writing classrooms. *The Writing Instructor*, pp. 19–28.

Ackerman, J. (1990). Students' self-analysis and judges' perceptions: Where do they agree? In L. Flower, V. Stein, J. Ackerman, M. J. Kantz, K. McCormick, & W. C. Peck (Eds.), *Reading-to-write: Exploring a cognitive and social process* (pp. 98–118). New York: Oxford University Press.

Flower, L., & Hayes, J. R. (1981). A cognitive theory of writing. *College Composition and Communication* 32, 365–7.

Canseco, G., & Byrd, P. (1989). Writing required in graduate courses in business administration. *TESOL Quarterly, 23* (2), 305–316.

Charles, D. (1984). The use of case studies in business English. In G. James (Ed.), *The ESP classroom—Methodology, materials, expectations* (pp. 24–33). Exeter, UK: Exeter Linguistics Studies, University of Exeter.

Durst, R. (1992, April). *Coming to grips with theory: Students' use of theoretical explanation in history writing.* Paper presented at the American Educational Research Association Conference, San Francisco, CA.

Flower, L. (1987). *The role of task representation in reading to write.* Tech. Rep. No. 6. Berkeley, CA: University of California, Berkeley, Center for the Study of Writing.

Flower, L., Stein, V., Ackerman, J., Kantz, M. J., McCormick, K., & Peck, W. C. (Eds.). (1990). *Reading to write: Exploring a cognitive and social process.* New York: Oxford University Press.

Johns, A. M. (1991). Interpreting an English competency examination: The frustrations of an ESL science student. *Written Communication, 8* (3), 379–401.

Matalene, C. (1985). Contrastive rhetoric: An American writing teacher in China. *College English, 47*, 789–808.

Mohan, B., & Oszust, V. (1991). *Learning tasks as language socialization: A knowledge structure analysis of business case decision making by L2 learners.* Unpublished manuscript, Department of Language Education, University of British Columbia, Vancouver, BC.

Raimes, A. (1985). What unskilled ESL students do as they write: A classroom study of composing. *TESOL Quarterly, 19*, 229–258.

Swales, J. (1990). *Genre analysis.* English in academic and research settings. New York: Cambridge University Press.

Toulmin, S.E. (1958). *The uses of argument.* New York: Cambridge University Press.

Uber Grosse, C. (1988). The case study approach to learning business English. *English for Specific Purposes, 7* (2), 131–136.

# APPENDIX A
## MANAGERIAL POLICY REPORT FORMAT

**Title Page** (centered)

    MPR # _____
    Case Name
    Student's Name
    Date

**Starting on page one**

To:      (The recipient of the report is specified on the assignment sheet.)

From:    (Your role is also specified on the assignment sheet.)

Date:

Subject: (Example: International Expansion Decision at Wolff-Frienman Corporation)

I. Problem Statement:

The Central Problem or Problems: A concise, specific statement.

II. Issues:

Provide a title for each issue. The issue should be analyzed and supported by case facts. *Simple narration* of the case situation is *not acceptable*. Where you have developed exhibits as evidence, refer to the exhibit and in the text briefly summarize or analyze the *significance* of the exhibit. Moreover, present all information relevant to the argument in the Issues section.

III. Alternatives:

Title each alternative appropriately.

Weigh the advantages and disadvantages of each alternative with skillful reference to the findings presented in the issues. Note that this step does *not necessitate restating evidence* already presented, but may include summaries and brief analyses of evidence when helpful to the reader's understanding.

*No new evidence* is introduced in the evaluation of alternatives. You should not include implementation of the alternative at this point, but you should include a clear summary of the alternative.

The content of the alternatives section may consist of:

a) All reasonable alternatives, including, in the final position, the one you are selecting for your recommendation, or

b) Only the reasonable alternatives which you evaluate but reject because they are not optimum.

## IV.  Recommendations:

If you used format *a* (above), now restate the title of the chosen alternative.

If you used format *b* (above), now introduce your recommendation with a title.

Under either the *a* or *b* plan, the recommendation must now be fully developed and must be accompanied by a persuasive, well-balanced, explicit defense. As with the alternatives, your recommendation should bear directly upon solving the central problem. If you used format *a* in the Alternatives section, do no simply repeat, verbatim, your final alternative. Use the Recommendation section to explore the important aspects of the preferred alternative and to persuade your reader of the alternative's validity.

Test the validity of your recommendation by seeing whether it will satisfy the definition of the central problem and whether it is closely associated with your issues.

## V.  Plan of Action:

You must now devise a step-by-step plan of action which sets forth in detail the means by which you propose to implement your recommendation.

The steps to be taken should be set out one-by-one, titled, and enumerated, showing an awareness of priorities of time and/or importance (short-term and long-term actions). A contingency plan should also be presented when appropriate.

## PAGE ONE OF THE ASSIGNED CASE
## NEW EDUCATIONAL CONCEPTS, INC.*

New Educational Concepts, Inc. (NECI) was incorporated in January, 1967 with an initial capitalization of $100,000 for the purpose of publishing "Education NEWSREPORT Magazine" and supplying consulting and

---

*Names and certain quantitative information have been disguised.

This case was prepared as the basis for class discussion rather than to illustrate either effective or ineffective handling of an administration situation.

related services to the education industry. By May 31, 1969, NECI reported earnings in excess of 20% on annual sales of over $1.5 million. Shortly thereafter the firm "went public" in what officers and directors considered an "exceptionally successful" transaction.

In late summer NECI's Board of Directors met to discuss a proposal calling for the commitment of up to $300,000 to establish a new subsidiary which would franchise a nationwide chain of preschool learning centers for children from ages two to six. The tentative name of the proposed new division was "Child Advancement Centers, Inc."

## Company Background

By mid-1969 NECI, in the opinion of its officers and directors, had established a reputation as a leader in the rapidly growing education industry. The company's first and major publication, *Education NEWS-REPORT*, was a highly regarded "trade journal" for elementary education teachers and administrators. Its success had been one of the factors which had enabled NECI to expand its organization to five major operating divisions as follows:

PUBLISHING DIVISION – The activities of NECI's Publishing Division focused primarily on the monthly *Education NEWSREPORT*. By 1969 the magazine had a circulation of over 20,000 educators. It had been used successfully by the company to launch several other more specialized educational publications and newsletters. One such newsletter, promoted in four issues of the *NEWSREPORT* prior to publication, had secured a paid prepublication circulation of almost 10,000 copies.

NECI officers believed that all of the company's publications served as an important liaison for the company with the professional field of education. Hundreds of news releases, newsletters, government reports, and magazines were inspected each month by the company staff, making NECI a clearing house and information center for the industry. Frequent requests for information were received from readers and answered by the staff as quickly as possible. Such inquiries often were the source of ideas for new opportunities for various NECI divisions.

## APPENDIX B
## GOALS OF THE INTERVIEWS FOR GUIDING
## THE QUESTIONS

**Data Collection 1:** Trying to find out what students do when they read the case.

1. Do they read the case straight through once before taking notes? Do they skim? Read the headings first? Read the beginning and ending first?
2. About how long does it generally take to read the case through the first time?
3. Was there information or background missing from the case that the students wished had been in the case (perhaps better explanation of day care centers, working mothers, etc.)? Was there alien information, or lack of information, resulting from cross-cultural differences?
4. Do they underline the case? At what stage of case reading? First reading? Later?
5. What kinds of things do they underline and why?
6. What do they do when they come across an unfamiliar word?
7. Did they study the exhibits or just glance through them? For what purpose?
8. Did they do any calculations at this stage? If not, when? For what purpose? Using what case information?
9. When does notetaking occur (on the first reading, second)?
10. What kinds of notes do they take (analytical, summary, queries, what?)?
11. Where do they take these notes? In the margin of the case? On separate paper?
12. Is there a more "formal" notetaking from which the paper is (will be) generated? If so, when are these notes made (is there a time lapse between the reading/jotting and the formal note taking?
13. At some stage, do they more or less deliberately organize these notes before writing? Do they refer to the case at this stage? If so, for what?
14. In this prewriting phase, do they deliberately try to identify problem, issues, and so on, with reference to specific points in the case? Ask them to give examples of the case points?

**Data Collection 2** (before the final draft is written): Trying to find out what students do as they generate a first (rough) draft.

1. Do they write something that is the equivalent of a first draft or rough draft?
2. When do they start this draft (after having done what) and how do they go about it?
3. Do they write an outline first (either "working" or more formal; how formal?)?
4. Have them describe a typical drafting session.

5. Do they write a whole draft first and then revise, or do they revise as they go?
6. How long do they typically spend at a drafting sitting? In total on drafting?
7. When and for what purpose do they refer to the case as they draft?
8. How do they use their notes as they draft?
9. Do they use a computer at any stage? When and for what?
10. Do they refer to the case during this stage? When and for what purpose?
11. Ask students to point to the portions (sentences or paragraphs) of the case that they referred to the most while drafting. (record page number, paragraph number, or read first line, so we can find it later)
12. Ask them to point out the portions of the case they didn't use while drafting.

**Data Collection 3** (after the paper has been submitted): Trying to find out what students do when they revise/edit/polish/create a final draft.

1. Have them describe the process of producing the finished report.
2. Did they refer to the case at any point while creating the final draft? While revising or editing the final draft?
3. How did they use the case at this stage?
4. Did they reread the whole case or portions of the case to check the accuracy of their analysis/conclusions? Have them point out which portions, if any.

## APPENDIX C
## VERSIONS OF SECTION "ISSUES" OF CHUNG'S REPORT
### OUTLINE

II. Issues
1. Good potential market size
   ( -. Shortage of preschool centers in the suburban community.
   -. There are over 15 M working housewives and 12 M children under six years of age in this country
   -. Social trend that more emphasis is put on the preschool education.

I. Good potential market size

The suburban communities in the U.S. are experiencing a severe shortage of preschool education systems at present. Even though there are two or three such schools, they all have waiting lists several years long.

In addition, the number of working housewives there is a trend that is increasing. It is known that the number of children under six years of age also amounts to 12 million. Furthermore, it is noticeable that the 1970s will see a 23% increase in the number of working mothers with children under six years according to a recent publication by the Department of Labor. There is another over 80% of a child's reasoning is fully developed before it is evidenced six years of age. These days, parents put more emphasis on preschool education than ever before, as a good premonitory sign.

(has been recently)

Accordingly, parent's growing interest in preschool education means the bright future of preschool education centers because it's parents' usually up to whether or not children can have a chance to attend preschool systems, especially this kind of private preschool center.

## II. Issues

### 1. Good potential market size

The suburban communities in the U.S.A are experiencing a severe shortage of preschool education systems at present. Even though there are ~~two~~ or three such schools in ~~the~~ each suburban community, they all have waiting lists several years long. In addition, there is a trend that the number of working housewives is increasing. It's noticeable that the 1970s will see a 43% increase in the number of working mothers with children under six years according to a recent publication by the Department of Labour. There is another ~~remarkable~~ point as a ~~good~~ premonitory sign of ~~vast~~ potential market of preschool centers. It ~~is~~ has been recently ~~evidenced~~ that over 80% of a child's reasoning ~~is~~ fully developed before six years of age. Accordingly, ~~nowadays~~ most of parents are inclined to ~~nowadays~~ put more emphasis on preschool education than ever before. Parents' growing interest in preschool education means the bright future of preschool education systems franchised ~~based on the franchise system~~

because it's usually up to ~~po~~ parents' decision whether or not children can have a chance to attend ~~an~~ efficient but a little expensive private preschool education center of this kind.

## FINAL PRODUCT

### II. Issues

#### 1. Good Potential market size.

The suburban communities in the U.S.A. are experiencing a severe shortage of preschool education systems at present. Even though there are two or there such schools in each suburban community, they all have waiting lists several years long. In addition, there is a growing trend that the number of working housewives is increasing. It's noticeable that the 1970's will see a 43% increase in the number of working mothers with children under six years according to a recent publication by the Department of Labor.

There is another remarkable point as a good premonitory sign of vast potential market of preschool centers. It has been recently evidenced that over 80% of a child's reasoning is fully developed before six years of age. In this context, most parents are currently inclined to put more emphasis on preschool education than ever before. Parent's growing interest in preschool education means the bright future of franchised preschool education system, for it is usually up to the parent's decision whether or not children can have a chance to attend an efficient but a little expensive private preschool center of this kind.

# CHAPTER 8

# Consciousness Raising and Article Pedagogy

**Peter Master**
*California State University Fresno*

This study investigates the article errors of advanced nonnative speakers of English from Southeast Asia in a series of written summaries produced for a graduate class in second language acquisition. Feedback was provided in the form of corrections and brief classroom discussions of the most frequent grammatical and stylistic errors, and subjects kept a record of all article errors in each summary. These errors were analyzed over four successive 3–4-week periods, revealing a significant decrease in errors between Periods 1 and 4. The results show that the most frequent error was the use of $\theta$ when *the* was required (one type of underspecification error), which tended to increase as a proportion of total errors over time. Some $\theta$-for-*the* errors were caused by the failure to recognize that certain noun phrases unique to the discourse community of second language acquisition are considered to be known or identified and hence require *the*. Comments from the participants are included to support the conclusion that consciousness raising in regard to the English article system is an appropriate pedagogy for advanced ESL students.

The problems that ESL/EFL students have with the English article system are well known. Numerous teaching methodologies have been put forth to

*I am deeply grateful to the international students in my Linguistics 241 classes at California State University, Fresno, for their help, their comments, and their enthusiasm for this project. I would also like to thank Vivi Sinou, Dave Parrent, Krystyna Montauk, Diane Belcher, and George Braine for comments on an earlier draft of this Chapter.

make the articles as a system more intelligible to the learner (cf. Master, 1990) although very few have been tested empirically for their effectiveness.[1] Even with increased attention to the system, however, a few errors always remain and it seems in general that it is almost impossible for nonnative speakers of English to arrive at the point where all article errors disappear, especially when their first languages do not contain an article system.

Article errors constitute what Burt and Kiparsky (1974) called "local" errors in that article misuse, in contrast to what they called "global" errors, rarely leads to miscomprehension. Faced with the formidable task of acquiring a second language, second language learners are quick to recognize which aspects of grammar cause a listener to fail to understand the message and which do not. The latter naturally receive less attention until the higher levels of proficiency are attained and even then errors persist. Where article errors really become apparent is in composition, especially in the academic setting where course grades are awarded primarily on the basis of written work. In this setting, attention to the article system is particularly important, as local errors such as articles, prepositions, and subject verb agreement, even though they do not affect understanding, can have a negative effect on the reader, especially non-ESL faculty, as they may leave the impression that the writer has inadequate control of the language (McGirt, 1984). For this reason, many ESL instructors feel they cannot ignore these errors.

Just as the grammar of English negation, with its reliance on the complex auxiliary system that must carry tense, aspect and number, has been shown to be an indicator of interlanguage level (Stauble, 1978), accuracy in using the article system, with its reliance on definiteness, countability, and number, appears to improve with increased proficiency (Master, 1987, Oller & Redding, 1972). For this reason, article errors that persist at high proficiency levels can provide a picture of the acquisition process at the upper end of the interlanguage continuum.

Error analysis as a basis for pedagogical instruction came under criticism (cf. Schachter & Celce-Murcia, 1977) because it ignored avoidance strategies and because it only viewed interlanguage in terms of the target language. However, even though it is said to have evolved into interlanguage analysis (Celce-Murcia & Hawkins, 1985), error analysis as a

---

[1]In Master (1986), I found significant improvement on an article test after systematic instruction in six aspects of the article system in a controlled study. Kimura and McCroskey (1991) also found significant improvement on an article test, particularly in regard to *the* with ranking adjectives and "identifying" postmodification (see Footnote 3), after implementing the binary system for teaching the English articles proposed by Master (1990) in a controlled study.

source of insight into language acquisition processes has never been entirely discarded (cf. White, 1984). Indeed, according to Gaies (1987),

> Second language research has come to attach great significance to the role of errors in acquisition. In the last fifteen years, errors have been viewed as windows to the language acquisition process; errors are seen as overt reflections of a learner's internalized knowledge of the language. They are furthermore regarded as an inevitable part of acquiring a second language; indeed, for some, errors are the best evidence that acquisition is taking place. (p. 333)

The subjects in the present study are at a late stage in their interlanguage development. Since all the subjects have high language proficiency (the average TOEFL score for the 19 subjects is 581), the most significant errors that occur are those local errors that were understandably ignored at earlier interlanguage stages. It is presumed that the errors that persist at this level will not only reflect the learner's knowledge of the language but also reveal the aspects of article usage that are the most difficult to learn and thus suggest what a pedagogical treatment might require.

A second reason for focusing on errors rather than accuracy is that the data for this study come from a series of summaries written over the course of a semester. Because there was no way to control the degree to which students copied noun phrases from the original source, accuracy rates could be misleading. Errors, on the other hand, would be more likely to reflect the subjects' control of the article system.

## RESEARCH ON THE ARTICLE ERRORS OF L2 STUDENTS WHOSE FIRST LANGUAGES DO NOT CONTAIN ARTICLES

Yamada and Matsuura (1982) investigated the article usage of Japanese speakers with advanced English proficiency, none of whom had been in English-speaking countries. They found in a modified cloze test that accuracy in the use of *the* and $\theta$ increased significantly from the intermediate level while indefinite *a* remained the most difficult for advanced learners. The most frequent errors are shown in Table 8.1. They conclude that the over use of *the* suggests that the primary problem of advanced Japanese speakers of English is overspecification (the use of *the* when $\emptyset$ or *a* is required).

Chaudron and Parker (1988) studied the article use of Japanese speakers in a free production task describing picture sequences. Although they discuss article usage in terms of production rather than error, their inclusion of the context of use and the performance of native speakers allows an estimation of article errors. The high percentage of *the* used in place of *a* or

TABLE 8.1. Article Errors of Advanced Japanese EFL Students

| Used | Required | Percent of Total Usage |
|------|----------|------------------------|
| the  | Ø        | 18.2 |
| the  | a        | 10.0 |
| Ø    | a        | 9.6 |
| Ø    | the      | 6.9 |
| a    | Ø        | 2.3 |
| a    | the      | 1.5 |

Ø supports Yamada et al.'s suggestion that overspecification was the primary difficulty of advanced learners.

Master (1987) studied the article errors of individual Japanese and Chinese speakers with advanced English proficiency in an informal spoken interview. The results are shown in Table 8.2.. The greatest percentage of errors for both speakers concerns the over use of Ø, suggesting that, contrary to the findings of Yamada and Matsuura and Chaudron and Parker, the problem in spoken interlanguage appears to be a type of underspecification (the use of Ø or a when the is required) rather than overspecification.

## The Present Study

The present study was motivated by the observation that the nonnative English-speaking students in a graduate class in second language acquisition, all of whom were from Southeast Asia, appeared to make fewer article errors over the semester as they received feedback on their summaries of course readings. The study analyzes all the article errors made and investigates the effect of detailed feedback on these errors in subsequent summaries, providing a longitudinal view of the type and frequency of article errors produced over time.

TABLE 8.2. Spoken Article Errors of Advanced Japanese and Chinese Speakers

| Used | Required | Percent of Total Usage | |
|------|----------|----------|---------|
|      |          | Japanese | Chinese |
| the  | Ø        | 1.4  | 0.7 |
| the  | a        | 0.3  | 0.7 |
| Ø    | a        | 9.1  | 4.1 |
| Ø    | the      | 4.9  | 1.5 |
| a    | Ø        | 0.6  | 0 |
| a    | the      | 0.6  | 0.7 |

Because summarization is the context in which the article errors were produced, the criteria for the generation of optimal summaries in the classroom bears consideration. According to Kirkland and Saunders (1991), "[s]ummarizing skills are essential to academic success" (p. 105). Because these skills include adequate reading and writing skills as well as control of vocabulary and grammar, "[s]tudents should not be expected to produce formal, graded academic summaries until they have at least a high — intermediate level of proficiency" (p. 108). The building of the necessary content schemata to write a summary requires that there be prereading activities, a series of readings, and classroom discussions, while the building of formal schemata requires training in quoting, paraphrasing, and source acknowledgment. Top-down processing must be emphasized in order to counteract students' tendency to rely on bottom-up processing, which often leads to lack of cohesion and plagiarism in the final product. Think-aloud models of summary generation processes plus sample written summaries can help in bringing about such an emphasis.

## METHOD

The subjects of the study were 19 graduate students from Southeast Asia, as shown in Table 8.3. They were all students in an ESL/Linguistics MA program. Four of the 19 were male, the remaining 15 female. The ages ranged from 22–41, with an average of 28 years. The time spent in the United States ranged from 6 months to 12 years, with a mean of 2.48 years. The TOEFL scores ranged from 547 to 623 with an average of 581. As part of the requirements for the course, each subject wrote a series of detailed summaries (approximately one per week) on the reading material for the class (e.g., Bickerton, 1984; Schumann, 1976; chapters from McLaughlin, 1987). Before the first summary was assigned, there was a presentation on the nature of summaries, the need to paraphrase as opposed to quoting the important points, and how to go about generating a summary. A model of a good summary was also provided. When the summaries were turned in, the instructor (the author) corrected all grammatical and stylistic errors and briefly discussed the most common types of errors when the summaries

TABLE 8.3. First Languages of Subjects

| | |
|---|---|
| Mandarin Chinese (CH) | 13 |
| Japanese (JA) | 4 |
| Javanese (JV) | 1 |
| Korean (KO) | 1 |

were returned in the next class. These discussions entailed pointing out the difference between using the count and noncount form of a word like *theory,* identifying the word *evidence* as a noncount noun and suggesting the word *argument* as a countable alternative, showing that the noun phrase $\emptyset$ + *interlanguage* referred to a generalized notion that was often the focus of research whereas *the* + *interlanguage* represented the interim language of a specific learner, and the like.

The subjects were provided with an article record sheet on which to keep track of all the article errors made throughout the semester. These errors were all clearly marked on the returned summaries. The record sheets were then collected and analyzed both synchronically and diachronically to determine what the most frequent errors were and which types persisted over the course of the study. Every article error was counted, even if it occurred in an identical noun phrase, because often an NP would have the correct article at one time and not the next and the focus was on the continuous control of the system, not just on whether a subject knew which article to use with any particular noun. At the end of the study, the subjects were also asked to comment on the process, specifically in relation to writing the summaries, receiving feedback on the summaries, discussing the errors in class, and keeping a record of article errors. No exercises or other specific focus on the article system was provided.

## RESULTS

The summaries used as the basis of measurement were typically 4–5 typed pages in length, averaging about 1,000 words each. A total of 261 summaries were analyzed (approximately 250,000 words). Each subject wrote an average of 14 ($m = 13.79$, $r = 10$–$19$) of 20 possible summaries and kept a record of every article error marked in the summaries.

### Total Article Errors

The total number of article errors in the corpus was 1,857. The breakdown is shown in Table 8.4. Table 8.4 shows that the greatest proportion of errors consisted of three types: the use of $\emptyset$ when *the* was required ($\emptyset$ for *the*), the use of *the* when $\emptyset$ was required (*the* for $\emptyset$), and the use of $\emptyset$ when *a* was required ($\emptyset$ for *a*). Together, these errors accounted for approximately 88% of all errors. The mean per subject per summary column in Table 8.4 represents the group average for the total errors each subject made divided by the number of summaries that subject wrote, as not all students produced the same number of summaries. The reasons for this were that if

TABLE 8.4. Article Error Distribution

| Used | Required | n | % | Mean per Subject per Summary |
|------|----------|---|---|------------------------------|
| Ø | the | 771 | 41.52 | 2.82 |
| the | Ø | 507 | 27.30 | 1.93 |
| Ø | a | 369 | 19.87 | 1.38 |
| a | Ø | 80 | 4.31 | 0.31 |
| the | a | 75 | 4.04 | 0.29 |
| a | the | 55 | 2.96 | 0.20 |
| Total Errors | | 1857 | 100.00 | 6.93 |

a student was making a presentation no summary was required that week and that a small number of summaries were simply not submitted.

*Ø-for-the* errors.    The greatest percentage of errors (41.52%) concerned the use of Ø for *the*, which is one of two possible underspecification errors, the other being *a* for *the,* which accounted for only 3% of the errors. Because they were so prevalent, Ø-for-*the* errors were also analyzed in terms of two broad categories: *standard* means of identifying a noun phrase and *academic* means of identifying a noun phrase. Standard errors are those that a speaker might make in any situation. Academic errors are those that would be only likely to arise in an academic setting, particularly in relation to the assumed knowledge of a specific field or discourse community. The term *identifying* comes from Master (1990), in which the use of *the* signals the singling out or "identification" of a noun phrase in contrast to the use of Ø and *a*, which signals the grouping of like others or "classification" of a noun phrase.

The standard category, which accounted for two-thirds of the Ø-for-*the* errors, includes the use of *the* with (a) ranking adjectives, (b) shared knowledge, and (c) identifying postmodification. Ranking adjectives include three subcategories: (a) superlatives (e.g., *the best, the most, the largest*), (b) sequence adjectives (e.g., *the first, the second, the next, the last*), and (c) unique adjectives (e.g., *the same, the only, the main*). Shared knowledge includes second or subsequent mention as well as those things of which we share knowledge either on a universal (e.g., *the sun, the ground*), regional (e.g., *the valley, the seaside*), or local (e.g., *the post office, the blackboard*) level. Identifying postmodification refers to nouns that are postmodified in such a way that the head noun becomes identified (e.g., *the book that I bought yesterday, the capital of France*). The number and percent occurrence of each of these errors is shown in Table 8.5. Table 8.5 shows that shared knowledge produced the greatest number of errors. Some examples from the summaries are shown below:

TABLE 8.5. Standard Underspecification Errors

| Measure | Shared Knowledge | Postmodified N | Ranking ADJ | Total |
|---------|------------------|----------------|-------------|-------|
| n | 226 | 182 | 52 | 460 |
| % | 49.13 | 39.57 | 11.30 | 100.00 |

CH (Sum. 9): "Negative forms will eventually . . . become more like *model language."

JA (Sum. 16): " . . . there will be no competition from *L1 parameter setting."

KO (Sum. 20): "Let's briefly look at some terms in *neurosciences."

In all three examples, the writers failed to communicate shared knowledge about the limitation of the set, that is, that there was only one model language, only one L1 parameter setting, and a limited set of neurosciences. This may have been so obvious that the writer did not feel that the English requirement to mark these NPs as known or "identified" was necessary.

Postmodified nouns were the second largest source of standard Ø-for-*the* errors. Some examples are shown below:

CH (Sum. 5): "He failed to identify *types of errors that occurred."

JA (Sum. 9): "*Researchers discussed above have been influenced by these ideas."

JV (Sum. 15): "This article discusses *analogy between pidginization and SLA."

In each of these examples the writer failed to realize that the postmodifying phrase served to identify the headnoun, which thus required *the*. The ranking adjective category accounted for the smallest percentage of standard Ø-for-*the* errors. Nevertheless, since there is only a small set of ranking adjectives, the number of errors with each ranking adjective was tabulated and is shown in Table 8.6. Table 8.6 shows that sequence adjectives account for more than half of the ranking adjective errors, especially the adjectives *first* and *second*.[2] Unique adjectives account for roughly a third of the errors, with the adjective *same* predominating as the most frequent culprit, accounting for nearly a quarter of all ranking adjective errors.

The academic category, which accounted for the remaining third of the Ø-for-*the* errors, includes three subcategories: (a) generic *the*, (b) academic terms, and (c) complex nominals with noncount modifiers. Generic *the*

---

[2]The adjectives *first* and *second* in relation to languages (i.e., a first language, a second language) are descriptive rather than sequence adjectives and were therefore not included in this tally.

TABLE 8.6. Errors with Ranking Adjectives

| Category | adjective | n | % |
|---|---|---|---|
| Superlative (n = 4; 7.7%) | best | 3 | 5.77 |
| | most | 1 | 1.92 |
| Sequence (n = 30; 57.7%) | first | 10 | 19.23 |
| | second | 8 | 15.38 |
| | third | 3 | 5.77 |
| | next | 4 | 7.69 |
| | following | 2 | 3.85 |
| | previous | 2 | 3.85 |
| | final | 1 | 1.92 |
| Unique (n = 18; 34.6%) | same | 12 | 23.08 |
| | only | 3 | 5.77 |
| | main | 1 | 1.92 |
| | principle | 1 | 1.92 |
| | whole | 1 | 1.92 |
| Total | | 52 | 99.99 |

occurs with a singular count noun to indicate a genre or class (e.g., *the learner, the computer*). Academic terms include phrases that are peculiar to the field of second language acquisition (e.g., *the Language Acquisition Device, the that-trace effect*). Complex nominals with noncount modifiers refer to a headnoun that is premodified by a noun that would be "classified" as a noncount noun if it occurred by itself (e.g., *the pidginization hypothesis, the pro-drop parameter*). These are shown in Table 8.7. Table 8.7 shows that "complex nominal" errors predominate, accounting for nearly half of the errors in this category. Some examples are shown below:

JA (Sum. 2): " . . . provides little information about *acquisition process."

CH (Sum. 4): " . . . another tendency . . . that should account for *language system . . . "

KO (Sum. 9): " . . . the role of *internal processing mechanism."

In all three examples, the zero article would have been correct if the singular count headnouns *process, system,* and *mechanism* had not been present.

TABLE 8.7. Academic Underspecification Errors

| Measure | Complex Nominal | Generic the | Academic Term | Total |
|---|---|---|---|---|
| n | 136 | 33 | 63 | 232 |
| % | 58.62 | 14.22 | 27.16 | 100.00 |

Initial calculations found generic *the* to account for roughly a third of the academic Ø-for-*the* errors. Seventy percent (76/109) of these were body parts (e.g., * brain, * amygdala), which only occurred in Summaries 19 and 20. Furthermore, 41/76 of these were produced by two individuals (the Javanese subject and a Chinese subject). Because these error scores had a disproportionate effect on the results, it was decided not to count any of the Ø-for-*the* errors with body parts for any of the subjects, and the adjusted figures are reflected in Table 8.7. Table 8.7 shows that 14.2% of the academic Ø-for-*the* errors concerned generic *the* and 39% of these occurred with possessive structures (e.g., *the learner's, the teacher's*), suggesting that some of the subjects may have thought that the definite article could not function as part of the possessive determiner structure.

Academic terms that were not included in any other category (several occurred in the "complex nominal" category) accounted for the remaining 27.2%. Some examples are shown below:

JV (Sum. 1): " . . . *inductive approach progresses from accumulation [of data]."
CH (Sum. 2): "*Natural order hypothesis is weak."
JA (Sum. 15): "Eckman advocates *Markedness Differential Hypothesis."

*A comparison of the errors of Chinese and Japanese subjects.* Because the majority of the subjects were speakers of Mandarin Chinese and Japanese, the errors were also tabulated separately to allow a comparison of these two groups in Table 8.8. The average TOEFL score for the Chinese group was 587, for the Japanese group 573. However, there was no significant correlation between TOEFL score and the mean errors per subject per summary of the entire group. Table 8.8 shows that both

TABLE 8.8. Article Error Distribution for Chinese and Japanese Groups

| | | Chinese (n = 13) | | | Japanese (n = 4) | | |
|------|----------|--------|--------|---------------|--------|-------|---------------|
| Used | Required | Errors | % | Mean/Subj/Sum | Errors | % | Mean/Subj/Sum |
| Ø | the | 465 | 41.15 | 2.54 | 186 | 39.32 | 3.13 |
| the | Ø | 341 | 30.18 | 1.94 | 100 | 21.14 | 1.80 |
| Ø | a | 216 | 19.12 | 1.22 | 105 | 22.20 | 1.79 |
| a | Ø | 41 | 3.63 | 0.23 | 35 | 7.40 | 0.66 |
| the | a | 48 | 4.25 | 0.28 | 17 | 3.59 | 0.32 |
| a | the | 19 | 1.68 | 0.11 | 30 | 6.34 | 0.49 |
| | Total | 1130 | 100.01 | 6.32 | 473 | 99.99 | 8.19 |

groups made the greatest number of errors in the first three categories, which account for 90.45% and 82.66%, respectively, of the total errors. However, the Chinese speakers as a group made fewer errors per subject per summary than the Japanese speakers, and the Japanese speakers tended to have more problems with *a* than did the Chinese speakers. Yamada and Matsuura (1982) found indefinite *a* to be the greatest problem for advanced Japanese learners as did Chaudron and Parker (1988), who suggested that, once *the* has been acquired, emerging *a* may also be overgeneralized and thus undermine some of the progress made with *the* (p. 19).

## Errors Over Time

The period over which the summaries were written was divided into four periods (Periods 1-4). A maximum of five summaries (mean = 3.42) was written during each period, which ranged from 3 to 4 weeks in length. This provides a longitudinal picture of the pattern of article errors over the duration of the study. These patterns were looked at in two ways: (a) as the mean number of errors per summary and (b) as the mean percentage of the total that each type of error accounted for.

*Mean number of errors per summary.* For each subject, the total errors in each of the four periods was divided by the number of summaries written in that period, providing a mean score for each error type in each period. The average score for the entire group in each period was then determined for each of the article error scores. This score represents the mean of a mean, which could skew the results in favor of those who wrote a larger number of summaries. To test this effect, a correlation was run between the mean error scores for each individual and the number of summaries written ($r = .45$, $p > .05$). The results show that there was no significant correlation between number of summaries written and the article errors per summary in each period for each subject. Hence, it was considered appropriate to calculate the means of each error type in each period for the entire group. The results are shown in Figure 8.1. Figure 8.1 shows that the mean number of total article errors for all subjects decreased significantly between Period 1 and period 4 ($p = .01$) in a t-test for dependent groups (the effect of the inclusion of Ø with body parts is shown by the dotted line). The patterns for the Chinese and Japanese groups are shown for comparison.

The means of the three most common error types, the use of Ø for *the* (A),

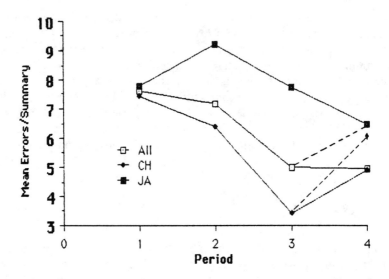

**Figure 8.1.**   Total article errors

*the* for Ø (B), and Ø for *a* (C) were also calculated. The results are shown in Figure 8.2. Figure 8.2 shows that for the entire group (all), the number of Ø-for-*the* errors (A) increased between Period 1 and Period 2 and then diminished between Period 2 and Period 4 (the effect of the inclusion of Ø with body parts is shown by the dotted line). The use of *the* for Ø (B) decreased between Periods 1 and 4, as did the use of Ø for *a* (C). Once again, the patterns of the Chinese and Japanese groups are included for comparison.

*Percentage of error type in each period.*   The percentage of errors of each type was calculated for each of the four periods by taking the number of errors of each type for all subjects in each period and dividing by the total number of errors in each period. The results are displayed in Figure 8.3. Figure 8.3 shows that the percentages of error types are fairly consistent across the four periods. The percentage of Ø-for-*the* errors consistently increases such that by Period 4, Ø-for-*the* errors account for over 60% of the total. When Ø with body-part errors are ignored, Ø-for-*the* errors fall to 48% in Period 4, but they still constitute by far the greatest percentage of errors overall. The only other error type to increase over time is the percentage of *a*-for-*the* errors, which increased from just over 2% of the total errors in Period 1 to just under 4% in Period 4 (to 5% if Ø with body-part errors are excluded), a relatively small increase.

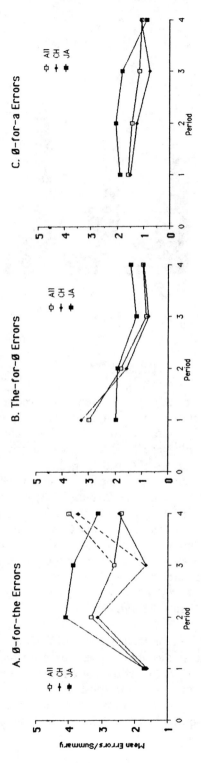

**Figure 8.2.** The three most common error types

195

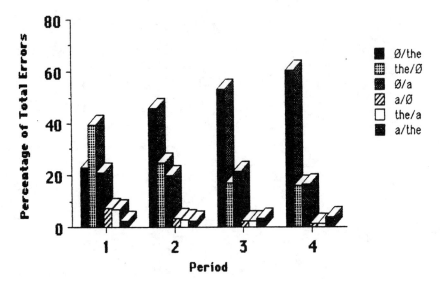

**Figure 8.3.**   Percentage of error type in each period

## DISCUSSION

The results of the present study are discussed in this section in relation to the research cited in the first section and in terms of the pedagogical implications. The distribution of article errors shown in Table 8.5 has several implications. First of all, since even learners with advanced proficiency continue to make article errors, the need for pedagogical focus on the article system is apparent, as many researchers have concluded (e.g., Grannis, 1972; Master, 1987; McEldowney, 1977; Pica, 1983; Whitman, 1974). More specifically, in a pedagogical treatment of the article system, it would seem that students have relatively little difficulty choosing *a* vs. *the* but a great deal of difficulty choosing *a* or *the* vs. Ø. Thus, the most useful focus from the student's point of view would be on how the zero article functions in English and under what circumstances Ø replaces *a* and *the*, and vice versa.

### Comparisons with Other Studies

The results both confirm and challenge the findings of Yamada and Matsuura (1982). Both studies agree in finding *a*-for-*the* errors to be the least frequent, *a*-for-Ø errors to account for a relatively small percentage of errors, and Ø-for-*a* errors to be the third most frequent type. The two studies disagree in that Yamada and Matsuura found overspecification (*the* for Ø and *a*) to be the source of most errors whereas the present study finds

Ø-overuse (Ø for *a* and *the*) to predominate. The difference may stem from the nature of the task. Yamada and Matsuura used a modified cloze test as an instrument whereas the subjects in this study had to generate summaries from readings. The former may have required more conscious contemplation of rules than did the generation of summaries, where the focus was much more on content than on grammar rules, as will be attested to by the subjects' comments in the conclusion. On the other hand, the difference in findings may stem from differences in the definition of advanced proficiency. In the present study, advanced proficiency is established by TOEFL score and the fact that the subjects were in a graduate program (a score of 550 is required by most graduate programs in the U.S.), whereas Yamada and Matsuura presumed their subjects, undergraduate English majors with 7 to 9 years of English studies, to be advanced without supplying an objective measure of their proficiency level.

The results are also not supported by Chaudron and Parker (1988) who, like Yamada and Matsuura (1982), found overspecification errors to predominate. Chaudron and Parker found a substantially lower accuracy (i.e., greater proportion of errors) in their advanced Japanese subjects than did Master or Yamada and Matsuura. They found a much higher proportion of *a*-for-*the* errors than did the other studies including the present one, and they found Ø-for-*the* errors to be the least frequent error, whereas the other studies found this type to range from the middle to the most frequent error. The disparity may again be the product of what is meant by *advanced*. Chaudron and Parker used three measures (verbs per T-unit, verb type-token, and performance on an exact imitation task) and placed subjects with at least one standard deviation above the mean in the advanced group. Thus, *advanced* means only in relation to the other subjects in the study and not in relation to a broader population.

Finally, the results are both confirmed and challenged by my study of spoken article usage (Master, 1987). The three least frequent errors in both studies were the same (*a*-for-Ø, *the*-for-*a*, and *a*-for-*the*) with a substantially lower degree of frequency compared to the other errors. Furthermore, as in the present study, the most frequent errors were Ø-over use (Ø for *the* and *a*) errors, although there is a significant percentage of *the*-for-Ø errors as well. The difference between the two studies is that Ø-for-*a* errors predominate in the spoken corpus whereas Ø-for-*the* errors predominate in the summary study. Both Master (1987) and Yamada and Matsuura (1982) report percentages of total usage (i.e., accuracy scores) and it is interesting that, whereas the percentages of Ø-overuse error scores are quite similar (Ø-for-*the* = 6.9% vs. 4.9%, respectively; Ø-for-*a* = 9.1% vs. 9.6%), the Ø-under use scores are quite different (*the*-for-Ø = 1.4% vs. 18.2%; *a*-for-Ø = 0.6% vs. 2.3%). Master (1987) determined advanced proficiency by the presence of a high proportion of analyzed *don't* auxiliary negative structures described by Stauble (1978) and said to characterize the high-mesolang interlanguage level but found overspecification errors to occur at an earlier stage of proficiency. The fact that the subjects in the present study made many more Ø-overuse errors than overspecification errors suggests that the advanced subjects in the other studies were at a lower proficiency level than supposed.

## Pedagogical Implications

The analysis of Ø-for-*the* errors suggests several areas that may benefit from pedagogical attention. The most difficult and intangible area and the one that caused the greatest number of errors is "shared knowledge." This requires a constant assessment on the part of the writer of what he or she presumes the reader to know. One example of what many advanced students with no article system in their L1s appear to do is to apply the correct shared knowledge article rules early in a paragraph but then fail to maintain the marking of the shared knowledge NP throughout the paragraph as English requires, perhaps reasoning that the reader must know by now what the writer is talking about so why should it require constant remarking? The failure to maintain the marking of shared knowledge NPs with *the* leads to Ø-for-*the* errors, as exemplified earlier in the sample sentence "Negative forms will eventually . . . become more like *model language." Since students quickly grasp the idea of first and subsequent mention in simple exercises, perhaps explicit models of this process in longer stretches of discourse may help students to apply the English requirement for continual marking of known NPs. The results also suggest that a clear explication of the "identifying" effect of certain types of postmodification may be useful as well as the need for *the* with certain frequently recurring ranking adjectives like *same, first,* and *second.* A comment from one of the Japanese subjects suggests the kind of tribulations students must go through to attain mastery of *the* and to avoid what I have called "standard" Ø-overuse errors:

> [Y]our explanation of the articles that are not influenced by contexts (*the* next or *the* following) were very helpful and I always remember those rules when I write. However, the articles which are determined by the contexts in which they are in are still hard for me to distinguish because I am not competent enough to apply your discussion to other contexts.

This comment would suggest that a pedagogical focus on "the articles that are not influenced by contexts," that is, ranking adjectives, "identifying" as opposed to "classifying" postmodification,[3] and the continual marking of noun phrases that have been "identified" for the reader, might provide students with easily applied rules of thumb to apply in selecting the article. Mastering the complexity of context-dependent article rules, however, may only come after years of exposure to native speakers and the automaticity of article rule application that will hopefully result.

The use of *the* in the "academic" category largely concerns shared knowledge within a specific field. This a curious phenomenon that may be better understood in light of genre analysis and discourse community (Swales, 1990). Let's take for example the NP *the Monitor Model*. For members of the discourse community of applied linguistics and second language acquisition, this NP describes the well-known model established by Krashen (1977). Part of our knowledge as members of this discourse community is that there is likely to be only one such model (especially when it is exalted with capital letters) and that a single, identified noun requires the article *the*. Second language acquisition is, however, a relatively young field. Let's imagine that in a few years there is another monitor model. There would then be a category of such hypotheses rather than a single example, and the article would now shift to *a*, (that is, a monitor model). Thus, membership in the discourse community, which graduate students can be presumed to seek, brings with it not only the knowledge of field-specific terms and their relative status within the community but also an assessment of the relative age of the discipline. Such a sophisticated sense is difficult for native speakers to achieve, let alone nonnatives with no article system in their native languages.

Of the three types of "academic" errors tallied, the most frequent was the use of Ø before a headnoun premodified by a noun that would be "classified" as a noncount noun if it occurred by itself (i.e., the complex nominal category). One implication of this error is that the subjects may have chosen the zero article because they did not look beyond the modifying noun in the complex nominal and thus produced NPs such as * *pidginization hypothesis* and * *pro-drop parameter*. Since in some ways this may be considered an article rule that is not determined by context, it may be

---

[3]"Identifying" vs. "classifying" postmodification is described as "limiting" vs. "defining" postmodification by Master (1990), and is exemplified in the following sentences (p. 472): (a) **The** water *in this glass* is dirty. [limiting or identifying]; and (b) A thermometer is **an** instrument *that measures temperature.* [defining or classifying]. In (a), the postmodifying phrase *in this glass* limits the scope to a known quantity. This indicates that the water has been identified and thus requires *the*. In (b), the postmodifying phrase *that measures temperature* defines the headnoun *instrument* as a member of a class that is differentiated by the postmodifying phrase. *Instrument* is therefore classified and requires *a* (θ for a noncount or plural noun), as is usually the case for the class word in a definition.

pedagogically fruitful to point out to advanced learners the "identifying" effect of reigning in a noncount noun by appending a singular countable category word such as *hypothesis, parameter, process, system, mechanism, model, rule,* and *effect.* A comment from one of the Chinese subjects supports this suggestion:

> The most helpful discussion is when examples are given to distinguish between using the article *the* and not using any article in different summaries, for example *the monitor* vs. *monitor theory, interlanguage* vs. *the interlanguage, nativization* vs. *the nativization process,* and *mesolect* vs. *the mesolect phase.*

Finally, teaching generic *the,* especially with body parts such as *the brain* and *the amygdala,* and pointing out the unique status of academic terms such as *the Monitor Model,* which thus become identified and require *the,* might help students to reduce the number of errors with this usage.

## ERRORS OVER TIME

The results of the errors over time analysis shown in Figures 8.1 and 8.2 suggest that although the mean errors per subject per summary decrease steadily over time, as do *the*-for-$\emptyset$ and $\emptyset$-for-*a* errors, $\emptyset$-for-*the* errors show an initial increase between Periods 1 and 2, and then decrease between Periods 2 and 4. Because a focus on the article system was being made in the classroom, perhaps the requirement to keep a record of article errors initially caused subjects to pay attention to the system and, in so doing, apply a faulty rule, which was then modified by the cumulative effect of feedback on and classroom discussion of the common article errors on subsequent summaries.

The percentage of error type in each period shown in Figure 8.3 shows that the proportion of $\emptyset$-for-*the* errors was the only one to substantially increase, although there was a very slight increase of *a*-for-*the* errors. For this reason, a detailed analysis was only provided for $\emptyset$-for-*the* errors as they appear to be the most logical area for pedagogical attention.

Nevertheless, $\emptyset$-for-*a* errors, the other category of $\emptyset$ overuse, did account for 19.9% of the total errors in the study. In this regard, Hiki (1989), who studied the *a* and $\emptyset$ errors of Japanese speakers in an editing test and questionnaire, found a significant relationship between accuracy in the use of *a* and $\emptyset$ and the type (i.e., bounded [= a tangible entity with a definite shape], abstract, mass, and proper) and the countability markedness ([= a preferred countability for every noun class in the learner's mind (p. 7)]) of the nouns to which they were attached. He found a difficulty order in which proper and mass nouns with *a* were the most difficult for his subjects, followed by abstract nouns with Ø and *a*, and finally bounded nouns with Ø, which led him to conclude that learners need basic training in being sensitive to the context when they choose an article (p. 23), especially for articles with abstract nouns. The problems with Ø-for-*the* errors in the present study also suggest that abstract nouns with Ø were a problem (Hiki did not investigate the use of *the*), as the errors with complex nominals, as well as the field-specific terms noted above, occurred primarily in NPs headed by abstract nouns.

## CONCLUSION

This study of the article errors in a series of academic summaries written by Southeast Asian students with advanced English proficiency has shown that article errors appear to decrease significantly over a relatively short period of time (one 15-week semester) if attention is paid to the article system. In this case, attention was applied not through detailed explanations and exercises but through constant feedback on the article errors in written summaries, brief classroom discussions, and the keeping of an article error record sheet by each subject. At the end of the study, the subjects were asked to comment on the effect that (a) preparing the summaries, (b) receiving feedback on the summaries, (c) discussing the errors in class, and (d) keeping an error record had on their understanding of the English article system. Some of these comments are shown below.

### 1. Preparing summaries

I can not catch any articles in the speech of the native speakers. So I have not learned any articles from speech at all. I have learned it by writing and may be some reading. I think the only way to acquire the articles is to do a lot of writing and to get feedback from native speakers repeatedly.

### 2. Receiving feedback

I cannot understand the usage of articles unless I receive feedback or correction from teachers. I think that it is very difficult for me to learn articles without instruction. However, it seems to me that instruction about articles is not enough. I can understand whether a word needs definite or indefinite articles in a certain situation when I receive feedback. But it seems to me that I have not yet understood the general concept of nouns or articles, so I make a mistake in the same word in a different context.

[Feedback] was helpful in terms of the whole thing: the content, the organization of summaries, etc. But in terms of the article system, not much [because] article system is more like a habitual thing to me.

Receiving feedback on the summaries and classroom discussion make me pay more attention to count and noncount nouns and the use of articles.

I was using so much energy to pay attention to the grammar (even though the article system is also part of it) and I had regarded the articles as not so important until you raised this issues.

## 3. Discussing errors in class

The brief discussion at the beginning of each class period helps me a lot. Although I have learned the basic article rules from Linguistics 171 . . . in certain circumstances I still have a hard time to determine which article is the most appropriate to use. However, from being exposed to the rules in each session [of this class], I think I have made some progress and I can see the improvement from the last few summaries.

Each of [the areas you want us to comment on] benefits the others. Error Record Sheet alone does not help me very much if the mistakes are not explained. As the same token, the correction on our summaries might lose its value if we just ignore the marks that the instructor makes. Only when they are complemented by [each other] can they achieve the greatest efficiency.

Overall discussing the errors in the class is a good teaching strategy. However, it takes time for me, as a foreign student, to tell some slight differences, for example, sometimes we use *the* before *interlanguage* but sometimes don't.

I am sure nouns after articles are very important in deciding to use what article or to use no articles at all. For nouns like *relationship, interlanguage,* they are very confusing to me, yet after instruction in class I have a general idea for better article-choosing in writing.

All the teachers in my undergraduate classes have not pointed out my article mistakes. I wish teachers in writing classes could formally teach the article system so that their students would have knowledge about the usage of articles before they actually get into their academic disciplines.

## 4. Keeping a record of article errors

Seeing the list was very depressing for me because I could see that I had not improved anything since the beginning of the semester and because the list looked like a pile of things I could not control.

It would have helped me more if I had recorded [the errors] every time I got my summary back. Though I did not write down the article errors as I should have done, I have been more sensitive to the use of article in different situations than before. This has made me pay more attention to the use of articles by native speakers.

During the course of keeping the record of article errors, I found out that some errors I made in the summaries were just careless mistakes. Most of them were due to the fact that I didn't proofread my paper . . . In the last two articles, I finally started to proofread the paper. I looked through each article in the summary and checked it with my notes when in doubt.

By keeping this article error record, I find the weak part of my grammar. Without being pointing out, I probably never pay much attention to the usage of articles. The reason is because articles were taught at early stages, and thus I assume them as a easy thing. In such an occasion, article acquisition tends to be fossilized. There are many rules that I know, but I still make mistakes. That means, my knowledge is not well integrated into interlanguage.

In addition to confirming many of the difficulties discussed in this study, these comments speak for the value of consciousness-raising in regard to the article system at the advanced level of English proficiency. Consciousness-raising, however, should not come about simply through rule presentation and exercises but through integrating feedback with writing. The subjects appeared to value the classroom discussion of errors, the narrow focus of which was possible only because all the students were writing the same kind of essay (a summary) on the same material. The integration of such a methodology into graduate classes may benefit the substantial numbers of nonnative speakers who are completing their graduate degrees in the United States and other English-speaking countries.

## REFERENCES

Bickerton, D. (1984). The language bioprogram hypothesis. *The Behavioral and Brain Sciences* 7 (2), 173–188.

Burt, M. K., & Kiparsky, C. (1974). Global and local mistakes. In J. Schumann & N. Stenson (Eds.), *New frontiers in second language learning*. Rowley, MA: Newbury House.

Celce-Murcia, M., & Hawkins, B. (1985). Contrastive analysis, error analysis, and interlanguage analysis. In M. Celce-Murcia (Ed.), *Beyond basics: Issues and research in TESOL* (pp. 60–77). Cambridge, MA: Newbury House.

Chaudron, C., & Parker, K. (1988, October). *Discourse markedness and structural markedness: The acquisition of English noun phrases*. Paper presented at the 13th Annual Boston University Conference on Language Development, Boston, MA.

Gaies, S. (1987). The investigation of language classroom processes. In M. Long & J. Richards (Eds.), *Methodology in TESOL* (pp. 329–338). New York: Newbury House.

Grannis, O. (1972). The definite article conspiracy in English. *Language Learning, 22* (2), 275–289.

Hiki, M. (1989). *The acquisition of the indefinite article and zero article by advanced Japanese EFL learners: The acquisition of the concept of countability.* Unpublished paper, University of Indiana, Bloomington.

Kimura, E., & McCroskey, C. (1991). *Research into teaching articles using Master's binary system.* Unpublished paper, University of Washington, Seattle.

Kirkland, M., & Saunders, M. (1991). Maximizing the student performance in summary writing: managing the cognitive load. *TESOL Quarterly, 25* (1), 105–121.

Krashen, S. (1977). Some issues relating to the Monitor Model. In H. Brown, C. Yorio, & R. Crymes (Eds.), *On TESOL '77* (pp. 144–158). Washington, DC: TESOL.

Master, P. (1986). *Measuring the effect of systematic instruction in the English article system.* Unpublished paper, University of California, Los Angeles.

Master, P. (1987). *A cross-linguistic interlanguage analysis of the acquisition of the English article system.* Unpublished doctoral dissertation, University of California, Los Angeles.

Master, P. (1990). Teaching the English articles as a binary system. *TESOL Quarterly, 24* (3), 461–478.

McEldowney, P. L. (1977). A teaching grammar of the English article system. *International Review of Applied Linguistics, 15* (2), 95–112.

McGirt, J. D. (1984). *The effect of morphological and syntactic errors on the holistic scores of native and nonnative compositions.* Unpublished Master's thesis, University of California, Los Angeles.

McLaughlin, B. (1987). *Theories of second language learning.* New York: Edward Arnold.

Oller, J., & Redding, E. Z. (1972). Article usage and other language skills. *Language Learning 21,* 85–95.

Pica, T. (1983). The article in American English: What the textbooks don't tell us. In N. Wolfson & E. Judd (Eds.), *Sociolinguistics and language acquisition* (pp. 222–233). Rowley, MA: Newbury House.

Schachter, J., & Celce-Murcia, M. (1977). Some reservations concerning error analysis. *TESOL Quarterly, 11* (4), 441–451.

Schumann, J. (1976). Second language acquisition: The pidginization hypothesis. *Language Learning, 26* (2), 391–408.

Stauble, A. M. (1978). The process of decreolization: A model for second language development. *Language Learning, 28* (1), 29–54.

Swales, J. (1990). *Genre analysis.* Cambridge, UK: Cambridge University Press.

White, L. (1984 March). *Universal grammar as a source of explanation in second language acquisition.* Paper presented at the 12th Annual University of Wisconsin-Milwaukee Symposium on Markedness, Milwaukee, WI.

Whitman, R. L. (1974). Teaching the article in English. *TESOL Quarterly, 8* (3), 253–262.

Yamada, J., & Matsuura, N. (1982). The use of the English article among Japanese students. *RELC Journal, 13* (1), 50–63.

# CHAPTER 9

# Holistic Scoring in ESL Writing Assessment: What Does an Analysis of Rhetorical Features Reveal?*

**Diane J. Tedick**
*University of Minnesota*

**Maureen A. Mathison**
*University of Utah*

The assessment of writing proficiency in both first language (L1) and second language (L2) contexts has been receiving increased attention in the past decade. As with all forms of assessment, validity is central to writing assessment. Hamp-Lyons (1990), in her substantive analysis of writing assessment issues, emphasizes the need to establish validity for the four major components of direct writing assessment: the task, the writer, the scoring procedure(s), and the reader(s). This chapter explores aspects of these various components while focusing primarily on the relationship between some rhetorical features of ESL students' essays written in response to two different tasks (one general and one pertaining to academic disciplines), and the holistic scores awarded to those essays. Simply said, our descriptive analysis of rhetorical features in the essays raises questions about holistic scoring, particularly as it relates to task differences.

Fifty ESL essays were examined on the basis of two rhetorical features: framing and elements of task compliance. The framing of an essay refers to the extent to which it provides enough context and appropriate development so as to meet a reader's expectations (Hoey, 1983; van Dijk & Kintsch, 1983). Examining elements of task compliance involved an analysis of the extent to which the writers were successful in carrying out the implied elements of the writing tasks.

---

*This chapter is a revised version of the paper presented at the annual meeting of the American Educational Research Association, Boston, MA, April 1990. Special thanks to Paul Prior for his insightful comments during the revision process.

Our analyses indicated that framing appeared to be a major variable contributing to the holistics scores subjects received on their essays. The general pattern was that subjects received higher holistic scores on the essays—regardless of prompt type—that they framed well enough for readers to be able to make predictions about the content to come. A few essays did not fit the general pattern, however. Our examination of the elements of task compliance led us to discover an anomaly in the holistic scoring. Some subjects who did not address the field-specific task were successful in that they achieved *high* holistic scores regardless of the fact that their responses did not address the task. Other subjects who did not address the task or who were judged to be off topic did *not* receive higher holistic scores. We offer two possible explanations to explain the anomaly. The first is that some writers may be successful in employing strategies that permit them at once to avoid doing the task specified in the prompt, and to get away with it. A second plausible explanation is that responses may lie on a continuum of acceptable/ unacceptable responses based upon with whom (reader or writer) authority resides.

We conclude with a number of recommendations. First, the issue of task comparability must be addressed in ways that reach beyond correlational studies that use holistic scores as the means for comparison. Secondly, we offer pedagogical implications related to the notion of framing. We end with questions about the validity of holistic scoring based on the anomalies that we discovered. We believe that writing assessment involves complex negotiation along dimensions like authority, subject-matter knowledge, and interest—dimensions that are distinctly cultural. It is time for teachers, researchers, and evaluation experts involved in ESL writing assessment to move beyond the limits that holistic scoring places on us.

## INTRODUCTION AND BACKGROUND TO THE STUDY

The assessment of writing proficiency in both first language (L1) and second language (L2) contexts has been receiving increased attention in the past decade. Direct measures have either replaced or been added to indirect measures, and large-scale assessments at global, national, and local levels have grown in popularity. Students from grade school to graduate school are required to demonstrate their writing performance by responding to essay writing tasks. Because important decisions, such as those regarding admission, placement, diagnosis, and achievement, are made on the basis of the results of writing assessments, there is a need for reliable data concerning the many factors that affect the measurement of writing ability (Brossell, 1986). As with all forms of assessment, validity is central to writing assessment. Hamp-Lyons (1990), in her substantive analysis of writing assessment issues, emphasizes the need to establish validity for the four major components of direct writing assessment: the task, the writer, the scoring procedure(s), and the reader(s). This chapter explores aspects of these various components while focusing primarily on the relationship between some rhetorical features of ESL students' essays written in response to two different tasks (one general and one pertaining to academic disciplines), and the holistic scores awarded to those essays. Simply said, our descriptive analysis of rhetorical features in the essays raises questions about holistic scoring, particularly as it relates to task differences.

For most large-scale assessments, holistic scoring procedures are followed (Faigley, Cherry, Jolliffe, & Skinner, 1985; Scherer, 1985; White, 1985). Yet, as a several scholars have noted, despite its widespread use, holistic scoring lacks a demonstrated theoretical foundation (Charney, 1984; Gere, 1980; Huot, 1990). One major question that has emerged in the literature relates to the effects of holistic training and monitoring procedures, which emphasize agreement and rapid reading. Charney (1984), Gere (1980), and Odell and Cooper (1980) have all argued that such procedures interrupt normal reading processes in ways that may impede raters in making sound choices about writing quality. In other words, reliability is bought at the cost of validity. Certainly reading research would suggest that readers' purposes, interests, and prior knowledge influence the way in which they interact with text, and, hence, would influence the judgments they make about writing (e.g., Anderson & Pearson, 1984; Rumelhart, 1980; Spiro, 1980). It may be argued that the relationship between the reader and the text is further complicated when the readers do not share the same native language and culture of the writers (e.g., Steffensen & Joag-Dev, 1984). For example, in this volume Bloch and Chi demonstrate how historical and political factors influence the use of citations and argumentation practices in Chinese academic discourse. What has often been considered a lack of contentiousness and originality in the texts of Chinese students writing in English may actually be attributed to particular rhetorical traditions that shape discourse in ways unknown to native English-speaking readers and writers.

In the development of direct assessment writing tasks, the research has focused on four broad factors related to topics: wording, mode of discourse, rhetorical specification, and subject matter.[1] Theoretical models

---

[1]For studies on the effects of changes in wording see, for example, Brossell and Hoetker Ash (1984), Greenberg (1981), and a number of studies summarized by Ruth and Murphy (1988). Different modes of discourse required by writing tasks have been found to produce varying

in the field of writing research include subject-matter knowledge as a central component (e.g., Bereiter & Scardamalia, 1987; Flower & Hayes, 1981). A number of studies in both L1 and L2 writing research have focused on the subject matter of the writing task and the degree to which a writer's prior knowledge about that subject matter affects his or her writing performance. Several L1 studies have demonstrated that prior knowledge of the subject matter of a writing task leads to an improvement in the quality of high school students' writing (Chesky, 1984; Chesky & Hiebert, 1987; Langer, 1984) and children's writing (McCutcheon, 1986). A study conducted with L2 students at the university level examined the effects of familiar and unfamiliar cultural contexts on writing. In this study, Winfield and Barnes-Felfeli (1982) found that cultural familiarity among subjects was found to have a positive impact on their writing.

The study described in this chapter is a follow-up to an ESL writing study conducted under large-scale assessment conditions, which examined differences in essays written in response to two different tasks (Tedick, 1988, 1990). This follow-up study provides a descriptive analysis of rhetorical features found in selected essays and compares them to the holistic scores assigned to the essays in the original study. It is important to begin with a brief description of the original study in order to provide a context for the study described in this chapter.

## THE ORIGINAL STUDY

The original large-scale repeated measures study was conducted to examine the effects of subject-matter knowledge on ESL writing performance (Tedick, 1988, 1990). One hundred and five international graduate students representing three levels of ESL composition courses (beginning,[2] intermediate, and advanced) at a large state-supported institution in the Midwest

---

degrees of syntactic complexity (e.g., Crowhurst & Piché, 1979; Quellmalz, Capell, & Chou, 1982) and varying degrees of sophistication in lexical choices (e.g., Neilsen & Piché, 1981). There has also been work in the area of the cognitive demands placed on writers for different discourse modes (Matsuhashi, 1982). Results on studies regarding rhetorical specification (i.e., specification of audience and purpose within the task) have been inconclusive. See, for example, Brossell (1983), Hoetker (1982), Plasse (1981), Rowntree (1977), and Witte, Meyer, Cherry, & Trachsel (1986).

[2]It should be noted that beginning students in the ESL program under study could very well be considered to be at the intermediate level in other intensive ESL programs at the university level. The majority of students come to in this program with a great deal of English study behind them as well as a strong educational background in their native languages. This is particularly true of the graduate students in the program, who are the focus of the original and present studies.

were asked to write in response to two topics, one general in nature and the other pertaining to their fields of study.

The general prompt was chosen from the repertoire of topics used by the ESL program for diagnostic examinations.

> In a recent news magazine, a famous educator argued that progress makes us lazy. Do you agree or disagree with this point of view? Explain why you believe that progress does or does not cause people to become more lazy or passive. Support your answer with specific reasons and examples.

Tedick created the field-specific prompt with two goals in mind: to develop a prompt that would (a) be similar in type to the first, and (b) encourage subjects to write about subject matter with which they were familiar.[3]

> Every field of study has controversial issues. Debate over these issues often occurs among professionals in the field and leads them to conduct research in order to look for evidence to support one position on the issue over another or others. Choose a current controversial issue in *your* field of study. Discuss the controversy and explain your position on the issue, being sure to provide examples to support your position.

In the first phase, subjects were asked to respond to the topic of general nature, and in the second phase, they were asked to respond to the topic pertaining to their fields of study.[4] The 210 essays were scored on the basis of (a) overall quality, as measured by holistic scores; (b) fluency, as

---

[3]It was a limitation in the original study (and, therefore, remains a limitation in the present study) that no measure of prior knowledge in the field was obtained. It is important to recognize that the individual subjects may have had differing degrees of knowledge in their fields of study. The subjects who were chosen for the original study were new to the United States; it will remain unknown whether some were also new to their fields. In addition, it may be that the students who participated had not yet dealt with controversies in their fields of study, or that they may have had extensive prior knowledge about the content of their fields of study, but little or no experience with writing arguments related to their fields of study (that is, discussing a controversy and supporting one side of the controversy over the other).

[4]The ideal way to control for testing effects involves randomly assigning the different levels of the treatment variable to subjects at the various times at which repeated measures are obtained (e.g., Campbell & Stanley, 1963). It was not possible, however, to exercise this control in the present study because the first writing measures were obtained during the actual administration of the diagnostic examination of the ESL composition courses. The tradeoff for attempting to conduct a study under normal circumstances in order to minimize the artificiality of highly controlled experimental conditions is that ideal experimental control suffers.

measured by overall length; and (c) syntactic complexity, as measured by the mean number of and mean length of T-units and error-free T-units.

The analyses indicated that the field-specific topic resulted in statistically significant increases in holistic scores, overall length, and mean length of T-units and error-free T-units. The field-specific topic also proved to be superior to the general topic with respect to its ability to discriminate among subjects in different course levels.

Although the original study has important implications for L2 writing assessment with respect to the effects of subject-matter knowledge on writing performance and to topic development, it is limited in terms of its explanatory power due to the fact that the analyses were strictly quantitative. In other words, increases in numbers representing holistic scores and average T-unit length do not *describe* the nature of the improved writing performance. We believed it would be useful to have descriptive data about the writing samples, data which might help us to understand what factors led the raters to award higher holistic scores to certain essays rather than to others. We are well aware that holistic scoring of writing is meant to be just that—holistic—however, research has repeatedly shown that features of texts (including handwriting, length, etc.) correlate with ratings.[5] Furthermore, recognizing that the judgments made during the holistic scoring session in the original study were supposed to take into account factors such as (a) content, (b) development, (c) organization, (d) the degree to which the writer effectively addresses the task, (e) appropriate use of the lexicon, (f) coherence, and (g) syntactic accuracy, variety, and complexity, we felt compelled to examine whether some of these factors did in fact appear to be related to the holistic scores that were awarded to the essays in the original study.

## THE PRESENT STUDY

An assumption underlying holistic scoring is that higher scores indicate greater quality of writing, and rhetorical features can be said to contribute to writing quality. In order to shed light on some factors that could have influenced the holistic scores awarded to selected essays from the original study, we decided to focus on rhetorical features. To conduct a complete analysis of the essays, it is necessary to examine both rhetorical and linguistic features.[6] A good deal of the L2 literature on writing has focused

---

[5]See, for example, Charney (1984) for a review of the studies on factors influencing holistic ratings.

[6]Linguistic analyses (including a syntactic analysis and a topical structure analysis) have been performed on the same 50 essays selected for the present study, but discussion of these analyses

on linguistic aspects, whereas rhetorical analyses (beyond those appearing in the area of contrastive rhetoric, e.g., Connor & Kaplan, 1987; Purves, 1988; and those select few conducted, for example, by Connor, 1990, and Scarcella, 1984) have often been neglected. Because of the frequent absence of rhetorical discussions in the L2 literature, we decided to begin by examining several features that would describe rhetorical aspects of selected essays from the first study, features that might provide insight into what Leki points out in this volume: " 'Good writing' is writing that meets particular requirements set for a particular readership at a particular time and place" (p. 41). Specifically, we wanted to know what types of features may have contributed to raters' judgments of students' so-called writing proficiency for academic purposes, that is, the rhetoric that would be evaluated as enabling students' college careers.

## Sample Selection

Pairs of essays written by 25 subjects, or approximately 25% of the 105 subjects who participated in the original study, were selected for the present study. We made this selection systematically, not randomly, because we wanted to obtain a sample that was representative of the original group. We chose ten subjects from both the beginning and intermediate groups (each of which was originally composed of 43 subjects) and five subjects from the advanced group (which originally had 19 subjects).

We decided to select pairs of essays on the basis of holistic scores, because the statistical analyses conducted in the original study indicated that of the six dependent variables investigated, the holistic scores revealed the greatest discriminatory power. We systematically selected essays from each level that would represent the relative percentages of essays receiving higher, lower, and equal scores across the two topics. In addition, we made every attempt to select subjects representing a range of native language groups and major fields found in the original study. Table 9.1 provides a list of the subjects selected and their corresponding native languages, major fields of study, and the scores they received on both the general (i.e., progress) essay and the field-specific essay.

## Analysis of the Essays

We examined the 50 essays on the basis of two rhetorical features: framing, and elements of task compliance. Our reasons for choosing to focus on framing and elements of task compliance stem from our experience as

---

is beyond the scope of this chapter. See Tedick and Dubetz (1991) for a complete description of the linguistic analyses and their results.

TABLE 9.1. Summary of Selected Subjects and Corresponding Characteristics

| Level | Subject | L1* | Major | Holistic Score Progress | Field |
|---|---|---|---|---|---|
| | 1 | Chinese | City/Reg Plan. | 2 | 2 |
| | 2 | Chinese | Civ. Eng. | 6 | 3 |
| | 3 | Japanese | Chem. Eng. | 4 | 7 |
| Beginning | 4 | Korean | Poli. Sci. | 7 | 5 |
| (n = 10) | 5 | Korean | Land. Arch. | 2 | 9 |
| | 6 | Chinese | TESOL | 4 | 12 |
| | 7 | Indonesian | Elec. Eng. | 5 | 7 |
| | 8 | Portuguese | HomeEc/Hous. | 2 | 8 |
| | 9 | Chinese | Art | 5 | 2 |
| | 10 | Chinese | Elec. Eng. | 7 | 7 |
| | 11 | Chinese | Elec. Eng. | 8 | 8 |
| | 12 | Burmese | Agriculture | 4 | 9 |
| | 13 | Chinese | German | 3 | 10 |
| | 14 | Chinese | Indus/Sys. Eng. | 6 | 4 |
| Intermediate | 15 | Chinese | Business | 4 | 12 |
| (n = 10) | 16 | Korean | Economics | 12 | 6 |
| | 17 | French | Metal. Eng. | 2 | 4 |
| | 18 | Chinese | Metal. Eng. | 3 | 11 |
| | 19 | Chinese | TESOL | 8 | 2 |
| | 20 | Korean | Computer Sci. | 5 | 9 |
| | 21 | Korean | Cinema | 3 | 8 |
| Advanced | 22 | Arabic | Civil Eng. | 4 | 10 |
| (n = 5) | 23 | German | Sociology | 7 | 7 |
| | 24 | Indonesian | Civil Eng. | 10 | 4 |
| | 25 | Chinese | Journalism | 5 | 11 |

*In Tedick's original study, 13 native language groups were represented: Chinese (65 subjects), Korean (19 subjects), Japanese and German (5 subjects each), Indonesian and Spanish (2 subjects each), and Burmese, French, Portuguese, Thai, Greek, Serbo-Croatian, and Arabic (1 subject each).

instructors of ESL composition and as holistic raters of ESL writing. These reasons are described further below. The analyses were conducted by the researchers and additional raters, who were asked to provide judgments for the framing analysis.

*Framing.* The first rhetorical feature we examined was what we referred to as the framing of the essays. The notion of framing is derived from the theoretical framework set forth by Hoey (1983) and van Dijk and Kintsch (1983), among others. Hoey, for example, suggests that

On the basis of (1) cultural and linguistic expectations about the type of discourse encountered and (2) what the writer/speaker has already said (including the title and the place of occurrence), a reader/listener hazards guesses as to the content to come and its relationship to what has preceded. In so far as they guess correctly, they have a smooth ride; in so far as they guess wrongly, their comprehension is slowed down to some extent. If they consistently guess wrongly, it can be doubted whether they properly comprehend at all, though the fault may lie with either encoder or decoder. (p. 170)

In this description, Hoey is simply highlighting the relationship between the reader and the text, mentioned earlier in this chapter. As readers of texts, holistic raters are expected to make judgments about the quality of writing based on their understanding of the text and their beliefs about what constitutes writing quality. One could argue that essays which are framed well, and thus, facilitate the reader's task, might be judged as reflecting greater quality than essays which are not framed well. This assumption led us to decide to choose framing as a rhetorical feature of interest to the present study.

Van Dijk and Kintsch (1983) conducted a study in which they asked readers to read paragraph fragments and then to write down what they thought would be a likely continuation of that paragraph fragment. They found that readers relied on how much context was provided in the paragraph fragment and how good the paragraph fragment was. They suggest that if a paragraph fragment is not well developed or does not provide enough context, the reader will rely on some salient phrase in order to construct a continuation. Building on the design used by van Dijk and Kintsch, we asked six native readers of English, who were graduate students in TESOL at a small liberal arts college in the East, to act as raters for the framing analysis.[7]

The six framing raters were asked to read the first paragraph of each essay and to respond to two questions. The first asked these raters to state what they predicted the topic of the essay to be. The second asked that they explain how they thought the essay would be developed by the writer. The first paragraph of each essay was typed onto individual pages along with the two questions. Each rater was randomly assigned 16 or 17 paragraphs and was given two weeks in which to complete the task independently. Steps were taken to achieve systematic multiple independent scoring, which

---

[7]It is important to note that the nature of the *writer*, the nature of the assigned writing *task*, the nature of the *reader*, and the nature of the *purpose* for which the writer writes and the reader reads (i.e., the contexts) are factors that interact with each other and that largely determine *how* the essays are read and interpreted. Given this framework, it would have been ideal to have been able to have raters from the original study to complete the framing analysis, but this simply was not possible. It is imperative that this limitation be kept in mind during the interpretation of the results of the framing analysis.

involves having two different readers score each essay independently.[8] After the raters completed their tasks, their responses were copied, and then the researchers independently examined them. First, we made judgments as to whether the two raters who were assigned to the same paragraph agreed with respect to their predictions of the topics and development. Secondly, we compared the raters' predictions with the actual essays and made judgments as to whether the raters' expectations for both topic and development were realized.

*Elements of task compliance.* The other rhetorical feature we looked at involved judgments regarding the extent to which the writers were successful in carrying out the implied elements of the writing tasks. We labeled this feature "elements of task compliance," and devised a list of the elements that we felt were called for in each prompt. Consistent in holistic rating scales is mention of the extent to which the writer is successful in addressing the assigned task. Once again, the assumption is that holistic scores will be higher for those essays that comply with the requirements of the writing tasks. We wanted to determine whether this was indeed the case with the essays we selected.

Upon examining the general prompt, we agreed that it called for four elements:(a) a definition of progress, (b) a position statement indicating the writer's agreement or disagreement with the famous educator, (c) reasons to support the position statement, and (d) examples. An examination of the field-specific topic led us to agree that it called for six elements of task compliance: (a) an identification of the field of study, (b) an identification of the controversy, (c) an identification of the two positions on the controversy, (d) an explanation or development of one or both positions, (e) a position statement indicating the writer's position on the controversy, and (f) reasons to support the position statement.

In order to conduct this portion of the analysis, we independently analyzed the 50 essays to identify the elements of task compliance called for in each prompt. Later we determined whether the position statements appeared at the beginning, middle, or end of the essays.

## Results and Discussion

Due to the limited number of subjects in this study, it was not possible to provide full statistical analyses of the results. Instead, the results are summarized descriptively and conclusions based on these descriptions are drawn. When warranted, interrater reliability coefficients were calculated

---

[8]See, for example, Tedick (1988) and White (1985) for a detailed explanation of procedures for achieving systematic multiple independent scoring.

using Cohen's kappa. This formula, which takes into account the percentage of chance agreement possible, is used to establish reliability when the data involve independent subjects, independent ratings by judges, and a nominal scale with independent categories (Cohen, 1960).

*Framing.* Because the six framing raters made judgments about both topic and development, and because the researchers had to determine whether those raters' expectations were realized in the actual essays, a total of four interrater reliability coefficients needed to be calculated for the raters' predictions. The Cohen's kappa coefficients and percentages of agreement between raters were high, ranging from .76 to .92 and 88% to 96%, respectively. The interrater reliability coefficients for our judgments as to whether the raters' predictions were realized in the actual essay were also high; percentages of agreement ranged from 85% to 100% (with coefficients ranging from .70 to 1.00).

The process of determining reliability for the judgments that made up the framing analysis was rather cumbersome, because each category (i.e., topic and development) involved a total of four judgments for each essay. This was necessary because *both* researchers had to judge whether the *two* raters' predictions for topic *and* development on each essay had been realized or not. For example, to determine if an essay's first paragraph successfully framed the development of the essay (i.e., what would come next), each of us had to independently compare the two raters' predictions with the original text. Thus, we each produced two judgments — one for each rater — for each category (topic and development), making four judgments per researcher per essay. The need to view the data in this way, then, created a total of eight judgments for each of the 50 essays, or 400 judgments in all. In order to collapse the data so that they would be comprehensible, we calculated the mean and standard deviations of the number of "yes" judgments to illustrate the mean number of instances where the framing raters' predictions were realized in the actual essays. Table 9.2 provides a summary of the results of this framing analysis. In addition, because mention of individual subjects' essays is useful for discussion, Table 9.3 provides a summary of the subjects, their holistic scores, and a listing of the most frequent judgment (collapsing the total of eight researchers' judgments) that the subjects received for both topic and development predictions on both essays.

An examination of Table 9.2 indicates that subjects at the beginning and intermediate levels were more successful in framing the essays they wrote in response to the field-specific prompt such that native readers of English were able to predict both the topics of the essays and how the writers would develop them. For example, the raters correctly predicted the topics of an average of 4.50 of the progress essays written by beginning subjects. They

TABLE 9.2. Summary of the Means and Standard Deviations of the Number of Essays for Which Framing Expectations Were Realized*

| | | Expectations Realized | | | |
|---|---|---|---|---|---|
| | | Topic | | Development | |
| Level | Topic | Yes | No | Yes | No |
| Beginning (n = 10) | Progress | 4.50 (.50) | 5.50 (.50) | 4.25 (1.48) | 5.75 (1.48) |
| | Field | 6.25 (.83) | 3.75 (.83) | 7.50 (.50) | 2.50 (.50) |
| Intermediate (n = 10) | Progress | 2.50 (.50) | 7.50 (.50) | 3.00 (1.00) | 7.00 (1.00) |
| | Field | 6.00 (1.00) | 4.00 (1.00) | 4.00 (.71) | 6.00 (.71) |
| Advanced (n = 5) | Progress | 3.25 (.83) | 1.75 (.83) | 3.25 (.43) | 1.75 (.43) |
| | Field | 2.50 (.50) | 2.50 (.50) | 2.75 (.83) | 2.25 (.83) |

*The original counts were not even because framing raters did not always agree in their predictions and researchers did not always agree in their judgments of whether those predictions matched the content of the texts. Therefore, the numbers in this table represent the means of the researchers' judgments, and the standard deviations for these means are given in parentheses.

also correctly predicted the development of an average of 4.25 of the same essays. In contrast, of the field-specific essays written by the same subjects, the raters correctly predicted the topics of an average of 6.25 and the development of an average of 7.50. The intermediate subjects' essays show an even greater difference for predicted topic (2.50 for the progress essays and 6.00 for the field-specific essays). Their field-specific essays also resulted in a slight improvement over their progress essays for framing with respect to development, though in both instances fewer of the raters' expectations were realized in the actual essays.

Only the advanced subjects did not appear to frame their field-specific essays better than they did their progress essays. In fact, as Table 9.3 indicates, the raters' predictions of topic and development for the field-specific essays were realized in the essays of only two of the five advanced subjects (subjects #21 and #23). The raters' predictions were not realized in the essays of another two (subjects #22 and #24). For the last subject (#25), one rater's predictions were realized, and the other's were not.

Of the two subjects whose first paragraphs were not framed in such a way for the raters to make accurate predictions of the topic and development,

TABLE 9.3. Summary of Individual Scores and Judgments for Framing

| | | | | Expectations Realized | | | |
| | | Holistic Score | | Progress | | Field-Specific | |
| Level | Subj. | Prog. | Field | Topic | Devel. | Topic | Devel. |
|---|---|---|---|---|---|---|---|
| | 1 | 2 | 2 | N | N | N/Y* | Y |
| | 2 | 6 | 3 | Y | Y | N | N |
| | 3 | 4 | 7 | N/Y | N | Y | Y |
| | 4 | 7 | 5 | Y | N/Y | Y | N/Y |
| Beginning | 5 | 2 | 9 | N/Y | N/Y | Y | Y |
| (n = 10) | 6 | 4 | 12 | N/Y | Y | Y | Y |
| | 7 | 5 | 7 | N | Y | N | Y |
| | 8 | 2 | 8 | N | N | Y | Y |
| | 9 | 5 | 2 | N | N | N | N |
| | 10 | 7 | 7 | Y | N/Y | Y | Y |
| | 11 | 8 | 8 | N | N/Y | N | N/Y |
| | 12 | 4 | 9 | N/Y | Y | Y | Y |
| | 13 | 3 | 10 | N | N | Y | Y |
| | 14 | 6 | 4 | N | N | N/Y | N/Y |
| Intermediate | 15 | 4 | 12 | N/Y | N/Y | Y | Y |
| (n = 10) | 16 | 12 | 6 | Y | Y | N/Y | N |
| | 17 | 2 | 4 | N | N | N/Y | N |
| | 18 | 3 | 11 | N | N | Y | N |
| | 19 | 8 | 2 | N/Y | N | N | N |
| | 20 | 5 | 9 | N | N | N/Y | N |
| | 21 | 3 | 8 | N | N | Y | Y |
| Advanced | 22 | 4 | 10 | Y | Y | N | N |
| (n = 5) | 23 | 7 | 7 | Y | Y | Y | Y |
| | 24 | 10 | 4 | Y | Y | N | N |
| | 25 | 5 | 11 | N/Y | N/Y | N/Y | N/Y |

*Both Y and N are reported to indicate cases in which either framing raters or researchers disagreed in their judgments. In most cases, the disagreements occurred between framing raters, not researchers.

one (subject #22) received a higher holistic score on the field-specific essay than he did on the progress essay, though the latter led to better predictions of topic and development on the part of the raters. In contrast, the other (subject #24) received a much lower score on his field-specific essay. An examination of the introductory paragraphs written by these subjects and the raters' predictions that were based on the paragraphs may shed some light on this apparent discrepancy in the general patterns found.

As the science is not stable, and as the theorems and ideas are subjected to changes and additions, we find controversial issues arising every day in most of the fields of science because every new idea or theorem will be approved or rejected by the scientists and professionals, and the tools for this fight are the researches conducted to support or reject this new idea. (Subject #22, advanced level)

This subject was clearly providing a general orientation to the overall theme of the prompt in order to introduce a controversial issue related to his field of study. The first sentence of his second paragraph was "One of the interesting controversial issues arising now is the use of pozolonic materials in the concrete making." He goes on to explain the arguments of those both for and against using these materials and discusses research to support the use of the materials. He ends with a general statement that relates back to his introductory paragraph. The raters, who were only given the introductory paragraph, could obviously not predict that his essay would discuss concrete making; the writer did not fail to frame his essay adequately. This is the only essay in which a frame was provided after the introductory paragraph.

Subject #24's introductory paragraph illustrates a very different case.

> It is still unclear why there are two driving rules in this world, namely right hand driving and left hand driving. People who drive on a particular side of the road never realize why they do it. If we ask them why they drive on that side of the road, they will almost give the same answer, which is that the rule tell them to do so. The authorities who enacts the rule, never gives or explains the reasons why they choose the particular side of the road as the legal side for driving.

Two different explanations may be offered to suggest reasons why this subjects' introductory paragraph did not lead the raters to predict the topic and development of his essay accurately. On the one hand, this paragraph may be a case of inadequate framing. Both raters' predictions appear to have been influenced by the subject's claim that people do things without questioning, because there are rules that tell them to do so. For example, one rater (B) predicted the topic of this essay to be "Things people do as habits." The other (rater A) predicted it to be "People habitually 'follow the rules' without even 1) questioning the rules; and 2) asking *why* there is such a rule in the first place." Similarly, these raters' predictions of the development of the essay focused on the notion of following rules. Their predictions follow.

**Rater B:** What happens if you don't follow the rules, or importance of knowing the rules.

**Rater A:** He may go on to give other examples of situations in which people unquestioningly conduct themselves according to certain rules without making inquiry about them.

Little did Rater A know that left-hand versus right-hand driving, which she thought was just one example, would be the focus of the entire essay (see essay in Appendix A). This illustration may exemplify van Dijk and Kintsch's (1983) claim that "if . . . [readers] are given an illformed, disorganized paragraph, they do not have a frame to base their continuations on and must rely instead on some salient detail that they find in the paragraph" (p. 330). This explanation may also, in part, explain why this subject's holistic score on the field-specific essay was so low.

On the other hand, it may be that the holistic raters had trouble recognizing the theme as a serious disciplinary issue, even though it might have been for this writer, whose field of study is civil engineering (see Table 9.1). This interpretation is supported by the evidence of the framing raters, neither of whom evidently recognized driving rules as the topic of this essay. This second possible explanation relates to the social, contextual nature of writing. That is, who the *reader* is, and what the *context* is will largely determine how a text is interpreted and, in assessment situations, how a text is rated. It may be posited that an informed reader, for example, a civil engineer, would have rated subject #24's essay very differently from the ways in which the lay readers rated it. This interpretation also might explain in part the holistic raters' low scores for this essay; that is, not recognizing the issue as disciplinary, they might have concluded that the essay did not respond appropriately to the prompt.

A quick perusal of subjects' holistic scores and judgments of framing (Table 9.3) shows a general pattern: Subjects received higher scores on the essays—regardless of prompt type—that they framed well enough for readers to be able to make predictions about the content to come. It is important to note, however, that a few subjects' essays (e.g., those written by subjects #14, #19, and #22) do not appear on the surface to fit this general pattern.

*Elements of task compliance.*   Recall that the researchers served as the raters for analyzing the elements of task compliance. Separate interrater reliability coefficients were determined for each element of task compliance. Therefore, a total of four coefficients were calculated for the judgments made on the progress essays, and a total of six for the judgments made on the field-specific essays. The percentages of agreement and corresponding Cohen's kappa coefficients for the identified progress elements of definition, position statement, reasons, and examples were 92% (.84), 100% (1.00), 80% (.45), and 76%, (.39), respectively. We achieved 100% agreement (with Cohen's kappa coefficients of 1.00) on our identifications of five of the six field-specific elements of task compliance and 92% agreement (Cohen's kappa = .83) on the sixth, the element labeled as "Reasons."

The individual judgments for the progress and field-specific essays are listed along with the corresponding holistic scores in Table 9.4. A brief scanning of the judgments in Table 9.4 reveals that the vast majority of the judgments were positive (i.e., "yes" judgments). In other words, viewed in this way, the data appear to indicate that there were not many differences with regard to the subjects' inclusion of the various elements. The data, however, are admittedly deceiving. That is, although they do indicate the existence of the elements, they do not indicate how (or whether) the elements were put together to convey the writer's message. Despite this limitation, a few points can be made about this analysis.

As Table 9.4 shows, more subjects were successful in including position statements in their progress essays than in their field-specific essays. In addition, in general, position statements in the progress essays tended to occur at the beginning of the essays, whereas in the field-specific essays, they tended to appear in the middle or at the end. The distinct places in which the position statements appeared in the essays may be due to the wording of the prompts.

In order to determine why a total of nine subjects did not include position statements in their field-specific essays, we took a closer look at these essays. Of the three beginning subjects' essays that did not contain position statements, we found that one subject's essay (#1) was not finished and that two (#2 and #9) were off topic. That is, the holistic raters who scored the essays in the original study (Tedick, 1988) judged the essays to be off topic.

Of the four intermediate subjects' essays that did not contain position statements, two subjects' (#16 and #17) essays were not complete, and two (#18 and #19) were off topic. The two advanced subjects' (#23 and #25) essays that did not contain position statements were also judged to be off topic by the holistic raters in the original study. All but one of the essays (that of subject #2) judged to be off topic did, in fact, contain position statements, but these statements did not meet the researchers' requirement that they specifically address the given task. Interestingly, some of these subjects (#9 and #19) were penalized (by receiving lower holistic scores) for being off topic, whereas others (subjects #18, #23, and #25) were not.

It is interesting that we had trouble agreeing on our judgments for the inclusion of reasons and examples in the progress essays written by beginning and intermediate subjects. The two columns referring to "reasons" and "examples" for the progress essay in Table 9.4 reflect our discrepancies (that is, "Y/N" judgments indicate that one of us judged an essay as containing an element while the other did not).

Close examinations of the progress essays that resulted in discrepant judgments on our part led us to believe that some of the discrepancies may have been caused by essays lacking coherence and/or clear organization, making it difficult for us to interpret the elements similarly. Upon

TABLE 9.4. Summary of Individual Scores and Researchers' Judgments for Elements of Task Compliance

| Level | Subj. | Holistic Score | | Judgments for Elements of Task Compliance | | | | | | | | | |
| | | Prog. | Field | Progress Essays | | | | Field Essays | | | | | |
| | | | | 1 | 2 | 3 | 4 | 1 | 2 | 3 | 4 | 5 | 6 |
| | 1 | 2 | 2 | Y | Y | N | Y | N | Y | Y | Y | N | N |
| | 2 | 6 | 3 | Y | Y | N/Y | Y | Y | N | N | N | N | N |
| | 3 | 4 | 7 | Y | Y | Y | Y | Y | Y | Y | Y | Y | Y |
| | 4 | 7 | 5 | N | Y | Y | N/Y | Y | Y | Y | Y | Y | Y |
| Begin. | 5 | 2 | 9 | N | Y | Y | Y | Y | Y | Y | Y | Y | Y |
| (n = 10) | 6 | 4 | 12 | N | Y | Y | Y | Y | Y | Y | Y | Y | Y |
| | 7 | 5 | 7 | N | Y | Y | Y | N | Y | Y | Y | Y | Y |
| | 8 | 2 | 8 | N | Y | Y | N | N | Y | Y | Y | Y | Y |
| | 9 | 5 | 2 | Y | Y | Y | N/Y | Y | N | N | N | N | N |
| | 10 | 7 | 7 | N/Y | Y | Y | Y | Y | Y | Y | Y | Y | Y |
| | 11 | 8 | 8 | N/Y | Y | Y | Y | Y | Y | Y | Y | Y | N/Y |
| | 12 | 4 | 9 | Y | Y | N | N/Y | N | Y | Y | Y | Y | Y |
| | 13 | 3 | 10 | Y | Y | Y | N/Y | Y | Y | Y | Y | Y | Y |
| | 14 | 6 | 4 | N | Y | N/Y | N/Y | N | Y | Y | Y | Y | Y |
| Inter. | 15 | 4 | 12 | N | Y | N/Y | Y | Y | Y | Y | Y | Y | Y |
| (n = 10) | 16 | 12 | 6 | Y | N | N | N | Y | Y | Y | Y | N | N |
| | 17 | 2 | 4 | Y | Y | Y | Y | Y | Y | Y | N | N | N |
| | 18 | 3 | 11 | N | Y | Y | Y | N | N | N | N | N | N |
| | 19 | 8 | 2 | N | Y | N/Y | N/Y | N | N | N | N | N | N |
| | 20 | 5 | 9 | N | Y | N/Y | Y | Y | Y | Y | Y | Y | N/Y |
| | 21 | 3 | 8 | N | Y | Y | N | N | Y | Y | Y | Y | Y |
| Advan. | 22 | 4 | 10 | N | Y | Y | Y | N | Y | Y | Y | Y | Y |
| (n = 5) | 23 | 7 | 7 | Y | Y | Y | Y | Y | N | N | N | N | N |
| | 24 | 10 | 4 | Y | Y | Y | Y | N | Y | Y | Y | Y | Y |
| | 25 | 5 | 11 | N | Y | Y | Y | N | Y | N | N | N | N |

Note: Progress Elements of Task Compliance: 1 = Definition; 2 = Position Statement; 3 = Reasons; 4 = Examples. Field Elements of Task Compliance: 1 = ID of Field; 2 = ID of Controversy; 3 = ID of 2 Positions; 4 = Explanation/Development of 1 or 2 Positions; 5 = Position Statement; 6 = Reasons.

examining some of the essays, we discovered that a number of them looked more like prewriting/brainstorming exercises rather than essays. In fact, several of the essays ended with new position statements different from those found at the beginning of the essays. It appeared as though the subjects ended up talking themselves into a different stance on the issue as they wrote their essays. (This interpretation is necessarily hypothetical in light of the fact that it was impossible for us to ask the writers to explain the processes they went through as they composed their essays.) The essay written by subject #14 provides a particularly interesting example (see Appendix A). This subject begins his essay by quoting the prompt and indicating at least partial support of the statement that progress makes people lazy. Then he makes a case for the need for progress and appears to contradict his original position statement. He finishes with a new position statement, that is "progress makes us comfortable." This apparent jumping may have led us to see different elements in the essay. Kantz (1990) reports similar interrater discrepancies in judgments on the coherence of certain L1 students' texts.

In contrast to our identifications of the elements of task compliance in the progress essays, our identifications of the elements for the field-specific essays were unusually accurate. A brief glance at the individual judgments for elements of task compliance (see Table 9.4) illustrates the overwhelming number of positive (i.e., "yes") judgments in this analysis. The essays that did not contain the majority of the elements were, not surprisingly, those same essays that did not contain position statements. As explained previously, these essays were found to be either incomplete or judged to be off topic. Of this group, essays that merit discussion are those that were awarded high holistic scores even though, in our opinion, they did not address the task specified. Two of these essays, one written by intermediate subject #18 and one by advanced subject #25, are presented in their entirety in Appendix A. They both received very high holistic scores of 11.

In contrast, other subjects (beginning subjects #2 and #9, and intermediate subject #19), who did not address the task specified in the field-specific prompt, received lower holistic scores on their essays. It is interesting to note that a number of subjects' progress essays were judged to be off topic by the holistic scorers in the original study (Tedick, 1988). An examination of some of these essays (written by intermediate subjects #13 and #15, and advanced subjects #21 and #25) revealed that their writers all had one thing in common: They all assigned a meaning to *progress* that differed from the one implied in the prompt. That is, they all approached the term *progress* from a personal achievement—one progresses when one learns—point of view (see, for example, subject #25's progress essay in Appendix A).

These examples illustrate an anomaly in the holistic scoring. Some subjects who did not address the field-specific task were successful in that they achieved *high* holistic scores regardless of the fact that their responses did not address the task. Other subjects who did not address the task specified (in some cases for the field-specific task) or who were judged to be off topic (in four cases for the progress task) did *not* receive higher holistic scores. Two possible explanations may be offered to explain the anomaly. The first is that some writers may be successful in employing strategies that permit them at once to avoid doing the task specified in the prompt, and to get away with it. A number of researchers have reported on a similar phenomenon shown by L1 writers, particularly with respect to content-area writing tasks or essay examinations (e.g., Bereiter & Scardamalia, 1987; Doyle, 1983; Nelson, 1989; Nespor, 1987; Tedick, Bernhardt, & DeVille, 1991). For example, Bereiter and Scardamalia describe what they refer to as the "knowledge-telling strategy" as one that writers use to tell what they know by employing key words in the question and following to some degree the form of the question. Although these writers do not answer the question as it was intended, they end up with acceptable scores. The field-specific essays written by subjects #18 and #25 could be examples of this phenomenon (see Appendix A).

A second plausible explanation is that responses may lie on a continuum of acceptable/unacceptable responses based on with whom (reader or writer) authority resides. One could argue that in an assessment situation, the raters of the essays have authority over the writers in that the ultimate decision of whether or not the essay meets acceptable standards lies with the raters. Such authority may shift, however, depending on the subject matter of the essay. The progress and field-specific tasks used in the present study resulted in essays that provide illustrations of the shift in authority.

The holistic raters clearly have the authority in reading essays written on the progress topic. Indeed, they judged four of the 25 progress essays as being off-topic because the writers applied a different meaning to the term *progress* in addressing the task (cf. Prior, this volume). Meaning is rooted in its prior use as much as it is forged in its present context. Words have histories that are socially situated. Thus, it could be argued that the progress task is culturally biased. That is, most if not all Americans would recognize that progress means technological advance in the context of this writing task. Yet, this definition is not absolute. It is interesting that in the four cases where the progress essays were judged to be off topic, the raters were not willing to entertain the writers' different interpretation for *progress* and to read the essays within that interpretation; they had the authority and chose to exercise it as such.

Alternatively, it may be argued that for some field-specific essays, such as that written by subject #18 (see Appendix A), the writers had authority over the raters. Subject #18's essay reads more like an abstract for a research study than a response to the field-specific prompt, yet it was not judged to be off topic by the holistic raters in the original study, and it received a high holistic score of 11. It could very well be that the raters were simply out of their league with the discussion of electron diffraction techniques; that is, the subject matter of the essay allowed the writer to retain authority over the raters.

A different example of writer authority can be seen with subject #25's field-specific essay (see Appendix A). Here it seems that interest on the part of the reader (or some kind of empathy with an issue of cultural currency) could explain why the holistic raters awarded a high score to the essay even though it did not address the task. The writer's authority in this case is manifested in her ability to engage the readers in the subject matter of her essay so much so that they ignored the fact that she did not respond to the prompt.

## PEDAGOGICAL IMPLICATIONS AND DIRECTIONS FOR FUTURE RESEARCH

The rhetorical analysis of the 50 essays has uncovered a variety of issues that would not have been considered had the holistic scores awarded to the essays in the original study been accepted at face value. The conclusions and questions we raise here remain tentative, because the analyses focused on the writing itself rather than on the writers and raters. Future research needs to continue exploring aspects of the processes readers go through as they score essays holistically, as has been the focus of a limited number of studies to date (Freedman, 1981, 1984; Huot, 1988; Janopoulos, 1987; Tedick, 1993; Vaughan, 1991). That said, we can make several points and raise several questions on the basis of this study.

First, the present study has led us to question the notion of task comparability. Different task types (having different underlying purposes and/or different subject matter) will elicit different kinds of writing; indeed, different academic disciplines elicit writing that is linguistically and rhetorically different, a theme implicit in every chapter in this volume. This question holds important implications for writing assessment. The TOEFL Test of Written English (TWE), for example, has used topics dealing with a variety of subject matters that are categorized under two topic types (compare/contrast, and graph/chart interpretation). Reid (1990) reported the results of a study comparing essays written on the distinct TWE topic types which revealed that they elicited different kinds of writing. These different kinds of writing, in turn, may have differing degrees of influence on the raters. Therefore, students randomly assigned to write on one topic over another may be at a disadvantage. This issue of task comparability must be addressed in ways that reach beyond correlational studies that use the holistic scores as the means for comparison (e.g, Carlson, Bridgman, Camp, & Waanders, 1985).

Secondly, framing appears to be an important variable contributing to the ways in which holistic raters scored the essays. In general, when subjects framed their essays well, they received higher holistic scores on those essays—regardless of prompt type. In addition, more subjects appeared, in general, to be more successful in framing the field-specific essays than they were in framing their progress essays. This finding has clear pedagogical implications. ESL students need to be taught how to frame their written work in ways that will facilitate the reader's comprehension. Certainly having students examine the ways in which essays in their particular academic fields are framed will help them to learn this important concept.

Finally, the different subject matter of the two topics raises some questions regarding the nature of the relationship between the readers and the writers and the ultimate effect on the holistic scores assigned to essays in the original study. The individual cases illustrated in this chapter particularly in the analysis of elements of task compliance (e.g., subjects #18, #24, and #25) are examples of anomalous holistic scoring. These cases reveal complex negotiation along dimensions like authority (e.g., #18 and #25's progress essay), subject-matter knowledge (e.g., #18 and #24), and interest (e.g., #25's field essay)—dimensions that are distinctly cultural. They also bring into question the validity of holistic scoring. We cannot continue to accept holistic scores at face value and assume that they are valid indicators of writing quality. We cannot continue to assume validity on the basis of reliability. It is time for teachers, researchers, and evaluation experts involved in ESL writing assessment to move beyond the limits that holistic scoring places on us.

## REFERENCES

Anderson, R. C., & Pearson, D. P. (1984). A schema-theoretic view of basic processes in reading comprehension. In D. P. Pearson (Ed.), *Handbook of reading research* (pp. 225–291). New York: Longman.

Bereiter, C., & Scardamalia, M. (1987) *The psychology of written composition*. Hillsdale, NJ: Erlbaum.

Brossell, G. (1983). Rhetorical specification in essay examination topics. *College English, 45,* 165–174.

Brossell, G. (1986). Current research and unanswered questions in writing assessment. In K. L. Greenberg, H. S. Wiener, & R. A. Donovan (Eds.), *Writing assessment* (pp. 168–182). New York: Longman.

Brossell, G., & Hoetker Ash, B. (1984). An experiment with the wording of essay topics. *College Composition and Communication, 35,* 423–425.

Campbell, D. T., & Stanley, J. C. (1963). *Experimental and quasiexperimental designs for research.* Boston, MA: Houghton Mifflin Co.

Carlson, S. B., Bridgman, B., Camp, R., & Waanders, J. (1985). *Relationship of admission test scores to writing performance of native and nonnative speakers of English* (Res. Rep. No. 19). Princeton, NJ: Educational Testing Service.

Charney, D. A. (1984). The validity of using holistic scoring to evaluate writing: A critical overview. *Research in the Teaching of English, 18* (1), 65–81.

Chesky, J. A. (1984). The effects of prior knowledge and audience on writing. *Dissertation Abstracts International, 45,* 2740A. (University Microfilms No. DA 8428407).

Chesky, J. A., & Hiebert, E. H. (1987). The effects of prior knowledge and audience on high school students' writing. *Journal of Educational Research, 80,* 304–313.

Cohen, J. (1960). A coefficient of agreement for nominal scales. *Educational and Psychological Measurement, 20,* 37–46.

Connor, U. (1990). Linguistic/rhetorical measures for international persuasive student writing. *Research in the Teaching of English, 24,* 67–87.

Connor, U., & Kaplan, R. B. (Eds.). (1987). *Writing across languages: Analysis of L2 text.* Reading, MA: Addison-Wesley.

Crowhurst, M. C., & Piché, G. L. (1979). Audience and mode of discourse effects on syntactic complexity in writing on two grade levels. *Research in the Teaching of English, 13,* 101–109.

Doyle, W. (1983). Academic work. *Review of Educational Research, 53,* 159–199.

Faigley, L., Cherry, R. D., Jolliffe, D. A., & Skinner, A. M. (1985). *Assessing writers' knowledge and processes of composing.* Norwood, NJ: Ablex.

Flower, L. S., & Hayes, J. (1981). A cognitive process theory of writing. *College Composition and Communication, 32,* 365–387.

Freedman, S. W. (1981). Influence of evaluation of expository essays: Beyond the text. *Research in the Teaching of English, 15,* 245–255.

Freedman, S. W. (1984). The registers of students and professional expository writing: Influences on teachers' responses. In R. Beach & L. S. Bridwell (Eds.), *New directions in composition research* (pp. 334–347). New York: The Guilford Press.

Gere, A. R. (1980). Written composition: Toward a theory of evaluation. *College English, 42,* 44–48.

Greenberg, K. L. (1981). *The effects of variations in essay questions on the writing of CUNY freshmen.* New York: City University of New York Instructional Resource Center.

Hamp-Lyons, L. (1990). Second language writing: Assessment issues. In B. Kroll (Ed.), *Second language writing: Research insights for the classroom* (pp. 69–87). New York: Cambridge University Press.

Hoetker, J. (1982). Essay examination topics and students' writing. *College Composition and Communication, 33,* 377–392.

Hoey, M. (1983). *On the surface of discourse.* London: George Allen and Unwin.

Huot, B. (1988). *The validity of holistic scoring: A comparison of the talk-aloud protocols of expert and novice holistic raters.* Unpublished doctoral dissertation, Indiana University of Pennsylvania, Indiana, PA.

Huot, B. (1990). Reliability, validity, and holistic scoring: What we know and what we need to know. *College Composition and Communication, 41* (2), 201213.

Janopoulos, M. (1987). The role of comprehension in holistic evaluation of second language writing proficiency at the university level (Doctoral dissertation, The Ohio State University). *Dissertation Abstracts International, 48,* 1137A. (University Microfilms No. DA 8717654).

Kantz, M. J. (1990). Promises of coherence, weak content, and strong organization: An analysis of the students' texts. In L. Flower et al. (Eds), *Reading-to-write: Exploring a cognitive and social process* (pp. 76–95). New York: Oxford University Press.

Langer, J. A. (1984). The effects of available information on responses to school writing tasks. *Research in the Teaching of English, 18,* 27–44.

Matsuhashi, A. (1982). Explorations in the real-time production of written discourse. In M. Nystrand (Ed.), *What writers know: The language, process, and structure of written discourse* (pp. 269–290). New York: Academic Press.

McCutcheon, D. (1986). Domain knowledge and linguistic knowledge in the development of writing ability. *Journal of Memory and Language, 25,* 431–444.

Neilsen, L., & Piché, G. (1981). The influence of headed nominal complexity and lexical choice on teachers' evaluation of writing. *Research in the Teaching of English, 15,* 65–73.

Nelson, J. (1989). *This was an easy assignment: Examining how students interpret academic writing tasks* (Tech. Rep.) Pittsburgh, PA: Center for the Study of Writing, Carnegie Mellon University.

Nespor, J. (1987). Academic tasks in a high school English class. *Curriculum Inquiry, 17,* 203–228.

Odell, L., & Cooper, C. (1980). Procedures for evaluating writing: Assumptions and needed research. *College English, 42,* 35–43.

Plasse, L. A. (1981). *The influence of audience on the assessment of student writing.* Unpublished doctoral dissertation, University of Connecticut, Storrs, CT.

Purves, A. C. (1988). *Writing across languages and cultures.* Newbury Park, CA: Sage.

Quellmalz, E. S., Capell, F. J., & Chou, C. P. (1982). Effects of discourse and response mode on the measurement of writing competence. *Journal of Educational Measurement, 19,* 241–258.

Reid, J. (1990, March). *Responding to different topic types: A quantitative analysis from a contrastive rhetoric perspective.* Paper presented at the Annual Convention of Teachers of English to Speakers of Other Languages, San Francisco, CA.

Rowntree, D. (1977). *Assessing students: How shall we know them?* London: Harper and Row.

Rumelhart, D. E. (1980). Schemata: The building blocks of cognition. In R. J. Spiro, B. C. Bruce, & W. F. Brewer (Eds.), *Theoretical issues in reading comprehension* (pp. 33–58). Hillsdale, NJ: Erlbaum.

Ruth, L., & Murphy, S. (1988). *Designing writing tasks for the assessment of writing.* Norwood, NJ: Ablex.

Scarcella, R. C. (1984). How writers orient their readers in expository essays: A comparative study of native and non-native English writers. *TESOL Quarterly, 18,* 671–688.

Scherer, D. L. (1985). *Measuring the measurements: A study of the evaluation of writing—An annotated bibliography.* (ERIC Document Reproduction Service No. ED 260 455).

Spiro, R. J. (1980). Constructive processes in prose comprehension and recall. In R. J. Spiro, B. C. Bruce, & W. F. Brewer (Eds.), *Theoretical issues in reading comprehension* (pp. 245–278). Hillsdale, NJ: Erlbaum.

Steffensen, M. S., & Joag-Dev, C. (1984). Cultural knowledge and reading. In J. C. Alderson & A. H. Urquhart (Eds.), *Reading in a foreign language* (pp. 48–61). New York: Longman.

Tedick, D. J. (1988). *The effects of topic familiarity on the writing performance of non-native writers of English at the graduate level.* Unpublished doctoral dissertation, The Ohio State University, Columbus, OH.

Tedick, D. J. (1990). ESL writing assessment: Subject-matter knowledge and its impact on performance. *English for Specific Purposes, 9,* 123–143.

Tedick, D. J., Bernhardt, E. B., & DeVille, C. (1991). Interpreting essay examination topics used for assessing content knowledge: Differences among test makers, test raters, and test takers. *Journal of College Reading and Learning, 24* (1), 63–80.

Tedick, D. J., & Dubetz, N. E. (1991, April). *Differences between ESL students' writing on two topics: A look at linguistic features.* Paper presented at the American Educational Research Association, Chicago, IL.

Tedick, D. J. (1993, April). *A multidimensional exploration of scoring processes: What influences raters' judgments of second language writing?* Paper presented at the American Educational Research Association, Atlanta, GA.

van Dijk, T., & Kintsch, W. (1983). *Strategies of discourse comprehension.* New York: Academic Press.

Vaughan, D. (1991). Holistic assessment: What goes on in the rater's mind? In L. Hamp-Lyons (Ed.), *Assessing second language writing in academic contexts* (pp. 111–125). Norwood, NJ: Ablex.

White, E. M. (1985). *Teaching and assessing writing.* San Francisco, CA: Jossey-Bass.

Winfield, F. E., & Barnes-Felfeli, P. (1982). The effects of familiar and unfamiliar cultural context on foreign language composition. *Modern Language Journal, 66,* 373–378.

Witte, S., Meyer, P., Cherry, R., & Trachsel, M. (1986). *Holistic evaluation: Issues, theory, and practice.* New York: Guilford Press.

# APPENDIX A
## SAMPLE ESSAYS

### Advanced Subject #24 — Field-Specific Essay

It is still unclear why there are two driving rules in this world, namely right hand driving and left hand driving. People who drive on a particular side of the road never realize why they do it. If we ask them why they drive on that side of the road, they will almost give the same answer, which is that the rule tell them to do so. The authorities who enacts the rule, never gives or explains the reasons why they choose they particular side of the road as the legal side for driving.

The question "which is the wrong side of the road" has never been answered for hundred of years. Physically, according to research, ninety percent of the people are right-handed. In the early days, a person who was approached by oncoming stranger tended to keep to left, a defensive position for a right handed person. A person also mounts on a horse from the left side, keeping him to the left side of the road. This physical condition formed the early rule of driving to the left of the road. But as the vehicles became larger, as the large horse-drawn wagon, the driver was seated to the left side of the wagon to enable him controlling the horses. This position lead the driver to keep to the right of the road. The two types of driving position has been carried over to the modern world.

The left-hand side driving is formed by physical nature, and the right hand side is formed by habit. In the modern world both of the driving rules are still used. It seems that there is not wrong side of the road, because there is no argument arise about the two rules. From the science and technology point of view, there must be differences between the two rules. The left hand driving is the right rule because it follows the human physical nature, while the right-hand driving is wrong because it is formed by the habit in the past.

### Intermediate Subject #14 — Progress Essay

Progress makes us lazy. That's right, in some aspects. In the morning we just pour some milk into the cereal for breakfast. For supper, we have microwave pizza. After that, we may just sit in front of TV during the whole night. In the office, we may sit in front of a computer. Writing and labor working are decreasing. Compared with our grandparents, we are lazy.

Why do we need progress? Walking to visit a relative lived far away from us is quite a hard job. So we want a easy way to do that. That is the reason why we have trains, cars, airplanes. We save the labor and time as the progress we make. Nobody wants to do the routine work, sitting there just plug something into the other, so we need a automatic machine. Need makes progress. What is the need. Need to do less labor work, to do something more quickly. The reason why we need to do things more quickly is we need more time to think, to do other works. We want to increase our productivity, to increase our income, to have more vacation. But that is not lazy. Lazy is just sit there and has no productivity.

We want to do things more easily, so we have need of progress. And progress makes us more time to do things we want to do. If we have more time, we will make more progress. So, we should say that progress makes us comfortable.

## Advanced Subject #25 — Progress Essay

In my own experience, progress does not make me lazy. It, however, makes me more active to work toward the specific objectives. I think that stagnation is more likely to cause passiveness, not progress.

During the period of time when I learned to play the piano, progress or improvement always propelled me to practice more industrially. I've never thought that improvement is the synonym of terminal. In the light of pursuing academic achievement, progress also results in stronger motive to purchase greater accomplishment. That is why a baby will not stop learning to run after it learns how to walk.

The process of learning is endless. Once someone's potential is developed during the energetic process, he usually becomes a more earnest and enthusiastic learner.

## Intermediate Subject #18 — Field-Specific Essay

The displacement vector of stacking faults in pyrite has been studied for a long time. Through the X-Ray and electron diffraction techniques, some researchers concluded that the displacement vector is [0.27, 0, 0], i.e., the displacement vectors lie in the 100 plane.

But, due to the peculiar diffraction property of pyrites, there are some forbident diffraction spots, and these diffraction spots are essential to verify experimently wheather the component of the vector normal to the 100 plane exists or not. Lacking of such diffraction spots, one can not says there is no such a normal component, one can only say such a normal component might not exist.

Although most of the pyrite lack of the necessary diffraction spots, one kind of pyrite came from a specific origin has an abnormal electron diffraction phenomenon. Due to this phenomenon, the forbident diffraction spots in other pyrites will appear in this kind of pyrite. With these diffraction spots, we can determine wheather the normal component of the displacement exist.

From the electron diffraction study by using the abnormal electron diffraction phenomenon of pyrite, our research group found that the normal component of the displacement vector does exist, and its value should be 1/2, i.e., the displacement vector should be [0.27, 1/2, 0]. This result is also consistent with the value deduced by mathematical calculation.

## Advanced Subject #25 — Field-Specific Essay

As a journalism major, I pay much attention to the problems on press development in a society.

In Taiwan, there has been a 38-year-old prohibition on newspaper establishment and pages of papers, although the government claims that it is kind of regularization instead of sanction. Such a politically-viewed policy has led Taiwan's press to monopoly and malignant competition. And the editorial policies of most existing print media are quite conservative. Even some privately owned newspapers are regarded as the mouthpieces of government.

After lifting the martial law and the ban on setting up political parties earlier this year, the government in Taiwan decided to recall the restriction on newspaper foundation and enlarge the limit to newspapers' page to six pages from next year. It is really an exciting change in the history of Taiwan's press although there might be some problems after that, for example, the originally well-running newspapers may become more powerful and monopolistic thus lead smaller papers to an end.

# CHAPTER 10

# A Comparison of the Use of Citations in Chinese and English Academic Discourse*

**Joel Bloch**
*Lake Superior State University*

**Lan Chi**
*Buchanan Ingersoll*

This chapter explores recent research in how citations are used in academic research papers as a basis for a study in comparative Chinese-language/English-language rhetoric. Specifically, we explore the question of the similarities and differences between how Chinese-language writers and English-language authors use source texts when writing in their own languages. Two factors are considered: the date of the citation and its function. The results show areas where there are both similarities and differences in the way these source texts are used. Most interestingly, the results show how Chinese-language writers are aware of the social context of their texts in much the same way as are English-language writers, although both these groups may express these relationships in different ways. In the second part of the chapter, we show how the use of the source texts in the Chinese texts reflects both the multiplicity of possible forms of rhetoric as well as how traditional forms of rhetoric have evolved from the time of Confucius to modern times. In the conclusion of the chapter, we suggest how the results of the study can be used as a basis for teaching academic writing to Chinese writers or any group of students who may not have experience with the Western traditions of academic writing.

Anecdotal evidence from teachers of Chinese students has argued that one of the main problems Chinese-speaking ESL students have with writing

---

*We would like to thank David Banks and Hao Lingxin for their assistance in preparing this chapter.

academic compositions is knowing how to use source texts (Basham, Ray, & Whalley, 1991; Comprone, 1990; Matalene, 1985). A common complaint from these teachers is that Chinese students often overrely on their source texts; they only recite back what the authors had already said, sometimes to the extent of plagiarizing these texts. The social and historical structure of Asian society has often been cited as a reason why students from Asian cultures in general have problems with taking critical stances in regard to source texts. Connor and Kramer (this volume) observe that in graduate management courses, Asian students may refuse to take critical positions because of their perception of feeling subordinate in the social structure of the business culture. Classical Chinese rhetoric has likewise been cited as a source for some of these problems (Cheng, 1985; Matalene, 1985; Scollon, in press).

Often examples from the teachings of Confucius or from the traditional Chinese civil service examinations have been used to support the argument that the root of the problem Chinese writers have with using source texts is the cultural norms that have characterized Chinese society at least since Confucius. Confucianism and the civil service examinations are both, in fact, logical sources of the problem. Confucianism has long been seen as a philosophy which places great emphasis on memorizing the classic texts and being able to recite them by heart. The famous Confucian dictum "I transmit but I do not create" (Chan, 1963, p. 31) seems to indicate that in traditional Chinese thinking, the ability to recite the content of the classic texts is more important than the ability to produce original ideas. It is this tradition of transmitting information but not creating new information that is often cited as the reason that Chinese students may have difficulty with the rhetorical demands of English-language compositions.

Unfortunately, many assumptions made about how Chinese students write were based on the errors they made when writing in a second language, especially English (e.g., Kaplan, 1988; Ostler, 1987; Reid, 1988). This methodological bias makes some claims vulnerable to charges that they ignored developmental factors such as whether Chinese writers had any experience writing academic essays (Mohan & Lo, 1985). If, as has been found with many NES students, they have little or no experience writing from sources (Applebee, 1984), it cannot be expected that these writers can produce acceptable academic writing, regardless of their cultural backgrounds. Moreover, much of the research has examined Chinese rhetoric only to the degree that this research can verify that L1 rhetorical transfer is the problem. This has meant that not only has positive transfer been ignored, but also any facet of Chinese rhetoric that does not support the basic premises of the research.

Recently, research has begun to look more closely at comparing first language (L1) and second language (L2) academic writing in hopes of eliminating this developmental factor. For example, studies comparing the introductions to Chinese and Western academic texts have shown that while there are structural similarities in the introductions of Chinese and Western academic texts, the one most significant difference is in how they use prior texts (Bloch, 1988, 1991). Although most of the American texts used in both studies cited several texts in their introductions, the Chinese texts used few if any citations in their introductions. This lack of citations could cause a significant problem since the misuse of prior texts may undermine the rhetorical strategies a writer uses in the introduction.

Given the types of criticisms that have been made of Chinese L2 writers, it is useful to consider more closely the Western model of citation use that these students are expected to emulate. In order to understand why these students may have problems with the rhetorical use of citations, it is also useful to understand the cultural tradition of rhetoric they bring to the writing task. The purpose of this chapter, then, is first to examine how Western writers use source texts to make new claims. The second part of the chapter will present results of a study comparing how citations are used in Chinese and American academic texts. The third part of the chapter interprets the results of this study in the context of the historical development of Chinese rhetoric.

## THE USE OF CITATIONS IN ACADEMIC WRITING IN THE WEST

### Rhetorical Views of Proprietary Claims

The citation of articles is part of the reward system that motivates writers to publish in the first place, what Mulkay (1972) calls the process of "social exchange" in an academic community. According to Mulkay,

> There is a growing body of evidence that within the scientific community information is exchanged for professional recognition. To put this more specifically, the evidence establishes four things: firstly, that scientists supply information to their colleagues; secondly, that they receive recognition in return; thirdly, that recognition is experienced as a reward; and fourthly, that recognition is forthcoming primarily for contributions which conform to current cognitive and technical norms. (p. 23)

Mulkay (1991) has since argued that an academic text must satisfy two basic premises: The text must exhibit "sameness" to account for what has been previously published while also exhibiting a "difference" from these same texts. The "sameness" demonstrates the connection between this chapter and what has been previously published while the "difference" demonstrates that the text has some originality. Especially in the sciences, there has been much research on the use of citations in accomplishing this "sameness/difference." How prior texts are used in creating networks of knowledge has been quantitatively analyzed in a variety of citation studies. Price (1986) has described extensively how science accumulates information through the practice of citation and the immediacy in which that information is useful. A more rhetorical view of citations has been proposed by Bruno Latour. Latour (1988) used metaphors such as military strategy, Byzantine politics, and billiards to describe strategies for which writers use source texts.

> Whatever the tactics, the general strategy is easy to grasp; do whatever you need to the former literature to render it as helpful as possible for the claims you are going to make. The rules are simple enough: weaken your enemies, paralyze those you cannot weaken . . . help your allies if they are attacked, ensure safe communications with those who supply you with indisputable instruments . . . oblige your enemies to fight one another; if you are not sure of winning, be humble and understated. (pp. 37–38)

Though a sociologist and not a rhetorician, Latour feels that the study of rhetoric is of importance in understanding how arguments are developed in scientific and technical texts. He argues that scientists use a variety of rhetorical strategies when making claims about their research. One such rhetorical strategy is what Latour calls the argument from authority, similar to what classical rhetoricians call ethos. Just as with using any form of ethos as support, it matters both who you are and what your background is.

Scientific discourse classifies authority in a text hierarchically so that a text in a scientific journal usually carries more weight than a text in the newspaper. The reason for this, according to Latour, is that texts do not exist as isolated entities but as part of large and complex networks. They are both the mechanism of transmittal of new information and the representation of the information itself (Hunter, 1990). Therefore to oppose an idea published in a particularly prestigious journal would be to oppose not only the person who wrote the article but the entire social network behind the writer, the editorial board, and referees of the journal, perhaps the funding agencies that gave money for the acknowledgment section (Latour, 1988). As a result, such opposition is both difficult and risky, and therefore, it would probably only occur infrequently.

## Using Citations Critically

One use of citations that is of particular interest to a comparative study of Chinese-and English-language texts is how citations are used critically. If the central focus of Chinese rhetoric is harmony (Oliver, 1962), then it could be presumed that Chinese writers would find it difficult to directly criticize others. The research on introductions by Taylor and Chen (1991), in fact, questions the degree of contentiousness found in Chinese rhetoric. On the basis of the results of their analysis, Taylor and Chen argue that perhaps Chinese scientists are not as contentious as their Western counterparts.

Western writers are also limited in how contentious they can be. Scientists are often careful in how they criticize others' research. Gilbert and Mulkay (1984) found that scientists used a contingent repertoire of phrases in their articles that expressed their opinions more politely than how these opinions had been previously expressed orally. Much like the levels of politeness often found in other types of speech acts, these phrases often indirectly stated what in private might have been stated more directly. Their finding can be illustrated by comparing how scientists express their opinions in interviews and how they express their opinions in published articles. For example, in a recent article in *Science* magazine discussing a current debate in geophysics, one scientist accuses another of misinterpreting the data. The second scientist responds that the interpretation of his opponent "lacks scientific rigor" (Kerr, 1989, p. 758). He goes on to say about his opponent that what "he sometimes lacks in experimental rigor, he makes up for by stimulating the community to think about the big questions . . . but you also have to learn the basic physics [of ultrahigh pressures]" (p. 758). This type of personal criticism, where both the methodology and the basic knowledge of another scientist is criticized, is unlikely to be found in a research article published in the same journal.

Within these constraints, it may sometimes be necessary to attack "enemies," those references that oppose the claims of the author. This attack can have many purposes. In some contexts, attacking those contradictions can establish the truth of a claim. In the introduction, an attack can be a way of establishing the reason another paper on this topic needs to be written. This exemplifies what Swales (1981, 1986, 1990) has called "opening a gap" in the prior research. By opening such a gap, the writer is implicitly arguing that the paper is necessary to correct a falsely held belief.

There are a variety of ways of opening a gap. As Gilbert and Mulkay (1984) showed, scientists are often very careful in how they criticize others' research. Critically attacking others' work is one of the more sensitive issues in the use of source texts. Ziman (1968) points out that scientists meticulously avoid personal attacks in order to maintain a free flow of information although, as is shown later, attacks can be made outside the scientific paper. Though Swales' work on introductions has shown that an attack on prior research is only one of several possible ways of justifying the publication of a paper, it, nevertheless, provides a powerful rationale for new research.

One such way is to divide those ideas one supports from those ideas one disagrees with. In the following quotation, Latour shows how an author can separate those ideas that are supportive from those that need to be attacked.

The now well established concept of a neurohumoral control of adenohypohyseal secretions by the hypothalamus indicates the existence of a hypothalamic growth-hormone-releasing factor (GRF) (ref 1) having somatostatin as its inhibitory counterpart (ref 2). So far hypothalamic GRF has not been unequivocally characterized, despite earlier claims to the contrary (ref 3). (p. 36)

Both references 1 and 2 are what Latour calls "black boxes," ideas already accepted in the discipline as true, and therefore there is no need to argue rhetorically. Reference 3, however, is attacked as false. By showing that this reference has not adequately solved the problem, the author has opened a "rhetorical gap" that can justify the publication of another paper on the topic. In these quotations from a recent paper on volcanic debris, Cashman and Fiske (1991) show that prior research, perhaps once acceptable, may no longer be considered valid.

1. Some workers have suggested that silicic magmas can only vesiculate significantly, and thus erupt explosively, at water depths of ten meters or less (8).
2. Discoveries in the past few years, however, provide strong evidence that pumice-forming eruptions can take place at much greater depth. (p. 275)

The gap here is less direct than shown in the previous example. The authors reflect in their selection of words extreme care in making such a criticism. They do not name those they criticize, a practice consistent with the general policy of the journal. The term "some workers" has no clear referent to identify the person being criticized while the reference they are attacking is numbered and not directly named. These strategies make the criticism of previous research as impersonal as possible. The authors go on to cite several research articles to support their claims. They criticize the earlier papers by showing that new data, perhaps obtained from more sophisticated technologies such as the use of submersibles, has replaced the old data. This strategy makes their criticism seem even less personal since the discovery of this new data is seen as being beyond these authors' control.

Direct attacks are often used, particularly on research methodologies, to undermine the significance of the claims an author has previously made. Hunter (1990) suggests that scientific claims cannot be opposed simply by saying they are wrong; instead, they can be attacked by saying that the procedures used to generate the claim are wrong or that the claims contradict some external evidence. For example, in these quotations from a statistics article on predicting the incidence of AIDS, the author criticizes previous approaches on methodological grounds.

> The first approach, simple extrapolation of the AIDS incidence curve (2), has two serious limitations. First, the estimates depend crucially on the mathematical function used as a basis for the extrapolation, and some functions can produce anomalous results (3). Second, extrapolation produces projections only of AIDS cases and HIV prevalence or incidence. (Brookmeyer, 1991, p. 37)

This quotation, again with no names mentioned in the text, directly attacks the previous research by showing the fallibility of the research methods used, making for a much stronger form of attack than found in the previous example.

The purpose of this attack is to oppose those ideas that might affect whether the reader accepts the author's claims. For example, in these two quotations, the writer uses citation (2) to oppose a potentially damaging citation (1), thus problematizing the prior research and opening a gap for the writer's own research.

> 1. This synthetic decapeptide material or the natural material were [sic] only weakly active in tests where the release of growth hormone was measured by a radioimmunoassay for rat growth hormone (two refs.).
> 2. However, the adequacy of the radioimmunoassays for measuring rat growth hormone in plasma has been questioned recently (ref. 8). (p.37)

Because the author had not used a "radioimmunoassay" for his prior claims, his results are still viable despite the contrary results in the first quote. In sum, the general strategy of citations is to do whatever is necessary to the prior literature to render it as helpful as possible for your own claims. For Latour, this process alone is not enough to establish a claim to be what Ziman (1968) has called "public knowledge." For a claim to become established, it itself needs first to be published and later cited by other authors. Thus, Latour argues, if a paper is ignored, that is, uncited, it is the same as if the claim were not true in that the claim will be discarded. Thus both the reading and the writing of an article is a rhetorical event. Though it may appear to a reader that she is reading an isolated article, she is in, fact, engaging in a social activity in which she interacts with various authors, all of them participating in bringing the reader around to a specific point of view.

## Plagiarism

One serious consequence of violating the rules and conventions of citation use is plagiarism. As stated previously, accusations of plagiarism have been the strongest charge laid against Chinese writers. Plagiarism is not, of course, limited to foreign students. Most schools have strict rules about plagiarism; some have honor codes that students must abide by or face dismissal from school. Plagiarism is not only confined to students. Recent scandals about researchers plagiarizing or fabricating data have been reported at several universities and government funding organizations (LaFollette, 1992). In a survey of recent cases of plagiarism in the Public Health field, Wheeler (1991) found that professionals caught plagiarizing received a variety of punishments, ranging from reprimands to resignations. One of the main excuses for plagiarizing, according to Wheeler, was the pressures of their job.

In the humanities, the debate over whether Martin Luther King plagiarized his dissertation shows that in specific rhetorical contexts there can often be only a fine line between intertextuality and plagiarism (cf. Cole, 1990; Miller, 1990). As with the scientists caught plagiarizing, the reasons may have been related to external pressures. Garrow (1991) suggests that one reason may have been King's way of "coping with an intellectual setting that was radically different from his own heritage and in which he may have felt an outsider" (p. 90). In their research on remedial writers, Hull and Rose (1989) draw similar conclusions about why one of their subjects plagiarizes her student essay. This kind of pressure to conform to the linguistic standards of an academic community may be similar to what foreign students feel when they are expected to produce high-quality research papers in a language they may have barely mastered.

Thus, plagiarism may be a compensatory strategy used both by novices just entering a field and experts well established in their disciplines. How does this, then, differ from the way plagiarism is valued in China? Underlying many of the assumptions about how Chinese writers use source texts is the assumption that the concept of plagiarism is understood differently in China than in the West, perhaps as a result of a different concept of what constitutes private property (e.g., Matalene, 1985). Therefore, plagiarism could be considered an expert strategy in Chinese writing, reflecting how composition has been traditionally taught in China. Matalene (1985) refers to the use of Confucian teachings in the civil service examinations as exemplifying places where rote memorization and plagiarism are considered acceptable. Thus it might appear that Chinese rhetoric does not place the same taboo on plagiarism that Western rhetoric does.

## RESEARCH STUDY

### Background

The previous discussion of academic writing and the use of citations in particular has raised several issues that can be used as a basis for a comparative study of English and Chinese rhetoric. Of particular interest here is whether Chinese writers use sources in the same way as American writers do. In order to further explore this question, a textual analysis of citation use was designed to examine three issues from both qualitative and quantitative perspectives.

1. Do Chinese and American writers cite source texts from the same time period? Price (1986) found what he called a recency factor in the dates of texts cited in scientific articles, meaning that most citations in English-language academic papers come from within a 5-year period. Because the Chinese have traditionally been taught to value traditional texts, it is therefore interesting to explore whether this recency factor holds for Chinese writers as for Western academic writers.

2. Do Chinese and American writers use citations in the same manner? Previously discussed research (Taylor & Chen, 1991) has questioned whether Chinese academics are as argumentative as Western academics.

It is the intent here to examine both whether there are similar numbers of citations used and, from a qualitative perspective, whether they were expressed in the same manner. Previous research, both theoretical (Needham, 1970, 1981) and empirical (Bloch, 1990), indicates that there may be differences across disciplines in how citations are used. According to Needham, the physical sciences in China have been strongly influenced by the Western model of empirical research. My prior research, however, has indicated that this may not be the case in the social sciences. The social sciences were never as developed as the physical sciences and when they did develop, they were subjected more to political pressures than were the physical sciences. Thus we have identified two key factors that need to be considered: the language (Chinese or English) of the writer and the area (physical science or social science) in which that writer is publishing.

### Limitations Of This Study

The purpose of this research was to see if there were differences between how prior texts were used in Chinese and English and not to make generalizations about either the disciplines or the journal itself. Therefore, it was not necessary to check to see whether the sample represented the population of articles in the journal, although this was the case for the articles in the social sciences. Coding for the content of citations has been criticized for being subjective and therefore lacking the validity of such research as counting citations. From the more theoretical arguments of Latour and others, it might be argued that the distinction between background and support articles was trivial in that all the citations were to some degree supportive. However, by carefully distinguishing the uses of citation differences, the degree of rhetorical effect might be distinguished. For example, a distinction was made between a citation showing how the methodology that is being used is valid, which was coded as background, and a citation showing how the results were consistent with previous results, which was coded as support. Thus I argue in the coding scheme that the latter example has more rhetorical force than the former.

## Materials

The sample of articles was designed to reflect possible disciplinary differences. A total of 60 articles were chosen for each language for a total of 120 articles. The articles were broken down according to the area in which they were written, either the physical sciences or the social sciences. Each of these areas was further divided into three disciplines for the social sciences—economics, sociology, and psychology—and three disciplines—physics, biology, and engineering—for the physical sciences. For each language, ten articles were chosen from each discipline in the physical sciences and in the social sciences. In both samples, the articles were randomly chosen from a sample of articles from the three journals. The articles were all published between 1989 and 1991, although this does not necessarily mean that the articles were written at the same time. The sample excluded letters, discussions, and laboratory reports.

Finding comparable samples is one of the most difficult aspects of cross-cultural research (Cole & Means, 1981). To try to minimize possible differences, journals were chosen in both English and Chinese that were considered prestigious for publishing theoretical articles in the discipline. The articles for the English language group were all chosen from issues of *Science* magazine published between 1990 and 1991. *Science* is the publication of the American Association for the Advancement of Science, one of the leading umbrella organizations in the United States. There are a variety of articles published in both the physical sciences and the social sciences. There was no equivalent journal to *Science* found in Chinese; therefore, based on recommendations from professionals in the field and from librarians as to what were considered to be important journals for publishing theoretical research, one physical science journal, *Zhongguo Kexue (Chinese Science)*, and two social science journals, *Shehui Kexue (Social Sciences)*, and *Jiaoyu Yanjiu (Educational Research)* were selected. As with *Science, Zhongguo Kexue* publishes theoretical articles in biology, physics, and technology, while the two social science journals similarly publish articles in economics, sociology, and psychology.

*Data analysis for Question One.*    First, each citation in the references was coded according to its age, that is, the difference between the date of the citation and the date of publication of the article in which it is found. Using Price's conception of a recency factor of 5 years or less, one category was created for citations within this age including those marked "in press." A second category for citations 15 years or older was created since previous research (Bloch, 1990) indicated that there may be a greater use of older citations by Chinese-language writers than by their English-language counterparts. A third category was also created for citations between 5 and 15 years.

Dates categorized as "personal communication" or "unpublished" were eliminated since it was difficult to determine exactly when the information was written. The Chinese articles did not always contain the date of the paper and these were not coded for this part of the experiment. An ANOVA was used to test each category of dates for significant differences using two factors — language and area — and one nested factor — discipline.

*Data analysis for Question Two.*    Since we were concerned here with the rhetorical strategies used by writers, only citation strategies were coded, not each individual citation as in the previous two parts. A citation strategy indicates that one or more source texts were cited for the same sentence. Each article was coded for the function of the citation using a modified version of the analysis of how source texts are used found in Kaufer, Geisler, and Neuworth (1989). Citations that did not refer to prior texts, such as explanatory footnotes, were eliminated. Each citation strategy was initially coded for one of the following functions:

- background
- support
- faulty path
- return path

The English language group was coded by two fluent English speakers. The Chinese language group was coded by two fluent Chinese speakers. Raters were given the following details to help them distinguish between the functions:

*Background*:(1) Anything not directly related to the argument the writer is making. (2) Citations referring to methodology. (3) Background information including definitions and explanations. (4) Historical references presented uncritically

*Support*: (1) Citations directly related to supporting the argument the writer is making. (2) Citations that support a point the author is making in the paragraph.

*Faulty*: (1) Citations the author disagrees with either partly or completely.

*Return*: (1) Citations that are used to support points of disagreement.

It was expected that there would be few citations in both the faulty and return. Preliminary attempts at coding the functions showed that it was difficult to achieve a high rater reliability between faulty and return codes because first there were few of them and second because without reading the article mentioned it was often difficult to tell exactly whether the citation was being used as a faulty path, one where the author disagreed with the citation, or as a return path, where the citation was used to support a point the author disagreed with. As a result, the number of citations coded as faulty and return were totaled together in a category called *critical*. This was justifiable since both categories were concerned with the critical analysis of prior texts, what the research is primarily concerned with. Using a sample of 10 percent of the citations, the revised coding scheme achieved a high degree of reliability (.86) for both the English-language group and the Chinese-language group. An ANOVA was then used to test each of the three strategies for significant differences using two factors — language and area — and one nested factor — discipline within area.

## RESULTS FOR QUESTION ONE

### Analyses of Data

The number of citations in each of the three categories of dates (pre-5, 5 to 15, and post-15) served as the dependent variable for this part of the study. There were three independent variables: language (English or Chinese), area (physical sciences or social sciences), and discipline nested within area (biology, technology, and physics nested within physical sciences and psychology, economics, and sociology nested within social sciences). There were three categories of dates: pre-5 years, 5 to 15 years, and more than 15 years.

### Results for Question I

Question I examines whether there were differences in the raw numbers of citations used first according to the area and second according to language. As Table 10.1 shows, the results from a repeated measures analysis of

TABLE 10.1. MANOVA for Between-Subject Effects for Raw Number of Citation Dates

| Source | DF | SS | MS | F Value | Pr > F |
|--------|----|----|----|---------|--------|
| Language | 1 | 13893.51 | 13893.51 | 126.14 | 0.0001 |
| Area | 1 | 2091.36 | 2091.35 | 18.99 | 0.0001 |
| Language*Area | 1 | 152.66 | 152.66 | 1.39 | 0.2416 |
| Discipline(Area) | 4 | 926.29 | 231.57 | 2.10 | 0.0852 |
| Lang*Disc(Area) | 4 | 808.45 | 202.11 | 1.84 | 0.1271 |
| Error | 112 | 12335.96 | 110.14 | | |

variance (MANOVA) for tests of between-subjects effects indicated overall significance for language and area. Each of the categories of dates was then analyzed separately. Table 10.2 presents a breakdown of the ANOVAs for each category (pre-5, 5 through 15, and post-15), showing significant differences for language and for area in category I (pre-5) and category II (5 to 15) and for language in Category III (post-15).

These results indicate that there were significant differences in the use of Category I and Category II citations in both the Chinese-language texts (CLT) and the English-language texts (ELT) and in both the physical and social science articles. A Tukey post-hoc analysis for language showed that the means for ELT were significantly higher than for CLT (see Table 10.3). A Tukey post-hoc analysis for area showed the means for physical sciences were significantly higher than the means for the social sciences.

A closer examinations of the means (Table 10.4) shows that within each language group, there were differences between the number of citations in Category I for the physical and social sciences. An analysis of the means for Category II (5 to 15 years) shows a similar pattern of differences between the physical and social sciences although the differences were not as pronounced (see Table 10.3). The means for Category III (post-15) were higher for the ELT but by only a small amount. As Figure 10.1 shows, the differences both within the ELT and between the ELT and the CLT decrease substantially with each respective category. When examined with language as a factor, the differences were also similar to those found in

TABLE 10.2. Significant ANOVA Findings for Raw Numbers of Citation Dates

| Variable | F | DF | Pr > F |
|----------|---|----|--------|
| Category I (pre-5 years) | 12.21 | 11 | .0001 |
| Language | 111.95 | 1 | .0001 |
| Area | 8.72 | 1 | .004 |
| Category II (5 to 15 years) | 7.26 | 11 | .0001 |
| Language | 41.84 | 1 | .0001 |
| Area | 19.63 | 1 | .0010 |
| Category III (post-15) | | | |
| Language | 4.11 | 1 | 0.0191 |

TABLE 10.3. Tukey Post-Hoc Comparisons for Categories I (pre-5) and II (5–15)

| Variable | Citation Means | Significant Differences |
|---|---|---|
| Category I | | |
| Language | | E > C |
| English | 29.102 | |
| Chinese | 3.590 | |
| Category II | | |
| Language | | E > C |
| Area | | E > C |
| English | 10.855 | |
| Chinese | 5.00 | |

TABLE 10.4. Average Number of Category I (pre-5) Dates

| Language | Physical Sciences | Social Sciences | Discipline | N | Mean | SD |
|---|---|---|---|---|---|---|
| English | 34.70 | 23.31 | Biology | 20 | 22.56 | 26.47 |
| | | | Technology | 20 | 19.68 | 22.70 |
| Chinese | 4.66 | 1.30 | Physics | 20 | 14.85 | 14.06 |
| | | | Psychology | 20 | 12.53 | 15.18 |
| | | | Economics | 20 | 14.05 | 17.47 |
| | | | Sociology | 20 | 9.80 | 14.34 |

Category I (see Table 10.5). Though not significant, the average number of citations in Category III was lower in the CLT group for both the physical and social sciences. Figure 10.1 illustrates the similarity of the numbers between all four groups, particularly when compared with the great differences in Category I.

The results here indicate that the date of the citation was a factor that distinguished the texts both according to language and according to area. The English-language writers in the physical sciences used more recent citations (pre-5 years) than their Chinese counterparts in the physical sciences and the English-language writers in the social sciences. Within the CLT group, the physical science writers likewise used more recent citations

TABLE 10.5. Average Number of Category II Dates

| Language | Physical Sciences | Social Sciences | Discipline | N | Mean | SD |
|---|---|---|---|---|---|---|
| English | 15.13 | 9.35 | Biology | 20 | 13.14 | 14.22 |
| | | | Technology | 20 | 7.95 | 6.69 |
| Chinese | 6.58 | 1.71 | Physics | 20 | 11.25 | 6.07 |
| | | | Psychology | 20 | 8.42 | 8.69 |
| | | | Economics | 20 | 3.85 | 7.82 |
| | | | Sociology | 20 | 2.55 | 3.92 |

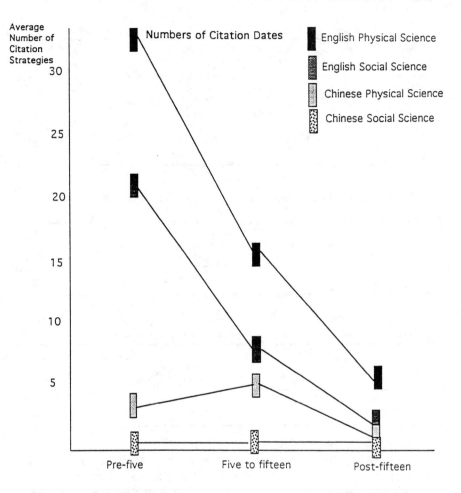

**Figure 10.1.**  This figure compares the average number of citation publication dates according to language and area.

than the social science writers. The significant results for area also indicate that the distinction made between articles written in the physical and social sciences did yield significant results. Though the distinction made between the physical and social sciences is somewhat arbitrary, the distinction did prove to be a factor in the dates of the citations. An analysis of the means in Category III (post-15) shows that there was a greater average number of older citations for the ELT in both the physical and social sciences (see Table 10.6).

The ratios between the use of citations in the ELT and CLT in each category show that a major area of difference can be found in the use of the Category I (pre-5) dates. Table 10.7 shows that in both the physical and

TABLE 10.6. Average Number of Category III (post-15) Dates

| Language | Physical Sciences | Social Sciences | Discipline | N | Mean | SD |
|---|---|---|---|---|---|---|
| English | 5.06 | 3.80 | Biology | 20 | 4.27 | 7.79 |
| | | | Technology | 20 | 3.10 | 2.57 |
| Chinese | 2.53 | 1.43 | Physics | 20 | 4.05 | 2.22 |
| | | | Psychology | 20 | 4.05 | 4.25 |
| | | | Economics | 20 | 2.50 | 6.35 |
| | | | Sociology | 20 | 1.30 | 1.59 |

TABLE 10.7. Ratios between the English and Chinese Use of Citations by Area

| | Physical | Social |
|---|---|---|
| Category I | 7.5–1 | 18–1 |
| Category II | 2–1 | 2.7–1 |
| Category III | 2–1 | 2.7–1 |

TABLE 10.8. Ratios of Category I (pre-5) and Category III (post-15) Citations

| | Ratios (X:1) | |
|---|---|---|
| | English | Chinese |
| Physical Sciences | 6.85 | 1.84 |
| Social Sciences | 6.24 | .91 |

social sciences, there was a far greater ratio in Category I (pre-5) than in Categories II (5 to 15) and III (post-15). These ratios indicate that in both the physical and social sciences there was a far higher number of Category I (pre-5) dates in the ELT; however, the differences between numbers was smaller in the other two categories.

An analysis of the ratio between the earliest (Category I) and the latest (Category III) dates also shows that a far greater number of early texts can be found in the ELT (see Table 10.8). As Figure 10.2 shows, the ratios in the ELT were far higher than the ones in the CLT. Figure 10.3 shows the ratios across languages in Categories I (pre-5) and III (post-5). Here it can be seen that in Category I (pre-5) there is a much greater ratio between the ELT and CLT in the social sciences. This indicates that there is a greater similarity in the physical sciences between the texts in English and Chinese on the use of recent texts. Surprisingly, there was little difference between the languages in the ratio of older texts.

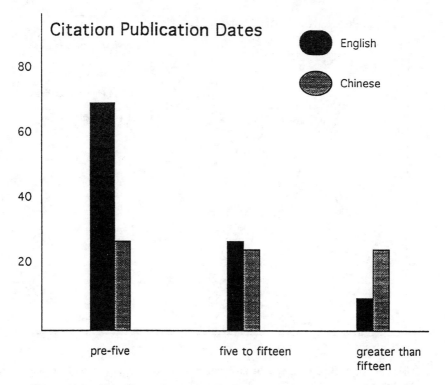

**Figure 10.2.** This figure shows the distribution of the percentages of citation publication dates according to language.

## Discussion

Question one examined whether there were differences in what Price (1986) called the recency factor in the use of citations. Three variables were examined: language, area, and discipline nested within area. It was not expected that there would be any difference in discipline and the analysis confirmed that there was no difference. Language and area, as well as the interaction between language and area, were found to be significant overall. It was found that the recency factor held for English language writers both in the physical and social sciences. On average the majority of citations had been published earlier than 5 years and, the English language writers used proportionately fewer older citations. The Chinese writers, on the other hand, used proportionately fewer newer citations and more older citations. Figure 10.1 shows that the proportions are almost inverse; that is, the proportion of new citations in the ELT and CLT is nearly the same as the proportion of old citations.

There can be a number of explanations for these differences. The first,

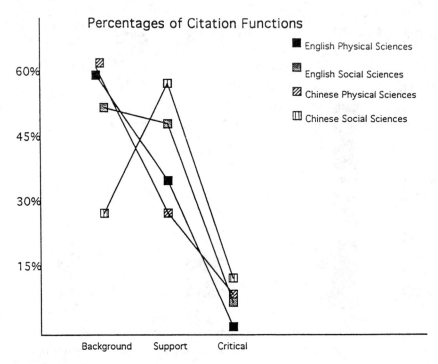

**Figure 10.3.** This figure shows the distribution of percentages of citation functions according to language and area.

which is consistent with arguments about the role of Confucianism, is that the Chinese writers, particularly those in the social sciences, are more likely to rely on older, classic texts than are the English-speaking writers. This would confirm the argument that Chinese writers are more tied to the past than their English counterparts. A second explanation, however, is that the Chinese writers have less access to a range of texts and therefore rely on the more traditional texts. One group of texts that all writers would have access to are Marxist texts. A second factor is that during the Cultural Revolution (1966-1976) little was published and many libraries were burned down.

The statistical analyses on the pre-5 citations showed no significance for area, which combines both CLT and ELT. Therefore, there was no post-hoc analysis for either group. There was, however, significance in the interaction between language and area, indicating that there is a difference when language and area are taken into account. Figure 10.2 shows that the slopes of the usage patterns also differ between the CLT and ELT. In addition, there are differences within the CLT that are not found in the ELT. The slopes of usage pattern in CLT are flatter than in the ELT, indicating that there is less of a distinction in the Chinese texts in regard to the dates of the texts. However, there still is a difference within the Chinese texts. The Chinese physical science texts used more pre-5 year texts and an interesting gap appears in the 5-to-15 category. The social science texts used almost no texts in this category while the physical science texts used more than in either group in the English-language texts. If these two categories are combined, then the Chinese-language physical science texts would look more like the English-language texts. Interestingly, there is no difference in either area of the Chinese texts in the post-15 category.

This is a somewhat unexpected finding and a finer analysis needs to be made. Overall, however, there is indication that the Chinese physical science texts are more like the English texts than are the Chinese social science texts. The similarities could be accounted for by a greater influence of Western thinking, especially since the Cultural Revolution. This reflects the more pragmatic approach toward the relationship between science and politics as reflected in the emphasis on what have been called the "four modernizations" as the dominant policy that would govern the importation of outside influences. The four modernizations refer to the modernization of agriculture, industry, the military, and science and technology. Some idea or process could be justified if it contributed to these modernizations. At the same time, this influence is not absolute.

The dissimilarities may also reflect the vagaries and contradictions of the political situation. The modernizations did not include the social sciences. Each of the social science disciplines is an area that would come under intense political scrutiny. All have to be accountable to Marxist theory. Sociologists have to be very careful about publishing problems in the society that socialist doctrine would admit to. Economists, too, have to accept socialism although they have the advantage of being able to situate their arguments within the recent liberalization programs. As recent events in China show, this advantage, however, can disappear quickly. Psychology, even in the area of education, has been a very difficult discipline to practice.

The gap in the 5-to-15 category may also be a result of the fact that the revival of the social sciences has been very recent. Though there is no data on this, it may be that very little was published or imported in these disciplines until the mid 1980s. Zhongshan University, one of the leading universities in southern China, did not enroll a graduate student in sociology until this period. Because there are so few sociologists publishing in China, the only texts the writers would have access to are either ones very recently imported or the classic texts of Marxist theory.

## RESULTS FOR QUESTION II

### Analysis of Data

Question II examines whether there were functional differences in how citations were used. Three distinct functions were identified: (a) the use of citations for giving background, (b) the use of citations for giving support to an argument, and (c) the use of citations for expressing a critical viewpoint. The numbers of citations in each of these three categories were used as the dependent variable. Strategy I included citation strategies used as background, Strategy II included those used as support, and Strategy III included those used as criticism (see above for definitions of each strategy). As with Question I, there were three independent variables: language (Chinese and English), area (physical and social sciences), and discipline nested within area (biology, technology, and physics nested within physical sciences, and psychology, economics, and sociology nested within social sciences).

## Results

A MANOVA for within-subjects effect showed significance at $p < .0001$. These results indicated that distinctions had been made between the three categories of citation strategies. These results give support to the validity of using these three categories as variables in the study. A MANOVA test criterion for testing the hypothesis of no category effect could then be conducted to test for between-subjects differences. Table 10.9 shows that the MANOVA for between-subjects effects showed significance for language and area but not for the interaction between language and area, discipline within area and the interaction of language and discipline within area.

ANOVAs were therefore run for each of the three categories of strategies (see Table 10.10). For background citations, there were significant overall main and also significant results for language, area, and the interaction between language and area. A post-hoc Tukey analysis showed significant differences of means for English-language articles and for the physical science articles. The ANOVA for support citations strategies showed an overall significance, but significant results were found only for language. A Tukey post-hoc analysis showed significantly more citations in the English-language articles (see Table 10.11). An analysis of the means shows that for

TABLE 10.9. MANOVA for Between-Subjects Effects for Raw Number of Citation Functions

| Variable | F | DF | Pr>F |
|---|---|---|---|
| Language | 71.67 | 1 | .0001* |
| Area | 9.16 | 1 | .0001* |
| Language and Area | 2.34 | 1 | .1293 |
| Discipline within Area | 1.21 | 4 | .3104 |
| Language and Discipline | .93 | 4 | .4470 |

TABLE 10.10. Significant ANOVA Results for Between Subjects Effects of Raw Numbers of Functional Categories

| Variable | F | DF | Pr > F |
|---|---|---|---|
| | 71.67 | 1 | .0001 |
| Background | 13.98 | 11 | .0001 |
| Language | 88.99 | 1 | .0001 |
| Area | 44.38 | 1 | .0001 |
| Language and Area | 14.58 | 1 | .0001 |
| Support | 3.97 | 11 | .0001 |
| Language | 31.78 | 1 | .0001 |
| Critical | 3.10 | 11 | .0012 |
| Language | 22.38 | 1 | .0001 |

TABLE 10.11. Significant ANOVA Results for Between Subjects Effects of Percentages of Functional Categories

| | F | Pr > F | Significant Differences |
|---|---|---|---|
| Strategy I (Background) | | | |
| Language (Chinese and English) | 14.16 | .0003 | E > C |
| Strategy II (Support) | | | |
| Language (Chinese and English) | 25.41 | .0001 | E > C |
| Strategy III (Critical) | | | |
| Language (Chinese and English) | 7.97 | .0057 | C > E |
| Discipline (Area) | 2.63 | .0380 | |
| Language*Discipline (Area) | 2.53 | .0447 | |

both the English-language articles and for the Chinese-language articles there was little difference between the number of support citations in the physical and social science articles. The ANOVA for citations in Strategy III also showed an overall significance with only significant results for language. The Tukey post-hoc analysis showed a significantly greater mean for the English-language articles than for the Chinese-language articles.

Figure 10.3 shows a fairly consistent distribution of support, background, and critical citations for both areas of the ELT and for the Chinese physical science texts. Only in the Chinese social science texts were there a lower number of background citations and a higher number of support citations. As with the data concerning dates of publication, this indicates a similarity across area in the ELT but not in the CLT. What is important for our comparison here is that the Chinese physical science texts show a greater similarity to the ELT than to the Chinese social science texts.

A breakdown of the different citation strategies gives further evidence for the differences between citation use within the CLT. Figure 10.4 shows that in both the ELT and CLT, there is a greater number of background than support strategies although the differences are smaller in the ELT. Figure 10.4 shows the differences in Strategy I (background). The background

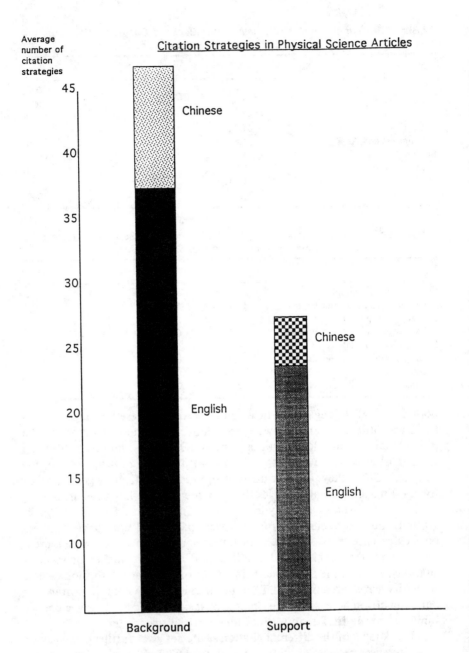

**Figure 10.4.** This figure compares the average number of citation strategies in the physical science articles for each language.

citations tended to show the larger context of the present text without giving direct support to a claim. Often this type of citation helps orient the reader and explain key points. As Figure 10.5 shows, there are differences both across areas and languages. Here again is evidence that there is more similarity across languages in the physical science texts than in the social science texts. Figure 10.6 shows, however, that in the social science texts, there is a similarity in the ratio of background and support texts although the numbers, particularly of background citations, are quite low in the CLT.

Another interesting finding concerns the use of critical citations. The question of whether Chinese writers can criticize other writers has been a controversial issue. Taylor and Chen (1991), who confined their study to article introductions, found an unwillingness on the part of Chinese writers to publicly criticize those they disagree with. As Figure 10.7 shows, the average number of critical citations was relatively low across all the texts. An analysis of the means shows that in the ELT, there were a greater number of Strategy III (critical) citations in the social sciences than in physical sciences. In the CLT, on the other hand, there were more critical citations in the physical science articles than in the social sciences. Thus, there is some evidence that Chinese writers can and do take critical positions, though not necessarily as often as the English-language writers do.

## Discussion

The results presented here are in response to a question that concerns whether there are differences across languages and areas of research in the use of intertextual knowledge. Three functions were chosen as independent variables to be tested across English and Chinese and physical and social sciences. It was intended that each of the categories would have a different degree of rhetorical impact. The citations in the background strategy would have less rhetorical impact than the ones in the support strategy. The critical strategy, including citations the author was criticizing and ones used to criticize others, was designed to ask whether there were patterns of critical thinking. While it was not tested whether these assumptions were true for each strategy, the results did show that there were significant differences between each of the categories.

As with the results of Question I, there was a far greater number of citation strategies used in the ELT than in the CLT. It was expected that the ELT would contain a variety of these patterns with large numbers of background and support citation moves and a few critical citation moves; however, less was known about how the Chinese writers used citations,

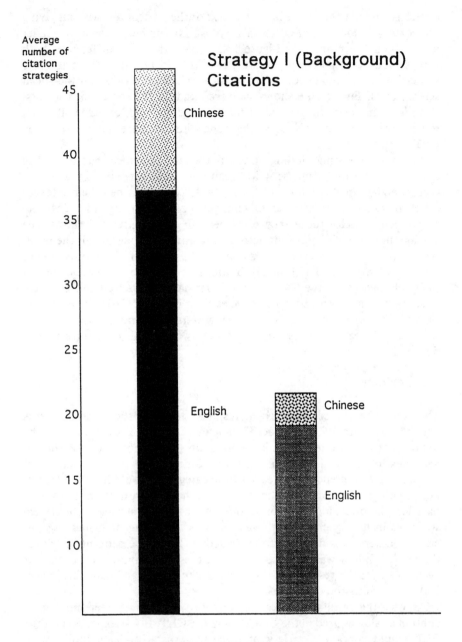

**Figure 10.5.** This figure compares the average number of Strategy 1 (Background) citations according to language and area.

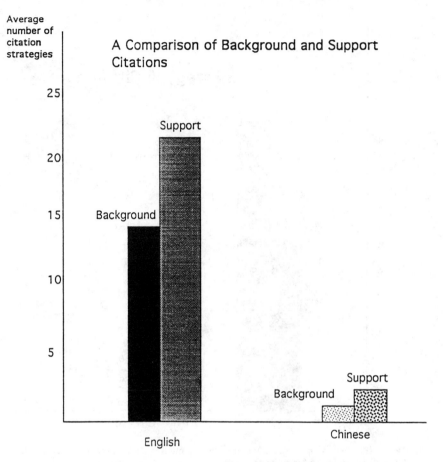

**Figure 10.6.** This figure compares the average number of citations for Strategy I (background) and Strategy II (support) in the social science articles.

especially critical ones. The anecdotal evidence discussed above concerning problems Chinese students have with taking critical stands indicated that Chinese writers might not use critical citations in the same way as do Western writers.

Although there was not significance for area, the distribution of citations shown in Figure 10.3 indicates that the significant differences in language may have resulted from the fact that the Chinese writers in the social sciences did not use a large number of background citations. For both the English and Chinese writers, there were many more background citations used in the physical sciences than in the social sciences and more used for background than for support. If the rhetorical distinction between the use

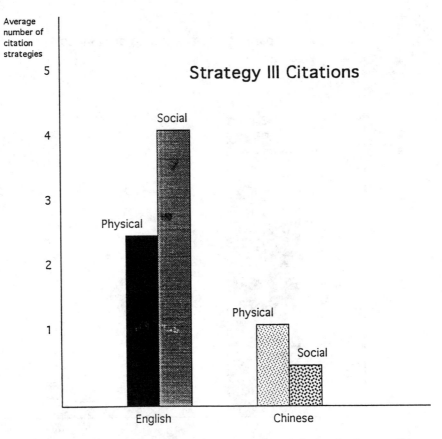

Average
number of
citation
strategies

**Figure 10.7.** This figure compares the average number of citations in Category III (critical) according to language and area.

of Strategy I (background) and Strategy II (support) citations is correct, then it could be concluded that the physical science writers were more concerned with laying out the background to their paper than in building support for their arguments. On the other hand, the social science writers, both in English and Chinese, used more citations for supporting their arguments, which could indicate a greater use of source texts for their rhetorical power. The differences within the CLT sample between the physical and social sciences indicate that the writers in these two areas may be using different strategies. The lack of background citations and the greater number of citations in the social sciences, in particular, could reflect both the general lack of articles discussed in Question I and a more pragmatic use of the available citations for more rhetorical purposes than orienting the reader.

## The Critical Use of Citations

Some of the more surprising and difficult to interpret findings were found in Strategy III (critical). These results had to be viewed more cautiously since there were relatively fewer numbers in this strategy compared to the other two categories. In the English-language articles, there were more critical citations in the social science articles than in the physical science ones. English-language writers in the physical sciences used very few critical citations. This is consistent with Kuhn's (1970) concept of paradigmatic shift in that it would be expected that such criticisms would only take place in a period of conflict between existing paradigms. The social sciences may be more frequently engaged in such conflict and therefore it would be expected that they would use more critical citations.

One of the reasons that might explain the lack of significance for area was that this distinction was not as great in the CLT. An examination of means shows that while there is some difference between the social and physical sciences in the CLT, the differences are not as great. The relative number of critical citations in the Chinese articles is higher than might be expected. There was more than one critical citation per article in the physical science articles and a little more than one for every two articles in the social science articles. This finding seems to contradict previous research by Chen and Taylor (1991), who found no critical citations; however, they examined only the introductions to articles. The placement of citations in a text is important since it has been argued that Chinese writers often defer making critical citations until an argument has already been made (Kaplan, 1988). However, here, we did not attempt to measure where in a text a citation was placed. Overall, these results indicate that taking a critical position seems to be considered an acceptable and important part of Chinese academic writing although, as will be discussed later, it may not be expressed the same way as in English articles.

Since the use of critical citations has been identified as an important problem in Chinese writers, we examined the CLT closely to see whether there were differences in how the Chinese expressed these criticisms. This analysis uncovered some intra-area differences in how Chinese writers expressed their criticism. For example in this citation from a biology article, the author finds that there has been much confusion about the duplicating point of the DNA cell and therefore there is a "gap" in what is known about this point.

It is obvious from the descriptions above that there is disagreement among the research results regarding the duplicating point of the DNA cell . . . There is no in depth analysis but only a general description of the area where the silver grain appeared. Therefore, there is no clear conclusion about the inner cell rDNA duplicated position up to date [11, 12, 16, 17] (Han, Jiao, & Xing, 1990, p. 820)

This style of the criticism is similar, even to the convention of how the articles discussed are referenced, to the English-language examples previously cited. There are no names cited, as is the custom in *Science*; however, the author is straightforward in his criticism of the inconsistencies of previous research.

The writers in the social sciences frequently used a more indirect strategy. In this example from a sociology paper, there is no naming of the work being criticized, even in the footnotes. "Some of the teaching materials divide social roles into the actual role and the ideal role, the conceptual role, and the actual role. It is worthwhile to reconsider and discuss these points" (Sun, 1991, p. 46).

The Chinese expression *shi zhide tuiqiao he shangcuo de*[1] (it is worthwhile to reconsider and discuss) is frequently used by Chinese writers to make an indirect criticism. There were other types of indirect criticisms found throughout the social science papers. Another frequent strategy was to say "Some people have said" without ever naming the people. Though we did not attempt to statistically measure directness and indirectness, these examples indicate that there may be differences in how writers in various areas express their criticisms.

## CHINESE RHETORIC AND THE USE OF CITATIONS

The results of this study indicate that a comparison between English and Chinese texts yields a complex series of results that show that it is difficult to make strong generalizations about the relationship between Chinese and English rhetoric. In this section of my chapter, we are going to examine whether these results about the use of citations in Chinese academic texts are consistent with an analysis of Chinese rhetoric.

### Social Harmony and Chinese Rhetoric

The results showing the use of critical or "faulty" paths challenge the idea that Chinese rhetoric lacks a critical nature. The supposed lack of conten-

---

[1]We have used the Pinyin form of romanization that is common today in Mainland China. Many authors, however, still use the Wade-Giles form. To avoid confusion, if a Chinese term is used from one of these authors, we use the Wade-Giles form with the Pinyin in parenthesis.

tiousness among Chinese writers has often been connected to the concept of social harmony (Chen & Taylor, 1991). Chinese rhetoric has often been identified with the idea of social harmony (Oliver, 1962). Thus in a society that values harmony how does one demonstrate that prior texts are inadequate or wrong? In this section, we examine how the concept of harmony may influence a particular writing strategy.

One of the clearest representations of harmony in Chinese society is the Confucian concept of "rectification of names" (*zheng ming*). This principle refers to the relationship between the role of the individual and the structure of society: individuals' actions should reflect their position within the society. "Let the ruler be a ruler, the minister be a minister, the father be a father, and the son be a son" (cited in Hansen, 1983, p. 73). A ruler, therefore, has certain obligations to the people, which if not carried out, means that the ruler is not fit to hold that office. It is this process of rectification that forms the basis for the importance Confucius places on order in a harmonious society (Bao, 1990). For Confucius, then, rhetoric could be used to resolve any potential conflict between an individual action and that individual's position in society (Hansen, 1983).

This need for rhetoric to aid in creating a harmonious society reflects the fundamental pragmatism of Chinese rhetoric (Garrett, 1991). Rhetoric needed some "use" or purpose to make it valuable. For the Confucianists in particular, rhetoric aided in creating harmony within a society at every level of social interaction. At the same time, rhetoric was often considered subordinate to action in Confucian thinking (e.g., Chi'en, 1986). Thus, individuals should be judged more on their deeds than on their words. As Xunxi expressed it.

> The wise ruler controls (the people) with power, guides them with the Way, instructs them with commands, enlightens them with the maxims (of the former sages) and prohibits them (from evil) with punishments. Hence his people are converted to the Way as though by supernatural power. What need has he of discourses and explanations. (cited in Chi'en, 1986, p.138)

This subordination of rhetoric to action reflects a skepticism about language. Chi'en (1986) argues that the Confucianists trusted language (at least as compared with the skepticism of the Daoists and Buddhists) but viewed its use as rhetoric as a last resort. This emphasis on the use of language and rhetoric to achieve social harmony has been considered a fundamental difference between Chinese and Western philosophy. Where both Plato and Aristotle emphasized the importance of rhetoric for obtaining agreement from the audience, Confucius emphasized the promulgation of a social hierarchy.

The relationship between the individual and the social hierarchy has also been one of the key differences between China and the West. Whereas the Western view has been dominated by the idea of a divine power that first created and now controls the universe, the Chinese world view focuses on individuals as parts of hierarchies. Social harmony was an important factor for that hierarchy to function. This view of hierarchies manifested itself in the Confucian view that society was a stratified system of often conflicting units that must be unified to achieve social harmony (Bodde, 1981). The Confucian concept of *zheng ming* best encapsulates this view of society. In a Confucian society, each member of that society plays a role and his or her actions are expected to conform to the expectations of that role. A teacher is supposed to act like a teacher and a student like a student. Thus Chinese students are socialized with strong and usually consistent views of how their teachers and they themselves should behave.

There have been many assumptions made about how argumentation in Chinese rhetoric is situated within a social and cultural context that values harmony, courtesy, and concessions (Leki, 1991; Matalene, 1985). These assumptions, however, do not mean that Chinese writers are not as contentious as are Western writers but that Chinese writers may express their disagreements in ways that differ from how they are expressed in Western texts. This argument is consistent with both the numbers and types of criticisms found in the Chinese texts previously discussed.

Our previous findings that critical or faulty citations were seldom found in the introductions but more often found later in the paper may be consistent with this conception of harmony. It has been argued that the presentation of argument is often indirect, with arguments sometimes postponed until the end of the paper (Kaplan, 1988). Our findings above do not strongly support these assumptions since we did not measure distance; however, these assumptions are still critical to understanding the relationship between Chinese and Western rhetoric since they are at the core of how culture may influence language.

## The Role of Precedent

The results showing that Chinese writers used greater numbers of older citations may not necessarily be a product of cultural differences but instead a product of the possible lack of availability of newer texts. Still, the greater use of older citations is strongly connected to the importance of argument from precedence. An earlier study of the use of citations in the introductions to articles (Bloch, 1988) found a significant use of citations from the "founding fathers" of Marxism — Marx, Engels, Lenin, and Mao. These citations were used not in place of original arguments but as warrants used to support an argument. One strategy for establishing a claim was to show how an argument is consistent with a quotation from Chairman Mao or one of the other leading figures.

Here again, there can be different explanations for why this strategy was so often used. There can be no denying that it is important in contemporary Chinese society to be politically correct and one way to demonstrate this correctness is to show consistency with the political views of these founding fathers. However, there is also a consistency with the use of precedence in traditional Chinese rhetoric. The use of citations in this way is related not only to the idea of social harmony but also to a more general view of how the past is valued.

While to some degree all societies use the past to justify present actions, it has been argued that Chinese writers are more dependent on precedent than their Western counterparts (Scollon, in press). According to Scollon, printing in China, unlike that in the West, was associated with reestablishing a connection with the past. In the West, on the other hand, it has been argued that literacy is sometimes accompanied by radical movements such as the Protestant Reformation, which, in part, resulted because more people could own their own copies of sacred texts with the invention of the printing press. Because there was a preference in Chinese rhetoric for arguing from precedence instead of logic, as was preferred by the Greeks (Nakayama, 1984), there is less need, therefore, for any formal system of invention in Chinese rhetoric (Garrett, 1989). This does not, however, mean that the Chinese did not value new and original arguments but that they supported these arguments through precedence, much the same as writers in many academic disciplines in the West.

The importance in Confucian rhetoric of precedence as a substitute for invention is a direct consequence of the Confucian view of history. Confucius viewed history as a "wise counsel" that could render a "communal verdict" that went beyond an individual's private opinion (Tu, 1989). Confucius' respect for prior texts, thus, reflects a view of history where the present is inherently inferior to the past. This sense of history also reflects *guanxi*, where an individual is connected not only to one's peers but also to one's culture and history. The idea of *guanxi* permeated all areas of thought. Therefore, any new argument must be connected with previous arguments. Thus, individuals may argue not just from their own opinions but also from what Tu calls the "collective memory" of history. As Cua (1973) points out, a good Confucian argument reflects what is also universally accepted behavior in the society. An argument must, therefore, be consistent with the accepted principles of the society, and therefore, it might be difficult to take contrary positions.

Confucian rhetoric does not rely as heavily on logic to justify a claim; instead it relies more on prior wisdom as the basis of argumentation. In particular, the most significant source of wisdom could be found in the classics (*ching*), such as the works of Confucius or particular works such as the *Inner Cannon of the Yellow Lord*, a founding text for the study of traditional Chinese medicine. Liu Hsieh (Xie), a major Confucian rhetorician writing in the fifth century, defines the *ching* in this way:

> By *ching* we mean an expression of the absolute or constant Tao or principle, that great teaching that is unalterable. Therefore the *ching* faithfully reflect heaven and earth, spirits and gods. They help to articulate the order of things and to set up the rules governing human affairs. In them is found both the secret of nature and spirit and the very bone and marrow of fine literature. (Liu, 1959, p. 17)

It is clear from this passage that Liu Hsieh (Xie), like Confucius, sees the classics as the source material for constructing new texts. Though China has changed from a feudal society to a Marxist one, the practice of relying on the sages is still an important factor in Chinese rhetoric. In a Marxist society, however, the sages have become the fathers of Marxism (e.g., Shen, 1989).

## Individualism

With all the emphasis Chinese rhetoric has on *guanxi* or connectedness to the past and the imitation of the sages, then what is the role of the individual author? The importance given to creating harmonious societies and the continual emphasis placed on China as a "collective" society could indicate that China does not value individualism to the degree it is valued in the West, particularly in the United States. Individualism in Chinese society would particularly affect the agency of the writer or the control the writer has over the text. The extent to which a culture values the "differences" between new texts and all other texts depends on to what degree the culture values the individual author.

As Zhang (1992) has argued, the importance of intertextuality in Chinese rhetoric empowers the authors of these traditional texts since groups of writers who were considered sages or wise men could be only carefully criticized if at all. This empowerment, in turn, lessens the power the individual has over the text. This relationship is, of course, true in other writing contexts. The degree of control an individual has over the text changes depending on the text. A writer has much control over a personal essay, some control over an academic essay, and less control over a technical text, where a clear understanding of the content is the most important aspect of the text. A writer who must acknowledge the intertextuality of a text by the citing of source texts may sometimes be more constrained in expressing individual or idiosyncratic ideas than a writer who does not. Thus, a writer of academic texts is constrained more than an essayist or a novelist and perhaps may have much difficulty in making novel claims, fearing that he or she may stand out from the group.

The role of individualism in Chinese society has itself been controversial. de Bary (1991) argues that while it is often felt there has not been enough individualism in Chinese society, it has been sometimes felt that there is too much individualism. de Bary points out that the term *individualism*, what the Chinese call *ko-jen chu-i* (ge-ren zhu-yi), was imported from the West. Since the Chinese imported their term for individualism, *ko-jen chu-i,* from the West, it could be argued that they did not value individualism, as the Sapir/Whorf hypothesis might predict; however, this does not mean that individualism and the rights due an individual were not important topics in China.

First, there is the question of whether the ideal of Confucianism reflected the actual role of relationships in Chinese culture. Pang (1988) argues that there was often a conflict between the real and ideal views of the relationship between the individual and the social order. She finds one interesting example of this in the 18th-century novel *The Dream of the Red Chamber*. In this novel, the protagonist, Jia Bao Yu, is torn between his true love and the woman his family had arranged for him to marry. When his lover dies, he marries, fathers a child, and passes the civil service examinations, thus fulfilling his filial obligations. However, after this, he disappears and never returns. Pang argues that this story illustrates the continual struggle in Chinese society between the needs of the individual and the individual's societal obligations. According to de Bary, Confucianism focused on the cultivation and self-fulfillment of the individual but within the individual's proscribed realm. Thus the individual was not set against the society but in harmony with it. Even from this brief analysis here, it can be shown that individualism has evolved from Confucian times to the present. Though individualism in Chinese society meant something different from what it meant in the West, it is again too narrow to define Chinese society as "collectivist."

## ALTERNATIVE VIEWS OF CHINESE RHETORIC

### The Writings of Hsi K'ang

When considering the possible influence of contemporary Chinese rhetoric on second language writing, it is important to understand the complexity of Chinese rhetoric, particularly that classical Chinese rhetoric was never as monolithic as is usually depicted. The data presented above indicate that in some areas of study, particularly the physical sciences, contemporary

Chinese rhetoric may have imported Western modes of writing, at least so far as the use of source texts is concerned. In this section of the chapter, we would like to argue that while this importation from the West may differ from the traditional Confucian use of source texts, it did not differ from all forms of Chinese rhetoric: There are alternative forms of Chinese rhetoric that use source texts in ways similar to those found in Western rhetoric.

We can see some of the tensions that have existed in Chinese rhetoric in the essays of Hsi K'ang, one of the leading members of the "Seven Worthies of the Bamboo Grove" during the third century. Hsi K'ang was a Daoist and not a Confucian, and his writings demonstrate some of the limits to which non-Confucians pushed Confucian ideas. In this way, we can see the development of rhetorical strategies that continue to resonate throughout Chinese history.

An excellent example of this use of source texts can be found in Hsi K'ang's essays. For instance, in "An Essay on Nourishing Life," the introduction shows a gap in the current knowledge about immortality, a strategy similar to what is found in a Western academic essay (Swales, 1990).

> In this world there are those who say that immortality can be attained by study and "no-death" brought about by effort. Others say that the extreme of old age is one hundred and twenty, and that in this past and present are the same — [claims] of going beyond this are all wild and absurd. (cited in Henricks, 1983, p. 22)

Hsi begins the essay by citing claims that he does not agree with. Here Hsi K'ang directly contradicts the admonition against criticizing traditional thinking. Hsi, in fact, is not considered to be an orthodox Confucian (Henricks, 1981, 1983). However, though he is critical, he does not directly name those he criticizes. This is a common strategy that might reflect either a reluctance to directly name those being criticized or an assumption that the reader knows the reference. The use of this strategy in Chinese texts is consistent with the argument that in a homogeneous culture, texts are more writer based than reader based since it is assumed that the reader shares the knowledge of the writer. This relationship is indicative of a more active, dialogic interaction between the writer and the audience (Garrett, 1991).

When Hsi wants to argue that people cannot live as long as it is theoretically possible to, he gives several practical examples relating to everyday life. For instance, he argues "When we take drugs to make us sweat we sometimes do not succeed. But when feelings of shame build up inside, perspiration pours out in streams" (Henricks, 1983, p. 23). After several such examples about how such entities never work out as planned, he concludes the paragraph by making a generalization using a metaphor that compares the relationship of the spirit and body to that of ruler and state.

> Speaking on the basis of this, the relation of essence and spirit to form and body is like that of the ruler to the state. When the spirit is disturbed on the inside, the form wastes away on the out, just as when the ruler is confused above, that state is chaotic below. (p. 24)

There is an interesting logical progression here from concrete examples to more abstract principles. This example refutes claims that Chinese argumentation lacks a logic or deals only with abstractions. However, in this example, even the abstract argument is compared to a concrete situation that the reader can identify with.

Later in the essay, Hsi K'ang demonstrates how an argument is situated in classical texts. He argues that an individual who is skilled at nourishing life will become harmonious with "the Great Accord": "He maintains this state with the one and nourishes it with harmony. Harmony and principle daily increase and he becomes one with the Great Accord" (p. 29).

According to Henricks' annotation on this essay, this citation comes from the work of Lao-Tzu. Again, there is no direct citation, perhaps on the assumption that the audience knows from where this reference comes. It is not clear what Hsi's intention was in this citation. By citing Lao-Tzu, he connects his argument to the writings of Daoism, thus creating that connection between his own argument and that of the past. In this way he is following the advice of Liu Hsieh (Xie) and Xunzi about the importance of the classic texts (*ching*) in argumentation. At the same time, he is relying on his own logic to argue his case; thus, it is not clear whether he is only citing the prior text to adhere to the expected format of an argument or whether he is actually using it, as would be used today, to show how his argument is consistent with previous arguments.

What we see in this example is that Chinese writers do not necessarily follow the teachings of Confucius in how they develop their arguments. We can see in the writings of Hsi K'ang the importance of logical argumentation and even how the writer can directly attack ideas that he may disagree with. At the same time, there are conventions of argumentation such as not naming sources or using the classics that seem more consistent with Confucianism. This example is important for demonstrating that Chinese rhetoric is not monolithic, that there are alternative and often contradictory forms of rhetoric. Thus, when discussing how contemporary writing is influenced by Chinese tradition, it is necessary to consider that there may be forms of rhetoric not different from what is found in the West.

## The Influence of the Civil Service Exams on Rhetoric

As discussed at the beginning of this chapter, one of the most important factors in the history of Chinese rhetoric is the role of the civil service examinations. The exams were the means by which an individual could obtain a government job. There was a series of local, regional, and national exams. The higher the exam passed, the better the job the individual could obtain. Matalene (1985), Scollon (in press), and others have cited the civil service exams as one of the major causes of the importance Chinese writers seem to give to the ancient texts. Although these exams were an important factor in establishing the memorization and recitation of traditional Confucian texts as a dominating factor in Chinese education, a brief study of the civil service examination can show how alternate forms for teaching composition have also developed along with alternative forms of rhetoric. The civil service exams, particularly during specific periods, mandated a restricted canon of texts (Nakayama, 1984). The examination system made knowledge of the Confucian classics the basis for obtaining a position. From an early age, children, particularly from those families who had a high ambition for their children, had to concentrate their study on what are called *The Four Books* and *The Five Classics,* which are the basic texts of Confucian thought.

The examinations influenced the literacy practices in general. Literacy practice for children involved the memorization of the classics as well as the copying of model texts to improve writing skills (Rawski, 1979). These practices reflected the importance of form in the evaluation of the civil service examinations. During the Southern Sung Dynasty, for example, candidates had to write a discussion (*lun*) on political and philosophical principles, answer policy questions (*tse*) involving history and classics, and compose a poem (*fu*) according to precise rules of composition (Chaffee, 1985). Particularly after 1400, writing well-structured essays using the *ba-gu-wen* (8-legged essay) form took precedence over the content of the essay (Elman, 1991). Though other types of schooling and other forms of literacy practice emerged parallel to those connected with the civil service examinations, the emphasis on memorization and the use of the *ba-gu-wen* achieves a hegemonic position in relationship to these other forms.

Along with Confucian rhetoric, the civil service examinations have often been cited as one example of how classical Chinese rhetoric still can influence second language writing. Although they were discredited at the beginning of the century with the fall of the Qing Dynasty, the assumption has been made that aspects of them still appear in the texts of Chinese students today. One such factor is the importance given to memorization. For the civil service examinations, the importance of memorization meant that individuals had to spend much time going over and over the classics, giving them an even greater significance. Thus, despite the existence of various strands of knowledge, both domestic and imported, Confucian philosophy emerged as dominant. Other types of literature were deemphasized or excluded from the canon. Buddhist teachings were either banned or used as objects of criticism (Zurcher, 1989). That some types of texts were elevated while others were marginalized can be assumed to have a significant effect on the development of rhetoric as well.

The civil service examinations, and the importance they gave to the memorization of the classics and the use of the *ba-gu-wen*, were not the sole forces affecting the development of Chinese rhetoric. The influence of the examinations on rhetoric was controversial throughout the Sung Dynasty. The *ba-gu-wen* form remained the center of controversy throughout both the Qing and Ming Dynasties, hundreds of years after they were first introduced. During the Ming Dynasty, the dominance of the *ba-gu-wen* as a form of writing was blamed for the decline of other forms of classical writing (Chou, 1988). Alternative forms for writing classical prose developed in response to the *ba-gu-wen* (Chou, 1988).

## The Influence of Neo-Confucianism on Rhetoric

We have tried here to show that Chinese rhetoric, rather than being monolithic, encompassed a variety of forms of thought, often reflecting the divergence of philosophical inquiry in Chinese society. Even Confucianism, the dominant form of rhetoric in many areas of Chinese literacy practice, was not a static form, but evolved in response to changes in Chinese society. One of the most important periods of such change for our discussion here is the development of Neo-Confucian thinking during the Sung Dynasty (960–1279). de Bary (1989, 1991), for example, analyzes Neo-Confucian philosophy in a way important for our understanding of Chinese rhetoric. Neo-Confucianism developed around the eleventh and twelfth centuries during the Sung Dynasty as a response to the growing influence of Buddhism. According to his view, there was a much larger role for critical thinking in Neo-Confucian thought than in more traditional Confucianism. This difference can be shown in an analysis of the terms used by Chu Hsi, a leading figure of Neo-Confucian thinking. Central to the process of learning for Chu Hsi was *ko wu chih-chih (ge wu zhi zhi)*, which can be translated as the "investigation of things and the extension of knowledge" (de Bary, 1989). This process differed from pure memorization in that it emphasized developing an insight into and understanding of what was being read.

According to de Bary, *ko* refers to the process of arriving at the principles of things and *chih* to the process of knowing. By defining *chih* as "knowing" instead of "knowledge," de Bary argues that more importance be given to the process of enlarging one's knowledge and developing an insight into the principles of what is learned instead of merely the memorization and recall of classic texts. He cites Chu Hsi from *The Great Learning (Da Xue Chang Chu)*: "Hence the initial teaching of *The Great Learning* insists that the learner, as he comes upon things of the world, must proceed from the principles already known and further explore them until he reaches a limit" (p. 197).

de Bary argues that Chu Hsi valued the students' abilities to judge for themselves so highly that he encouraged them to question even the classics. In the following passage from the *Wen-chi*, Chu Hsi presents a more critical view of how the classics should be read than has been found in some of the traditional texts on learning.

> [I, Chu] have found that sages and worthies of antiquity taught people to pursue learning with one intention only, to make students understand the meaning of moral principle through discussion, so that they can cultivate their own persons and extend it to others. The sages and the worthies did not wish them merely to engage in memorizing texts or in composing poetry and essays as a means of gaining fame or seeking office. Students today obviously do the contrary [to what the sages intended]. The methods of the sages and worthies employed in teaching are all found in the Classics. Dedicated scholars should by all means read them frequently, ponder them deeply and then inquire into them and sift them. (cited in de Bary, 1989, p. 203)

Chu deemphasizes the memorization of texts and in its place proposes that the way to understand the classic texts is through discussion, what de Bary describes as a "creative interaction" (p. 204). Thus, Chu deemphasizes the memorization and rote recitation of prior texts, preferring a more balanced relationship between the individual and the texts whereby the individual is expected to examine these canonized texts more critically. In another passage, Chu Hsi writes that "merely to memorize what one has recited and to have extensive information, but not to understand principle or to reach the point of thorough understanding and penetration, is to chase after what is small and forget what is great" (Chu & Lu, 1967, p. 52).

Chu Hsi saw literacy as an integral part of the education process. He criticized contemporary education as training students to impress others instead of cultivating the self. The emphasis on memorization was part of this focus on impressing others. Chu was particularly critical of writers excessively concerned with style, comparing them to "stage entertainers," since they are primarily concerned with pleasing other people. Thinking, in contrast to memorization, was the critical aspect of achieving the virtuous qualities laid down in the teachings of Confucius.

Chu wrote that "the virtue of thinking is penetration and profundity. When you think for a long time, penetration will naturally come about" Chu & Lu, 1967, p. 93). Thinking and reflection, however, are not enough. "One should try to formulate his own understanding in words because the process of articulating one's thoughts in words may clarify them" (cited in de Bary, p. 58). Chu here makes a connection between rhetoric and learning that has only appeared in Western rhetoric in recent times. This connection is similar to what was found in the writings of Hsi K'ang discussed previously. This discussion of Neo-Confucianism, does, however, present evidence that while the memorization of canonical texts was an integral part of the educational process, there were other practices equally valued. Thus, to say that memorization dominates the Chinese educational system ignores alternative practices presented here. Moreover, it ignores the fact that while memorization, even in conventional Confucian educational systems, may have been appropriate for younger children, it was not necessarily so for older children. A study of educational practices during this period shows that while younger children often memorized the classics, the older students were expected to apply what they had learned to the issues and problems of the day (Chaffee, 1985).

More important for this discussion is that Neo-Confucianism developed as an alternative form of learning to the traditional educational system designed to train individuals for the examination system. The Neo-Confucian academies were designed more for the moral and philosophical development of the individual. The dichotomy between the two was expressed in the essay "Admonitions for the Young and Ignorant": "If examination preparation is used to educate human talent, [the talented] will not know the essentials of action, so how can they be employed [by the government]" (cited in Chaffee, 1985, p. 7). Neo-Confucian scholars often could recognize the importance of the examinations, but at the same time criticize how the examinations distorted the learning process. In a speech at the famous White Deer Hollow Academy in Changsha, the Neo-Confucian scholar Liu Chiu-yuan admonished its students to not compromise their learning when they took the examinations.

Students look at the state examination as something to which they aspire. Very few can regard it with contempt. What they read is superficially the books of the sages; but what they aspire to is entirely different from what the sages said. . . . Students who perceive that this is not the right attitude for a man, and who make efforts to avoid falling in with mean fellows, must repent and exert themselves strenuously in behalf of righteousness when they enter the examination hall. They will be able to write on their papers what they have learned and what they have determined to do, and they will not deviate from the ways of the sages. (cited in Chaffee, 1985, p. 92)

Liu Chiu-yuan clearly placed more importance on the individual's own critical faculties than on the memorization of texts. For the Neo-Confucianists, this way of thinking was consistent with the teachings of Confucius.Chu Hsi does not deviate from the traditional Confucian focus on the sages; instead he differentiates between making a superficial recitation of what the sages said and coming to a deeper understanding of their wisdom.

There are many additional aspects of the debate over rhetoric that we have not covered here. In the 20th century, there has been the May 4th movement (Gunn, 1991) and the Communist revolution, both of which have had a profound impact on writing and the teaching of composition. Here, our goal has been to show in this discussion that Chinese rhetoric is not monolithic but that there are contending strands that have existed since Confucius. How this continuing debate over Chinese rhetoric affects contemporary rhetoric is an extremely complex issue that we have only superficially examined here.

## Implications for Teaching

Johns (this volume) suggests that the analysis of academic genres, including the role of citations, is an important part of a curriculum for initiating students into academic communities. My research suggests a number of areas for curriculum design for courses or programs that have large numbers of Chinese students.

1. Students need to understand the social context of the area or discipline the student is entering. We have shown here that the use of source texts in English-language texts reflects specific cultural attitudes that may or may not be similar in Chinese culture.

2. Students need to understand the rhetorical importance of source texts in their writing. The citing of a text is not just a convention but an integral part of the writer's argument.

3. Since English-language texts contain a variety of uses for citations, it is important for students to understand that source texts can be used in different ways.

4. The constraints of a genre, such as how to phrase a criticism, need to be directly taught, since there are sometimes clear cultural differences in how such criticisms are expressed.

5. The representation of what writing an academic research paper entails needs to be made explicit. Too often students are led to assume that a research paper is simply a regurgitation of facts from other authors. Students need to be trained specifically in analyzing those claims of an author they agree with and those they disagree with.

These suggestions argue for a composition curriculum that integrates reading and writing. Reading in the composition class need not be simply about learning facts but about how writers think through the problems they are addressing. In this way, the ESL composition class can break out of what Swales (1990) called the "ghetto of remediation" where ESL teaching only serves the needs of other academic departments and becomes a place where students come to understand what it means to be a contributing member of their chosen field.

## CONCLUSION

Olson (1977) wrote that the academic research paper is a manifestation of the long tradition of logic in Western culture. In this chapter, we have attempted to show how Chinese research is comparable by focusing on one aspect of the rhetoric of the academic paper, the use of citations. The purpose was not to show that one rhetoric lacked something the other one had but instead to show that each form of rhetoric reflects the cultural traditions in which it developed. In making this comparison, we have offered a view of rhetoric in this chapter that differs in many ways from previous research in contrastive rhetoric, yet reflects the concerns that teachers have raised concerning how Chinese students learn to write in English. We have attempted to show in this chapter through historical and empirical methods that Chinese rhetoric is as complex and ever changing as is Western rhetoric. Chinese students, particularly those who come to the West to study, are usually highly literate Chinese. They also bring a 2, 000-year old tradition of rhetoric to their second language writing process. Any attempt to make clear-cut and definitive conclusions concerning where Chinese rhetoric is affecting second language writing should be viewed with skepticism. At the same time, we have pointed out areas where problems Chinese ESL writers have been shown to have are consistent with their rhetorical traditions.

Research comparing the rhetorical traditions of different cultures has survived for over 25 years as a paradigm explaining second language writing. However, it has had to adapt itself to both changes in how second language learning is viewed and how literacy, in general, is viewed. Prior (this volume) has called for new approaches to contrastive rhetoric as a means for this paradigm to continue to develop. To continue to do so it must take into account new directions in the teaching of both L1 and L2 composition. We have suggested here a number of areas of research, such as the sociology of science and the historical study of Chinese rhetoric, as sources of information for research in comparative rhetoric and its implications for second language composition teaching. Regardless of the approach used, research must continue to explore the implications of new approaches to language learning as well as new approaches to rhetorical study in order for contrastive rhetoric research to contribute more to the ESL classroom than what Raimes (1991) has called a "heightened awareness" of the rhetorical traditions the ESL student brings to the classroom. By doing so, contrastive rhetoric can continue to contribute to the discussion of how students learn to write in a second language and what types of writing should be taught in the ESL classroom.

## REFERENCES

Applebee, A. N. (1984). *Contexts for learning to write: Studies of secondary school instruction*. Norwood, NJ: Ablex.

Bao, Z. M. (1990). Language and world view in ancient China. *Philosophy East and West, 40*, 195–219.

Basham, C., Ray, R., & Whalley, E. (1991). *Cross-cultural perspectives on reader/writer orientations*. Paper presented at the 1991 Conference on College Composition and Communication Convention, Chicago, IL.

Bloch, J. G. (1988). *Academic writing in Chinese and English: Is there a difference?* Paper presented at the 1988 Conference on College Composition and Communication Convention, St. Louis, MO.

Bloch, J. G. (1990, March). *Univeralism versus particularism: The relationship between Chinese and English rhetoric*. Paper presented at the 1990 Conference on College Composition and Communication Convention, Chicago, IL.

Bodde, D. (1981). *Essays of Chinese civilization*. Princeton, NJ: Princeton University Press.

Brookmeyer, R. (1991). Reconstruction and future trends of the AIDS epidemic in the United States. *Science, 253*, 37–42.

Cashman, K. V., & Fiske, R. S. (1991). Fallout of pyroclastic debris from submarine volcanic eruptions. *Science, 253*, 275–280.

Chaffee, J. W. (1985). *The thorny gates of learning in Sung China: A social history of examinations*. New York: Cambridge University Press.

Chan, W. T. (1963). *A source book in Chinese philosophy*. Princeton, NJ: Princeton University Press.

Cheng, P. G. P. (1985). *An analysis of contrastive rhetoric: English and Chinese expository prose, pedagogical implications, and strategies for the ESL teacher in a ninth-grade curriculum*. Unpublished doctoral dissertation, The Pennsylvania State University, University Park, PA.

Ch'ien, E. T. (1986). *Chiao Hung and the restructuring of neo-Confucianism in the late Ming*. New York: Columbia University Press.

Chou, C. P. (1988). *Yuan Hung-Tao and the Kung-An school*. Cambridge, UK: Cambridge University Press.

Chu, H., & Lu, T. C. (1967). *Reflection on things at hand* (W. T. Chan, Trans.). New York: Columbia University Press.

Cole, M., & Means, B. (1981). *Comparative studies of how people think*. Cambridge, MA: Harvard University Press.

Cole, S. C. (1990). Martin Luther King Jr., and his sources [Forum]. *PMLA, 105*, 1125–1126.

Comprone, J. (1990 March). *Dialogues of self and text: Asian and American perspectives on rhetoric*. Paper presented at 1990 Conference on College Composition and Communication, Chicago, IL.

Cua, A. S. (1973). Reasonable action and Confucian argumentation. *Journal of Chinese Philosophy, 1*, 57–75.

de Bary, W. T. (1989). Chu Hsi's aims as an educator. In W. T. de Bary & J. W. Chafee (Eds.), *Neo-Confucian education: The formative stage* (pp. 186–218). Berkeley: University of California Press.

de Bary, W. T. (1991). *Learning for one's self*. New York: Columbia University Press.

Elman, B. A. (1991). Political, social, and cultural reproduction via civil service examinations in late imperial China. *The Journal of Asian Studies, 50,* 7–28.

Fang, L. Z. (1992 April). *Politics and science in China.* Paper presented at the University of Pittsburgh.

Garrett, M. (1988, November). *Mediations on invention East and West.* Paper presented at the SCA Conference, New Orleans, LA.

Garrett, M. (1991). The Asian Challenge. In S. K. Foss, K. A. Foss, & R. Trapp (Eds.), *Contemporary perspectives on rhetoric* (2nd ed.). Prospect Heights, IL: Waveland Press.

Garrow, D. J. (1991). King's plagiarism: Imitation, insecurity, and transformation. *Journal of American History, 20,* 86–92.

Gilbert, N., & Mulkay, M. J. (1984). *Opening Pandora's box.* Cambridge, UK: Cambridge University Press.

Gunn, E. (1991). *Rewriting Chinese: Style and innovation in 20th century Chinese prose.* Palo Alto, CA: Stanford University Press.

Hansen, C. (1983). *Language and logic in ancient China.* Ann Arbor: University of Michigan Press.

Han, S., Jiao, M. D., &, Xing, M. (1990). Yang-Cong He-ren di Chao Wei Jie-gou yu rDNA Fu-zhi Wei-Zhi (The Micro-sculpic structure of Onion Core and rDNA Replication Position). *Chinese Science, 8,* 818–821.

Henricks, R. G. (1981). Hsi K'ang and argumentation in the Wei, and a refutation of the essay "Residence is unrelated to good fortune." *Journal of Chinese Philosophy, 8,* 169–224.

Henricks, R. G. (1983). *Philosophy and argumentation in third-century China: The essays of Hsi K'ang.* Princeton, NJ: Princeton University Press.

Hull, G., & Rose. M. (1989). Rethinking remediation: Toward a social-cognitive understanding of problematic reading and writing. *Written Communication, 6,* 139–154.

Hunter, A. (1990). Rhetoric in research, network of knowledge. In A. Hunter (Ed.), *The rhetoric of social research.* New Brunswick, NJ: Rutgers University Press.

Kaplan, R. B. (1988, June). *The Chinese connection.* Paper presented at the 1988 Summer TESOL Meeting, Flagstaff, AZ.

Kaufer, D. S., Geisler, C., & Neuwirth, C. (1989). *Arguing from sources: Exploring issues through reading and writing.* San Diego: Harcourt Brace Jovanovich.

Kerr, R. A. (1989). A wizard of middle Earth under fire. *Science, 246,* 758–760.

Kuhn, T. (1970). *The structure of scientific revolutions (2nd ed.).* Chicago: The University of Chicago Press.

LaFollette, M. C. (1992). *Stealing into print: Fraud, plagiarism, and misconduct in scientific publishing.* Los Angeles: University of California Press.

Latour, B. (1988). *Science in action.* Cambridge, MA: Harvard University Press.

Leki, I. (1991). Twenty-five years of contrastive rhetoric: Text analysis and writing pedagogies. *TESOL Quarterly, 25,* 123–143.

Liu, H. (1959). *The literary mind and the carving of dragons: A study of thought and pattern in Chinese literature* (trans. by V. Y. C. Shih) New York: Columbia University Press.

Matalene, C. (1985). Contrastive rhetoric: An American writing teacher in China. *College English, 47,* 789–808.

Miller, K. D. (1990). Composing Martin Luther King, Jr. *PMLA, 105,* 70–82.

Mohan, B., & Lo, W. A. (1985). Academic writing and Chinese students: Transfer and developmental factors. *TESOL Quarterly, 19,* 515–534.

Mulkay, M. J. (1972). *The social process of innovation.* London: Macmillian.

Mulkay, M. J. (1991). Don Quixote's double: A self-exemplifying text. In S. Woolgar (Ed.),

*Knowledge and reflexivity: New frontiers in the sociology of knowledge* (pp. 81–100). London: Sage Publications.

Nakayama, S. (1984). *Academic and scientific traditions in China, Japan, and the West* (J. Dusenberry, Trans.). Tokyo: University of Tokyo Press.

Needham, J. (1970). *Clerks and craftsman in China and the West*. Cambridge, UK: Cambridge University Press.

Needham, J. (1981). *Science in traditional China: A comparative perspective*. Hong Kong: The Chinese University Press.

Oliver, R. (1962). *Communications and culture*. Springfield, IL: Thomas.

Olson, D. R. (1977). From utterance to text: The bias of language in speech and writing. *Harvard Educational Review, 47*, 257–281.

Ostler, S. E. (1987). English in parallels: A comparison of English and Arabic prose. In U. Connor & R. Kaplan (Eds.), *Writing across languages: Analysis of L2 text* (pp. 169–182). Reading, MA: Addison-Wesley.

Pang, L. O. Q. (1988). To abide in harmony: Family and the individual in Confucian China. In *Chinese social relationships: The ideal versus the real* (pp. 7–11). Honolulu: Center for Chinese Studies.

Price, D. J. (1986). *Little science, big science . . . and beyond*. New York: Columbia University Press.

Raimes, R. (1991). Out of the woods: Emerging traditions in the teaching of writing. *TESOL Quarterly, 25*, 407–430.

Rawski, E. S. (1979). *Education and popular literacy in Ch'ing China*. Ann Arbor: University of Michigan Press.

Reid, J. M. (1988). *Quantitative differences in English prose written by Arabic, Chinese, Spanish, and English students*. Unpublished doctoral dissertation, Colorado State University,

Scollon, R. (in press). Eight legs and one elbow: Stance and structure in Chinese English compositions. *In Launching the literacy decade*.

Shen, F. (1989). Culture: Identity as a key to learning composition. *College Composition and Communication, 40*, 459–465.

Sun, T. H., (1991). Dui "She-hui Jiao-Se" di Zhi-xue Si-kao (Philosophical Thought on "Social Roles"). *Social Science, 4*, 44–47.

Swales, J. (1981). *Aspects of article introductions*. Birmingham, UK: University of Aston.

Swales, J. (1986). Citation analysis and discourse analysis. *Applied Linguistics, 7*, 39–56.

Swales, J. (1990). *Genre analysis: English in academic and research settings*. Cambridge, UK: Cambridge University Press.

Taylor, G., & Chen T. G. (1991). Linguistic, cultural, and subcultural issues in contrastive discourse analysis: Anglo-American and Chinese scientific texts. *Applied Linguistics, 12*, 319–336.

Tu, W. M. (1989). The Sung Confucian idea of education: A background understanding. In W. T. de Bary & J. W. Chafee (Eds.), *Neo-Confucian education: The formative stage* (pp. 139–150). Berkeley: University of California Press.

Wheeler, D. L. (1991, July 3). US has barred grants to 6 scientists in past two years. *The Chronicle of Higher Education*, pp. A1, A5–A6.

Zhang, L. (1992). *The tao and the logos: Literary hermeneutics East and West*. Durham, NC: Duke University Press.

Ziman, J. M. (1968). *Public knowledge: An essay concerning the social dimension of science*. London: Cambridge University Press.

Zurcher, E. (1989). Buddhism and education in T'ang Times. In W. T. de Bary & J. W. Chafee (Eds.), *Neo-Confucian education: The formative stage* (pp. 19–56). Berkeley: University of California Press.

# PART III

# Pedagogy

# CHAPTER 11

# Teaching Classroom and Authentic Genres: Initiating Students into Academic Cultures and Discourses

**Ann M. Johns**
*San Diego State University*

This chapter first presents some of the problems faced by English for Academic Purposes (EAP) instructors when attempting to promote "the process" in their classrooms. It then describes efforts to balance process, written product, and transfer of learning in academic English (adjunct) classes for diverse freshman students through the introduction of classroom genres (e.g., the essay examination) and authentic genres (texts that serve communicative purposes among experts). Two assignments, one for each genre type, are described, with subtasks outlined. Conclusions are drawn about the successes of this approach and suggestions for extending it to other contexts, especially through the use of portfolios, are made.

> The models of literacy are like those of Monopoly or checkers; they can be taught and learned without any great psychic damage to the learner. Violating them, however, can mean a forfeit.
>
> —Purves, 1991, p. 36

The Process Movement, which originated in native-speaker contexts in the 1960s and continues into the 1990s, has benefited the teaching and learning of ESL writing immensely. For the first time in modern history, ESL teachers have began to think of writing as *writing*, not merely as an afterthought in the teaching of spoken language or an outgrowth of the study of reading and translation. The earliest realization of the Process Movement, Expressivism, enabled teachers to encourage students to develop freedom and fluency through the use of ungraded journals, poetry, and other writer-generated texts (Elbow, 1981; Johns, 1990; Urzua, 1986). Cognitivism, the second phase of the Process Movement, encourages student planning for writing, self-reflection, and thoughtful revision of written drafts (Flower, 1989; Mlynarczyk, 1991). The introduction of Expressivism and Cognitivism into ESL has led to research in composing (Kroll, 1990; Raimes, 1985, 1987; Zamel, 1983), to improved teaching and learning, and sometimes to more equitable testing for second language students (Hamp-Lyons, 1991; Tierney, Carter, & Desai, 1991). Despite its considerable contributions, some ESL teachers have begun to question the centrality of "the process" in an academic reading and composition curriculum. There are a number of reasons for teacher concern, some of which will be discussed here.

One issue has been raised in the native-speaker camp, as well: In the late 1980s, criticisms of the stance of the hard-line process advocates—and the way in which the "writing process" had been codified in school curricula— began to appear in *College English* and *College Composition and Communication*. Practitioners began asking whether the students' processes should be the be-all and the end-all of writing instruction and whether self-expression and exploration of writer processes and meaning discovery should crowd out issues such as audience and rhetorical purpose. A neglected topic, because of its role in the discarded current-traditional rhetoric (Johns, 1990), is form; for in process teaching, form has become secondary (Zamel, 1984) as the writer is encouraged to explore meaning in texts. In an important article, " . . . who took the form out of content?", Coe argues that form should continue to be a central consideration in the teaching of writing, for it is necessary for student access to various literacies.[1] Coe tells us that

> Like language, form is social. One function of discourse communities is to prescribe and prefer forms. Learning conventional forms, often by the tacit process of "indwelling", is a way of learning a community's discourse, of gaining access. For a form implies a strategy of response, an attitude, a way of sorting factors, sizing up situations. (1987, p. 19)

Coe and others (see Purves, 1991; Swales, 1990) do not suggest that teachers and students return to the empty forms of the current-traditional days, for example, the "comparison/contrast," "description," or "cause/effect" vessels into which content is poured. Instead, a much more sophisticated notion of form is suggested, consisting of the macrostructures and moves of texts as they reflect the conventions, the contents, and the

---

[1]See also Jacoby, Leech, and Holten (this volume) for a discussion of the importance of forms and their rhetorical purposes.

habits of minds among initiated readers within discourse communities (Dudley-Evans, this volume; Swales, 1981, 1990). Thus, when contemporary rhetoricians speak of form, they are referring to a generalized organizational structure that is identified by and serves the communicative purposes of a discourse community. Within many of our students' science classes, for example, there is what is called the lab report. Engineers identify grant proposals and bids as important texts (Johns, 1993). Academics write research papers appropriate for their disciplines, and so on. As the interest in these genres and the interaction of content, form, and values within communities grows, so does the literature. Bazerman's *Shaping Written Knowledge* (1989), a discussion of how writing and knowledge is shaped by discourse communities, has been well received, as has Bazerman and Paradis's (1991) edited volume on writing in the professions. Myers (1985, 1989) has written a number of important articles on textual "forms" and their functions in the sciences. Jolliffe's edited volume on writing in academic disciplines (1988) includes papers on "form." And there are many other examples, including those in this volume, for example, Braine and Dudley-Evans. Thus, in theoretical, pedagogical, and research contexts, forms have appeared again in considerably different guises: as genres, with structure, language, conventions, nonlinear text, and specialized argumentation.[2]

In addition the neglect of form, there are other concerns voiced by ESL practitioners when they express their doubts about accepting "the process" as central to their classrooms. It goes without saying that most ESL writers are different culturally and linguistically from native English speakers. If we are to accept the arguments of contrastive rhetoric, for example, that the organization of discourses and the values realized in texts, even within the same genres, can differ among cultures[3] (Bloch & Chi, this volume; Connor & Kaplan, 1987; Leki, 1992), then we must devote more time to assisting students in understanding English texts and their cultural and linguistic contexts. If style or register is not transparent to the nonnative speaker, then we must devote class time to academic styles within discourse communities and the purposes they serve (Elbow, 1991). The relationship between tense and discourse function, long an interest in English for Specific Purposes (Swales, 1985; Tarone, Dwyer, Gillette, & Icke, 1981) must also be taken into consideration in a class for ESL students.

In addition to being troubled by the topics that "process" classes address, academic teachers also question the methods. As Horowitz (1986a) has

---

[2]See Belcher, this volume, for an interesting discussion of argumentation within genres across disciplines.

[3]It has also been argued that similarities across languages exist within disciplines (see, e.g., Eggington, 1987).

noted, some nonnative speaking students are not familiar or comfortable with the inductive orientation of process-centered approaches or with a personal search for meaning. Many have lived with deduction and "removed writing" in their past lives—and they feel quite comfortable with their past experiences.

For these reasons, then, some academic ESL teachers have decided that teaching "the process" as it appears in most textbooks is not enough, and in some cases, it is clearly inappropriate.[4] The need for an alternative, genre-based approach is most evident for teachers of graduate students (Belcher, this volume; Swales, 1990). At the graduate level, students have selected their majors, and research and writing for their majors is essential to their success. Thus, focused teaching for research papers and other genres becomes a necessity. For, as Dillon (1991) suggests, "Scholars are constituted as authors by their disciplinary discourse. . . . The works and views they must refer to, the very issues they can address, are "given" by the state of the disciplinary discussion at the time" (1991, p. 158).

However, for those of us teaching undergraduate students, the requirement to step above and outside the Process Movement in order to empower our students is also essential, for they are confronted constantly with university writing demands that are at odds with approaches and assignments in their process-centered classrooms. (Johnson & Roen, 1989; Leki, this volume) Some of our students' academic writing tasks do not allow for careful revising or editing; others do not encourage self-expression; others do not allow for choices about form or content (Horowitz, 1986b). Perhaps most obvious of these antiprocess tasks is the essay examination question, which is basically a knowledge display (Hounsell, 1984; Horowitz, 1986a, 1986b).

Nonetheless, Spack (1988) has argued, quite convincingly, that teaching principles of academic writing to undergraduates is problematic. Often, students have not chosen a major, or they have little experience with the demands, topics, knowledge claims, and values of the discipline they have chosen. Having never been exposed to a writing class in their home country (see Dubin & Kuhlman, 1992; Leki, 1992, pp. 39–46, 88–104), or having written only in their high school English classes, they have little knowledge of the intellectual and linguistic requirements of academic discourses.

---

[4]It appears that these arguments would not have to be made in Australia, where the genre approach is evident at all levels of education. A teachers' book explaining this approach (Derewianka, 1990), suggests that primary school students ask the following questions of texts for a reading/writing class:

What do you think we might use this sort of text for?

What could we call it?

How is this text different from x text?

Look at the beginning of the text. What is the writer doing here? What does the beginning tell the reader?

Teachers of these novice ESL students, seeking to break the "process" barrier, ask these questions: What should I teach? What can students at this level learn that will enable them to approach academic discourses and discourse communities with some confidence?

## ACADEMIC DISCOURSE AT THE FRESHMAN LEVEL

It would be impossible to suggest the answers to these questions for all undergraduate students and contexts, but I can report some successes in a freshman "package" that has been in existence at my university for the past six years, a program enrolling culturally and linguistically diverse students for their first semester that has increased their retention into second-year enrollment from 20% to more than 50%. To be assigned to this program, the students must be "at risk": They have scored below 400 on the SAT verbal or failed the freshman-level composition examination that would enable them to enroll in the first general education composition course.

## THE PROGRAM: ASSUMPTIONS AND PURPOSES

Each fall, we offer a "transition package" for this population: 10 to 12 English reading/writing adjunct classes attached to required classes in the core general education (GE) curriculum (e.g., introductory political science, cultural geography, or psychology).[5] The GE classes become a springboard for development in the adjunct class of study skills, as well as for discussion and study of academic genres, ways of speaking, argumentation, use of data, knowledge claims, and other issues that separate the new student, and even the more experienced one (see Pearson-Casanave, 1992), from the initiated academic. We have based the curriculum in these adjunct classes on some shared assumptions, though the manner in which we conduct these classes depends, in large part, upon the nature of the general education class in which the students are enrolled.

The assumptions are these:

1. The students are entering a new culture, with a generalized set of academic rules that apply to discourses (Dillon, 1991; Elbow, 1991) and another, related set that applies to the disciplines and individual classrooms. The rules are not always agreed on, nor are they written in stone: Changes occur constantly in the literacy practices of the disciplines. As in all cultures, there are defined roles (e.g., teacher/student, writer/reader) and

---

[5]For discussions of adjunct and nonadjunct classes, see Brinton, Snow, and Wesche (1989) or Jacoby, Leech, and Holten (this volume).

implicit expectations for how individuals in these roles interact, either in speaking or in writing.[6]

2. With these roles come values, implicitly held by expert writers. Among the values suggested in the literature for general academic English are the "rhetoric of objectivity" (Dillon, 1991), thus the preference for use of the third person; the "rubber-gloved quality of voice and register," and the requirement for using caution, especially when making knowledge claims (Elbow, 1991).

3. Ways of writing and speaking, and the resulting genres, depend upon the communicative purposes of the participants in the disciplines (Swales, 1990). Often, even "non-writing" (Raimes, in Horowitz, 1986a) such as that found in essay examinations, is guided by an academic instructor's sense of important disciplinary topics and concepts. Written text is often accompanied by nonlinear text, for example, graphs and charts, containing information that is central to the understanding of the genres of the disciplines.

## GOALS AND APPROACHES: CLASSROOM AND AUTHENTIC GENRES

At the freshman level, and during most of their undergraduate careers, students may occasionally be exposed to the authentic texts employed to communicate among experts in a discipline (e.g., the bid, the proposal, the memo, the report, or the journal article), but they are seldom asked to write in these genres. Instead, most academic faculty, who know only the assignments of their own university experience, require students to produce texts that are reminiscent of their own undergraduate experience rather than of the discipline they have chosen, texts that I will call "classroom genres" (CGs).[7] These include, as Horowitz (1986b) and others have noted, the essay examination, the summary or summary critique, an annotated bibliography, class lecture notes, a research project, and a synthesis of sources. For very prac-

---

[6]See, for example, Bloch and Chi (this volume) and Matalene (1985), for the implications of these roles for Chinese students attempting to produce academic English.

[7]My students and I were particularly surprised one semester when a young instructor, fresh out of graduate school, required essays much like those in the typical nonadjunct English class for the geography class. I suggested that my students not use a wordy introduction in their essays as they had in English classes, but instead, employ a sentence like "The purpose of this paper is to. . . . " I also suggested that they provide headings throughout the essay so that the teacher could quickly follow their arguments, for he had more than 200 papers to read.

I was wrong. The geography instructor, believing that the only acceptable genre for undergraduates was the English class essay, marked my students down for their practical introductions and their use of headings. "You failed," the students reported to me. And I had.

Paul Prior (this volume) notes that the assignment of classroom rather than authentic genres can also be characteristic of graduate classes. Apparently, many faculty have no interest in initiating their students into the discourses of their disciplines.

tical reasons, then, one goal in our freshman classes is to enable students to discover the rules and the purposes for the CGs that determine their grades.

Mastering of CGs may provide the basis for assisting students in studying authentic genres (AGs), texts that serve real communicative purposes among professionals in the discipline. However, unless the academic English instructors encourage student understanding of the connections and possible transfer of skills among all academic genres (Johns, 1988) and the importance of student openness to genre possibilities, their students may be locked into an undergraduate pattern, an inability to move beyond the requirements of the CGs to initiation into an academic or professional discourse community. Therefore, the second goal of the adjunct class is to expose students to AGs and to the possibilities they present for intellectual interaction among the initiated in discourse communities.

Thus, we strive to encourage student flexibility. By the time our students leave our classes, they should grasp the general purposes for CGs and AGs. If they are to understand and produce what is expected in their classes, they must know how to analyze the classroom context and the texts important to that context. They should know what questions to ask and how to get answers that will assist them in coming to terms with the new texts and the cultures that these texts represent — and to manipulate these texts for their own purposes (see Johns, 1992).

In this chapter, I will discuss two of the adjunct writing class assignments developed for a group of freshman students enrolled in an entry-level geography class. Of particular importance to this discussion is the interaction between CGs and AGs and the development of an investigative approach to the issue of genres. It must be noted that although assignments related to CGs and AGs were the central focus of the class, extensive use was also made of the contributions of the Process Movement — especially in the areas of peer review and student reflection in the portfolios — for developing personal as well as academic literacies is central to student success (Brandt, 1990; Johns, 1992).

The general education geography class in which these students were enrolled was much like other large core classes: Students listened to lectures and took notes, read a textbook, and were administered a number of examinations, principally in the multiple-choice format. They were also given take-home essays as part of their evaluation. Little was deliberately done by the professor to initiate students into the discipline; nothing was provided that would increase their awareness of authentic genres.

## PORTFOLIO STRUCTURE: COMBINING CGS AND AGS

In order to enrich the students' experience and support our goals, we require an Academic Task Portfolio (ATP) in our adjunct classes. Writing and reading portfolios vary considerably from context to context (Belanoff & Dickson, 1991; Hill & Parry, 1992); however, most share certain elements (Paulson, Paulson, & Meyer, 1990; *Quarterly of the National Writing Project*, 1990), and our ATPs are no exception. Each ATP is a collection of student work, representative of the goals of the program. Entries are varied and written over time. Each entry (in our case, there were five, carefully marked by dividers) includes the various drafts of the text, related materials (e.g., interview notes and a map for the migratory history paper) and a reflection (Hebert, 1992). At the end of the semester, the portfolios are considered in the assessment process (see Hamp-Lyons, 1991; Tierney et al., 1991).[8]

In this adjunct program, all portfolios contained the same task types (emphasized below); however, tasks varied depending upon the nature of the general education class with which the adjunct reading/writing class was integrated. For the students in the geography class, the following reading/ writing assignments task entries, with their reflections, were included in the portfolio:

1. *A data-driven paper* (interview, data analysis): migratory history.
2. *A library assignment*: Writing from sources: journals and academic books in geography.
3. *An abstract or summary:* Abstract of a journal article in geography.
4. *An out-of-class essay:* Longer paper, assigned by the content instructor.
5. *An in-class examination response:* Written under time constraints in the geography class.

I will discuss two of these assignments, the data-driven research paper (a CG) and the abstract (based on an AG) and how these assignments were designed to meet the class goals.

## Assignment 1: A Data-driven Paper (CG)

The data for the students' papers in this task category can be gathered in a number of ways. Most adjunct faculty choose observation (e.g., of a student demonstration on campus) or interview. In all cases, the students must prepare for and create a classroom genre considerably different from the standard composition class essay and must employ terms and topics from their general education classes.

---

[8]For a useful, ongoing discussion of portfolio projects in a variety of contexts at all levels of instruction, subscribe to *Portfolio News*.

For the geography students, I assigned an interview paper on the topic of migration, with the following goals:

1. to wean students away from their fixation upon the 5-paragraph essay, a carryover from the current-traditional period and their earlier composition class experiences,
2. to develop within students a sense of the requirements of academic writing,
3. to enable students to develop and draw from an interview to produce an academic paper,
4. to increase student awareness of their writing processes as they approach different tasks.

As we began the project, the students and I reviewed issues related to migration within their geography textbooks and lectures. First, we identified terms and concepts that dealt directly with migration, for example, "chain and step migration," and "push and pull factors." Then, we searched for related terms, for example *acculturation* and *assimilation*, and their various realizations (e.g., economic, religious, linguistic, political).

After compiling this list of vocabulary and concepts, many of which would appear in the paper, students were asked to identify either an individual or a family who had migrated to the United States. Because many of my students are recent immigrants, they were permitted to use their own families as subjects. The assignment was

Write a migratory history of an individual or family that has come to the United States within the last ten years. In the introduction, state the purposes for your paper. Then, briefly describe the geography of the area and culture of that family in their home location, e.g., Laos. Next, discuss the manner in which the family migrated to the United States. Finally, discuss the acculturation or assimilation factors that define the family as presently constituted. Note, in particular, the differences between the generations born in this country and those who migrated.

Your grade will be based upon how well you follow directions in the assignment, use of detail and example to demonstrate the results of your interview data, and your use of geography terms.

The students devoted the next two weeks to writing interview questions (in groups) and practicing interviews with fellow students, identifying their subjects, organizing and analyzing their notes, and preparing their first drafts. Using a peer revision sheet based upon the assignment presented above, the students evaluated each others' first drafts for content, remarking on the absence of geography terms, the lack of detail, or the failure to include a purpose in the introduction. Together, we discussed how this assignment was unlike most of those they had completed in writing classes: The prompt was more explicit and the paper was, by necessity, organized differently from 5-paragraph essays or book reports that the students had been accustomed to completing in high school.

After the peer reviews, the second versions of the paper were completed. Another revision resulted in a third draft, after which the students wrote a reflective paper on the assignment, a paper that would later become a part of their academic task portfolios. In the reflection, students discussed (a) why they had chosen a particular family as their subject, (b) the difficulties they had in completing the assignment, and (c) some of the successes they had experienced, particularly in producing the text. We concluded this task with a recapitulation in which I argued that there are all kinds of academic tasks, and that students should be sufficiently flexible to adapt to the task requirements presented.

## Assignment 3: Writing an Abstract for an AG

The second assignment discussed here begins with an authentic genre, a published research article, provided by a faculty member in the geography department. This article did not deal directly with concepts and issues from the students' human geography course. Instead, it was selected because it was readable, "typical of article structure." It also demonstrated the breadth of the discipline and its core values and concepts. For all geographers, for example, site is central, thus maps are an integral part of the discussion, whether the text discusses birds (as in the article) or human migration (as in the case of their textbooks).

Whereas the first assignment provided a transition from personal to academic writing and an introduction to a CG using academic style, this authentic article opened the door to a number of possibilities, including the integration of CGs and AGs, a further study of the nature of academic writing, of the structure of introductions (Dudley-Evans, this volume; Swales, 1981), and of practice of summarizing and abstracting, an important skill at every level of academic life.

Because this genre was new to the students, we spent a considerable amount of time studying the text. We noticed, for example, that the title, "The Potential for Conservation of Polynesian Birds through Habitat Mapping and Species Translocation" was quite revealing[9], identifying not only the topic but the site and the methodology. From the title, we went to other titles in the list of references at the end of the article, discovering what

---

[9]Huckin (1987) has argued that titles in scientific articles are becoming increasingly informative. This is certainly the case here.

these titles revealed. This activity provided an opportunity to practice referencing styles. Students were asked to write a bibliographic entry for this article, using the style reflected in the article references. This activity led to a discussion of how different types of references are cited and the importance of always requesting a style sheet from a faculty member when a paper requiring references was assigned.

Having removed the abstract from the paper, I then took students to the introduction, asking them to work in groups to segment it into "moves," that is, establishing the territory, establishing a niche, and occupying the niche (see Dudley-Evans, this volume; Swales, 1981, 1990). Initially, the students found this exercise very difficult; however, by the time our class activity ended, they had began to understand how the moves were signaled and why they were important to an introduction of this type.[10] We then scanned the text to find the headings, noting which of these headings that might be characteristic of geography ("Description of the Study Area") and which might be contained in any research article (e.g., "Materials and Methods," "Results," "Conclusions"). We then studied the special characteristics of the maps in this article, noting geography terms and predicting text from what the maps portrayed.[11]

A final exercise in the initial reading was a discussion of citation, which we approached from three angles. The first was the manner in which citations are inserted into texts, that is, the syntax. We found sentences in which citations were included, and read them aloud:

"Griffith et al. (1989) found that . . ."

"The eight southern islands contain the bulk of land area (Johnston, 1953; 1955)."

"Floristic studies have been published for Rorotonga (Cheesman, 1903; Wilder, 1935)."

In each case, we discussed the syntax and the focus, that is, whether citations were author or information prominent (See Weissberg & Buker, 1990, pp. 43–45). Later, we would practice citation sentences when developing another CG, a short library research paper.

The second view of citations comes from work of DuBois (1988) and others (see, e.g., Amsterdamska & Laydesdorff, 1989; Bavelas, 1978). In

---

[10]Understanding the purposes of introductions — and writing them — is demanding for us all, but particularly for ESL students. See, for example, Scarcella (1984).

[11]One of my students told me that before he enrolled in this cultural geography class, he thought maps were "the truth", that there was just one kind of map for all purposes. This "Polynesian Birds . . . " article, and much that he learned in his geography class, opened his eyes to the ideologies and informational possibilities of map-making.

this work, citation is seen as revealing a complex set of social and authority relations among members of a discourse community. We began discussing whom the authors might cite if they were aware of the importance of these relations. They suggested the authors' teachers, leaders in the discipline, and people with whom the author agrees.[12]

After this purposeful skimming of the AG, the students were ready for their own writing. As noted earlier, I had omitted the abstract, and now I asked them to write one. However, rather than leaving them to create their own summary of the text, I provided a set of moves, based upon the article headings, to guide their efforts. In the summaries, students were to include sentences about the *purpose*, *questions*, *methodology*, *results*, and *conclusions*. I omitted the discussion of site, though if I were to make the assignment again, I might not have done so. This abstract assignment was a very difficult one, students found. Most did not get to the core of the article, that is, they could not summarize each major section in a sentence or two. Instead, most concentrated upon the argument for conservation which appeared in the justification for the study.

We compared the students' work with my own abstract of the article and with the abstract written by the authors, which interestingly enough, contains opinion and argument. A discussion of variation in summary and abstracting ensued, and students came away with an understanding that summary texts differ depending on their purposes.

After reviewing the paper and writing the abstract, students were asked to take the information within the article to create a professional genre, a formal letter. Placing themselves in the roles of the authors of "The Potential for Conservation . . . " paper, whose purposes are to obtain grants and publish their findings, the students wrote a letter to the Tonga Parliament, discussing their findings and suggesting measures for conservation of wildlife. Again, the students had difficulty. Writing persuasive letters, particularly letters of this type, is a formidable task. As in the case of the abstract, I also wrote a letter, so that we could compare my approach with theirs.

## CONCLUSION

Teaching issues in academic discourse to undergraduate students is demanding. Because they are still naive about academic language and values, because they must enroll in a variety of different classes in different disciplines to meet their general education requirements, and because they

---

[12]A personal note: This paper follows the rules: My reference list includes my Journal co-editors (Dudley-Evans & Swales) and those colleagues with whom I agree (a long list).

are assigned tasks (e.g., essay responses) in their academic classes that are not required of mature professionals in discourse communities, making decisions about what and how to teach becomes problematic.

We believe that we may have found some of the answers in our adjunct classes as we integrate the study of classroom genres (CGs) and the authentic genres (AGs) of the disciplines in which the students are enrolled. Through reading and discussion of texts, we can prepare students to

1. Ask the appropriate questions of content faculty, for example, about the organization of unfamiliar genres, about citation and referencing style, and about academic language.
2. Understand the limited purposes of CGs and the expectations of faculty in undergraduate classes.
3. Understand more about the nature of authentic genres and the purposes they serve within communities.
4. Be flexible—not to cling to one referencing style, one summary style, or one text organization. Instead, students need to be open to styles and texts of all kinds.
5. To begin to analyze the importance of audience in writing, to understand that audiences have different expectations depending on their individual personalities and their roles within a community.

Thus, though the contributions of the Process Movement have enriched the teaching of ESL writing greatly, adopting them as a core for an academic discourse class can shield students from real-life writing only temporarily. If we can make genres the class focus and teach variety and openness to texts, we may more appropriately prepare students for the demands of their academic classrooms and their professional lives.

## REFERENCES

Amsterdamska, O., & Laydesdorff, L. (1989). Citations: Indicators of significance? *Sciento-metrics, 15*, 449–471.

Bavelas, J. B. (1978). The social psychology of citations. *Personality and Social Psychology Bulletin, 16,* 274–283.

Belanoff, P., & Dickson M. (Eds.).'(1991). *Portfolios: Process and product.* Portsmouth, NH: Boynton-Cook.

Bazerman, C. (1989). *Shaping written knowledge.* Madison: The University of Wisconsin Press.

Bazerman, C., & Paradis J. (1991). *Textual dynamics of the professions.* Madison: University of Wisconsin Press.

Brandt, D. (1990). *Literacy as involvement: The acts of writers, readers and texts.* Carbondale, IL: Southern Illinois Press.

Brinton, D. M., Snow, M. A. & Wesche, M. B. (1989). *Content-based second language instruction*. New York: Newbury House.

Coe, R. M. (1987). An apology for form: Or, who took the form out of process? *College English, 49*, 13–28.

Connor, U., & Kaplan, R. B. (1987). *Writing across languages: Analysis of L2 texts*. Reading, MA: Addison-Wesley.

Derewianka, B. (1990). *Exploring how texts work*. Maryborough, Victoria, Australia: Primary Teaching Association

Dillon, G. L. (1991). *Contending rhetorics: Writing in academic disciplines*. Bloomington/Indianapolis: Indian University Press.

Dubin, F., & Kuhlman N. (Eds.). (1992). *Cross-cultural literacy*. Englewood Cliffs, NJ: Regents/Prentice-Hall.

DuBois, B. L. (1988). Citation in biomedical journal articles. *English for Specific Purposes , 7*, 181–194.

Eggington, W. (1987). Written academic discourse in Korean: Implications for effective communication. In U. Connor & R. B. Kaplan (Eds.), *Writing across languages: Analysis of L2 text* (pp. 115–138). Reading, MA: Addison-Wesley.

Elbow, P. (1991). Reflections on academic discourse. *College English, 53*, 135–155.

Elbow, P. (1981). *Writing with power: Techniques for mastering the writing process*. New York: Oxford University Press.

Flower, L. (1989). *Problem-solving strategies for writing* (2nd ed.). San Diego, CA: Harcourt Brace Jovanovich.

Franklin, J., & Steadman, D. W. (1991). The potential for conservation of Polynesian birds through habitat mapping and species translocation. *Conservation Biology, 5* (4) 506–552.

Hamp-Lyons, L. (1991). Issues and directions in assessing second language writing in academic contexts. In L. Hamp-Lyons (Ed.), *Assessing second language writing in academic contexts* (pp. 323–330). Norwood, NJ: Ablex.

Hebert, E. A. (1992, May). Portfolios invite reflection; from students and staff. *Educational Leadership*, 58–61.

Hill, C., & Parry, K (1992). A test at the gate: Models of literacy in reading assessment. *TESOL Quarterly, 26*, 433–462.

Horowitz, D. M. (1986a). Process not product: Less than meets the eye. *TESOL Quarterly, 20*, 141–143.

Horowitz, D. M. (1986b). What professors actually require: Academic tasks for the ESL classroom. *TESOL Quarterly, 20*, 445–462.

Hounsell, D. (1984). Learning and essay writing. In F. Marton, D. Hounsell, & N. Entwistle (Eds.), *The experience of learning*, (pp. 103–125) Edinburgh, UK: Scottish Academic Press.

Huckin, T. (1987 May). *Surprise values in scientific discourse* (Eric No. ED284291). Presented at the 38th Conference on College Composition and Communication. New Orleans, LA.

Johns, A. M. (1993). Written argumentation for real audiences: Suggestions for teacher research and classroom practice. *TESOL Quarterly. 27*, 73–90.

Johns, A. M. (1992). Toward developing a cultural repertoire: The case study of a Lao college freshman. In D. Murray (Ed.), *Diversity as resource: Redefining cultural literacy* (pp. 183–201). Arlington, VA: TESOL.

Johns, A. M. (1990). L1 composition theories: Implications for developing theories of L2 composition. In B. Kroll (Ed.), *Second language writing: Research insights for the classroom* (pp. 24–36). Cambridge, UK: Cambridge University Press.

Johns, A. M. (1988). The discourse communities dilemma: Identifying transferable skills for the academic milieu. *English for Specific Purposes, 7*, 55–60.

Johnson, D. M., & Roen, D. H. (1989). *Richness in writing: Empowering ESL students*. New York: Longman.

Jolliffe, D. A. (Ed.). (1988). *Advances in writing research, Vol. 2: Writing in academic disciplines.* Norwood, NJ: Ablex.

Kroll, B. (Ed.). (1990). *Second language writing: Research insights for the classroom.* New York: Cambridge University Press.

Leki, I. (1992). *Understanding ESL writers: A guide for teachers.* Portsmouth, NH: Boynton/Cook/Heinemann.

Matalene, C. (1985). Contrastive rhetoric: An American writing teacher in China. *College English, 47,* 789-808.

Mlynarczyk, R. (1991). Is there a difference between personal and academic writing? *TESOL Journal, 1,* 7-10.

Myers, G. (1985). The social construction of two biologists' proposals. *Written Communication, 2,* 219-245.

Myers, G. (1989). The pragmatics of politeness in scientific articles. *Applied Linguistics, 10,* 1-35.

Paulson, F. L., Paulson, P. R. & Meyer, C. A. (1990, February). What makes a portfolio a portfolio? *Educational Leadership,* pp. 60-63.

Pearson-Casanave, C. (1992). Cultural diversity and socialization: A case study of a Hispanic woman in a doctoral program in sociology. In D. Murray (Ed.), *Diversity as resource: Redefining cultural literacy* (pp. 148-182). Arlington, VA: TESOL.

Purves, A. C. (1991). Clothing the emperor: Towards a framework relating to function and form in literacy. *Journal of Basic Writing, 10,* 33-53.

*The Quarterly of the National Writing Project and the Center for the Study of Writing.* (1990). *12* (3).

Raimes, A. (1985). What unskilled ESL students do as they write: A classroom study of composition. *TESOL Quarterly, 19,* 229-258.

Raimes, A. (1987). Language proficiency, writing ability and composing strategies: A study of ESL college student writers. *Language Learning, 37,* 439-468.

Scarcella, R. (1984). How writers orient their readers in expository essays: A comparative study of native and non-native English writers. *TESOL Quarterly, 18,* 671-688.

Spack, R. (1988). Initiating ESL students into the academic discourse community: How far should we go? *TESOL Quarterly, 22,* 29-52.

Swales, J. M. (1981). *Aspects of article introductions.* Birmingham, UK: Language Studies Unit, University of Aston.

Swales, J. M. (1985). *Episodes in ESP.* New York: Prentice-Hall.

Swales, J. M. (1990). *Genre analysis: English in academic and research settings.* New York: Cambridge University Press.

Tarone, E., Dwyer, S. Gillette, S., & Icke, V. (1981). On the use of the passive in two astrophysics journal papers. *ESP Journal, 1,* 123-140.

Tierney, R. B., Carter, M. A., & Desai, L. E. (1991). *Portfolio assessment in the reading-writing classroom.* Norwood, MA: Christopher Gordon.

Urzua, C. (1986). A child's story. In P. Rigg & D. S. Enright (Eds.), *Children and ESL: Integrated perspectives* (pp. 93-102). Washington, DC: TESOL.

Weissberg, R., & Buker, S. (1990). *Writing up research: Experimental research report writing for students of English.* New York: Prentice-Hall/Regents.

Zamel, V. (1983). The composing processes of advanced ESL students: Six case studies. *TESOL Quarterly, 17,* 165-187.

Zamel, V. (1984). The author responds. *TESOL Quarterly, 18,* 154-157.

# CHAPTER 12

# Common-core and Specific Approaches to the Teaching of Academic Writing

**Tony Dudley-Evans**
*The University of Birmingham*

This chapter describes an approach to the teaching of academic writing to international students at a British university. The approach draws on the insights arising from both genre analysis and language-subject cooperative teaching. Three types of teaching are described, common-core teaching of general academic language and discourse, specific classes related to assignments in specific departments and the "writing club," in which students' writing is reviewed by peers. The common-core teaching makes use of the findings of genre analysis and teaches both the conventions and the lexico-grammatical forms relevant to each section of the thesis and reports that students have to write. The specific classes are team taught by a subject and a language teacher and involve discussion of the strategies and language appropriate to subject-specific tasks required in the subject course. The writing club sessions involve peer review of students' writing by other graduate students of different disciplines.

## INTRODUCTION

The approach to the teaching of writing to international students at the University of Birmingham described in this chapter draws its inspiration from the work of genre analysis (Swales, 1981, 1990) and from the insights gained through collaborative teaching with subject teachers (de Escorcia, 1984; Johns & Dudley-Evans, 1980). Genre analysis provides information about the discourse conventions of the general academic community, while the insights from the collaborative teaching show how these conventions are adapted to meet the particular concerns of specific disciplines.

The approach involves three types of teaching. The first is classroom-based teaching of language and conventions related to the general requirements of the academic community. The second is more specific work in certain departments designed to prepare students for the actual writing tasks required of them, such as examination answers, assignments, and theses. The third is "writing clubs," in which students bring in subject-specific pieces of writing which they are actually working on for comment by the rest of the group. The students involved are almost invariably graduate students studying a 1-year Master's, or students doing a PhD, or in a few cases an MPhil by research. They come from a variety of backgrounds. Many come from EFL countries in which they will have studied at school and undergraduate level in their national language, for example, the countries of Latin America; countries in the Far East, such as China, Japan, Thailand, and Indonesia; and some countries in the Middle East. Others come from ESL countries in which much, if not all, of their schooling and certainly their undergraduate courses will have been taught in English. Singapore, the former British colonies in Africa, and the Indian subcontinent are good examples of the latter.

The experience of writing in English will vary considerably; some students, mostly from ESL situations, will have considerable experience in writing undergraduate-level tasks, such as the essay, the laboratory report, or a short thesis. Others, usually rather older, will have published, probably with some help from a translator or a correction service, a few articles in English. Others from EFL situations will have had little or no experience with writing in English. Clearly, there is a wide range of ability and classes at different levels are run to cater to this.

The classes described here are run by the English for Overseas Students Unit at the University of Birmingham, which provides a language support service for international students, mostly at the graduate level. We are thus preparing students to write "authentic" genres rather than the "classroom" genres that undergraduate students write (Johns, this volume). Students attend either *presessional* courses which concentrate on the key study skills of listening, reading, note taking, speaking in both academic and nonacademic contexts, and project writing; or *insessional* courses, which concentrate on academic writing, listening comprehension, social English, and some remedial grammar and pronunciation work. Subject-specific classes are also run in key departments. Lecturers are also available for individual consultations, which tend to be concerned with students' writing difficulties, and are thus similar to the writing clinics described by Benson and Heidish (this volume).

The underlying theoretical basis for much of the teaching of academic writing can be found in *genre analysis*, especially the research of Swales (1981, 1990). Indeed, the relationship between the more theoretical work of genre analysis and its application to the teaching of academic writing has always been close. Swales, in his initial work on the 4-move pattern found in article introductions, begins by attributing his wish to explore the article introduction in greater detail to his dissatisfaction with "the pious, prescriptive and ill-found nature of the materials dealing with the *Introduction* sections of such pieces of academic prose" (Swales, 1981, p. 1). Early work of my own (e.g., Dudley-Evans, 1978, 1985), although very much more materials-oriented, exhibited some of the features of genre analysis, particularly its concern with the relationship between language and the structure of the Introduction and Discussion of Results sections, and its aim to go beyond the more generalized findings of discourse analysis about cohesion, and the rhetorical acts of description, definition, classification, and generalization taught in textbooks such as *The Focus Series* (Allen & Widdowson, 1974), *Academic Writing Course* (Jordan, 1980), and *Communicate in Writing* (Johnson, 1981).

The advantage of an approach that draws on the work of genre analysis is that it strengthens students' rhetorical awareness of the texts they have to write. This increase in awareness may be of the general expectations of the academic community, or of the particular expectations of the discourse community of which the student is aspiring to become a member. By *general expectations*, I am referring to the patterns of organization or schemata that apply to the various sections of either the journal article or the Master's or PhD thesis across a range of disciplines, and what Johns (this volume, p. 282) refers to as "the rhetoric of objectivity." By *particular expectations*, I am referring to the ways in which the generalized schemata need to be adapted to meet differing expectations and requirements in different disciplines. The former can be taught in generalized classes; the latter can clearly only be explored in subject-specific groups or in one-to-one tutorials (see Rymer, 1988, and Prior, this volume, for more detailed discussion of the composition processes of scientists and graduate students).

## TEACHING PROCEDURES IN THE COMMON-CORE CLASS

In the first type of teaching, that is, the classroom-based common-core teaching, three particular procedures for the teaching of appropriate communicative skills for academic writing have evolved. The first is the development of rhetorical awareness of the conventions that pertain to the overall structure of a journal article or thesis. The second is the teaching of a range of linguistic forms for the expression of the writer's purpose within each section. The third is the conversion of the rhetorical and linguistic awareness into the ability to order one's ideas and data into logical "narratives" in the appropriate form expected by the discourse community. These three stages approximate the two objectives of the syllabus described by Jacoby et al. (this volume, pp. 353–354) to deal with "the textual conventions and routine lexical phrases found in each section" and "the cognitive and rhetorical challenges that each section presents to beginning scientists/writers."

The first of these, the development of rhetorical awareness, is developed by exercises in which students are encouraged, through a series of questions, to think about the patterns of organization of a text and the reasons why those patterns are favored by those in the discourse community. In a sense, the students are asked to carry out a short piece of discourse or genre analysis designed to introduce them to various general aspects of academic style. A typical example follows:

1. Consider the following examples of discussion of results.

**Example 1**

*Aim of experiment*: To determine the modulus of elasticity for several materials by using circular bending.

*Summary of Final Results*

|                                         | Mild Steel | Tool Steel | Brass | Dural |
|-----------------------------------------|------------|------------|-------|-------|
| Modulus of elasticity (E) from experiment (kN/mm$^2$) | 205 | 207 | 104 | 72 |
| Generally accepted value | 207 | 207 | 97 | 70 |

**Discussion of Results**

Comparison of the experimentally determined values of modulus of elasticity with those generally quoted for these materials mostly shows a good agreement. The value obtained for brass which is 104 kN/mm$^2$ is somewhat higher than the quoted value of 97 kN/mm$^2$.

It must be realised, however, that no exact comparison is possible when the composition and treatment of the beam made of brass are not known.

The slight lack of straightness in the beams seemed to have no effect on the quality of the individual graphs or on the modulus of elasticity. As the determined values of modulus of elasticity are close to those generally accepted, it may be stated that the circular bending test is a suitable method for determining the elastic modulus of any material. This type of test is more economical than a full scale tensile test, as there is no need to have an expensive tensile testing machine, no need to have the specimens machined with precision, and the test can be carried out quickly.

(a) Underline the phrases which are used to express comparison with gener-ally accepted values.
(b) How does the writer explain the difference between the result for brass and the generally accepted value?
(c) What is the writer's purpose in the final paragraph?
(d) What tense is used in this discussion? Are there any verbs which are not in that tense? Can you think of a reason for this?

(Dudley-Evans, 1985, pp. 24–25)

The second procedure in the common-core class makes use of the various *move analyses* of different sections of the journal article or thesis. In the same way as Jacoby et al. (this volume), we begin with the relatively straightforward rhetorical challenge of the Method section and then move on to the more difficult task of writing the Introduction and the Discussion sections. The move analyses have provided the foundation for the develop-ment of exercises that develop both the rhetorical awareness referred to earlier and the ability to express ideas in the appropriate academic style and language. The first and still the most influential of these analyses is the 4-move model that Swales (1981) proposed for the article introduction, as outlined here:

Move 1    Establishing the field
Move 2    Summarizing previous research
Move 3    Preparing for present research (by indicating a gap, a possible extension or raising a question)
Move 4    Introducing present research

My own research into the patterns of organization of the MSc thesis (Dudley-Evans, 1986) has shown that the introduction of the thesis is longer and rhetorically more complex than that in the journal article. The pattern I found consists of six moves:[1]

Move 1    Introducing the field
Move 2    Introducing the general topic (within the field)
Move 3    Introducing the particular topic (within the general topic)

---

[1] The model was also used by Berkenkotter, Huckin, and Ackerman (1991) to help a NS graduate student entering the Rhetoric program at Carnegie Mellon University.

Move 4    Defining the scope of the particular topic by:
    (i) introducing research parameters
    (ii) summarizing previous research

Move 5    Preparing for present research by:
    (i) indicating a gap in previous research
    (ii) indicating a possible extension of previous research

Move 6    Introducing present research by:
    (i) stating the aim of the research
      or
    (ii) describing briefly the work carried out
      plus
    (iii) justifying the research
    (iv) indicating thesis structure[2]

Research into the Discussion section (Dudley-Evans, in press; Hopkins & Dudley-Evans, 1988; Peng, 1987) has shown that the discussion does not follow a fixed pattern with a favored order of *moves*, as with the introduction, but is made up of a number of *move cycles* (Jacoby, 1987) that combine two or more of the following moves:

1. *Information Move*: The writers present background information, which may draw on theory relevant to the research, the aim of the research, the methodology used, and previous research that is felt to be necessary to the understanding of what follows in the move cycle. This move is often placed at the beginning of a cycle, but may appear at any point of the cycle.

2. *Statement of Result*: This move either presents a numerical value or refers to a graph or table of results. It is frequently the first move in a cycle and is followed by one or more moves that comment on the result. It can, however, appear later in a cycle in support of a *claim*.

3. *Finding*: The function of a *finding* is essentially the same as a *statement of result* in that it is followed by a series of moves that comment on it. The basic difference is that a finding does not present actual figures but an observation arising from the research. As with a *statement of result*, it may also act as a support for a *claim*.

4. *(Un)expected Outcome*: The writers make a comment on the fact that a result is expected or, much more frequently, unexpected or surprising.

5. *Reference to Previous Research*: The writers either *compare* their results with those found in previous research or use the previous research as *support* for their own *claims* or *explanations*.

---

[2]"Outlining thesis structure" is a later addition to the model.

6. *Explanation*: The writers give reasons for an unexpected result or one that differs significantly from previous research.

7. *Claim*: The writers make a generalization arising from their results, which is their contribution to the ongoing research on the topic. This is often referred to as a *knowledge claim*. Claims tend to be presented cautiously, that is, using modal or other hedged phrases.

8. *Limitation*: The writers introduce a caveat about a result or finding, or the methodology followed, or a claim made.

9. *Recommendation*: The writers make suggestions about future lines of research or possible improvements to methodology followed in the present research.

The key move cycles are those involving *statement of results* or *findings* followed by a *reference to previous research*, or a *claim* also followed by a *reference to previous research*.

These move analyses form the basis of exercises in academic writing courses in various ways. At the first stage, students' awareness of them is both tested and developed through "unscrambling" or "reordering" exercises in which they are asked to put the sentences presented in a jumbled order into the correct order. In the example that follows, the sentences have to be reordered to form an article introduction:

Put the following sentences into the correct order to form an article introduction (based on published materials prepared by M. J. St. John):

a. Furthermore, an impression has been gained from remarking investigations (Murphy, 1978) that more extreme differences in marking standards are revealed when previous marks and comments are removed from scripts.

b. The aim of this investigation was to test this view by comparing the results of re-marking two sets of scripts, one set with previous marks and comments on them and the other set with these removed.

c. In fact, Pilliner suggests that if the second examiner is aware of the marks awarded by the first examiner, then this invalidates the independence of the two assessments of the scripts.

d. There are many situations where examination scripts are marked by one examiner and then re-marked by another examiner.

e. Removing the Marks from Examination Scripts before Re-Marking them. Does it Make any Difference?

f. It has been suggested by Pilliner (1965) that one of the critical factors which affect the re-marking of scripts is whether or not the second examiner is aware of the marks awarded by the first examiner.

g. It would seem that, however much an examiner tries to ignore the judgments of a previous examiner, his own impression of the scripts is bound to be influenced.

h. One examiner may be checking on the marking standards of the other examiner (Black, 1962), or else the marks of the two examiners may be averaged in order to attempt to produce a more reliable assessment (Wiseman, 1949; Wood and Quin, 1976).

After this, the correct order is discussed and the 4-move model introduced and explained. This is followed by detailed practice of the language used to express each of the four moves.[3]

An excellent example of this type of exercise comes in Weissberg and Buker's (1990) *Writing Up Research* (pp. 48–49):

The following citations are taken from Stage 11 of the introduction to a research report from the field of nutrition. The citations are given here in scrambled order. Number the citations in the order you feel they should appear in the literature review for this report (Weissberg & Baker, 1990, pp. 48–49):

---

[3]In the latest version of the model (Swales, 1990) there are three *moves* and various *steps* within each move:

| | |
|---|---|
| *Move 1* | *Establishing a Territory* |
| Step 1 | Claiming centrality |
| | and/or |
| Step 2 | Making topic generalisation(s) |
| | and/or |
| Step 3 | Reviewing items of previous research |
| *Move 2* | *Establishing a Niche* |
| Step 1A | Counterclaiming |
| | or |
| Step 1B | Indicating a gap |
| | or |
| Step 1C | Question raising |
| | or |
| Step 1D | Continuing a tradition |
| *Move 3* | *Occupying the Niche* |
| Step 1A | Outlining purposes |
| | or |
| Step 1B | Announcing present research |
| | Announcing principal findings |
| Step 2 | Indicating Research Article structure |
| Step 3 | |

As yet, I have found that the 3-move model, although much tighter and more complete from an analytical point of view and more sensitive to the social roles of the academic writer, is less immediately accessible to international students learning to write than the original 4-move model. I currently use the original 4-move model with the addition of Steps 2 and 3 in Move 3 of the 3-move model.

## FOOD HABITS OF UNDERGRADUATE STUDENTS AT
## NEW MEXICO STATE UNIVERSITY

A. _____ Young and Storvick (1970) surveyed the food habits of 595 college freshmen in Oregon and found that the men generally had better diets than the women.

B. _____ Litman et al. (1975) reported that green and yellow vegetables and liver (all nutritionally desirable foods) were not liked by teenagers in Minnesota public schools. They also found that teachers have almost no influence on their students' food habits.

C. _____ Studies of the food habits of young school children have shown that the diets of grade school children are often deficient in ascorbic acid, calcium and iron (Lantz et al., 1958; Patterson, 1966).

D. _____ A review of the literature indicates that food habit studies have been conducted with students from a variety of different age groups.

E. _____ Young (1965) examined the nutrition habits of a group of young school children and found that their mothers lacked information about the importance of milk and foods rich in ascorbic acid.

F. _____ Studies done with adolescent children report similar findings (Ohlson and Hart, 1970; van de Mark and Underwood, 1972).

G. _____ A number of studies have been conducted using both male and female college students as subjects.

The third type of activity in the common-core classes involves more of a deep-end approach in which students are asked to write a simulation of either a full report or a full section of an article or thesis based on some data or information provided. They are given no specific guidance but have to draw on both what has been taught in the rest of the course and their own experience to write up the data or information appropriately. It has been found that these exercises, an example of which is shown below, are very successful in helping students bring together and consolidate both what they have learned from the materials and their overall knowledge of writing within science and technology. The example that follows is taken from a course on laboratory report writing (Dudley-Evans, 1985, pp. 32–37).[4] The course is similar to that described by Braine (this volume):

**Writing Practice**

1. Imagine that you have carried out an experiment to determine the boiling points of various liquids. Look at the results in the table below and write a paragraph discussing the results. Follow the pattern of the previous discussion in this unit, and use the expressions introduced. The source of the published values is again Kaye and Laby.

---

[4]To save space only the results have been presented here. In the original, notes on the *theory* and *procedure* are also provided.

| Liquid | Experimental Melting Point (mean value in °C) | Published Value (°C) |
|---|---|---|
| Ethyl Alcohol | 78.3 | 78.5 |
| Turpentine | 175 | 161 |
| Ether | 34.5 | 34.5 |
| Water | 94 | 100 |

## Writing a Full Report

You are going to write a full report of the experiment which compares the values of central vertical deflection of a beam with the deflection predicted by simple bending theory. Read through the theory, the instructions for carrying out the experiment and the results.

## Theory

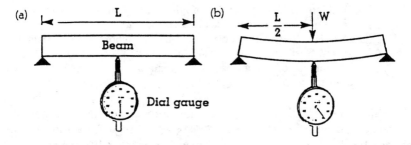

The theory relating to the experiment is as follows:

The assumptions involved in the development of simple bending theory for a straight beam are:

(a) the material remains elastic;

Add loads in steps.

Read dial gauge.

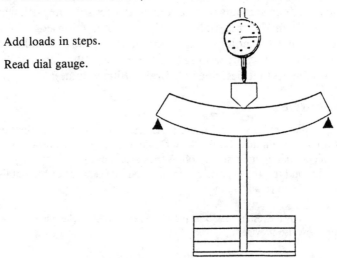

2. (a) Compute for each value of added load, the observed additional central deflection by subtraction of the zero reading from the current dial gauge reading.

(b) Calculate the second moment of area I from the formula: $I = \dfrac{bd^3}{12}$

(c) Use the formula $\Delta = \dfrac{WL^3}{48EI}$ to predict the additional deflection caused by the extra load for each value of load applied.

(d) Plot a graph of observed deflection against predicted deflection.

Imagine that you have carried out the experiment and have obtained the following readings, results and graph.

**Readings, Results and Graph**

Measurements by vernier caliper

| Depth of beam (mm) | Width of beam (mm) |
|---|---|
| 25.02 | 14.98 |
| 25.08 | 15.12 |
| 25.10 | 15.04 |
| 25.20 | 15.06 |
| 25.10mm (Average depth) | 15.05mm (Average width) |

$E = 210 \times 10^9$ N/m² (given)

Sensitivity of dial gauge = 0.01 mm/div

| Readings | | | Calculated Results | | |
|---|---|---|---|---|---|
| Load on hanger kg | Dial gauge reading | | Vertical force N | Observed deflection (mm) | Predicted deflection (mm) |
| 0 | 1342 | | 0 | 0 | 0 |
| 5 | 1368 | | 49.0 | 0.26 | 0.25 |
| 10 | 1395 | | 98.1 | 0.53 | 0.49 |
| 15 | 1419 | | 147.1 | 0.77 | 0.74 |
| 20 | 1444 | | 196.2 | 1.02 | 0.98 |
| 25 | 1480 | | 245.2 | 1.38 | 1.23 |
| 30 | 1498 | | 294.3 | 1.56 | 1.47 |
| 35 | 1522 | | 343.3 | 1.80 | 1.72 |

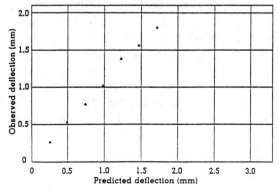

Central deflections of a simply-supported beam

3. Write a full report of the experiment with the title, the aim, a short description of the theoretical basis, the procedure, the readings, results and graphs, a discussion of the results, and a short conclusion. For the theoretical basis, use the explanation of theory on PO; for the procedure, describe the diagrams and calculation on PO; and for the discussions, say whether the results are consistent with the values predicted by bending theory.

The greater independence that students need to develop in order to tackle tasks of this kind leads to consideration of issues such as the importance of adopting a critical stance in presenting data (Connor & Kramer, this volume) and the difference between *knowledge telling* and *knowledge transforming* (Bereiter & Scardamalia, 1987; Cumming, this volume).

## TEAM-TAUGHT WRITING CLASSES

The second type of writing class mentioned in the introduction is the specific work done in departments running Master's courses that have large numbers of international students. This usually involves the working together of a language teacher and a subject teacher to help students with specific writing tasks, such as examination answers, assignments, and theses.[5] The team-taught sessions are thus similar to adjunct classes taught in the United States (see Brinton, Snow & Wesche, 1989; Crandall, 1987; Johns, this volume) and also have much in common with the Writing Across the Curriculum movement (Young & Fulwiler, 1986). The main difference is that they involve the actual working together of the subject teachers and language teachers in the same classroom.

The advantages of a team-taught approach are many and each of the three types of participants in the sessions — the students, the subject teacher, and the language teacher — gain particular insights from the sessions.

The students gain three particular kinds of insight. First, they are able to understand more fully what is required in the set tasks in terms of content, organization, and language. Secondly, they learn to apply the general knowledge of genre conventions and other aspects of writing they have gained from the general classes to actual assignments or examination

---

[5]For a full description of this type of work see Johns and Dudley-Evans (1980), Dudley-Evans (1984), Houghton (1984), and de Escorcia (1984).

answers. Thirdly, the students gain insights into the particular expectations and definition of the writing task (see Prior, 1991, this volume).

The subject teacher is able to see firsthand the difficulties the students face in understanding and carrying out the task that he or she has set and it is not unusual for the subject teacher to realize that the wording of an examination question or the instructions for the writing of an assignment are potentially confusing and need to be tightened up in the future.

The language teacher gains a fuller understanding of what the department or the subject teacher requires of students and of the difficulties students have in meeting those requirements. These insights come from discussion with the subject teacher in preparing the session and through participation in the actual classroom interaction, both of which provide an understanding of the culture of the discipline that cannot be gained through purely "desktop" research.

The actual sessions involve the preparation of a suitable and relevant task by the subject teacher which forms the basis for classroom discussion of the appropriate strategies for carrying out the task. In the case of an examination question, this will include discussion of issues, such as the meaning of the question, the points to be included in the answer, the ordering of those points, which technical terms need to be defined, and which do not. In the case of an assignment, discussion will revolve around questions such as which sections should be included and the way in which they should be structured. As an example of how the sessions work, I describe in a little detail a team-taught session that was built around the task:

*Laboratory Reports*
This is a short exercise to assist you in preparing laboratory reports for the soils assignment.

*Exercise*
Your brief is to give an appropriate compaction specification (i.e. % age, M.D.D. [maximum dry density] and moisture content) for a material which is available from a borrow pit and which will be used somewhere in the highway structure. You should follow the report layout suggested.

*Notes/Information*
1. The job is called Nata-Maun Road, Botswana
2. The material has already been classified by B.S. 1377 'Soils for Civil Engineering Purposes' tests nos. 1 to 7, and has been described as a brown clayey gravel with sand inclusions, well graded with a PI of 5. The natural moisture content is 12%.
3. Compaction test results are available (BS 1377 test nos. 12 and 13):

| Test No. 12 | Standard Compaction | Test No. 13 | Heavy Compaction |
|---|---|---|---|
| Moisture content % | Dry Density Mg/m | Moisture content % | Dry Density Mg/m 4 |
| 4 | – | 4 | 2.00 |
| 6 | 1.90 | 6 | 2.12 |
| 8 | 1.99 | 8 | 2.17 |
| 10 | 2.08 | 10 | 2.15 |
| 12 | 2.06 | 12 | 2.08 |
| 14 | 1.96 | 14 | 1.98 |

*SUGGESTED LAYOUT*

PROJECT LAYOUT
EXTENT OF INVESTIGATION
DESCRIPTION OF SAMPLE AND LOCATION IN THE HIGHWAY
TEST METHOD TO BE USED
TABLES OF RESULTS
CALCULATIONS
COMMENTS ON TEST METHOD
SUMMARY OF RESULTS WITH APPROPRIATE COMMENTS AND/
   OR EXPLANATION
REFERENCES

This task was prepared by the subject teacher and discussed with the language teacher (myself) in a short preparation session. In the class itself, the discussion focused on four sections, the *project title*, the *extent of the investigation*, *comments on the test method* and the *summary of results with comments and/or explanation*.

The initial suggestion made by the students for the title was:

Compaction Specification for the Nata-Maun Road, Botswana.

It was decided that this was not sufficiently detailed and the final decision was:

*The Nata-Maun Road, Botswana*
*The Site Investigations (materials testing)*
*Compaction Specification—Borrow Pit Material*

In the discussion of what should be included in the section called *extent of the investigation*, it was quickly decided that the fact that the government had gone ahead with the building of the Nata-Maun Road and that borrow pit material had been identified for the material should be mentioned. It was also decided that the section should state that the report would give results of compaction tests and provide appropriate compaction specifications for the material. A lively discussion then ensued on the question of whether the actual compaction value recommended should be stated at this early stage. It has been noted that writers of journal articles increasingly tend to announce their principal findings in the introduction (Swales & Najjar, 1987), and this was the reason why the language teacher raised the question. It was eventually decided, however, that in a project report it was not appropriate to include the recommendation in the introduction, but merely to state that the recommendation would be presented in the report.

Students were asked to plot the graph of the results before there was any discussion of the test method and results. The task thus had a reality from the point of view of the subject, as well as from the point of view of the language. In the section on *comments on the test method*, it was decided that the following points should be discussed:

1. the suitability of the sampling and pre-treatment methods
2. the appropriateness of the B.S (British Standard) to Botswana
3. the reasons for the use of two compaction methods
4. the reproducibility of the results and the link between the laboratory and field results

The comments on the results were then discussed and it was decided that it should include the following steps:

1. a summary of the main results
2. a comment on the results in relation to the natural moisture content and PI
3. a statement of the assumptions made about availability of machinery for the compaction of the material and the ability of the material to 'wet up'
4. an explanation of the results
5. the recommendation of the compaction specification

Note that the actual specification is placed at the end of the section and acts as a climax to it.

I have described the session in some detail in order to show how the planning of the report integrates discussion of subject content with analysis of the ordering of the steps in the argument in each section that was dealt with. The basis of this is a belief that we cannot separate the two aspects, and that an understanding of the rhetorical features of writing the report is as important as the content. For example, the questions of whether the recommendation about the compaction specification should be included in the *extent of investigation* section and, subsequently, where it should be placed in the *comments on results* section are as important as the actual value suggested for the specification. This kind of issue is dealt with very effectively through the working together of the subject and the language teacher. Furthermore, the discussion of the strategies for answering the question is integrated very closely with the consideration of the genre conventions in a way that combines very effectively product and process approaches to the teaching of writing.

## THE WRITING CLUB

The two types of writing class described above have been based on flexible prescriptions about the organization of writing tasks and the structuring of the different sections of the actual text drawn from the work of genre analysis and the more specific insights drawn from the team-taught sessions. To this extent they may be considered to focus more on the *product* or forms of writing. The other type of writing class that I wish to describe follows a stronger *process* orientation.

It would appear that in the United States there has recently been some rediscovery of form and the importance of a social dimension in a system in which the teaching of strategies for planning, audience consideration, and revision (e.g., the process approach described by Flower & Hayes, 1980) has long predominated (Johns, 1990, this volume). In Britain the opposite would appear to be the case. Teaching of academic writing to international students has tended to concentrate on *product*, typically the expression of functions such as cause & effect, description, definition, classification, and so on (Johnson, 1981; Jordan, 1980) or, latterly, moves as described earlier in this chapter or, by Jacoby et al. (this volume). It is only more recently that writing process has played a more important role in writing courses (see Bloor & St. John, 1988; Robinson, 1988).

The writing club sessions are thus an example of an emphasis on process within a course that aims to help students develop an awareness of the forms of writing expected by the discourse community that they are aspiring to join. The sessions are organized after the classes on the genre conventions of the thesis and article have been completed, and, therefore, assume that the students have some knowledge of the conventions and the ways in which they are expressed. The procedure is that a student produces a piece of writing for the session, which is usually part of a particular writing task, essay, report, or chapter of a thesis that he or she is preparing. This is copied and distributed to the group, which, either individually or in pairs, discusses the writing and makes suggestions for improvement. It has been found that the suggestions range from correction of spelling through to restructuring of the argument where it has been found to be unclear. The suggestions are then discussed with the writing teacher acting as a kind of referee. The groups consist of students from one discipline or, more usually, from a range of disciplines.

The writing club can be seen as an adaptation of the use of reformulation in the writing class (Allwright, 1988; Cohen, 1983). In Allwright's procedure, one piece of writing is taken out of a class set and rewritten or reformulated by a native speaker of English, either the actual teacher of the group, or a colleague in the English department or a native speaker student competent in writing academic English. The reformulation does not change the content of the original writing but corrects problems both at the level of the sentence and at the discourse level. The reformulated text is then distributed along with the original text and the differences discussed. The discussion focuses particularly on the reasons for the changes made. After this, all students revise their original drafts in the light of the discussion. Allwright (1988, p. 115) argues that "reformulation offers an excellent way of promoting student discussion on the key issues of academic writing" and "promote the autonomy that is the necessary aim of the sort of writing course my students need."

The writing club classes change the emphasis away from reformulation by writing teachers or their colleagues to discussion of first drafts by fellow students. It thus has much in common with the system of peer review or peer response used in L1 or L2 composition classes in the United States (Belcher, 1990; Frodesen, this volume). The particular advantage of this approach over the reformulation approach is that it focuses on the needs of the reader trying to grasp the meaning of the text. Although the students in the multidiscipline class do not belong to the same discourse community as the writer, they do belong to the general academic community and will have an understanding of the general requirements which that community has of the genre that the writer is using. They are also relatively experienced readers and can point to weaknesses in the argument presented. Nonetheless, the difficulties of interpretation and of readers being unable to comment critically on texts from a discipline very different from their own referred to by Belcher (1990), do occur. However, I would argue that the advantages of the writer having to present an outline or a sample of his or her work to a sympathetic, though non expert audience far outweigh the disadvantages, especially in the British system where the PhD is purely a research degree and students may communicate on academic matters only with their advisor. It would appear that many students feel less threatened by a situation in which the peers commenting on their writing do not have expertise in the subject area.

If the main focus of the first two types of writing class described in this chapter is on providing students with strategies appropriate to tasks that they will be undertaking in the future, the discussion in the writing club focuses on an actual piece of writing that a student has completed, albeit as a first draft. The focus is on the effectiveness of the writing and on whether it has both met the needs of the audience and satisfied the expectations of the academic community.

## CONCLUSION

The three types of teaching described in this, chapter—the common-core class, the specific team-taught class, and the writing club—attempt to synthesize the findings of applied research and classroom-based experience. They attempt to integrate both a product and a process approach to the teaching of academic writing and adopt a social constructionist standpoint (Johns, 1990), the underlying assumption of which is that students learning to write in a discipline need to be introduced to the ways in which knowledge is created and communicated in their discipline.

The overall approach has developed in a British English for Specific Purposes context, but has, I believe, much in common with the teaching of writing skills to native speaker undergraduate students at universities in the U.K. or U.S., and, in particular, with those courses that have a Writing Across the Curriculum (WAC) orientation. Both are essentially concerned with the socialization of students into the general academic community and into a specific disciplinary culture. Both also explore ways in which the knowledge we have gained about how the conventions of a discipline shape its discourse can be translated into classroom materials and activities. The main difference is at the language level; ESP courses are designed for students with less than native speaker competence in using the grammatical and lexical system of the language, while WAC courses are usually designed for native speakers. The overlap between the two movements is nonetheless quite large and the opportunities for exchange of ideas and materials between the two are considerable.

## REFERENCES

Allen, P., & Widdowson, H. (1974). *The focus series: English in physical science* Oxford, UK: Oxford University Press.

Allwright, J. (1988). Don't correct—reformulate. In P. Robinson (Ed.), *Academic writing: Process and product* (ELT Document 129, pp. 109–116) London: Modern English Publications.

Belcher, D. (1990). Peer vs. teacher response in the advanced composition class. *Issues in Writing, 2* (2), 128–150.

Bereiter, C., & Scardamalia, M. (1987). *The psychology of written composition.* Hillsdale, NJ: Erlbaum.

Berkenkotter, C., Huckin, T., & Ackerman, J. (1991). Social context and socially constructed texts. In C. Bazerman & J. Paradis (Eds.), *Textual dynamics of the professions* (pp. 191–215). Madison: University of Wisconsin Press.

Bloor, M., & St. John, M. J. (1988). Project writing: The marriage of product and process. In P. Robinson (Ed.), *Academic writing: Process and product* (ELT Document No. 129, pp. 85–94) London: Modern English Publications.

Brinton, D., Snow, M. A., & Wesche, M. B. (1989). *Content-based second language instruction*. New York: Newbury House/Harper & Row.

Cohen, A. D. (1983). Reformulating compositions. *TESOL Newsletter, XVII* (6), 1–5.

Crandall, J. (1987). *ESL through content-area instruction*. Englewoods Cliffs, NJ: Prentice-Hall/Regents.

de Escorcia, B. A. (1984). Team teaching for students of economics: A Colombian experience. In R. Williams, J. M. Swales, & J. Kirkman (Eds.), *Common ground: Shared interests in ESP and communication studies* (ELT Document 114, pp. 105–114) Oxford, UK: Pergamon Press.

Dudley-Evans, A. (1978). Report writing. In R. R. Jordan (Ed.), *Pre-sessional courses for overseas students* (ELT Document 75/2). London: The British Council.

Dudley-Evans, A. (1984). The team teaching of writing skills. In R. Williams, J. M. Swales, & J. Kirkman (Eds.), *Common ground: Shared interests in ESP and communication studies* (ELT Documents 114, pp. 127–134) UK: Oxford, Pergamon.

Dudley-Evans, A. (1985). *Writing laboratory reports* Melbourne, Australia: Nelson Wadsworth.

Dudley-Evans, A. (1986). Genre analysis: An investigation of the introduction and discussion sections of Msc dissertations. In M. Coulthard (Ed.), *Talking About text* (Discourse Analysis Monograph, No. 13, pp. 128–145). Birmingham, UK: The University of Birmingham.

Dudley-Evans, A. (in press). *Genre analysis: An approach to text analysis for ESP*.

Flower, L. S., & Hayes, J.R. (1980). The cognition of discovery: Defining a rhetorical problem. *College Composition and Communication 31* (1), 21–32.

Hopkins, A., & Dudley-Evans, A. (1988). A genre-based investigation of the discussion sections in articles and dissertations. *English for Specific Purposes*, 7, 113–122.

Houghton, D. (1984). Overseas students writing essays in English: Learning the rules of the game. In G. James (Ed.), *The ESP classroom* (Exeter Linguistic Series, Vol. 7, pp. 47–57). Exeter, UK: University of Exeter.

Jacoby, S. (1987). References to other researchers in literary research articles. In A. Dudley-Evans (Ed.), Genre analysis and ESP. *ELR Journal* (Vol. 1). Birmingham, UK: The University of Birmingham.

Johns, A. (1990). L1 composition theories: Implications for developing theories of L2 composition. In B. Kroll (Ed.), *Second language writing*. Cambridge, UK: Cambridge University Press.

Johns, T., & Dudley-Evans, A. (1980). An experiment in team-teaching of overseas postgraduate students of transportation and plant biology. In *Team teaching in ESP* (ELT Document 106, pp. 6–23). London: The British Council.

Johnson, K. (1981). *Communicate in writing*. Harlow, UK: Longman.

Jordan, R. R. (1980). *Academic writing course*. Glasgow, UK: Collins.

Peng, J. F. (1987). Organisational features in chemical engineering research articles. In A. Dudley-Evans (Ed.), Genre analysis and ESP, *ELR Journal* (Vol. 1), Birmingham, UK: The University of Birmingham.

Prior, P. (1991). Contextualizing writing and response in a graduate seminar. *Written Communication*, 8, 267–310.

Robinson, P. (1988). *Academic writing: Process and product* (ELT Document 129) London: Modern English Publications.

Rymer, J. (1988). Scientific composing processes: How eminent scientists write journal articles. In D. A. Joliffe (Ed.), *Advances in writing research*, Vol. 2: Writing in *academic disciplines* (pp. 211–250). Norwood, NJ: Ablex.

Swales, J. M. (1981). Aspects of article introductions (ESP Monograph, No. 1). Burmingham, UK: Aston University.

Swales, J. M. (1990). *Genre analysis: English in academic and research settings*. Cambridge, UK: Cambridge University Press.

Swales, J. M., & Najjar, H. (1987). The writing of research article introductions. *Written Communication, 4*, 175–192.

Weissberg, R., & Buker, S. (1990). *Writing up research*. Englewoods Cliffs, NJ: Prentice-Hall/Regents.

Young, A., & Fulwiler, T. (Eds.). (1986). *Writing across the disciplines: Research into practice*. Upper Montclair, NJ: Boynton/ Cook.

CHAPTER 13

# The ESL Technical Expert: Writing Processes and Classroom Practices

Philippa J. Benson
Peggy Heidish
*Carnegie Mellon University*

In this chapter, we focus primarily on the teaching of writing to adult nonnative speakers of English in graduate programs who have developed high levels of expertise in specific content areas and who have the opportunity to teach and/or publish. We begin with an outline of some of the strengths and weaknesses of empirical research in reading and writing across languages, emphasizing that these kinds of studies fall short of clarifying what nonnative writers need to function naturally in American discourse communities. We move on to discuss how incorporating information from research on writing processes can be used in composition classes for adult ESL technical experts. We also explore the idea of how ESL technical experts can be empowered as writers by becoming more acutely aware of themselves as experts. A final section presents a perspective on how explicit instruction about American classroom pedagogy can work to clarify and reinforce the communicative functions of discourse strategies commonly used in English text. Throughout the chapter we provide examples of how some of these perspectives might be incorporated into classroom practice.

In the United States, nonnative speakers of English are playing increasingly important roles in the classroom and in the workplace. A high proportion of these students and professionals are specialists in their fields — particularly in the sciences and technology — and are taking on roles, either in the workplace or classroom, that require them to convey their knowledge and expertise both orally and in writing. In this chapter, we are concerned primarily with the teaching of writing to nonnative speakers of English who are adults in graduate-level programs, who have developed relatively high levels of expertise in specific content areas, and who have the opportunity to teach and/or publish. These students have both different problems and different resources than many other English as a second language (ESL) composition students, in that they often have a certain degree of proficiency in their academic fields while, at the same time, they are often hampered in their ability to effectively communicate that knowledge. We address the difficulties these students have in producing effective written communication which occur not only because they may not have adequate control of their own writing process, but also because they may not fully understand culturally-based communicative practices, particularly those used in instructional settings.

We preface our discussion by outlining some of the strengths and weaknesses of empirical research in reading and writing across languages, emphasizing that these kinds of studies fall short of clarifying what nonnative writers need to function naturally in American discourse communities. We move on to discuss how incorporating information about findings from research on writing processes can be used in composition classes for adult ESL technical experts. We also explore how ESL technical experts can be empowered in their roles as writers by becoming more acutely aware of themselves as technical (or subject matter) experts. Finally, we discuss how explicit instruction about American classroom pedagogy can work to clarify and reinforce the communicative functions of discourse strategies commonly used in English text. In addition to providing some insight into functional aspects of written texts in English, instruction about communicative strategies used in teaching can be beneficial to ESL technical experts, many of whom will eventually teach American students. Throughout the chapter, we provide examples of how some of these perspectives might be incorporated into classroom practice.

## THE LIMITS OF EMPIRICAL STUDIES OF CROSS-LANGUAGE READING AND WRITING

Over the past decade, developments in reading and writing research across languages reflect the trend to move beyond a myopic concern with the language learners' knowledge of grammatical structures to a more broad-based consideration of the learners' abilities to appropriately use those structures in social and cultural settings. Both within and beyond the realm of second language teachers and researchers, *contrastive rhetoric* has often been used as a multidimensional term to describe the wide variety of studies in linguistics, reading theory, composition theory, and rhetoric concerned with the development of communication skills across languages and cultures. Until relatively recently, however, many comparative language studies were primarily concerned with the development of skills in acquiring and manipulating the structural rather than cultural aspects of language. In linguistics, for example, cross-language studies have tended to investigate comparative forms and functions of language structures, such as Xu's (1987) study of the differences in the referential functions of Chinese and English demonstratives in discourse, or Cumming's (1984) challenge to the traditional notion of "sentence" through a comparison of the notion of sentence in different writing systems. However, an increasing number of studies are looking beyond the sentence to the discourse level, including Hinds's (1979, 1983) explorations of differences in organizational patterns in Japanese and English discourse, and Kaplan's (1987) revision of his earlier notions of differences in the expression of cultural thought patterns in discourse to include an understanding of the differences in terms of a broader movement in the study of orality and literacy.

Similarly, in reading studies, research has moved from a concern with understanding the development of particular skills in isolation, such as in vocabulary development (e.g., Higgins, 1985), to a more connectionist view of reading and writing. This perspective on reading and writing as skills that should be taught together parallels developments in the teaching of literacy skills to native speakers (Bereiter & Scardamalia, 1984; Crowhurst, 1991). Arguments for this shift in cross-language research are articulated in recent publications by Carrell (1987) and Carrell, Devine, and Eskey (1988), who argue for an integrative model of reading and writing across languages, and by Bernhardt (1991) who reviews the growing and merging lines of research concerned with reading–writing relationships in second language learning. Because Steffenson's (1979) pioneering work on the effect of background knowledge on reader recall of culturally biased texts, a large number of experimental and descriptive studies have investigated the effects of both culture and topic knowledge on the development of second language reading and writing skills (e.g., Carrell, 1983; Flick & Anderson, 1980; Mohan & Lo, 1985; Parry, 1987; Smith, 1987).

Composition researchers have also been investigating the development of second language writing skills more vigorously during the last decade, including both studies of individual factors and studies exploring the connection of reading and writing on the development of second language proficiency. They have focused on, for example, differences in composition processes (Friedlander, 1987; Jones & Tetroe, 1987), and on the relationship between first and second language development (Edelsky, 1983) and competence (Krashen, 1984; Skibniewski & Skibniewski, 1987). Other studies of second language composition have looked at text structure, syntactic semantic factors, testing, and instruction (Bernhardt, 1991). The boundaries of the field of contrastive rhetoric have been gradually increasing to include, among others, cross-language studies of word recognition, text structure, oral/aural differences, testing, instruction, and a myriad of other factors in linguistics, reading, and composition theory related to the acquisition of second language reading and writing skills.

As research expands in these three areas, a number of fundamental problems have begun to emerge. First, there is little theory that serves to bind the related, yet quite divergent, goals of linguistic, reading, and composition researchers. Second, and not surprisingly, there are widely divergent practices in experimental methodology that provide results that, by design, are at best difficult to compare and, at worst fundamentally flawed. For example, many studies have not controlled for differences in the level of second language proficiency of the subject, for the potential effects of differences in the writing systems of the first language of subjects, or for potential effects in differences between the cultural contexts of language use. Therefore, critical moves in the development of second language literacy studies need to be made toward building a unified theoretical groundwork that will be usable in a variety of disciplines and toward the honing of experimental methods and designs. One of these moves may well be to look beyond factors that can be empirically manipulated and verified to other aspects of context, culture, and communication; those beyond language aptly described as the human activity of languaging (Becker, 1986).

Without question, the need for both more research and more proven pedagogical tools has been recognized and is being addressed, as evidenced by the creation of the new periodical *Journal of Second Language Writing* (Ablex) and by the publication of this volume. The lean pickings of robust studies of the development of second language literacy skills underscores the needs of students in ESL composition classes: Without a firm grounding in proven pedagogical methods for teaching writing skills to nonnative speakers, ESL composition teachers and their students have been left to fend for themselves.

In their efforts to build sound pedagogy, many ESL composition researchers and teachers have turned to first language composition research as a guide. As mentioned earlier, over the past several decades, first and second language composition studies have mirrored each other, at least in part, with first language studies taking the lead in both volume and potential application. A review of citations in second language composition studies inevitably offers substantial evidence of the influence that first language composition research has had on molding the directions of second language composition studies. For example, virtually every chapter in this volume draws on first language composition research, including, to name a few, work by Applebee (1983), Bartholomae (1985), Bazerman (1988), Bereiter and Scardamalia (1987), Durst (1987), Hayes and Flower (1980), and Witte and Faigley (1981). This historical connection of first and second language composition research points to the potential of applying similar pedagogical methods in both arenas.

## WRITING AS PROCESS

A general, powerful, and influential model of first language composition research includes the perspective on the writer as working through an individual cognitive process that is situated in a social context. Until the 1970s, most first language writing research was focused on the study of the finished product. The 1980s brought a shift in focus to an interest in the organization of the process of writing including (Hayes, 1989):

1. The task environment (i.e., the writing assignment and the text produced so far).
2. The writer's long-term memory including content knowledge, knowledge of genre, and knowledge of audience.
3. The writing process.

Initially, composition researchers gave a great deal of attention to writing as an individual cognitive problem-solving skill, focusing on the writing process in literate adults as a complex and recursive process weaving through stages of planning, sentence generation, and reviewing, with each stage containing addition recursive subprocesses, such as organizing and editing (Hayes & Flower, 1980). Researchers found that as writers mature, planning and revision become increasingly important subprocesses in the overall composing process.

Although the idea of writing as a strategic process is well-known by many English composition teachers, the idea has not trickled down easily into the community of teachers of writing to nonnative speakers of English. As Johns (this volume) points out, "Despite its considerable contributions, some academic ESL teachers have begun to question the centrality of 'the process' in an academic reading and composition curriculum" (p. 278). We argue here that, although overemphasizing process is certainly not a wise pedagogical strategy, teaching writing as a manageable and changeable process can be a powerful idea for many ESL composition students, particularly those who have concentrated on developing their expertise in their scientific or technical disciplines and have placed development of language skills low on their priority scale.

These writers do not feel confident in their ability to use language to express that expertise or to manage their own production processes. Many ESL technical experts, in fact, have had little formal training in writing, either in their native language or in English. Understandably, since their concentration has been on developing skills in their technical fields, they have become accustomed to having success measured by their abilities to solve quantitative, not communicative, problems. However, as these students move into the latter phases of their graduate education, many begin to be poignantly aware that the strength or weakness of their writing skills will have great impact on their futures as professionals. Needless to say, many of these students enter the composition classroom with a great deal of motivation.

Although some students may have had training in writing particular genres (e.g., abstracts, introductions, summaries) few have been given the opportunity to think of writing—in any language—holistically, as a multi-faceted process that they can purposefully manage. The lack of any emphasis on process has left many of these writers with a focus only on form, whether grammatical or discoursal, and, in turn, often with no real sense of control, with no direct link to an ability they feel is intuitive or natural. This lack of confidence felt by many adult ESL technical writers may, in fact, be underscored since many view their abilities in writing juxtaposed with the relative sense of assurance they feel in their areas of expertise. Distanced by default, many adult ESL technical writers continue to think of writing as a process of translating words and filtering meaning from one language to another.

Specific explanation of writing as a manageable process can not only enrich these students' notion of writing, but can also give them a method of diagnosing where they have problems in the process of moving from a blank page to a completed final text in English. The difficulty in getting ESL composition students to adopt a broader view of writing as process is in finding ways to loosen their grip on the focus on the written product and its form, that which is so often viewed as the immediate measure of success in many writing classes. Despite the fact that a few ESL composition textbooks (e.g., Leki, 1989; Raimes, 1987) do stress writing as a process, the majority of texts do not. Those texts that do focus on writing as process, cannot, however, replace the impact of a classroom where students are consistently encouraged to carefully inspect and reflect on their own writing process to see where they have the greatest ease and where the greatest difficulty. In other words, the idea of writing as process presented in a text alone most likely will not broaden adult students' focus on form unless the process orientation is consistently underscored throughout the composition curriculum.

We present here several tools teachers can use to weave the idea of writing as a manageable process into the composition classroom. For more than 2 years, we have used these methods at Carnegie Mellon University (CMU) both in our ESL Writing Clinic and in composition classes for nonnative speakers in graduate programs. Our discussion and comments are based on our work developing and using these tools.

One way to begin a composition course, or any kind of tutoring in writing with ESL students, is to have students fill out a questionnaire about their background in English, their current use of the language, and their current motivation for studying writing. The questionnaire can also be used as the basis for an initial interview the instructor or a teaching assistant can conduct with each student. The questionnaire could include questions such as those presented in Figure 13.1.

Through this questionnaire, instructors can get a fairly sound picture of the student's background in English and of their motivations and goals for study. Information about students' native language and their current course load can also help teachers both instruct and evaluate students throughout the writing instruction. Students from countries that have fairly standardized curriculum for English study (e.g., People's Republic of China, Japan) often have much the same background, while students from countries with less standardized courses of study may have training that varies widely. The questions regarding students' background in English language training can provide information useful for the instructor to begin to identify where and why students may have particular problems in writing and can also be used to prompt students to reflect on their training in writing, both in their native languages and in English. In a surprising number of cases, students have had little training in writing in their native language, a deficit that can affect their abilities to create in English. Questions about how much and what kind of experience students have in listening and speaking provide information about how much acoustical knowledge of English the students have which, we have found at the CMU ESL Writing Clinic, can significantly bear on their writing abilities. Information about how much and what kinds of materials students read also can provide insight into students' overall literacy skills and practices. (Other potential uses for this questionnaire are discussed later in this chapter.)

In addition to prompting students to reflect on their previous training in writing, the questionnaire can be used as a tool for introducing the idea of writing as a process. Whether this questionnaire is completed as an in-class exercise, or through a dialogue with the instructor or a teaching assistant, the question about writing process (marked in bold in Figure 13.1) can be foregrounded or followed with an explanation, perhaps by using a supplementary graphic such as Figure 13.2. In introducing the notion of writing as

Carnegie Mellon University
ESL Center
Writing Clinic Questionnaire©

Date _____                                    Courses this semester ____ .
Student name _____
Dept & status (UG/MA/PhD)_____
Native language/s or dialect/s _____
Months/years U.S. _____

BACKGROUND

  • How long have you been studying English?
            High school _____    University _____    Other _____

  • Describe your language study at each level (e.g., High School, University)
            Speaking / Listening / Reading / Writing

  • In your native language, how much writing instruction have you had and/or
    how much academic or professional writing have you done?

  • How much reading of English did you do before you came to the States?
    (both personal interest and school related)

CURRENT LANGUAGE USE

  • How much and when do you use English in school? (Speaking/writing/reading)

  • How much and when do you use English outside of school? (Speaking/writing/reading)

  • Outside of school-related texts, what kinds and how much English language
    material do you read?

  • What kind of writing do you need to do now?

  • What part of the writing process gives you most difficulty?
    Brainstorming? Generating initial drafts? Reviewing?  Revising?

MOTIVATION/ATTITUDE

  • Do you like to write in any language?

  • What are your professional goals?

  • How much time do you want to dedicate to improving your English writing skills?

**Figure 13.1.**  A version of the questionnaire used in initial interviews with students attending the ESL Writing Clinic at Carnegie Mellon University (reprinted with permission).

process, the instructor can briefly review each of the ideas in the boxes in Figure 13.2, many of which will probably be discussed in more detail during the full course of writing instruction. At this time, an instructor might also introduce the idea of differences between strategies used by novice writers and expert writers, examples of which are given in Figure 13.3. In addition, examples of writers who have problems at different stages in the process might be given. For example, one student could be described as having writer's block, freezing in the initial drafting stage, perhaps because he did not fully understand what his purpose in writing was or did not have a

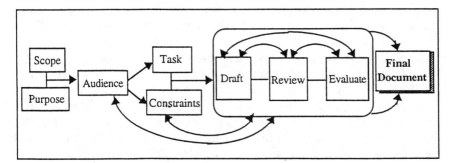

**Figure 13.2.**   A generalized scheme of the process of creating a document.

| Stage | Inexperienced writers | Experienced writers |
|---|---|---|
| Inventing/ Exploring | Don't consider exploring useful or important, and decide on approach to a text quickly | Spend considerable time exploring and evaluating alternative ideas, organizations, and approaches to developing a text |
| Planning/ Organizing | Often make few plans before beginning to write | Plan extensively before drafting |
|  | Prefer not to outline | Plan by making notes, sketches, diagramming both ideas and organizations |
|  | Develop plans while writing | Revise plans while writing |
| Drafting | Are preoccupied with grammar and mechanics in drafts | Are not much concerned with grammar and mechanics in drafts |
|  | Focus on topic and text, not on entire writing situation | Frequently stop to rescan, reread, and reflect on organization and content of text in terms of its appropriateness to audience, purpose, design, and constraints |
|  | Do not often rescan and reflect |  |
|  | Write from their own point of view, rather than that of reader | Are able to view draft from the point of view of the intended reader/s |
| Revising/ Editing | View revising and proofreading as largely similar | Tend to revise more extensively at sentence/paragraph level |
|  | Tend to revise locally at sentence or word level | Are concerned with effectiveness of text for reader |

**Figure 13.3.**   Example of different strategies research has shown novice and expert writers tend to use during different phases of the composing process (Adapted from Burnett, 1990).

well-developed concept of his audience. Another writer could be described as expecting an inappropriate degree of development in her first drafts, resulting in her spending too much time checking drafts for grammar and spelling instead of evaluating them in terms of, for example, the text's audience or purpose. Yet another writer could be portrayed as a poor planner, consistently forgetting to leave enough time for the final grammar and spelling checks, resulting in his submitting texts full of errors that he actually has the ability to detect and revise. By focusing on problems writers have in terms of process rather than form, ESL composition students can begin to break their conception of skill in writing as equivalent to skill in producing grammatical sentences.

In addition to not having reflected on their past training in writing, we have found, through hundreds of interviews of nonnative writers conducted at the CMU ESL Writing Clinic, that few have ever reflected on their writing as a process, either in their native language or in English. This finding is particularly true for those writers in graduate programs in technology and the sciences. Since the model of writing portrays the entire process of writing as a set of interrelated skills, rather than as an unapproachable "talent," the model may appeal to many adult graduate students who are beginning to see the implications of writing beyond the classroom. As students' view of the activity of writing broadens, they may also begin to see similarities in the problems they have writing in their own language with problems they have writing in English. In time, one hopes students may change their idea of improving their writing in English to improving their writing—period.

By introducing the notion of writing as a recursive and strategic process that can take place in a generally similar fashion in every language, students begin to see the process—as a cognitive task, as a social task, as a personal activity—as a more tangible series of skills they can consciously and systematically improve.

## ESL WRITERS AS TECHNICAL EXPERTS

In addition to encouraging students to revise their notion of writing as a process, adult ESL students in technical and scientific disciplines can also be usefully encouraged to revise their notion of themselves as writers. Second language writers are coping with two kinds of writing problems: writing in a second language and writing as technical experts. However, many ESL composition students think of themselves much more as struggling with second language problems rather than with more general writing problems, problems that any writer in technical or professional settings might have in producing prose for readers who do not share their expertise. In other words, many ESL composition students hold fast to their image of themselves as *students*, tending to see themselves as apprentices and nonexperts, and not perceiving of themselves as having any real authority, even over their own texts. This tendency to downplay expertise can be particularly prevalent in students from cultures where humility is valued as a personal characteristic. Although a few ESL students do come into composition classes brimming with confidence about their skills in technical areas, that confidence often does not move into the domain of writing.

To counter this perspective, second language writers can benefit from changing their notion of themselves as second language writers to thinking of themselves as technical writers, faced with many of the same writing and revising problems as their native-speaking counterparts. Instructors can begin to nurture this perspective of students as technical writers and to underscore the importance of students' appreciation of their own expertise by using the questions in the questionnaire discussed earlier. For example, by prompting students to elaborate on their school-related activities — perhaps conducting experiments or writing conference papers or proposals — composition instructors can give students feedback that many are unlikely to get in their academic peer groups or department: how far they have developed as experts, rather than how far they have to go as professionals. By asking students to discuss their professional goals, including what kinds of materials they imagine themselves needing to write in the future, students also have the opportunity to envision themselves in the authority roles they will be assuming sooner rather than later.

However, instructors must tread a fine line in encouraging students to approach their writing tasks with a sense of expertise rather than a sense of inadequacy. The trick is to get students to acknowledge their expertise in certain domains while at the same time not forgetting that they are perhaps less than expert in writing. One way to accomplish this task is to go back to the process model of writing and again stress the differences between novice and expert strategies in producing text. An instructor could, for example, draw on the research of Flower, whose popular composition textbook (1989) points out that writers whose skills are still developing often produce "writer-based" prose. Flower explains that writer-based prose is rooted in the writer's "failure to actively imagine the point of view of someone else" as they write (p. 191). Writers who are highly expert in technical fields often produce this kind of writer-based prose because their material is often complicated. In initial drafts, these writers concentrate on organizing their knowledge for themselves and often have much less concern for how understandable their text might be to another reader (Huckin & Olsen, 1991). After creating initial drafts, less skilled writers move on quickly to become concerned with word-level problems and the form of the text, neglecting consideration of the appropriateness of the generated text to its intended readers.

The move to concentrate on the form of sentences is particularly prevalent in ESL composition students who often think of their writing problems as existing primarily on the sentence level. The lack of awareness of the importance of making global adjustments for nonexpert readers, coupled with a learned tendency to focus on sentence structures, often obscures ESL writers' abilities to detect the need to reorganize their texts for readers who do not share their content knowledge expertise. First language studies show that expert writers, on the other hand, revise early drafts on more global levels with great attention to the readability of the text by other readers (Freedman, Dyson, Flower, & Chafe, 1987).

The idea of needing to adjust text for different readers is a particularly difficult one for some non-English speaking graduate students in technical fields not only because they are not quick to acknowledge their own expertise, but also because they are often writing for peers or instructors. When writing for peers or instructors, students will often assume that their readers will 'know what they mean' even if their texts are not particularly clear. However, if writers can acknowledge readers as having different perspectives on or background knowledge about the information being presented, they may also be more willing to admit that their expertise is unique and that they should not make quick assumptions about how readers will interpret their texts. Again, and importantly, ESL technical writing students may be more willing to attack more global kinds of text problems if they realize that they and their native-speaking counterparts are all tackling the same kind of problems in adjusting texts to readers.

## ESL WRITERS AND CLASSROOM CULTURE

During the 1980s the interest in individual cognition in the writing process, the recursive stages of planning, generating sentences, and revising broadened further to include a concern with writing as a contextualized social activity. Freedman and her colleagues (1987) note that along with a more fine-grained picture of the cognitive processes involved in responding to writing tasks, research of the writing process of individuals revealed that

> Writing is a functional ability that begins well before the school years as stories, messages, and greetings are drawn and written — and that ways in which young children approach writing are related to the language and literacy tasks to which they were exposed in their home and community environment . . . learning and instruction for people of all ages can only be understood within the complexities of the communicative environments in which those processes naturally occur. (p. 1)

ESL researchers and teachers are increasingly recognizing that communicative patterns are reflections of cultural practices and that, in particular, these unique cultural practices manifest themselves in the classroom (Freed, 1991, Stewart, 1972). Learning and teaching in classroom settings not only requires communicative competence of the participants (facility with language structures and vocabulary) but, as part of that competence, the pragmatic knowledge of social and cultural behavior patterns for the interpretation, expression, and negotiation of meaning (Savignon, 1991). In other words, from a young age, readers and writers are oriented to understanding and discussing facts, beliefs, and values in specific, culturally defined ways.

Regardless of how knowledgeable nonnative speakers may be about discipline-specific content areas, they may not be able to effectively communicate that knowledge, either in speaking or writing, because of their lack of familiarity with more general communicative patterns in U.S. academic and work environments. One of the communicative environments most unfamiliar to many ESL students when they arrive to study in the United States is, in fact, the American classroom. Through their student years, many nonnative speakers of English continue to socialize primarily with groups from their home cultures, learning to interpret and respond to academic practices in U.S. schools through their own cultural norms. This method of adjusting to different demands of the classroom can begin to show its flaws, however, when graduate students are called upon to teach or present information at conferences and other professional meetings.

In recent years, the increasing numbers of foreign teaching assistants in American classrooms have made it obvious that different assumptions about communicative practice are at work in different cultures. One example is in the roles and relationship of teacher and student. These differences in assumptions have led to misunderstandings in the classroom and other instructional settings which have, in turn, prompted an increase in research focusing on the problem of nonnative speakers as teachers, as well as the development of training programs and materials to deal with classroom communicative problems, which are often rooted in cultural differences (e.g., Byrd, Constantinides, & Pennington, 1989; Wennerstrom, 1989). In fact, the problem of cultural differences in pedagogy has become severe enough that 13 states have passed laws requiring that nonnative speakers pass English language proficiency tests before being allowed to teach (Thomas & Monoson, 1991). Note, however, that despite their intention, most state exams test only proficiency in speaking and not overall communicative competence in the classroom.

The idea of coupling teaching about pedagogy with teaching writing skills becomes timely as researchers from a variety of disciplines converge on the idea that effective teaching methodology in American classrooms does indeed reflect some more general communicative styles of American speakers (Andersen & Powell, 1991; Pratt, 1991). For example, Sarkisian (1990) suggests that assumptions about the classroom behavior that Americans take for granted must be consciously learned by both foreign students and teachers. These assumptions include expectations about the amount of appropriate participation in the classroom (a lot in the U.S. compared to some cultures), the role of the teacher (for American students, someone who can be questioned or challenged), and the amount of feedback expected from students (for American teachers, a lot of feedback compared to some cultures). In turn, these assumptions can also be seen in terms of expectations readers have of texts.

Expectations about participation in classroom discussions is one specific example of different expectations about appropriate communicative behavior that can be seen both in terms of classroom practice and in terms of writing. For example, many foreign students often feel that they should participate only when they can present completely new information into a discussion (Heidish, 1990). American students, on the other hand, feel free to engage in classroom discussions more broadly, by demonstrating prior knowledge to make connections to known ideas, rewording teacher's statements to clarify their own understanding, and making links to group knowledge to extend and support the ongoing topic of discussion.

Consider a student who perceives that participation in discussion is valuable only if the information offered is new and that information already known or shared among an audience is not appropriate to interject into an argument. Not only might this student appear dormant in class, but he or she may also produce texts that seem stilted and lack flow. The classroom behavior and the problems in production of coherent text may both be rooted in the lack of value put on the sharing of information known to be common knowledge to the audience. In terms of text in particular, students placing minimal communicative value in articulating shared information may find it difficult to digest basic principles for creating readable prose in English, such as the need for transitions that reword or summarize, or the given/new tenet in writing which suggests that writers "put information that is new to the reader into a framework of information already known to the reader" (Huckin & Olsen, 1991, p. 396).

A glance through any number of popular technical and professional writing textbooks reveals consistent advice to writers to contextualize new information, acknowledge counter arguments, and include examples and alternative wording of information to accommodate different audiences (e.g., Burnett, 1990; Keene, 1987; Olsen & Huckin, 1991). Second language writers may have difficulty understanding how and why these principles function in English text, in part due to the communicative norms learned in their home cultures. However, if these students learn how shared information functions in American classroom discourse, not only might they be able to participate in classes more productively, but they also may be able to be better teachers and to better understand how they can use information already known to their readers to lend coherence to their writing. In addition, ESL students' abilities to frame sound written arguments may also improve as they become accustomed to the idea that in U.S. classrooms knowledge is seen as negotiable and relative and that questioning and debating are not only appropriate behaviors but are also seen as necessary skills to develop as a learner. In short, one potentially powerful way for students to appreciate principles of coherence and readability in English language expository prose is to learn about the value and role of providing background knowledge in productive classrooms.

Another example of differences in communicative practice that is obvious in the classroom and also in written discourse is the idea of "getting to the point." As Althen (1988) pointed out: "To understand the way that Americans talk about things, it's necessary to understand about the 'point'. . . . Speakers and writers are supposed to 'make their point clear,' meaning that they are supposed to say or write explicitly the idea or piece of information they wish to convey" (p. 30).

Althen proceeds to say that language learners from many other cultures work under a different concept of how to convey "the point" of discourse. He points to African traditions of using stories to convey meaning, rather than blatant or explicit statements of "the point." Althen also refers to the Japanese preference of speaking indirectly, leaving the listener to draw on cultural and context knowledge to determine meaning. Other authors such as Hinds (1983) have also explored this tendency toward indirectness as exhibited in Japanese prose.

Stewart (1972) noted that culture may influence not only classroom behavior but also thinking style.

> Foreign students are frequently described by American instructors as lacking "analytical thinking." In writing papers, theses and dissertations, the students tend to be subjective and descriptive. They avoid analysis and, when compelled to do so, make inappropriate generalizations. A less frequent complaint, usually made about some European students, is that they are too theoretical, disparage facts, and ignore methods for collecting data. These two observations suggest that the preferred American pattern of thinking — that which is dominant in the academic world and, to a great extent, represents the cultural norm — lies in-between theoretical speculation and empirical description. (p. 22)

Although this perspective on alignments between culture and thinking style is a broad generalization, many ESL composition teachers do find that some students, particularly those who are just beginning to write for larger audiences (i.e., conference papers or articles for refereed journals) find adjusting to the genres preferred by their discourse communities difficult. These difficulties may be rooted in differences in cultural preferences for articulating knowledge.

The main point in providing these examples is to show that highlighting culturally specific classroom practices can drive home communicative norms that function in both spoken and written discourse. If students can see how communicative norms function in immediate and natural settings, such as in making explicit statements of purpose or in using rewording and redundancy, they may in turn be able to understand how these communicative features work in English language text for English language readers.

## CHANGING THE IMAGE OF ESL TECHNICAL WRITERS

All the perspective mentioned here — teaching writing as process, teaching writers to view themselves as experts, and teaching writers to compare effective communication in writing with effective communication in classrooms — require renewed effort to be woven into the composition classroom. Many of the graduate-level ESL students who enter our classrooms think that they will be facing the task of improving their control over English grammar and form. As teachers, we often accommodate this expectation by spending a substantial portion of time focusing on matters of form, without invoking other messages about writing to counterbalance and contextualize the importance of structure and form. What we are suggesting here is that adult students who will soon be teachers or researchers themselves may benefit most from a course in writing in which they are taught primarily to change their image of themselves as ESL writers to that of technical experts who must be able to communicate their knowledge clearly and within appropriate communicative norms to readers — and students in classrooms — who do not share their expertise.

## REFERENCES

Althen, G. (1988). *American ways: A guide for foreigners in the United States.* Yarmouth, ME: Intercultural Press.

Althen, G. (1991). Teaching "culture" to international teaching assistants. In J. Nyguist, R. Abbot, B. Wulff & J. Sprague (Eds.), *Preparing the professoriate of tomorrow to teach* (pp. 350-355). Dubuque, IA: Kendall/Hunt.

Applebee, A. (1983). *Contexts for learning to write.* Norwood, NJ: Ablex.

Andersen, J. F., & Powell, R. (1991). Intercultural communication and the classroom. In L. Samovar & R. Porter (Eds.), *Intercultural communication: A reader* (pp. 208-214). Belmont, CA: Wadsworth.

Bartholomae, D. (1985). Inventing the university. In M. Rose (Ed.), *When a writer can't write* (pp. 134-163). New York: Guilford.

Bazerman, C. (1988). *Shaping written knowledge: The genre and activity of the experimental article in science.* Madison: University of Wisconsin Press.

Becker, A. (1989). A short essay on languaging. In F. Steier (Ed.), *Method and reflexivity: Knowing as systemic social construction.* London: Sage.

Becker, C. B. (1986). Reasons for the lack of argumentation and debate in the Far East. In L. Samovar & R. Porter (Eds.), *Intercultural communication: A reader* (pp. 234-243). Belmont, CA: Wadsworth.

Bereiter, C., & Scardamalia, M. (1984). Learning about writing from reading. *Written Communication,* 1, 163–188.

Bereiter, C., & Scardamalia, M. (1987). *The psychology of written composition.* Hillsdale, NJ: Erlbaum.

Bernhardt, E. B. (1991). Developments on second language literacy research: Retrospective and prospective views for the classroom. In B. Freed (Ed.), *Foreign language acquisition research and the classroom* (pp. 221–251). Lexington, MA: DC Heath.

Burnett, R. E. (1990). *Technical communication* (2nd ed.). Belmont, CA: Wadsworth.

Byrd, P., Constantinides, J., & Pennington, M. (1989). *The Foreign Teaching Assistant's Manual.* New York: Macmillan.

Carrell, P. L. (1983). Three components of background knowledge in reading comprehension. *Language Learning, 33,* 183–207.

Carrell, P. L. (1987). Text as interaction: Some implication of text analysis and reading research for composition. In U. Connor & R. B. Kaplan (Eds.), *Writing across languages: Analysis of L2 text* (pp. 47–55). Reading, MA: Addison-Wesley.

Carrell, P. L., Devine, J. & Eskey, D. E. (1988). *Interactive approaches to second language reading.* New York: Cambridge University Press.

Crowhurst, M. (1991). Interrelationships between reading and writing persuasive discourse. *Research in the Teaching of English, 25,* 314–338.

Cumming, S. (1984). The sentence in Chinese. *Studies in Language, 8,* 365–395.

Durst, R. (1987). Cognitive and linguistic demands of analytic writing. *Research in the Teaching of English, 21,* 347–376.

Edelsky, C. (1983). Segmentationandpunc.tu.a.tion: Developmental data for young writers in a bilingual program. *Research in the Teaching of English, 17,* 135–156.

Flick, W. C., & Anderson, J. (1980). Rhetorical difficulty in scientific English: A study in reading comprehension. *TESOL Quarterly, 14,* 345–351.

Flower, L. (1989). *Problem-solving strategies for writing* (3rd ed.). New York: Harcourt.

Freed, B. (Ed.). (1991). *Foreign language acquisition research and the classroom.* Lexington, MA: DC Heath.

Freedman, S. Dyson, A., Flower, L., & Chafe, W. (1987). *Research in writing: Past, present, and future* (Tech Rep. No. 1) Berkeley: Center for the Study of Writing, University of California.

Friedlander, A. (1987). *The writer stumbles.* Unpublished doctoral dissertation, Carnegie Mellon University, Pittsburgh, PA.

Furey, P. R. (1986). A framework for cross-cultural analysis of teaching methods. In P. Pyrd (Ed.), *Teaching across cultures in the university ESL program* (pp. 15–28). Washington, DC: National Association for Foreign Student Affairs.

Hayes, J. R. (1989). Writing research: The analysis of a very complex task. In D. Klahr & K. Kotovsky (Eds.), *Complex information processing: The impact of Herbert A. Simon* (pp. 209–234). Hillsdale, NJ: Erlbaum.

Hayes, J. R., & Flower, L. (1980). Identifying the organization of writing processes. In L. Gregg & E. R. Steinberg (Eds.), *Cognitive processes in writing* (pp. 3–30). Hillsdale, NJ: Erlbaum.

Heidish, P. (1990). *Teaching and learning across cultures* (University Learning Occasional Series). Pittsburgh, PA: Carnegie Mellon University Teaching Center.

Higgins, J. (1985). Hard facts: Notes on teaching English to science students. In J. Swales (Ed.), *Episodes in ESP* (pp. 28–34). Oxford, UK: Pergamon Institute of English.

Hinds, J. (1983). Contrastive rhetoric: Japanese and English. *Text, 3,* 183–195.

Hinds, J. (1979). Organizational patterns in discourse. In T. Givon (Ed.), *Syntax and semantics L2: Discourse and syntax* (pp. 135–157). New York: Academic Press.

Hofstede, G. (1986). Cultural differences in teaching and learning. *International Journal of Intercultural Relations, 10,* 301–320.

Huckin, T. N., & Olsen, L.A. (1991). *Technical writing and professional communication for nonnative speakers of English* (2nd ed.). New York: McGraw Hill.

Jones, S., & Tetroe, J. (1987). Composing in a second language. In A. Matsuhashi (Ed.), *Writing in real time* (pp. 34–57). New York: Longman.

Kaplan, R. B. (1987). Cultural thought patterns revisited. In U. Connor & R. B. Kaplan (Eds.). *Writing across languages: Analysis of L2 Text* (pp. 9–20). Reading, MA: Addison-Wesley.

Keene, M. L. (1987). *Effective professional writing.* Lexington, MA: DC Heath.

Krashen, S. D. (1984). *Writing: Research, theory, and applications.* Oxford, UK: Pergamon.

Leki, I. (1989). *Academic writing: Techniques and tasks.* New York: St. Martin.

Martindale, D. (1960). *The nature and types of sociological theory,* Boston, MA: Houghton Mifflin.

Mohan, B. A., & Lo, W. (1985). Academic writing and Chinese students: Transfer and developmental factors. *TESOL Quarterly, 19,* 515–534.

Olsen, L., & Huckin, T. (1991). *Technical writing and professional communication* (2nd ed.). New York: McGraw-Hill.

Parry, K. J. (1987). Reading in a second culture. In J. Devine, P. Carrell, & D. E. Eskey (Eds.), *Research in reading in English as a second language* (pp. 59–70). Washington, DC: TESOL.

Pica, T., Barnes, G., & Fingers, A. (1990). *Teaching matters: Skills and strategies for international teaching assistants.* New York: Newbury.

Pratt, D. D. (1991). Conceptions of self within China and the United States: Contrasting foundations of adult education. *International Journal of Intercultural Relations, 15,* 285–310.

Raimes, A. (1987). *Exploring through writing: A process approach to ESL composition.* New York: St. Martin.

Sarkisian, E. (1990). *Teaching American students: A guide for international faculty and teaching fellows.* Cambridge, MA: Danforth Center for Teaching and Learning, Harvard University Press.

Savignon, S. J. (1991). Research on the role of communication in classroom-based foreign language acquisition: On interpretation, expression, and the negotiation of meaning. In B. Freed (Ed.), *Foreign language acquisition research and the classroom* (pp. 31–45). Lexington, MA: DC Heath.

Skibniewski, L., & Skibniewski, M. (1987). The writing processes of intermediate/advanced language learners in the foreign and native languages. *Sinica Anglica Posnaniensia* (Vol. XIX). Poznán, Poland: Adam Mickiewicz University.

Smith, L. (1987). *Discourse across cultures: Strategies in world Englishes.* New York: Prentice.

Steffensen, M. S., Joag-Dev, C., & Anderson, R. (1979). A cross-cultural perspective on reading comprehension. *Reading Research Quarterly, 15,* 10–29.

Stewart, E. (1972). *American cultural patterns: A cross-cultural perspective.* Yarmouth, ME: Intercultural Press.

Swales, J. (1990). *Genre analysis: English in academic and research settings.* Cambridge, UK: Cambridge University Press.

Thomas, C., & Monoson, P. (1991). Issues related to state-mandated English language proficiency requirements. In J. Nyguist, R. Abbot, B. Wulff, & J. Sprague (Eds.), *Preparing the professoriate of tomorrow to teach* (pp. 382–392). Dubuque, IA: Kendall/ Hunt.

Wennerstrom, A. (1989). *Techniques for teachers.* Seattle: University of Washington Press.

Witte, S., & Faigley, L. (1981). Coherence, cohesion, and writing quality. *College Composition and Communication, 32,* 189–204.

Xu, Y. (1987). A study of referential functions of demonstratives in Chinese discourse. *Journal of Chinese Linguistics, 15,* 132–155.

# CHAPTER 14

# Negotiating the Syllabus: A Learning-Centered, Interactive Approach to ESL Graduate Writing Course Design

**Jan Frodesen**
*University of California, Santa Barbara*

Graduate nonnative English speakers face writing tasks in their programs that often differ greatly from writing assignments demanded of undergraduate ESL students. As Belcher (1990a) has noted, graduate students also tend to differ from the undergraduate population in their level of cognitive development and their approaches to learning. For these reasons, graduate ESL courses that help to initiate writers into their field-specific research communities and provide them with relevant writing practice can best address the needs of this ESL population. Graduate students enrolling in required ESL courses often include international students who have recently entered their programs and have not yet started a major writing project. Consequently, the syllabus for such a course must not only address writing needs across disciplines but also adapt to various stages of students' involvement in their graduate programs.

This chapter describes a learning-centered approach to developing a graduate ESL writing course. This approach assumes that learning is not only a cognitive but a social process of negotiation between the individual and society; a learning-centered course design is a negotiated and dynamic process in which changing and developing needs interact with the target situation to influence the syllabus as the course progresses (Hutchinson & Waters, 1987). Components of course design discussed in this chapter include: (a) establishing course content and identifying needs, (b) negotiating assignments through contract proposals, (c) creating feedback channels for ongoing course development, (d) developing discourse analysis activities to examine field-specific and cross-disciplinary conventions, (e) designing peer response activities that address difficulties students experience in responding to writing outside their disciplines, and (f) responding to and assessing field-specific writing.

Graduate nonnative English speakers (NNS) who are required to take ESL composition in American universities face reading and writing tasks in their programs that often differ greatly from those emphasized in undergraduate ESL composition courses. While some universities do offer undergraduate ESL courses in English for science and technology, and some general ESL courses provide practice in writing across the curriculum, the typical undergraduate ESL composition course focuses largely on composing processes and rhetorical strategies for developing general essay writing skills in response to cultural or social themes, as evidenced by current composition texts used in ESL classrooms (e.g., Columbo, Cullen, & Lisle, 1992; Raimes, 1987; Spack, 1990). In contrast, the writing tasks for graduate students may include technical reports, grant proposals, summaries of research, conference papers, contributions to panel discussions, critical reviews of published research, or literature reviews of current developments in their disciplines. These writing tasks require knowledge of different genre-based conventions; they may also demand awareness of discipline-specific writing conventions such as the organization of reported research (Hopkins & Dudley-Evans, 1988; Swales, 1990).

It is no wonder, then, that NNS graduate students, upon finding themselves in required ESL writing courses developed primarily for undergraduates, often resent the demands of such courses, which they see as largely irrelevant to their needs and as taking them away from coursework in their disciplines. This attitude seems especially common with entering NNS international graduate students in the sciences, whose initial coursework may have few extended writing assignments. Although it is true that much language use is similar across the disciplines, and, consequently, that ESL instructors should be careful not to overemphasize language differences among fields (Hutchinson & Waters, 1987), it is also not difficult to understand, for example, an electrical engineering student's doubts that writing creative journal entries and composing essays on the meaning of friendship will prepare her for writing an analysis of forced overflow oscillations in digital filters. A lack of experience in essay writing may also cause international graduate students to feel out of place in traditional ESL composition courses; many of these students enter American graduate schools directly from their native countries, without having received the kind of composition instruction typically found in U.S. secondary schools and colleges.

Graduate NNS students differ from undergraduates not only in their writing needs but in other ways that argue in favor of providing instruction for them apart from undergraduate ESL populations whenever possible. They tend to be experienced writers in their disciplines, especially those who are in PhD programs. As Belcher (1990a) pointed out, graduate students are generally more mature, more advanced in cognitive development, and more focused in their intellectual pursuits than undergraduates are. Graduate students approach reading and writing assignments in their disciplines from an established knowledge base of technical language and field-specific topics. For all of these reasons, graduate ESL courses that help to initiate writers into their field-specific research and to provide them with relevant writing practice can best address the needs of this NNS population.

In some university contexts, it is possible to offer a graduate course solely on thesis or dissertation projects (Richards, 1988). Although such a course can obviously serve the needs of some graduate students, it is usually offered without credit to students who have advanced in their programs rather than as a course meeting university ESL requirements. A required ESL course, in contrast, will typically include at least some international students who have just entered their programs and have not yet started a major writing project, let alone a thesis. It may also include students in Master's degree programs who do not have to submit a thesis to satisfy requirements for their degrees. Thus, the instructor creating a syllabus for a required graduate ESL course is challenged in ways that he or she would not be in developing a more narrowly focused course, such as thesis/dissertation writing or editing, in which highly motivated students enroll voluntarily with clear expectations. The syllabus for a required course must not only address writing needs across disciplines; it must adapt to students' various stages of involvement in the larger academic community and in their specific disciplines; it must address varying student motivation and expectations; it may also have to meet specific English or ESL departmental requirements for composition credit.

This chapter reports on a graduate ESL writing course that was developed using a learning-centered approach. It served as an alternative to an ESL writing course developed primarily for undergraduates. As defined by Hutchinson and Waters (1987), a learning-centered approach assumes that learning is not only a cognitive but a social process of negotiation between the individual and society. A learning-centered course design is a negotiated and dynamic process in which changing and developing needs interact with the target situation to influence the syllabus as the course progresses. Feedback channels, created to provide frequent evaluation, constitute an important component of this approach, since learners' needs vary over time.

Elements of course design that will be described in the following sections include: (a) establishing course content and identifying needs, (b) negotiating assignments through contract proposals, (c) creating feedback channels for ongoing course development, (d) developing discourse analysis activities for exploring both field-specific and cross-disciplinary academic writing conventions, (e) designing peer review activities that address some of the difficulties students experience in responding to writing outside their disciplines, and (f) responding to and assessing field-specific writing.

The course description presented here draws largely from a writing course that I developed at the University of California, Los Angeles for graduate students who were required to take ESL composition on the basis of a diagnostic exam. Sixteen students enrolled in this course, representing the humanities, social sciences, biological sciences, and physical sciences. All but one were international students who planned to return to their native countries, which included Indonesia, Hong Kong, Taiwan, the People's Republic of China, Korea, and Israel. The majority (12) were doctoral students; their residency in the United States ranged from 3 weeks to 6 years. Four students enrolled in the course optionally; they had already satisfied the university's ESL requirement but wanted another writing course in preparation for their careers or for dissertation writing. Because the course design developed partially from students' input throughout the 10-week course, my discussion will include students' reactions to and evaluations of activities where they may help to illustrate the process of negotiating the syllabus.

## COURSE CONTENT

The extent to which course content is specified before the course actually begins, as well as the kinds of writing activities, may depend on a several variables including (a) university or departmental ESL requirements, (b) the instructor's preferences for structuring writing assignments, (c) the length of the course, and (d) the instructor's experience with and assessment of NNS graduate students' writing needs across disciplines.

The first three of these variables especially may influence the degree to which the course is structured prior to input from the students. Some required graduate ESL courses may need to parallel in certain respects the requirements for undergraduate courses offered at the same level. There may be, for instance, requirements on the number of papers or even the kinds of papers required.

The teacher's preferences for structuring writing activities may also affect the flexibility of the course. He or she may feel more comfortable assigning specific genres, such as the research proposal or the critical evaluation, which students can explore through both reading and writing in their disciplines, rather than having students work on actual writing assignments in their degree programs or on theses/dissertations in progress. This structuring could allow for more group-centered lessons in the classroom on major writing assignments, more common ground for peer review, and more uniform methods of evaluation than would a course in which students worked on different writing projects assigned in their disciplines.

Other teachers may prefer a more open course design with students engaged in various projects they have been assigned or have chosen based on anticipated academic or professional needs. Belcher (1990b) notes that actual field-specific assignments have the advantage of providing the student feedback from a content-area expert without having to make special arrangements. This course design could combine some group instruction, focusing on common rhetorical strategies, the analysis of form–function relationships, or other shared writing needs, with workshop sessions devoted to individual, pair, or small-group conferences, depending on the disciplines represented.

Another influence on course requirements is the duration of the course. For short (10 weeks or less) courses, it may be more critical to assign an initial common writing task relevant to all disciplines so that the class is immediately engaged in a meaningful writing activity. This buys time for negotiating other writing tasks to be completed later in the term. Even with tasks that are structured as to genre, students can have a role in choosing the topics and can contribute to genre definition by exploring the purposes of these genres, that is, the contexts in their fields that call for them, as well as the rhetorical moves that create them.

In the 10-week course that I developed, I used a uniform assignment for the first paper, an annotated bibliography addressing a research question. This assignment was designed to give students practice in providing background information, defining a research question, and practice in summary. For new students, the assignment oriented them to library sources and to bibliographic citation conventions in their disciplines. Two other major papers were negotiated through written proposals and conferences. These papers had minimum and maximum page requirements. If students desired, both papers could be sections of a longer project, such as the introduction and the methodology sections of a thesis. Students were required to submit a proposal, two drafts and a final revised paper for each writing project. Only the final revision was graded. Students were also required to keep an academic journal, which will be described later, to complete brief text analysis assignments and editing assignments, and to participate in peer review activities.

## NEEDS ANALYSIS

In defining *learner needs*, Hutchinson and Waters (1987) distinguish *target needs*, "what the learner needs to do in the target situation," and *learning needs*, "what the learner needs to do in order to learn" (p. 54). They further categorize types of target needs, identifying *necessities, lacks,* and *wants. Necessities* concerns the forms of communication demanded of the learner in the target situation and the linguistic features associated with these forms. *Lacks* refers to the gap between what the learner already knows and what he or she needs to know. Finally, *wants,* a category sometimes overlooked in course development, considers the subjective views that learners may have of their needs and lacks, views that may differ considerably from the instructor's assessment.

Information gathering to determine target needs and learning needs for the writing course described here included asking students to complete a questionnaire, class discussion, and individual conferences. The questionnaire requested personal data such as native country and language, length of residency in the U.S., status in their degree program, ESL courses taken, motivations for taking the course, and expectations. It asked students to identify their writing strengths and weaknesses, the types of writing that were most difficult for them, and any aspects of English that were particularly troublesome. It presented a list of academic writing skills for students to rank in terms of learning priorities. Finally, it asked them to describe any ongoing writing projects they had undertaken in their disciplines or writing tasks that they would be expected to complete during the quarter. Prior to filling out the questionnaire, students were given an opportunity to ask questions about any items on the form, and terms that might be unfamiliar were explained. (See Appendix A for a sample questionnaire.) The information obtained from this questionnaire was used as the focus for initial individual conferences to discuss learner needs and to negotiate writing tasks and goals for the course.

Both conferences and class discussion of course structure served to further reveal students' expectations and target needs, especially students' wants. A primary instructor goal for the course was to give students as much opportunity as possible to define their own assignments and to work on projects that were actually required by their programs or undertaken for professional development, whether dissertations, term papers, experiment reports, or conference presentations. Two unanticipated (although, in retrospect, not surprising) reactions by several students to this course structure were: (a) anxiety about having to define their own assignments, and (b) resistance to writing in their disciplines. The first response came from students who had taken other ESL composition courses at the university, in which they had been assigned readings and paper topics. These students' learning backgrounds, both EFL and ESL, had accustomed them to traditional methods and to the authority of the teacher. While by the end of the course they came to appreciate the opportunity to choose their own topics, the causes of their anxiety needed to be addressed in negotiating writing projects. The second unexpected response, one student's resistance to writing in his disciplines, reflected both expectations of what a university ESL course should be and personal motivations for learning English. The student, a native of Taiwan who had just entered a Master's program in atmospheric science, objected to writing in his field and chose to write personal essays for his major writing tasks. He believed that he needed to develop "general English," not field-specific English. If a syllabus is to be truly a negotiated one, such expectations and learning motivations cannot be ignored. Hutchinson and Waters (1987), in their discussion of target needs, stress that "there is no necessary relationship between necessities as perceived by sponsor or ESP teacher and what the learners want or feel they need" (p. 57). This is not to say that the instructor should make no demands unless they are agreeable to all (the very fact of being required to take an ESL course may be undesirable to some), but that instructor and student may have conflicting perceptions of target or learning needs. Instructors need to be aware of students' views so that they are acknowledged in the process of negotiating coursework.

## NEGOTIATING ASSIGNMENTS

Major writing assignments were negotiated in three stages. The first consisted of individual conferences outside of class. These conferences focused on discussing the responses students had provided in the questionnaires about their expectations, their motivations, the writing needs they had identified, and their current writing projects. I also used this opportunity to find out more about the students' disciplines and their degree programs. If students were not engaged in any ongoing writing projects or had not been assigned major papers in their courses, I helped them to explore and identify possible future needs or, as in the case of the student who resisted field-specific writing, to clarify writing development goals and to relate them to the student's academic and professional goals.

In the second stage, students submitted written proposals outlining the papers they planned to work on. They presented background information on the topic, a description of the type of writing project (e.g., review of the literature for a thesis, analysis chapter of a dissertation, critical review of published research), the academic context (e.g., course term paper, conference presentation, professional development), the objectives, the intended audience, and the proposed length.

The final stage involved my reading and approval of the proposals, including suggestions and guidelines for completion and, for some, questions I had to which students responded in conferences during class. Once approved, students were expected to treat the proposals as a course contract, subject to future negotiation through conferences.

## CREATING FEEDBACK CHANNELS

As mentioned in the introduction to this chapter, because the course design of a learning-centered approach is a dynamic process, it must incorporate opportunities for the learners' evaluation of their progress and their responses to the learning tasks so that the course can adapt to needs as they develop or change. Because the learning-centered approach is a negotiated process, these channels should also allow teacher feedback about course developments and students' work, other than the traditional methods of grading revised assignments.

The primary modes of feedback in the graduate ESL writing class were individual conferences, journals, class discussion, and midterm evaluations. Conferences were scheduled outside of class time to negotiate assignments, discuss drafts of major writing projects, and provide help with special needs, such as grammatical problems. For the academic journals, roughly half of the topics were assigned; for the others, students could write about either the ESL course or topics related to their disciplines and their writing development.

In the academic journals, students were asked to evaluate a variety of class activities, such as peer response and discourse analysis exercises. Occasionally they were asked to respond to readings, which, among other objectives, provided information on their attitudes toward language use. For example, they were asked to respond to an essay by Zinnser (1984) extolling simplicity in language and to evaluate an example of language use in their disciplines by Zinnser's standards. A Chinese student wrote how relieved he was to find out that native speakers of English also had trouble writing simply and clearly. Others raised questions about straying from the academic styles commonly found in their disciplines. Journals were collected biweekly and brief responses written for each entry.

In addition to journals and conferences, informal class discussion also served as feedback on class activities. For example, students occasionally evaluated the usefulness of a language exercise for their own writing development or discussed advantages/disadvantages of some component of a structured activity, such as pair work vs. small-group work in peer response. Finally, the midterm evaluations provided an opportunity for students to comment anonymously on the course and the instructor and to suggest changes for the remainder of the term. Frequent and varied methods of feedback allow students to be true participants in the process of learning and help the teacher develop and guide the course in ways that consider learners' intellectual and emotional responses as well as learning tasks.

## DESIGNING CLASS ACTIVITIES

If a graduate ESL writing course is designed with a genre-based syllabus, the nature of at least some group instruction is defined by the syllabus. For a course in which students are engaged in a variety of negotiated projects, one-on-one student–teacher conferencing will obviously be a central component. For both types of courses, however, teachers can use group activities to familiarize students with formal and rhetorical conventions in their field-specific discourse communities and to help them see how these conventions relate to the larger academic community. A survey of graduate faculty by Casanave and Hubbard (1992) indicates that many NNS graduate students have problems with discourse-level aspects of writing in their fields, including organization and development. ESL instructors can also assign out-of-class activities that encourage students to be ethnographers of the discourse in their disciplines. Finally, group activities can help students develop grammatical and lexical competence through discourse analysis, editing, and revision practice. Although global features of writing are more important than local features, grammatical accuracy remains a problem for NNS graduate students and a concern of graduate faculty (Casanave & Hubbard, 1992).

The following are suggested activities. Sample assignments for some of them are given in Appendix C.

1. Students interview their faculty advisors to get information about the roles of writing and publication in their fields, stylistic preferences of their fields, and to learn about their advisors' writing histories and processes.

2. Students locate academic or technical journal articles on topics of interest. Using guides created by the instructor, they analyze formatting conventions such as references to sources, explanatory notes, references to technical terms, types of headings and subheadings used.

3. Students bring to class an article or paper from their field in a specific genre or part of one, for example, a research abstract, introduction to a thesis, a critical review. In pairs or groups, they analyze the rhetorical moves of two or three of the papers, identifying similarities and differences.

4. Students compare grammatical coding of rhetorical moves in research abstracts from academic journals in their fields. For example, they examine the use of passive voice vs. first person "we" in describing research methodology. Students then write an abstract based on their own work or an assigned reading. This helps to familiarize students with the stylistic preferences of their discipline or of a specific journal in their field.

5. In cloze exercises, with certain grammatical features replaced by blanks in authentic texts, students choose appropriate forms and discuss

their choices. Such exercises can teach, for example, discourse motivations for verb tense or article usage, the use of logical connectors and the use of cohesive devices such as pronouns, demonstratives, and lexical repetition to express information previously given or known to the reader ("old information").

6. In groups or as a class, students can edit grammatical problems in sentences that the instructor has selected from their drafts. The instructor can focus on a particular type of problem across texts (e.g., verb tenses, prepositions) or indicate what different types of problems need to be edited. As with other exercises, editing is most successful when it is carefully guided.

7. Students can revise sentences to achieve clarity. They can revise short texts to create cohesion by adding conectors or substituting reference forms for repetition. They can revise for emphasis and focus. Williams's (1989) text *Style: Ten Lessons in Clarity & Grace* is excellent for this purpose.

These suggestions represent only a few of the possibilities for group activity in the ESL graduate writing class. Whatever the instructor chooses, work on general writing skills and strategies as well as field-specific investigation is helpful for most students who are required to take ESL.

## DEVELOPING PEER RESPONSE ACTIVITIES

Peer response, in which students read and comment on each others' work in progress, is now a common component of writing courses at all levels in the United States. The central problem confronted when including peer response in ESL graduate writing courses is an obvious one: Unless students are members of the same specialized academic discourse community, they may find it difficult to interpret each others' prose and almost impossible to say anything about it of a critical nature. Belcher (1990b) reported that even when graduate NNS students were matched across classrooms with others from their disciplines, the quality of peer response was frequently vague or lacking a critical perspective. Nevertheless, the majority of the students in Belcher's study appreciated having another audience, which gave them a chance to rethink the assignments.

In many contexts, such as the course I offered, it is not possible to group all students by discipline. Even so, peer response activities which draw on the writer's expertise and recognize the reader's limitations can provide graduate NNS students the opportunity to discuss their work orally with a nonthreatening audience, an activity that can be very beneficial especially for the new NNS graduate student, who may have had little previous experience speaking in English about topics in her discipline.

Peer response also encourages students to view their writing critically and to see how different perspectives can inform their work, even if they do not agree with their reviewers. As Herrington and Cadman (1991) have noted, "the value of peer-review exchanges can be realized as much in instances where a writer decides not to follow a peer's advice as where she does" (p. 184). One of the students in my course, a Korean woman in a biostatistics Master's program, observed how different the critical perspectives of her peer responders, public health students, were, both from hers and each others'. She also noted how these differences could be beneficial in collaborative work:

> Because of my training, I am very sensitive to the cause and effect. But Fauziah and Asril are different from me. Fauziah is very cautious about the proof to the statements and Asril is very precise about the statements that he makes. That is my observation and it may be wrong, but I think if we can work together on a paper or project, we may omit a lot of mistakes that each of us would make when we do it alone.

For peer response to be successful in mixed discipline groups, review activities need to be carefully structured. The tasks should not make demands that exceed most students' estimation of their abilities to perform them. I was reminded of this last point by students' journal entries after completing the annotated bibliography assignment. Students commented that they felt unqualified to critique their classmates' annotated bibliography drafts. Not only did they find it difficult to evaluate the summaries since they had not seen the source material, but some noted that they could not judge whether bibliographic entries appropriately addressed a research question out of their area of expertise.

The next peer response sessions were more successful, at least in terms of student evaluation of their benefits. This was due in large part, it appeared, to a multistage response process. For the second major paper, students were paired according to the same or related disciplines as much as possible. In cases where this was not possible, I paired students by English proficiency level. For example, two fairly advanced level students paired together were doctoral students in Chinese history and neuroscience. Despite a lack of common ground in their studies, they evaluated their peer response session very positively since the activity gave them an opportunity to explain orally in English their topics, the objectives and audience for their papers, and their difficulties in writing. For the third paper, students were paired or put in groups of three, depending on preferences they had indicated in a journal assignment.

The peer response activities for each cycle included the following:

1. *Pre-peer response exercises* (one class session)
   (a) Writers take turns explaining their projects, stating the type of

paper, topic, purpose, and the intended audience. They provide background that might help their classmates better understand the paper and summarize their main rhetorical strategies. The listener takes notes.

(b) After both students have discussed their papers, they summarize orally what their papers have in common and how they differ.

(c) Each student drafts a set of questions (a peer response guide) for his/her classmate to address. They may choose questions from a sample guide in addition to ones they make up.

(d) Each pair exchanges response guide drafts. In the roles of responders, students check their understanding of the questions and their ability to answer them. They offer any suggestions they have for the final draft of the guides and return them to the writers.

(e) Each student revises his or her response guide based on the discussion and gives it to the responder along with a copy of the draft. (For the actual instructions given students for this activity, see Appendix B.)

2. *Peer response*

(a) Outside of class, each student reads his/her classmate's draft and writes answers to the set of questions on the peer response guide.

(b) At the next class session, pairs meet to discuss their responses and afterward exchange the guides they have written for writers to use in further revision of their drafts.

3. *Evaluation*

As a journal assignment, students evaluate their peer response experiences as well as the process itself.

Students in my course responded enthusiastically to the discussion part of the pre-editing exercises; in general, they felt that explaining their papers before the actual responding session improved the final peer response discussion and that the feedback they got was helpful. There was less consensus about the value of writing their own response guides; although one student termed it "a good and progressive idea," others felt insecure about their ability to create their own questions, even with the sample guide, and requested more sample questions.

This response and others referring to lack of experience in peer review reveal that many NNS graduate students have had few opportunities to read and comment on their peers' work. Although these students often express confidence about writing in their fields, they are sometimes very hesitant to critique their peers' drafts. This may be the case even among students who are writing in the same disciplines. Since peer review is an important part of professional and academic life in many fields, graduate ESL courses can be of great service to NNS students by providing practice in this socialization process.

To guide students in developing peer review skills, well-structured activities and instructor modeling of the process are essential. Focusing on aspects of writing that students feel qualified to respond to can prevent frustration or resistance to peer response. Making responses progressively more demanding of students' linguistic and composition knowledge as the course progresses will help them further develop their abilities. Feedback from students on their experience with peer response can provide input for judging the effectiveness of techniques used to structure activities and for modifying procedures, if needed, so that they are responsive to previously unidentified or changing needs.

## RESPONDING TO AND ASSESSING FIELD-SPECIFIC WRITING

Most university ESL teachers have probably experienced feelings of inadequacy in responding to a student's field-specific paper due to unfamiliarity with the topic and with technical terminology. Although ESL teachers may not be able to represent the expert audience for whom students have written their papers, they can provide feedback about rhetorical development and language use. Belcher (1990b) provided evidence that ESL teachers' assessment of student writing may sometimes be closer to the views of the content-area teacher than the students' self-assessment is.

Individual conferences with students about proposals for writing assignments and, later, about their drafts, offer opportunities for students to share their expertise with the teacher and to explain the content, purpose, and audience for their papers. In fact, using a conferencing technique similar to that described earlier in the pre-peer response exercises can help the instructor become familiar with the student's research agenda and some of the technical language in their fields. Conferencing thus becomes a collaborative learning activity, with the teacher willing to learn from the student what is necessary to be as helpful an advisor as possible. As with peer response discussion, students' discussion of their work in conferences with instructors not only helps the responder understand the writing better, but assists students in developing oral skills of explaining, clarifying, and defending their ideas, skills needed for their academic and professional advancement.

As for final evaluation of field-specific work, again the instructor must decide what he or she can honestly assess in the student's work, as well as what language objectives have been established for the course, and create criteria for evaluation accordingly. Judging a student's paper in an English class by criteria other than that used by the content-area instructor is not uncommon. ESL students, both undergraduates and graduates, report that some content-area instructors pay little or no attention to grammar or mechanics in evaluating their papers, especially in the sciences. In evaluating the papers for the course described here, I used a departmental rubric designed to evaluate ESL writing in organization, content, grammar, mechanics, and expression, making adjustments where necessary for the various kinds of writing. Evaluation was also based on paper requirements outlined in the syllabus and on the agreement negotiated in the proposals.

## CONCLUSION

Johns (1990) pointed out the lack of negotiated learning in most university contexts: "[T]he entire agenda is set by the faculty members, with little or no input from students" (p. 212). Students who do not conform to this learning model are, Johns claims, often considered "cultural outsiders." Although Johns is describing undergraduate courses, her comments are relevant to graduate courses as well. We can assume that many international graduate students must feel like "cultural outsiders" trying to adapt to the norms and demands of American universities in general and their discipline's discourse community in particular. They may sense that their own academic traditions are not accepted or respected. And, perhaps for the first time, they may feel that they are judged "language deficient" by being required to take an ESL course, although in their native countries they may have been considered proficient users of English as a foreign language.

This description of the learning-centered approach to a graduate ESL class has attempted to demonstrate that there is much to gain by encouraging students to be active participants in and evaluators of their learning processes, by helping them to be ethnographers of their disciplines, and by giving them the language instruction that will increase their confidence as writers and their sense of being insiders in American universities. By negotiating the syllabus in a graduate ESL course, we invite our students to be collaborative learners and encourage them to make their voices heard in the conversation of the academic community.

## REFERENCES

Belcher, D. (1990a, August). The case for teacher–student/author conferencing in field-specific writing by graduate students. *TESOL Newsletter*, pp. 11–12.

Belcher, D. (1990b). Peer vs. teacher response in the advanced composition class. *Issues in Writing, 2 (2)*, 128–150.

Casanave, C., & Hubbard, P. (1992). The writing assignments and writing problems of doctoral students: Faculty perceptions, pedagogical issues, and needed research. *English for Specific Purposes*, *11* (1), 33–49.

Columbo, B., Cullen, R., & Lisle, B. (1992). *Rereading America: Cultural contexts for critical thinking and writing* (2nd ed.) New York: St. Martin's Press.

Herrington, A., & Cadman, D. (1991). Peer review and revising in an anthropology course. *College Composition and Communication*, *42*, 184–199.

Hopkins, A., & Dudley-Evans, T. (1988). A genre-based investigation of the discussion sections in articles and dissertations. *English for Specific Purposes*, *7*, 113–121.

Hutchinson, T., & Waters, A. (1987). *English for specific purposes: A learning centered approach*. Cambridge, UK: Cambridge University Press.

Johns, A. (1990). Coherence as a cultural phenomenon: Employing ethnographic principles in the academic milieu. In U. Connor & A. Johns (Eds.), *Coherence in writing: Research and pedagogical perspectives*. Alexandria, VA: TESOL.

Raimes, A. (1987). *Exploring through writing: A process approach to ESL composition*. New York: St. Martin's Press.

Richards, R.T. (1988). Thesis/dissertation writing for EFL students: An ESP course design. *English for Specific Purposes*, *7*, 171–180.

Spack, R. (1990). *Guidelines: A cross-cultural reading/writing text*. New York: St. Martin's Press.

Swales, J. (1990). *Genre analysis: English in academic and research settings*. Cambridge, UK: Cambridge University Press.

Williams, J. M. (1989). *Style: ten lessons in clarity & grace* (3rd ed.) Boston, MA: Scott, Foresman and Co.

Zinnser, W. (1984). Simplicity. In C. Muscatine & M. Griffith (Eds.), *The Borzoi college reader* (5th ed.). New York: Alfred A. Knopf.

## APPENDIX A
## NEEDS ANALYSIS QUESTIONNAIRE

Name _____

Native country _____ Native language _____

Your graduate department _____

     Program: M.A. _____ Ph.D. _____ Other (Describe) _____

How long have you been at [university] _____

How long have you been in the U.S.? _____

Which, if any ESL courses have you taken at [university]?

Please write brief responses to the following:

1. What are your main reasons for taking this course?
2. What kinds of writing (research papers, reports, collaborative projects, conference papers, etc.) do you most frequently do in your graduate work?
3. In general, what types of source materials do you read/use in your research/writing? (That is, do you primarily read academic jour-

nals, business reports, literature, textbooks, other books, or other written sources?)

4. What courses are you taking this term?
5. Are you working on any writing project(s) in your program now? If so, please describe and state when you plan to have it (them) completed.
6. What do you think are your writing strengths?
7. What do you think are your writing weaknesses?
8. What kinds of academic writing are most difficult for you?
9. Please indicate by number your priorities for developing the following academic writing skills.
   1 = very important  2 = somewhat important
   3 = not very important

   _____ using appropriate rhetorical strategies (e.g., comparison, definition, argumentation) for developing content
   _____ improving other organizational skills (ordering information, using cohesive devices effectively, using appropriate formats for discourse type)
   _____ paraphrasing/integrating source materials in research
   _____ writing abstracts, summaries
   _____ writing critical reviews of research
   _____ reporting on your own research
   _____ improving ability to analyze/evaluate readings
   _____ revising word/phrasing choices for conciseness, appropriateness
   _____ improving accuracy of grammatical structures in English
   _____ improving knowledge of mechanics conventions in English (punctuation, citation)

## APPENDIX B
## PRE-PEER RESPONSE EXERCISES

Main goals: To provide your peer response reader with background information about your paper. To construct individual response guides that reflect as much as possible the writer's desires for feedback and the reader's background.

I. Discovering Similarities/Differences
   A. Taking turns, briefly explain to each other the following (Listeners: take notes on this paper):

1. The kind of paper you are writing (e.g., research report, part of dissertation, review, essay, feasibility study, etc.)
2. The topic of your paper (What is it about?)
3. The purpose of your paper (e.g., does it intend to advance an argument about a particular theory, to offer a critique of an established position, to introduce a new idea, to report or evaluate research findings, to explain a process involving new technology in your field?)
4. The intended audience for your paper (e.g., colleagues with considerable knowledge of your topic, people in your academic discipline but not necessarily with a great amount of knowledge of your topic, college educated persons, etc.).
5. Background information about your topic. Given your classmate's background, what might help him/her understand your paper better?
6. The main rhetorical strategies of your paper (e.g., is your paper primarily analysis, argumentation, classification, explanation of a process, description? To develop your main points, do you define? Compare/contrast? Discuss causes and/or effects? Describe processes? Present examples?)

B. Based on the information in A, briefly summarize (orally) what your papers have in common and how they differ.


II. Drafting a Peer Response Guide
   A. Using the sample response guides and your own ideas, draft a set of questions to which you would like your peer editor to respond. When possible, formulate your questions so that they require more than a yes/no answer. (e.g., instead of "Is my thesis clear?" you could ask "What do you think my thesis is?") Comment on its strengths and/or weaknesses regarding clarity, focus, appropriateness to the development of the rest of the paper, etc. Write at least 4–5 questions.
   B. Give your response guide questions to your responder to read. Take turns responding to the questions below.

   Questions for responders to consider:
   Do you understand what you are being asked to evaluate?
   Do you think you can provide the feedback requested?
   Do you have any suggestions for additions to the list?
   Could the writer give you more information that might help you to respond?
   C. Return guides to writer for revision.

III. Writing Final Response Guide (Out-of-Class)
   A. Revise your response guide based on your discussion and on any "second thoughts" you may have about feedback you would like.
   B. Type your questions, leaving space for your reader to write responses. Bring two copies of this guide to class: one for your reader, one to turn in to me.

## APPENDIX C
## EXCERPTS FROM SAMPLE ASSIGNMENTS

*Faculty interview*

You are in the process of preparing to make important contributions to your field through your teaching and research. You will need to publish your research and other contributions in the theoretical framework of your discipline. Since your faculty advisors are already quite successful at communicating their ideas in writing, we would like you to interview your faculty advisor.

Interview questions:

1. In your opinion, what is the function of writing and publication in your field? Why?
2. How did you learn to write texts that are of publishable quality?
3. What writing process do you use when you are writing an article to send out for publication? Do you write multiple drafts? If so, how many? From whom do you get feedback?
4. What types of texts have you published?
5. Do you have any advice for me regarding stylistic preferences or bugaboos in our field or the publications in our field?

(Developed by Christine Holten)

*Academic Writing Formats and Citations*

Locate an article from a professional journal in your academic field. Write responses to the questions below.

Title of article: _____

Author(s): _____

Title of journal, date: _____

Page numbers

1. What kind of article is it (e.g., research report, review of literature, analysis, argumentation?)
2. Does the article have an abstract at the beginning? If yes, approximately how many words?
3. What headings and subheadings are used in the article?
4. Are footnotes given on the bottom of the page or at the end of the article?
5. How are footnotes indicated within the text?
   _____ by number   _____ by author, date, page
                                    e.g., (Smith, 1989:20)
6. Is there a "Bibliography" or "References" section at the end of the article?
   _____ Bibliography   _____ References
7. Give an example of citation form for a footnote:
8. Give an example of citation form for a bibliographical or reference entry:
9. How are technical terms indicated? (Italics? quotes?)

*Annotated Bibliography*

Prepare each of the following:

1. A one-paragraph proposal setting forth a question to be researched, a plan for doing so, and a summary of appropriate background information.
2. A provisional title for the proposed research paper.
3. An annotated bibliography of 3 to 5 appropriate sources.

You will *not* be carrying through the actual research, but this preliminary work should help prepare you for future research. An annotated bibliography is an alphabetically arranged list of sources, each written in proper bibliographical form and followed by a brief summary and/or critique of the source.

*The Grammar of Abstracts*

The following abstracts, or parts of abstracts, are from some of the articles you turned in from professional journals in a variety of disciplines.

1. After reading each abstract, in the blanks provided, identify one of the following styles indicated in parentheses:
   a. (I/WE) The abstract uses first person "I" or "we" and other subjects plus active verbs; no passive verbs are used as main clause verbs.

b. (3RD) The abstract uses "the author" or "this paper" (study/ research, etc.) and other subjects plus active verbs; no passive verbs are used as main clause verbs.

c. (PASS) The abstract uses passive verbs as main clause verbs and avoids first person subjects ("I," "we") or reference to the paper itself: "this paper/study," etc.

d. (MIX) The abstract uses mixed structures: that is, some reference to the writer(s) or the paper itself is made ("I," "we," the author," "this study") *and* passive verbs are used as main clause verbs.

2. Which of the four "styles" above is the most common for this group of abstracts?

3. What considerations might affect your decision to use either first person or passive constructions in an abstract?

CHAPTER 15

# A Genre-Based Developmental Writing Course for Undergraduate ESL Science Majors*

**Sally Jacoby, David Leech, Christine Holten**
*University of California, Los Angeles*

Discourse analysis has enhanced our understanding of the structure, rhetoric, and language of written genres, the most researched of which is the experimental report. Studies of such texts have investigated the frequency and function of lexical and grammatical forms (e.g., Trimble & Trimble, 1982), as well as features of the macrostructure, including the discourse moves of each subsection (e.g., Dudley-Evans, 1986; Peng, 1987; Swales, 1990). Although some pedagogical materials have resulted (e.g., Dudley-Evans, 1985; Weissberg & Buker, 1990), undergraduate science majors still struggle to meet the demands of scientific writing. Their writing courses too often do not prepare them to tackle scientific writing because they are focused on acquainting them with basic academic rhetorical modes, generic academic essays, and a model of the composing process which may not be applicable to that of proficient scientific writers (Parkhurst, 1990). Language-based courses focus mainly on introducing ESL writers to the frequent vocabulary and syntactic structures found in scientific discourse (e.g., Master, 1986). These approaches do not familiarize beginning science students, who are simultaneously developing writers and second language learners, with the complex linguistic demands of the experimental report or the sophisticated combination of description and persuasion necessary in scientific argument.

---

*An earlier version of this chapter was presented at the 1991 Annual Meeting of the American Association for Applied Linguistics, New York City.

Drawing on genre analysis, we outline a course for undergraduate science majors which introduces the fundamentals of the experimental research report while simultaneously addressing the needs of developing ESL writers. The instructional sequence breaks this complex genre down into manageable, yet nonprescriptive rhetorical strategies and linguistic patterns for the four subsections of the research report — introduction, methods, results, and discussion — ordering the presentation of each new subsection according to its conceptual and communicative difficulty. The tasks designed to teach each subsection encourage students to discover the link between purpose, discourse patterns, and linguistic features by examining authentic samples. The writing assignments foster increasing independence as students learn to meet scientific discourse conventions while working through the process of planning, executing, revising multiple drafts, and providing criterion-based feedback to their peers. Model tasks to teach the conventions and language of each subsection will be presented.

## INTRODUCTION

The scientific research report, comprised of an abstract, introduction, methods and materials, results, and discussion sections, is certainly one of the mainstays of the natural and physical sciences, and is also an important text type in the social sciences. Students in these disciplines at all levels of tertiary education, and particularly undergraduate science majors, must acquaint themselves with all or parts of this genre during their academic training. Learning the writing conventions of this genre presents a particular challenge to the large number of undergraduate science majors whose first language is not English. The ESL Service Courses at UCLA have thus designed and implemented a specialized English for Science and Technology course to teach this text type to second language undergraduate science majors. The course began as a nonadjuncted course[1] with content drawn mainly from the social and natural sciences. An adjuncted version[2] of this

---

[1] A nonadjuncted course is a free-standing course akin to many composition and ESL courses that base the development of the content and assignments for the course on the language and writing needs of the students enrolled. The nonadjuncted course implemented at UCLA differs from most regular composition courses only in that its content and assignments are drawn from a given field.

[2] An adjuncted course is a composition or ESL course tied to a content course. At UCLA, students enrolled in the EST composition course were simultaneously enrolled in an undergraduate biology laboratory course, Biology 5L, and assignments and content for the ESL course were taken directly from the labs and lectures in the biology course.

EST writing course was later developed, with the ESL course content drawn from a beginning-level biology laboratory course for undergraduates.

Since the students enrolled in such a course are typically developmental writers (more than 50% of the students placing into this course at UCLA are long-term immigrants who are inexperienced writers both in their first and second languages), the course must not merely introduce them to the formal aspects of scientific writing, it must also address their needs as developing writers.[3] These needs, which must be addressed in the EST course simultaneously with teaching scientific writing conventions, include idea generation, strategies for revising beyond the sentence and word level, shaping texts and information to meet rhetorical and audience demands, and responding effectively to their own and others' writing.

The dual mandate of teaching general writing skills and the conventions of scientific writing provides an interesting challenge for curriculum developers in that they must tailor the instruction in the textual conventions of the scientific research report to the language and writing needs of developmental second language writers who are also novice scientists. This challenge leaves us with what many in the second language composition world might consider an uneasy partnership: an emphasis on *product* within a course designed to help students master the writing *process* (Hamp-Lyons, 1986; Horowitz, 1986; Liebman-Kleine, 1986; Reid, 1989).

## Considerations in Designing an EST Course for Undergraduates

In order to establish a successful teaching scope and sequence that would simultaneously acquaint students with the textual conventions of the research report and enhance their general writing skills, we brought to bear our knowledge of the linguistic, conceptual, and rhetorical challenges each section of the genre poses to L2 undergraduates. We then designed a syllabus and course materials to help students meet these challenges. We first considered what discourse studies reveal about the textual conventions of the various subsections of the research report.

*The Textual Conventions and Routine Lexical Phrases Found in Each Section.*    Luckily, the scientific research report is one of the most well-researched genres on both the discourse level and the lexicosyntactic level (Swales, 1990). This research reveals that each subsection of the research report has its own unique set of conventions and patterns. Swales

---

[3]The constraints under which we teach EST are very different from those special-purpose courses which teach scientific writing to practicing scientists who are already both skilled writers in their L1 and skilled scientists.

(1981) carried out extensive analysis of the discourse structure of the introduction subsection, Dudley-Evans (1986) has added to our understanding of the workings of discussion sections, and the rhetorical structures of the methods/materials and results sections have been a longstanding feature of many technical writing texts and studies of EST discourse (e.g., Master, 1986; Trimble & Trimble, 1982)

Our task as curriculum and materials designers was to make the research findings on the research report's text formats at the lexical, grammatical, sentence, paragraph, subsection, and whole-text levels accessible to and "usable" by these undergraduate writers. The importance to second language writers of learning about text formats both at the discourse and at the grammatical and lexical level cannot be underestimated. Purves and Purves (1986) point out that certain parts of the activity of writing need to become "chunked" (habitual or unconscious) so as to relieve the cognitive demands of composing. Carrell (1987) also distinguishes two types of schemata—content and textual schemata—and emphasizes the importance of the latter in reading comprehension. The rhetorical structures and lexicosyntactic routines common to certain text types or genres can quite easily (even tacitly) become automatic for experienced L1 writers with rich reading backgrounds. The inexperienced L2 writers enrolled in our courses, on the other hand, have had little prior exposure to the sorts of text types they must read and write in an undergraduate science program.

*The Cognitive and Rhetorical Challenges That Each Section Presents to Beginning Scientists/Writers.*    Because our students are undergraduates and inexperienced writers, we needed to consider the cognitive challenges as well as the writing challenges posed by each section. We were aided in our task by the research of Hayes and Flower (1987) on the cognitive aspects of the writing process, in particular their findings regarding the planning phase of the writing activity. Their research has found two types of knowledge that are key to planning any piece of writing. The first is *topic knowledge.* To write a successful introduction and hypothesis and to explain experimental results requires an understanding of the physical processes being studied and the variables being manipulated in the given experiment. A relatively simple biology experiment designed to provide beginning biology students with the opportunity to study leaf transpiration, for instance, assumes knowledge of the complex processes of transpiration and photosynthesis, both of which take up pages of explanation in introductory botany textbooks. While mastery of this knowledge and its incorporation into the scientific report may seem relatively straightforward, it is not to beginning scientists and novice writers.

The second type of requisite knowledge which Hayes and Flower discuss is that of *writing strategies.* An essential writing strategy mastered by all skilled writers is the ability to direct one's own writing and revising processes. Conventional wisdom would have it that the writing process of working scientists, because this type of writing is so highly stylized, is a linear one; a task of simply recording what they did and observed in the laboratory. Had we built our EST course on this conventional wisdom, we would have omitted needed attention to the development of the students' writing process. Indeed, a recent study by Rymer (1988) of the composing processes of highly published natural scientists strongly suggests that the linear model of scientific composing is a misconception, for she finds instead that the scientists studied exhibited a full range of composing behaviors, from linear composing to detailed planning to recursive and detailed revision.[4] For the scientists in Rymer's study, writing was not simply a means of reporting their findings and experimental method, but a means of discovering "new ideas about their experimental results and what the science means" (p. 244).

While the composing behaviors of undergraduate science majors cannot be equated with those of accomplished writers of scientific research, the composing behaviors reported on by Rymer expand our understanding of the ways in which a process approach to writing complements the teaching of scientific report conventions. We therefore used these findings, combined with our own experience and knowledge of the needs of developing L2 writers, to elaborate course materials that would help students direct their own writing and revising processes. Like most developing writers, our students begin the course with little awareness of their own writing processes. The course thus incorporates the development of strategies used by skilled writers. These strategies include prewriting, planning, and organizing before putting pen to paper; information review and synthesis; and content and rhetorical analysis of professional and peer text models. Students also learn the criteria by which to judge the success of their own drafts and those of their peers by using criteria checklists for each subsection, criterion-referenced and reader-based peer response guides, and self-evaluation forms. Finally, emphasis is put on revising for meaning beyond the sentence and vocabulary level through resequencing and reorganization activities and teacher-guided revision of sample drafts.

Another important consideration for skilled writers is how to shape information both to suit the needs of an audience and to accomplish their own rhetorical purposes. This ability is as crucial to writing research reports as it is to other forms of academic writing because the experimental paper is a highly "rhetorical enterprise," serving "both as the vehicle for giving

---

[4]Using questionnaires, Rymer (1988) asked nine practicing scientists to report on their composing practices. In addition, she used protocol analysis to study the composing processes of one experienced scientist.

meaning to [experimental] observations and for persuading the scientific community that those observations are truths" (Rymer, 1988, p. 212). Shaping scientific discourse to meet the expectations of readers and to persuade them is undoubtedly the most cognitively and rhetorically difficult part of research report writing for both novice and expert writers. The various subsections of the research report taken together demand that the writer/researcher interpret raw data and observations, synthesize previous research findings and methodologies, evaluate research findings in order to distinguish those that are significant from those that are nonsignificant, and contrast present research findings and methodologies with those of previous related studies. In short, the writer/researcher undertakes all this to persuade the larger scientific community of the significance of his/her new research.

## CURRICULAR SCOPE AND SEQUENCE

In developing the curriculum for this EST composition course, we carefully considered the cognitive and rhetorical demands that each subsection of the research report would place on our students. Resulting from this analysis we developed a scope and sequence of instructional units and writing assignments through which the subsections are not taught in their actual published order. Instead, the course sequence moves from the methods and materials section, the least demanding subsection, to the introduction and the discussion subsections, the most demanding writing tasks. The instructional sequence is as follows:

Introductory Unit—Summary and Abstract[5]
Writing Assignment 1—Methods and Materials
Writing Assignment 2—Results
Writing Assignment 3—Introduction
Writing Assignment 4—Discussion
Final Writing Assignment—Summary and Abstract

The soundness of this instructional sequence is corroborated by research findings outlining a sequence that some working scientists follow when preparing articles for publication. The sequence of writing tasks adopted by

---

[5]The sequencing of the summary and abstract instructional unit varies in the adjuncted and nonadjuncted version of the course. It is the first instructional unit in the nonadjuncted version of the course so that students can become acquainted with the entire scientific research report and its subsections as they analyze and summarize model abstracts. In the adjuncted version, on the other hand, the instructional unit on abstracts is taught last, mirroring the actual composing sequence of working scientists (Rymer, 1988).

the expert scientist in Rymer's (1988) protocol study, for instance, consisted of sketching out figures of lab results, writing the materials/methods and results sections, writing the introduction and title followed by the discussion section, and ending with the abstract. Further, this scientist considered the introduction, discussion, and abstract so crucial to the article that he alone—not members of his research team—undertook to compose them.

Once the overall scope and sequence of the EST course was determined, we developed various activities that would teach not only the discourse and linguistic conventions of each subsection within a process-based curriculum, but also some of the variations possible in each case.

## PEDAGOGICAL APPLICATION:
## THE DISCUSSION SECTION

In the following section, we focus primarily on the instructional unit designed to teach the discourse structure and lexical and grammatical features of the discussion section because it is the most demanding and nuanced of the five sections. Research on discussion sections has revealed that this part of the research paper is highly complex in purpose and organization, in what must be accomplished through its content, and in the many subtle and conventional linguistic formulations used to carry it off (e.g., Dudley-Evans, 1986; Peng, 1987; Hopkins & Dudley-Evans, 1988; Weissberg & Buker, 1990). As Figure 15.1 shows, a writer faced with the communicative task of "discussing results" is actually faced with a number of interlocking subtasks: Composing this culminating section of a research

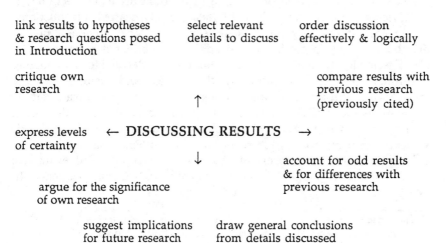

link results to hypotheses & research questions posed in Introduction

select relevant details to discuss

order discussion effectively & logically

critique own research

compare results with previous research (previously cited)

↑

express levels    ← DISCUSSING RESULTS    →
of certainty

↓

account for odd results & for differences with previous research

argue for the significance of own research

suggest implications for future research

draw general conclusions from details discussed

**Figure 15.1.**   The complexity of a discussion section

report thus demands an effective blending of selection, ordering, citation, summary, paraphrase, description, reporting, evaluation, critique, argument, and persuasion.

The pedagogical problem facing us when we began to develop this unit was how to induct novice second language writers, who are also novice scientists, into the textual, intertextual, rhetorical, and communicative complexity of the discussion section. The following instructional sequence and sample materials were designed to do just that.

## Overview of the Discussion Unit

The discussion section of the research report is introduced in the course as the second phase of a larger assignment linking the introduction and discussion sections. By the time students begin this unit, they have already produced the first draft of an introduction section. The entire introduction/ discussion assignment is based on materials excerpted and prepared from a study with which the students are not familiar in detail[6] or have not previously read. As part of the introduction unit, students are presented with brief summaries of some of the previous studies that informed the current study, are asked to deduce a possible next research direction and hypotheses, and then compose first drafts of an appropriate introduction section.

Following teacher and peer feedback on these first drafts of the introduction, the students are then presented with a schematic display of the current study's results, usually in the form of a table or graph. Subsequent activities and materials prepare them to write up the discussion section that will discuss these results in light of their already drafted introductions. Figure 15.2 shows how the 16-step sequence of the discussion unit is distributed among product-oriented and process-oriented component cycles: Essentially, this unit (as are the other units) is devoted to familiarizing the students with the conventions (both rhetorical and linguistic) and the criteria which inform discussion sections so that they can in turn use these conventions and criteria both as they analyze and evaluate actual discussion sections, and as they compose and revise their own writing. To this end, students are exposed to different kinds of authentic samples and to differentially displayed forms of the genre conventions and evaluative criteria at various points throughout the entire instructional sequence. In

---

[6]The nonadjuncted version of the course draws information and materials for the students to use in drafting introduction and discussion sections from published studies, while the adjuncted version draws information and materials from the experiments that students are actually conducting in their biology laboratory class.

| Genre Conventions | Models for Analysis | Assignment Preparation | Planning | Drafting | Feedback |
|---|---|---|---|---|---|
| 1) Discussion about Discussions | 2) two authentic published discussions | 3) review of data, introduction draft, and reference list | 4) possible discussion outlines | 5) first draft of discussion | 6) evaluate two peer drafts with criteria check-list; receive feedback from two peers and teacher |
|  | 7) two graded student-produced discussions from Bio. Department |  |  |  | 8) general first draft feedback to class from teacher |
|  |  |  | 9) first draft stock-taking | 10) second draft: combining both first drafts with reference list | 11) evaluate two peer drafts with open-ended form and conference; receive feedback from two peers and teacher |
| 12) final draft rating criteria |  |  | 13) second draft stock-taking | 14) third (final) draft | 15) self-evaluation |
|  |  |  |  |  | 16) teacher rating and feedback |

**Figure 15.2.**   Sequence of discussion unit

addition, students reflect on their progress and revise their writing at different stages of the sequence.

## Conventions and Criteria

Several documents which distill the conventions and evaluative criteria of the discussion section are distributed throughout the unit sequence to accompany various analysis, planning, composing, and feedback activities which the students engage in. The first of these documents, "Discussion about Discussions" (see Appendix A for excerpt), introduces the unit and becomes the students' basic reference for analyzing the organization and language of authentic published discussion sections and for composing their own first drafts. The "Discussion about Discussions" document incorporates a simpler version of the 11 discussion section moves (many cyclical) found in the research of Dudley-Evans and his students (e.g., Dudley-Evans, 1986; Hopkins & Dudley-Evans, 1988; Peng, 1987). While the list of seven moves in our version suggests a possible linear order, students are free to order their own discussion sections as simply or as complexly as suits their communicative goals.

After producing their first drafts, students receive feedback from the teacher and two classmates via the "Check-List for First Draft Feedback" (see Appendix B for excerpt). Most of the feedback on this form is elicited through yes/no questions drawn, for the most part, from the criteria outlined in the "Discussion about Discussions" document. The answers to these criterion-referenced questions, combined with open-ended suggestions, concretize for the students just which mechanical, linguistic, organizational, and content matters ought to be attended to in producing a competent discussion section.

As students are exposed to more and more samples, and as they receive and give feedback based on genre-specific conventions and criteria, they become better equipped to compose relevant and open-ended feedback for their peers. Thus, second drafts (including a revision of the first draft of the introduction) are evaluated by two class members and the teacher via a more open-ended feedback form, the "Second Draft Feedback" (see Appendix C). These completed forms are returned in a face-to-face conference attended by each trio of writers/peer evaluators and by the teacher.

The fourth document which reinforces the genre conventions expected even in student-composed discussion sections is the "Final Draft Rating Scale" (see Appendix D for excerpt), made up of three separate 6-point rating scales (Content, Control of Organization, Linguistic Control). This assignment-specific, criterion-referenced scale is distributed to the students before they revise their final drafts so that they are familiar with the scale to be used in grading their assignment.

## Authentic Samples

The documents which detail the various genre conventions and criteria for discussion sections are used in conjunction with the rhetorical and linguistic analysis of eight different authentic samples of discussion sections: (a) two published samples written by research scientists; (b) two authentic final drafts, written by undergraduate, lower division biology students who are L1 writers and accompanied by the marginal responses and grade assigned them by biology faculty; and (c) two first drafts and two second drafts, all written by L2 classmates in response to the class assignment. Students are thus exposed to different levels of expertise, to a variety of discussion section formats, and to the comments of actual faculty members teaching in the natural sciences, as well as to the feedback of their classmates and teacher.

Moreover, having two discussion section samples for each level of expertise allows the students to note variation and creativity in organizational plans, linguistic choices, and overall quality, and to further apply, and hopefully internalize, the common criteria relevant to the evaluation of discussions written by student writers and professionals alike. The published samples are thus selected to reflect typicality as well as deviation from "models," although the student-composed samples are selected to reflect drafts which successfully adopt the genre conventions and those which are less successful because they either omit, confuse, or only partially satisfy the requisite discourse expectations of the genre.

## Self-Reflection and Unit Assessment

Many of the classroom activities involving analysis of text samples, composition planning, and feedback are interactionally organized, but the unit sequence also provides for self-reflection so that individual students can assess their own sense of progress and mastery. Just before beginning the second draft revision, for instance, students respond to a "Taking Stock Exercise" (see Appendix E) which refocuses the student's attention not only on assessing his or her own draft in light of the samples examined and the feedback given, but also on setting concrete goals for revision. A similar form is distributed prior to revising the final draft.

The last self-evaluation form is handed in with the third (and final) draft of the assignment. This "Final Revision Self-Evaluation" (see Appendix F for excerpt) helps students reflect on what they have learned, what they feel they have not yet mastered, and how the unit may have helped or hindered their learning process. These self-assessment instruments provide valuable information to both student and teacher. They allow the student to consciously reflect on his or her writing process and progress as a writer of scientific discourse. In turn, through these self-assessment activities, the teacher is able to monitor the effect of the various forms of consciousness-raising throughout the course and is provided with ongoing course assessment, especially as each unit draws to a close.

## TEACHING LEXICAL PHRASES FOR WRITING DISCUSSION SECTIONS

Because it is aimed at second language writers, our course also intentionally focuses on the linguistic tools students need to write discussion sections. Embedded in every phase of each instructional unit is attention to "bottom up" grammatical and lexical issues. By way of example, we will focus on some of the teaching materials and activities developed for one particular linguistic aspect of the discussion section: the way conclusions are asserted — strongly or weakly, deductively or hypothetically — within any of the various moves of this subsection (Dudley-Evans, 1986). After all, conclusions are what discussion sections are fundamentally all about.

To express their conclusions, expert writers of scientific discourse make certain lexical choices, which, as in spoken discourse, range from idioms and cliches to highly flexible clause frames (Nattinger, 1988; Nattinger & DeCarrico, 1989). These choices in lexicon and phrasing reflect a writer's certainty regarding the research findings themselves and serve to guide readers' interpretations of the conclusions drawn from the findings. These phrases are a helpful means for dealing with the textual, intertextual, and rhetorical complexities of any discussion section (see, for example, the discussions of the intersection of grammar, lexis, and rhetoric in Hanania & Akhtar, 1985; Myers, 1985, 1989, 1991; Thompson & Ye, 1991). The following conclusion, taken from an actual published discussion section, illustrates several of the lexical choices a writer might make to put forward the significance of a given experimental result:

> These data suggest that, at least during development, the presence of estrogen receptor alone is insufficient for the induction of either vitellogenin synthesis or the receptor itself. (Reigel, Aitken, Martin, & Schoenberg, 1987, p. 1289)

In this sentence, the authors/researchers argue that "the presence of estrogen receptor alone is insufficient . . . itself," but they embed this conclusion in a tentative introductory clause aimed at making their claim more acceptable to their readers. They express this tentativeness in several ways. First, they choose to build their sentence around the verb *suggest*. The choice of this verb sets up an epistemic frame of less than full certainty within which to understand their claim. Secondly, the writers modify their claim with the adverbial phrase *at least during development* to indicate that the claim should be viewed as valid within given parameters. However, the words *at least* in the phrase lend slightly more certainty and potentially wider applicability to their conclusion. Moreover, the subject of the introductory clause, *these data*, focuses the readers' attention on the observable data rather than on the inferential process of the researchers themselves. It is from such lexical choices that a writer can build grammatically, logically, and discursively effective expressions of thought.

## Writing Decision: Choosing Lexical Phrases

One of our pedagogical aims in focusing on the lexical and grammatical phrasing of scientific discourse is to demonstrate that the language used by scientists to report their work is consciously designed to serve rhetorical and persuasive purposes. A second instructional aim is to expand the students' lexical repertoire of words and phrases useful in reporting research and making claims from research findings. However, our approach is not simply to have students memorize phrase or word lists and stick them into their writing as needed. Instead, the pedagogical activities are designed to help second language students understand and express their own nuanced meaning in language which is grammatically correct, lexically sophisticated, and typical of academic style and register.

Figure 15.3 is intended to represent a postulated thought/choice process which a writer engages in, either during the original drafting of the article or subsequent to editorial feedback, and shows the complex interrelationship between rhetorical/persuasive function and linguistic form:

## DISCUSSION SECTION

DISCOURSE MOVE:  COMPARING RESULTS TO
PREVIOUS FINDINGS

Deductive Conclusion:  "My results contradict Dazzo and
Hubbell's (1975) finding."

Phrasing Decisions:

Stance:     uncertainty (e.g., may suggest)
Topic:      my results   ( = X )
Comment:    rejection of previous
            findings (new look at
            old information)  ( = Y )

Possible lexical phrases, e.g.,

| TOPIC | COMMENT |
|-------|---------|
| X | suggests that Y |
|   | Y = Z should be considered |

possible sentence format:

*The presence of R. Trifoli in the streptomycin-treated medium may suggest that Dazzo and Hubbell's (1975) rejection of R.t. as a candidate for co-specific symbiosis with soybeans should be reconsidered.*

**Figure 15.3.**    Choosing lexical phrases

Following Figure 15.3, we might posit that a writer has reached a point in the discussion section in which she wants to compare her experimental results with the previous research findings of Dazzo and Hubbell (1975) and argue that her results contradict Dazzo and Hubbell's finding. To achieve this, she needs to translate her meaning into at least one appropriate, accurate, and clear sentence. Depending on how sure the writer is that her experimental results support her claim and how cautiously she wishes to package her claim for readers, she must consider how strongly or weakly to phrase her conclusion. In this particular case, the writer has selected the lexical items *suggest* and *may*, thereby setting up a stance of uncertainty and softening of her assertion.

Another decision concerns the topic of the sentence. Observing the text convention of discussion sections which focuses on present research results, the writer has topicalized her results, making the research findings the subject of her sentence while the argument that Dazzo and Hubbell's previous research claim "should be reconsidered" is relegated to the predicate slot (comment) of the sentence.

A third decision concerns how to express the contradiction and rejection of Dazzo and Hubbell's findings. The writer has chosen the verb *reconsider*, modifying it with the modal *should*, both of which soften her rejection of Dazzo and Hubbell's finding. Finally, by putting the entire verb phrase, *should be reconsidered*, in the passive voice, the writer has shifted the burden of criticism off herself onto the unstated agent, that is, the scientific community at large, to reconsider Dazzo and Hubbell's previous research findings.

## Classroom Activities

The activities outlined below are some of the tasks which have been designed to help students make intelligent and rhetorically informed choices about their use of lexicon and grammar in scientific writing. Activities which can increase student awareness of lexical phrases include: (a) analysis of sample texts produced by professionals and students, (b) peer editing focused on lexical and syntactic choices, and (c) practice sentence production and editing using phrases suggested by the teacher. Examples of (a) and (c) are given below. (See Appendices B and C for examples of peer editing tasks which include a focus on lexical and syntactic choices.)

## Text Analysis of Lexical Phrases

In the sample text analysis activity below, the students are first asked to rhetorically analyze a sentence found in a published discussion section by answering a series of questions:

TEXT: These data suggest that, at least during development, the presence of estrogen receptor alone is insufficient for the induction of either vitellogenin synthesis or the receptor itself. (Reigel, Aitken, Martin, & Schoenberg, 1987, p. 1289)

Self-Learning Questions for Class Discussion

1. What message is conveyed by the writer's choice of the words "these data suggest"?
2. What stronger phrase could the writer have used?
3. What are some words/phrases that mean the same thing as "suggest"? [HINT: You should be able to find some in the sample discussion sections we have studied!]
4. Try substituting these other words/phrases in the sentence. Which ones require you to change the sentence structure?
5. Does the voice or attitude of the original sentence change when you substitute these alternate words/phrases? If so, how?
6. When and why might these phrases be used in your own writing?

## Sentence Production and Editing

Following such an activity, students are given samples of student writing which state conclusions, but which state them poorly. Working in pairs, students rewrite the student samples, critically applying their emerging knowledge of words and phrases commonly chosen to express conclusions in scientific writing and making the grammatical and syntactic changes these choices entail:

Editing Tentative Conclusions

There are many words or phrases used to express tentative conclusions in scientific writing. Writers phrase a conclusion tentatively when they are fairly sure that it is accurate and can be supported by data, but wish to express their claim to readers in a somewhat guarded fashion.

With another student, work on rewriting the conclusion sentences found in the student writing samples so that they more cautiously and tentatively express the writer's comparison of his/her research findings with previous research. Try using the words and phrases we have been discussing and those in the list provided below.[7] Be prepared to present your work to the class. Please also tell us your ideas about how writers might use these words or phrases when stating conclusions.

---

[7]A list of lexical phrases may be provided which gives further useful language for the writers. An exercise involving a much larger text with several different discourse moves could also provide for interesting class discussions of the relative merits of different lexical phrases in context.

*1. X appear* that/to . . .

**Example:** It *would appear* that Rx is R. melitoti, which is co-specific with alfalfa.

Alternatives:
    appears to be similar to
    appears to be related to
    appears to be involved in
    appeared due to
    apparently depends on
    the apparent cause of X may be

*2. X suggest* that . . .

**Example:** The results *suggest* that symbiotic bacteria are important to some plants.

Alternatives:
    they suggest the possibility that
    we therefore suggest that
    there is nothing in our data to suggest that

USE: When tentatively sure the conclusion is accurate and can be supported by the data, but still guarded. Usually used to refer to present work.

From the student's point of view, learning to manipulate the conventional and nuanced language of scientific argument provides a means of entry into the writerly aspects of discussion sections. When students are made aware of the usefulness of particular lexical and grammatical choices, they enthusiastically learn to incorporate them into their drafts. In fact, one study has shown that L2 students already attend to these lexical routines, collecting them on their own as they read (Shaw, 1991). Intentional instruction, however, allows the language teacher to move students beyond their word lists to an understanding of the appropriate, strategic uses to which these phrases can be put to produce clear, coherent, and persuasive scientific texts.

## CONCLUSION

Drawing on genre analysis, our course introduces the fundamentals of the research report while simultaneously addressing the needs of developing second language writers. The instructional sequence breaks this complex genre down into manageable, yet nonprescriptive rhetorical strategies and lexicosyntactic patterns for the four subsections of the research report, ordering the presentation of each subsection according to its conceptual and communicative difficulty. The tasks are designed to encourage students to discover the link between argument, discourse patterns, and linguistic features by having students examine authentic samples, produce their own texts, and edit one another's drafts. Our course as a whole is designed to present the scientific research report in all its rhetorical, textual, linguistic, and cognitive complexity to second language undergraduates who are both novice scientists and novice writers. Rather than ignore or reduce this complexity, our approach has been to find systematic ways of engaging students in discovering the richness of scientific argument so that they can successfully produce their own first attempts at experimental report writing.

## REFERENCES

Carrell, P. L. (1987). Content and formal schemata in ESL reading. *TESOL Quarterly, 21*, 461–482.

Dazzo, F. B., & Hubbell, D. H. (1975). Antigenic differences between infective and noninfective strains of Rhizobium trifolii. *Applied Microbiology, 30* (2), 172–177.

Dudley-Evans, T. (1985). *Writing laboratory reports*. Melbourne: Nelson Wadsworth.

Dudley-Evans, T. (1986). Genre analysis: An investigation of the introduction and discussion sections of MSc dissertations. In M. Coulthard (Ed.), *Talking about text* (pp. 128–145). Birmingham, UK: English Language Research.

Hamp-Lyons, L. (1986). No new lamps for old yet, please. *TESOL Quarterly, 20*, 790–796.

Hanania, E. A. S., & Akhtar, K. (1985). Verb form and rhetorical function in science writing: A study of MS theses in biology, chemistry, and physics. *ESP Journal, 4*, 49–58.

Hayes, J. R., & Flower, L. S. (1987). On the structure of the writing process. *Topics in Language Disorders, 7*, 19–30.

Hopkins, A., & Dudley-Evans, T. (1988). A genre-based investigation of the discussion sections in articles and dissertations. *ESP Journal, 7*, 113–121.

Horowitz, D. J. (1986). Process not product: Less than meets the eye. *TESOL Quarterly, 20*, 141–144.

Liebman-Kleine, J. (1986). In defense of teaching process in ESL composition. *TESOL Quarterly, 20*, 783–788.

Master, P. A. (1986). *Science, medicine, and technology: English grammar and technical writing*. Englewood Cliffs, NJ: Prentice-Hall Regents.

Myers, G. (1985). The social construction of two biologists' proposals. *Written Communication, 2*, 219–245.

Myers, G. (1989). The pragmatics of politeness in scientific articles. *Applied Linguistics, 10*, 1–35.

Myers, G. (1991). Lexical cohesion and specialized knowledge in science and popular science texts. *Discourse Processes, 14*, 1–26.

Nattinger, J. (1988). Some current trends in vocabulary teaching. In R. Carter & M. McCarthy (Eds.), *Vocabulary and language teaching* (pp. 62–82). London: Longman.

Nattinger, J., & DeCarrico, J. (1989). Lexical phrases, speech acts and teaching conversation. In P. Nation & R. Carter (Eds.), *AILA Review: Vocabulary acquisition* (pp. 118–139). Amsterdam: Free University Press.

Peng, J-F. (1987). Organisational features in chemical engineering research articles. *English Language Research Journal, 1*, 79–116.

Purves, A. C., & Purves, W. C. (1986). Viewpoints: Cultures, text models, and the activity of writing. *Research in the Teaching of English, 20*, 174–197.

Reid, J. (1989). English as second language composition in higher education: The expectations of the academic audience. In D. M. Johnson & D. H. Roen (Eds.), *Richness in writing: Empowering ESL students* (pp. 220–234). New York: Longman.

Reigel, A. T., Aitken, S. C., Martin, M. B., & Schoenberg, D. R. (1987). Differential induction of hepatic estrogen receptor and vitellogenin gene transcription in *Xenopus laevis*. *Endocrinology 120* (4), 1283–1290.

Rymer, J. (1988). Scientific composing processes: How eminent scientists write journal articles. In D. A. Jolliffe (Ed.), *Writing in academic disciplines* (pp. 211–250). Norwood, NJ: Ablex.

Shaw, P. (1991). Science research students' composing processes. *ESP, 10*, 189–206.

Swales, J. (1981). *Aspects of article introductions*. Birmingham, UK: The University of Aston, Language Studies Unit.

Swales, J. (1990). *Genre analysis*. Cambridge, UK: Cambridge University Press.

Thompson, G., & Ye, Y. (1991). Evaluation in the reporting verbs used in academic papers. *Applied Linguistics, 12,* 365–382.

Trimble, M. T., & Trimble, L. (1982). Rhetorical-grammatical features of scientific and technical texts as a major factor in written ESP communication. In J. Hoedt, L. Lundquist, H. Picht, & J. Qvistgaard (Eds.), *Pragmatics and LSP, Proceedings of the third European Symposium on LSP* (pp. 199–216). Copenhagen: LSP Centre of the Copenhagen School of Economics.

Weissberg, R., & Buker, S. (1990). *Writing up research: Experimental research report writing for students of English*. Englewood Cliffs, NJ: Prentice-Hall.

# APPENDIX A[8]
## DISCUSSION ABOUT DISCUSSIONS (EXCERPT)

**Purpose**: Discussion sections are the *thinking* part of the research paper because in this section the researcher must explain her/his results and interpret their meaning as an advancement of knowledge.

The *organization* of the Discussion section is looser than that of the Introduction section, but it generally includes most or all of the following important moves:

1. A brief *recapitulation* of the purpose and main results of the present research.
2. Indication as to whether *hypotheses were confirmed or not confirmed.*
3. *Detailed discussion of particular results* and what they prove or suggest about the phenomenon being studied, with *comparisons*

---

[8]Appendices A–F and all sample exercises appearing in this chapter are taken from materials which have been under development since Fall 1990 for use in the ESL Service Courses at the University of California, Los Angeles. They are reproduced here with the permission of the UCLA ESL Service Courses.

*and contrasts* to results and explanations found in previous research studies.

4. A plausible account or *explanation of anomalous*, unexpected or missing results.
5. Discussion of the *possible flaws in the methodology* of the present research and how they might have influenced the results.
6. Summary of the most important *conclusions* to be drawn from the results, ordered by level of certainty.
7. Suggestions of what *implications* the conclusions have for future research, other research questions, related areas of inquiry, and real-world problems (if relevant).

# APPENDIX B
## CHECKLIST FOR FIRST DRAFT FEEDBACK (EXCERPT)

Reader's Name_____    Writer's Name _____

**Format**

1. Is the draft typed?
2. Is the length OK?
3. Is there a subtitle which says Discussion?

**suggestions:**

**In-Text Citations**

1. Are in-text citations used?
2. Do citations correctly & consistently follow the citation format?
3. Are all previous studies cited which could be used in the Discussion?

**suggestions:**

**Organization**

1. Are all move transitions clearly marked?
2. Is there an opening summary section?
3. Does the Discussion move logically from the results & conclusions of this study to implications for larger questions?

**suggestions:**

**Content**

1. Is it clear which hypotheses were confirmed and which not?
2. Is there a discussion of why results did not support any non-confirmed hypotheses?
3. Are anomalous/unexpected results discussed and explained?
4. Is it clear which conclusions the writer is more/less confident about?
5. Are results/explanations compared/contrasted with previous research?

**suggestions:**

**Strengths**
What do you think the writer did especially well in this draft?

**Language**
Mention 4 language problems or problematic sentences (and their precise location in the draft). For each case, *specify what bothers you and suggest how the writer might solve the problem.*

## APPENDIX C
## SECOND DRAFT FEEDBACK

Reader _____    Writer _____

**Format**
Format:
Title:
Cover Page:

**References**
Reference List:
In-Text Citations:

**Introduction**
Content:
Organization:
Language & Mechanics:

**Discussion**
Content:
Organization:
Language & Mechanics:
What is the most successful aspect of the Introduction?

**Successful Aspects**
What is the most successful aspect of the Introduction?
What is the most successful aspect of the Discussion?

**Priority Revision**
What is most in need of revision in the Introduction?
What is most in need of revision in the Discussion?

## APPENDIX D
## FINAL DRAFT RATING SCALE (EXCERPT)

[Each subscore ranges from 6 (highest) to 1 (lowest)]

### Content: Discussion

6 — Your discussion is informative and complete containing a summary of the purpose and main results of the present research, confirmation/disconfirmation of the hypothesis, discussion of the results, conclusions that can be drawn, explanation of surprising results, flaws in the methodology, and the implications for further research. There are no unnecessary, inaccurate, or unclear statements and the reader is never confused about the relationship of results to conclusions drawn.

4 — Your discussion is somewhat incomplete with occasional missing, inaccurate, unnecessary and/or unclear statements in the summary of the purpose and main results of the present research, confirmation/disconfirmation of the hypothesis, discussion of the results, conclusions that can be drawn, explanation of surprising results, flaws in the methodology, and the implications for further research. The reader is occasionally confused about the meaning of the individual components (moves) and/or the relationship of results to conclusions drawn.

### Control of Organization: Discussion

6 — a. The components (moves) in your Discussion section are logically organized and well-balanced.
b. There are clear transitions between all components (moves) of your Discussion section.
c. Each component (move) in your Discussion section is internally well-organized.
4 — a. The components (moves) of your Discussion section are logically organized but quite unbalanced.

b. Several of the components (moves) in your Discussion section are not clearly or smoothly connected.

c. More than one component (move) in your Discussion section requires internal organization.

## Linguistic Control: Discussion

6 – a. Your Discussion section exhibits excellent control of language. Grammatical structures are well-chosen for the summary task. Most verbs are in the appropriate tense.

b. You use academic vocabulary well and consistently to express your ideas in your Discussion section.

c. You successfully balance both simple and complex sentence patterns with coordination and subordination in your Discussion section, achieving a concise style.

d. You use transitions/logical connectors successfully in your Discussion section to achieve coherence and sentence flow.

e. You report objectively and use your own words (except for general scientific terminology) in your Discussion section.

f. Sources are cited correctly in your Discussion section and there are very few mechanical and typing errors.

4 – a. Your Discussion section exhibits good control of language. Grammatical structures are usually well-chosen to convey your ideas, although readers occasionally notice various language and verb tense errors.

b. You usually use academic vocabulary well and consistently in your Discussion section, but the reader notices occasional incorrect or imprecise word choices and/or nonacademic style.

c. While your sentences are usually well constructed in your Discussion section, you occasionally use too many simple sentences or incorrectly construct complex sentences. In several places, your style is wordy or repetitious.

d. You usually use transitions/logical connectors successfully to achieve coherence and sentence flow in your Discussion section, but some may be missing or occasionally incorrect.

e. You usually report objectively and use your own words (except for scientific terminology) in your Discussion section, but you occasionally copy the language of the original article too closely.

f. You are not consistent in the way you cite sources in your Discussion section, and there are several mechanical and typing errors.

## APPENDIX E
## TAKING STOCK EXERCISE (FIRST DRAFT)

Now that you are more familiar with what actual Discussion sections look like (including less successful ones) and have evaluated two classmates' first drafts, how do you feel about your own first draft?

What are some of your plans for revision?

## APPENDIX F
## FINAL REVISION SELF-EVALUATION:
## INTRODUCTIONS & DISCUSSIONS (EXCERPT)

## Discussions

1. What did you learn about writing a Discussion for a research paper that was new to you?
2. What was easy for you in writing your Discussion?
3. What was difficult?
4. What do you feel you have pretty well mastered about writing a Discussion?
5. What do you feel you have not yet mastered?
6. Was there anything confusing or frustrating about the unit on Discussions? If so, what?
7. What do you feel you have learned that will be useful in university courses other than English courses?
8. What suggestions do you have for improving the unit on Discussions?

CHAPTER 16

# Fostering Writing Expertise in ESL Composition Instruction: Modeling and Evaluation*

**Alister Cumming**
*Ontario Institute for Studies in Education*

This chapter argues that instruction for adult second language learners needs to account more fully for writing expertise as a specialized human capacity in academic settings. The chapter first presents two vignettes, derived from previous research on second language writers, that contrast — in Bereiter and Scardamalia's (1987) terms — *knowledge-telling* and *knowledge-transforming* approaches to composing. The chapter then explains why, and suggests how, second language teachers can prompt *knowledge-transforming* strategies in their classroom functions of *modeling* and *evaluating* students' writing. The final portion of the chapter describes preliminary findings from case studies that have started to implement and assess a specific approach, based on five thinking prompts, to model writing expertise among adult ESL students in classroom, tutoring, and computer environments. Far from being a simple innovation, this research shows the adoption of expertise-based writing instruction to vary considerably with such factors as teachers' beliefs and instructional focuses, stu-

*An earlier version of the first portion of this paper was presented as a plenary address at the Three Rivers TESOL Association's First Annual Conference, Indiana University of Pennsylvania, November 10, 1990. I thank Jim Cummins, Margaret Early, Bernie Mohan, and Dan Tannacito for urging me to consolidate some of these ideas. I am especially grateful to graduate students working on the current research for data collection and analyses as well as useful discussions of the theoretical and pedagogical ideas presented in the latter part of this chapter: Susanna Lo, Donna Patrick, Abdolmehdi Riazi, Hiroko Saito, Ling Shi, Kiyomi Shimabukuro, and Christina Xu. Acknowledgements are due also to the teachers and students participating in this research. Funding for the current research has been provided by The Social Sciences and Humanities Research Council of Canada through grant 410–91–0722.

dents' backgrounds and experiences writing, the aspects of writing processes attended to, and the type of instructional environment.

This chapter argues that ESL writing instruction needs to account more fully for writing expertise as a unique human capacity, particularly for adult students preparing for or pursuing academic studies. A substantial amount of recent research indicates that writing skills form a specific kind of expertise that transfers across first and second languages, is relatively distinct from proficiency in a second language, entails certain kinds of schematic and procedural knowledge, and has particular potential for learning a second language. The significance of these fundamental aspects of second language composing may be ignored by conventional approaches to language instruction based on conversational or comprehension processes or by conventional approaches to composition instruction based only on mother tongue norms. Most importantly, ESL teachers in academic settings need to know how to use instructional strategies that will foster expertise in second language composing and how to vary their instructional functions appropriately for learners who may have greater or lesser expertise in writing. However, while research on student writing performance has advanced considerably in recent years, studies are only now beginning to address the many pedagogical complexities of developing explicit instructional approaches that will foster ESL writing expertise.

The chapter first presents two vignettes portraying experiences characteristic of adult ESL learners while they compose, as constructed from the findings of research studies tracing the writing processes of Francophone learners of English (Cumming, 1989, 1990a), Anglophone learners of French (Cumming, Rebuffot, & Ledwell, 1989), Punjabi learners of English (Cumming & Gill, 1991), and Anglophone learners of Japanese (Uzawa & Cumming, 1989). The vignettes contrast two distinct approaches to composing—knowledge telling and knowledge transforming (as defined by Bereiter & Scardamalia, 1987)—which mark differences in the thinking strategies used by adult second language learners who are able, to greater or lesser extents, to write effectively in academic tasks. The chapter then suggests how these two approaches to composing relate to second language proficiency, knowledge in academic domains, and potential for second language learning.

The major portion of the chapter describes how ESL writing instructors can direct their teaching toward fostering knowledge transforming—rather than knowledge telling—strategies in their students, in order to promote the development of writing expertise suitable to academic studies. These suggestions are described in reference to two pedagogical functions common to second language composition instruction: modeling and evaluation. Examples are drawn from case studies of experienced ESL teachers' verbal routines in classroom settings (Cumming, 1992; Cumming & Gill, 1991), practices for evaluating compositions (Cumming, 1990b), and organizing self-assessment among their students (Cumming, 1986), as well as preliminary analyses of ESL teachers and students using five procedural facilitation prompts in three types of instructional environments: natural classroom settings, tutoring sessions, and a word-processing program. However, these recent studies indicate that ESL writing instruction aiming to foster students' writing expertise needs, like any educational innovation, to address and accommodate a variety of complex situational and individual factors.

## TWO VIGNETTES

1. Danielle turns on the power bar. She glances out the window while the machine boots up. Her apartment looks down on a small lake, where ducks circle the edge of the trees. Danielle has been waiting for this since she got home! The ideas she had on the bus have been circling around in her mind, like the ducks. She can grab one. Or maybe she was thinking of that too much at dinner tonight; her roommates told her she hardly spoke. But they're all Anglos. They live here, so they can chat away with each other. But Danielle wasn't just distracted. The ideas were like ducks, and she had to write them down, to capture them in her thoughts, before she could stop them circling and circling. Now was her chance.

As the word-processing program pops across the screen Danielle's fingers pounce on the keyboard. Her fingers cluck away at the keys. So what's the main issue? She has to convince her English teacher that the video today was wrong. It was just misconceived. How to start in on that? *Qu'est-ce que c'est le mot en anglais?* What's that word in English? No, a better way to do this is to start with the main point. No, that's the wrong word. It's *particuliere* in French. Do they say *particular* in English? How about *especially*? Yes, that's firmer. Now put the phrase the other way around. Is the spelling right? *Bien.* Okay, where is this going to lead? Save that idea for the end. What do I really want to say about it? *Qu'est-ce que je veux dire?* I don't want to sound too heavy. Okay, so I'll put the adjective here. Let's go back over that again. How does it sound? Does English take a preposition with this? On? In? It must be *on*. I'm sure the French phrase is different. What's the best way of saying this? Will the teacher believe this? Probably. She has to make her understand. So this part has to fit better with the opening sentence.

Danielle's eyes are glowing now, her mind is intent, and the computer screen becomes the lake. Her fingers fly across the keyboard chasing the ducks faster and faster. She's on to it now and won't stop until it's time to sleep.

2. Abdullah closes the pages. The crisp, clean pages of the textbook, still stiff on the outer edges, are sealed for now. In front of him are his notes: blue marks scribbled over the yellow lined note pad. They look messy. Everyone complains about his hand script, even in the letters he sends home. But enough of that, Abdullah has a summary to prepare for history class tomorrow. The chapter on the Russian Revolution. And the seminar leader is so sticky about the summaries. Ten points for each summary, one every week. But Abdullah now has two pages of notes. All those names! Two pages of names and places and dates. It would be tough enough in Arabic. Abdullah was always poor at writing in Arabic. But now in English too! You get a name, then a date, then a place, than another name. What fits with what? But the notes are the easy part. Just read and write it down. Why is he doing this? Why does he have to take this course to get into the commerce program anyway?

Abdullah's eyes rummage across the yellow pages. Where to start? Okay, St. Petersburg. He had a friend who went there once. Or was is it somewhere else? Oh, well, write down the title of the chapter. That's easy. What else? Okay put the first sentence. That's the same as the title. Now, what else? Just names and places and dates. Okay, what else? Well, put the first name. What place? Okay. What date? Who cares about the spelling. Okay. That's that. Now what else? Okay, the next name. Okay. What else? Who cares what order this is in? Just get it done. Copy out the sentence. Russia? This is not the same Russia as on the TV recently. The line-ups, the frosty breath, the woolen coats. Remember the TV news clips. No, forget those distractions: Get on with the summary. Okay, what else? What else? How does everybody else do this? Abdullah does not know. He jots down a few more names and dates and places. Then he shoves his pages away. He has got to get this into the typist first thing in the morning so she can have it ready for the afternoon class.

## Knowledge Transforming and Knowledge Telling

Danielle and Abdullah demonstrate two common but very different approaches to composing in a second language. In terms of Bereiter and Scardamalia's (1987) theory of writing expertise, my portrayal of Danielle displays the characteristics of a *knowledge-transforming* model of composing, whereas Abdullah shows the characteristics of a *knowledge-telling* model. Abdullah's knowledge-telling approach may suffice to perform many academic tasks at a competent level, but Danielle's knowledge-transforming approach is probably necessary to achieve full expertise in writing and to learn fully from the processes of composing in academic studies.

Research into the cognitive processes of writing in second languages indicates that such expertise in composing develops relatively independently of people's proficiency in a second language but nonetheless exerts a crucial influence on how well they are able to write in a second language (Cumming, 1989, 1990a, 1990b; Cumming & Gill, 1991; Cumming, Rebuffot, & Ledwell, 1989; Cummins, 1991; Hornberger, 1989). ESL students' cognitive processes of writing may be difficult to discern in the superficial features of the texts they produce, but the extent of ESL students' writing expertise proves to bear significantly on evaluations of the quality of their written work (Cumming, 1989, 1990b). An important implication for ESL instruction in academic settings is that students who have not yet developed a knowledge-transforming approach to composing may have to be prompted to do so through instructional approaches aimed specifically at this goal. Such instructional approaches may differ substantively from those of helping students to acquire the vocabulary, syntax, discourse conventions, and other aspects integral to conversational dimensions of the second language.

When Abdullah writes, he tells the knowledge he has about something, but he does not refine that knowledge, use it to achieve new goals, or to transform his thinking. As my depiction of Abdullah in a note-taking task illustrates, he can compile and sequence information bit by bit from given sources into a text. But his text will probably not be planned much in advance, nor will he revise it very much. Indeed, looking at the pages he produces, one would probably see few items crossed out, changed, or edited. This is because his writing is largely a telling of his thoughts on a topic as they occur to him, as in a spoken monologue. His mental strategy for composing involves finding or retrieving pieces of information then, asking himself, what's next? Then he finds another piece of information — virtually by association with the last bit — writes that down, then asks himself again, what's next? Abdullah's strategy for gathering declarative information could be called a "copy–delete" strategy rather than synthesis of ideas (Brown & Day, 1983).

Abdullah's strategy for controlling his writing procedures conforms to what Bereiter and Scardamalia (1987) call a "what next" strategy, rather than the complex use of goals and plans as characterize expert writing. People who write from such a knowledge-telling model in their mother tongue tend to approach writing this way in their second language, too (Cumming, 1989; Cumming & Gill, 1991, Cumming, Rebuffot, & Ledwell, 1989;). Note also that Abdullah doesn't use his native Arabic very much when he writes in English, perhaps because a teacher told him he needed to think in English when he wrote. Or perhaps he just tells the knowledge he has obtained from reading, without utilizing other kinds of knowledge or thinking strategies he has.

Danielle, in contrast, approaches her writing task with considerable expertise. She is a published author in her native French; she uses the diverse composing strategies she has developed in French to write skillfully in English as well. Writing is a mental challenge she enjoys, something which occupies her thinking well before she sits down to write. She sees writing as a way of solving a mental problem she has set for herself, clarifying her own thinking. But these processes also have social goals— convincing her teacher of something and demonstrating herself in these circumstances.

Danielle focuses intently on choosing the right words to achieve her purposes in writing. She puzzles over almost every word while thinking out complex aspects of her ideas, what her text will accomplish, and how the parts of the text cohere. Indeed, she attends to several of these dimensions of her writing at the same time. Danielle's thinking also switches frequently between her native French and her second language as she musters all the mental resources she can to achieve the goal of saying the right thing. Similarly, Danielle analyzes her language usage extensively, correcting herself, revising to improve her text while she is also improving her thoughts, as well as her sense of the impact she expects her text to have on someone reading it. Like Abdullah, Danielle tells the knowledge she has. But above and beyond that, Danielle also makes that knowledge problematic, performing ongoing mental operations on it and thereby transforming her own knowledge along with the text she composes. As a consequence, to look at Danielle's handwritten texts, one would typically see an array of crossed-out words, rearranged passages, and revised phrases—all reflecting her mental and textual efforts to refine her expression.

Of course, Danielle's and Abdullah's composing processes will interact to some extent with the proficiency they have in English, the knowledge they have of the subject matter they are writing about, and affective variables like their interest in, feelings about, or personal commitment to their writing tasks. But for argument's sake, let us assume that each of these variables is equivalent between the two individuals (if such a thing is possible): Each is writing about a topic they have only limited knowledge of, they are writing in conditions of instrumental motivation created by their educational situations, and they have equal levels of conversational proficiency in English as determined by interview and grammatical tests.

In the context of academic studies in a second language, what distinguishes the quality of either person's approach to composing is the extent to which they are able, or are not able, to use their knowledge in reference to texts. Danielle's writing expertise prompts her to make new knowledge out of ideas she is busily formulating mentally. She is skilled at putting her ideas into text forms; she may even have difficulty doing so outside of a textual environment. In contrast, Abdullah treats writing more as a kind of translation from one medium to another, as my metaphor of summary writing suggests. Abdullah can encode his knowledge in texts, but he does not use writing to consolidate new ideas, to synthesize his own thoughts, or to reach new insights. He does not treat writing as an opportunity to learn, although he certainly can incorporate knowledge transmitted to him through reading.

In short, substantive differences appear in people's capacities *to learn through writing* depending on the approach to composing they adopt (Cumming, 1990a; Flower & Hayes, 1984; Scardamalia & Bereiter, 1986). This distinction is important because it provides a more principled basis for academically oriented composition instruction than the futile notion that ESL students will simply learn to write by writing or that they will simply learn the language by using it.

For example, Abdullah may well be learning some history, at least enough to pass the course. His summary writing is a means of structuring the information he reads. But, because Abdullah merely transposes, rather than critically analyzing or interrelating the information he writes, it is doubtful that Abdullah actually reconstructs his knowledge in this process. Similarly, in regards to learning English, Abdullah does very little analysis of the language he uses and therefore probably learns little English while he writes. Little evidence appears of his searching for appropriate words, comparing English forms to his native Arabic, or analyzing his emerging text metalinguistically. So it is difficult to see how such learning could happen (Cumming, 1990a). In the terminology of second language acquisition theory, it is hard to see how Abdullah's "comprehensible input" could become "language intake."

In contrast, Danielle would appear to be learning a considerable amount while she composes. She actively consolidates and reconstructs her own ideas, even though she is not writing directly in reference to new language input in the way that Abdullah is. As she reformulates her ideas, improves upon them, and conveys them to her teacher to read, Danielle reaches new understandings for herself, further develops her self-control over her composing skills, and builds her self-confidence in her capacities to take a position on issues she judges important. Danielle probably also learns quite a bit of English, too. She does three things frequently while she writes which could facilitate what Swain (1985) calls *comprehensible output* — in juxtaposition to Krashen's (1982) ideas of *comprehensible input* in a second language.

First, Danielle actively searches out the best choices of words or phrases for her writing. This process leads her to analyze aspects of the vocabulary she knows, to assess subtleties of their sense and appropriateness, and to extend her own lexical resources. Second, Danielle switches between her native French and English frequently, comparing phrases, making important distinctions between aspects of the two languages, and consolidating her thoughts in relation to both linguistic codes. Third, Danielle analyzes her own written text extensively, correcting errors she may have made, forming her own sense of accuracy in the language, and ensuring that her use of language corresponds to her intended meanings. In these ways, Danielle's writing expertise enables her to think about her writing in ways that could help her to consolidate and gain greater control over her second language knowledge as well (Cumming, 1990a; Gass, 1988; Ringbom, 1987).

## IMPLICATIONS FOR ESL WRITING INSTRUCTION

To understand how teachers can productively account for these aspects of writing expertise, distinctions can be made between two integral functions of ESL composition teaching: (a) modeling writing for students, and (b) evaluating students' writing.

### Modeling Writing

*Modeling* broadly refers to anything that a teacher may do to display writing for the purposes of helping students learn. Modeling practices may focus on the textual, cognitive, or social aspects of composing. Most proponents of the recent pedagogical shift from product-oriented to process-oriented composition instruction have argued that instructional modeling in reference to text or language models alone is insufficient to foster students' learning in this domain because attention is also required to the cognitive processes and social conditions of composing.

*Text modeling* in second language composition instruction has conventionally provided students with models in the form of syntactic paradigms, essays written by professional authors, or specific rhetorical patterns—which students are asked to analyze and then emulate in their own writing. Many recent discussions of teaching ESL writing in academic contexts have emphasized the importance of modeling texts that closely resemble the types of tasks which learners will have to perform in their academic studies (Early, 1990; Hammond, 1987; Horowitz, 1986; Swales, 1990; as well as chapters in this volume by Bloch & Chi; Braine; Dudley-Evans; Jacoby, Leech, & Holten; and Johns). This pedagogical emphasis properly stresses how learners need to acquire familiarity and practice with the specific text types relevant to their academic studies. Moreover, instructional modeling at the rhetorical level of text discourse would appear to initiate students into the norms of academic activity while preserving the integral complexity of written communication for academic purposes.

Preserving the holistic complexity of composing is especially important for text-based instructional modeling because of the tendency for this approach to fragment the processes of composing into routine steps or language manipulation exercises, as in *controlled composition* or *sentence-building* tasks. Fragmenting writing tasks in this way probably promotes the kind of knowledge-telling strategies that Abdullah employs, or worse, it forces students like Danielle, who already use knowledge-transforming strategies, into adopting less productive approaches to composing. To foster knowledge-transforming strategies, students have to approach composition tasks holistically, allowing themselves to determine appropriate goals, complex representations, uses of their existing knowledge, and ongoing decisions while they compose (Cumming, 1989, 1991a; see also Belcher's argument for critical writing tasks in this volume). For students like Abdullah, these mental strategies for composing may have to be prompted while he writes (for example, using modeling techniques described later), a situation that would not be possible in sentence manipulation or controlled composition tasks which eliminate the need for such strategies altogether.

*Cognitive modeling* in writing instruction involves demonstrating and practicing the kinds of thinking processes that experienced writers use so that students can become aware of, and can practice, the complex mental activities that characterize expert composing (Bereiter & Scardamalia, 1987; Cumming, 1986, 1989, 1990c). Without explicit modeling of the cognitive processes of composing, students cannot obtain information about the effortful planning, decision making, or revising activities that they need to use to develop writing expertise. Such information about the cognitive aspects of composing is not readily retrievable for students from reading text models, teachers' feedback on compositions, or just watching other people write. So instructional approaches to cognitive modeling usually involve displaying, then enhancing, the mental strategies that people use while they write. Such modeling may involve teachers' verbalizing what they think about while they write a composition in front of a class (Cumming, 1986), students' analyses of their own thinking processes in groups of peers (Cumming, 1986; Dudley-Evans, this volume), rehearsal of invention or revision strategies in tutorial settings (Spack, 1984), or use of special questions or prompts to guide students' thinking in expertlike ways while they compose (Cumming, 1986).

The qualities of writing tasks assigned in classes also influence the thinking processes that students are encouraged to perform while composing. For instance, studies of mother tongue (Durst, 1987) and second language (Cumming, 1989) writing have both found that tasks like analytic arguments produce more extensive, complex thinking in students' mental activities while composing than, for example, summary tasks. Moreover, writing tasks can be devised to elicit specific kinds of mental processes characteristic of expert composing. One such example appears in Burtis,

Bereiter, Scardamalia, and Tetroe's (1983) tasks that provide a dramatic, complicated concluding sentence for which students are asked to compose an appropriate narrative text. As their research indicates, setting such challenging goals for composing requires students to engage in significantly more "means–ends" planning (to create a text that satisfies several relevant but contradictory goals) than would otherwise occur in their narrative writing.

For students like Danielle who have already developed writing expertise and effective second language learning strategies, cognitive modeling by a teacher would want to encourage, not restrict, existing approaches to composing. That is, it would be futile to force students like Danielle to go piecemeal through a prescribed learning routine in a doctrinaire way, such as fixed stages of planning, drafting, and revising a composition. Danielle's own approach to composing is already more sophisticated, complex, and productive than could be prescribed through such instruction. Instead, a teacher might want to capitalize on Danielle's expertise by having her model how she composes to other students who are less skilled writers, perhaps by having Danielle think aloud while she writes amid a small group of peers, explaining how she approaches a particular task, or working with other students to coach them on their writing. Further, teachers would want to ensure that students like Danielle work on tasks that challenge their composing skills, potential to learn through writing, and capacities to define and expand substantive knowledge (see chapters by Belcher, Connor & Kramer, and Johns, this volume).

For inexpert writers like Abdullah, modeling strategies for composing is crucial since he is probably unaware of the alternative kinds of thinking he could use to guide his writing or learning. For this reason, text models may have limited value in helping Abdullah to refine his thinking strategies while he composes (as suggested in Schneider & Fujishima's case study of Zhang in the present volume). The following sequence, described in Cumming (1986), is one approach to cognitive modeling that could be taken instead. A first step would be demonstration by a teacher who performs the kind of summary writing task that Abdullah needs to do for his history course. As the teacher talks aloud to display her thinking while writing, students take note of key strategies they observe. Next students attempt a similar task, working in small groups with common language backgrounds to identify the thinking strategies they use, or could have used more productively, for content learning, language learning, improving their texts. From this basis, individual students decide on goals for improving their own summary writing, then practice these in subsequent writing tasks, monitoring their own achievement of the goals. The teacher may then help students to put their chosen strategies into the form of prompts on cue cards to guide themselves as they write, such as: How can I relate these ideas to each other? What do I want my reader to believe? What's a better word for this? (Bereiter & Scardamalia, 1987).

*Social modeling* in composition instruction involves creating contexts for writing which will foster students' expertise and their purposeful uses of writing. As many researchers have observed, classroom situations tend to reduce second language composition to routine work that may have little relevance to students, their motivation for using writing, or their potential for developing writing expertise (Cumming, 1990c; Cumming & Gill, 1991; Cummins, 1984; Edelsky, 1986; Moll & Diaz, 1987). Skilled ESL writing instructors appear to counter this tendency in their classes by alternating proactive and responsive teaching strategies with whole class, individually focused, and peer groupings, while focusing on students' accomplishing and discussing writing tasks in a workshop-like environment (Cumming, 1992).

Classroom processes that appear particularly important to support the social development of writing expertise in academic settings are writing tasks that aim to accomplish specific purposes related to students' academic or professional concerns, peer groups that provide support for developing the qualities of each others' writing, and students coming to feel they are gaining control over their own learning and writing processes, as well as their broader capacities to use literacy purposefully. In academically oriented composition classes, these conditions can be created through projects involving group reports; research in libraries and other data sources; or interviewing professors, support staff, and other persons in the local academic community (Cumming, 1984; see chapters by Dudley-Evans; Frodesen; Jacoby, Leech, & Holten; and Johns, all this volume). Likewise, interactive dialogue journals are an instructional approach that create their own social context for literate communications based on students' expression of personal, academic, or intellectual interests to which teachers can model responses that foster individuals' writing expertise (Peyton, 1990). Treating writing from a critical, problematic perspective also appears integral to ensuring that students not only can identify and interpret their substantive knowledge, but also analyze its validity and values and use their knowledge to shape their own positions and responsibilities in the world (Belcher, this volume; Walsh, 1991).

## Evaluating Writing

Two approaches to student evaluation have dominated ESL composition instruction over the past decades: (a) error identification or correction, and (b) holistic or analytic rating of students' compositions. Both approaches are useful, either for the purposes of normative assessment or in helping teachers to understand their students' performance. But questions need to be asked about the extent to which either approach helps to foster ESL students' development of writing expertise (Cohen & Cavalcanti, 1990; Cumming, 1990b; Leki, this volume; Raimes, 1990; Zamel, 1985).

Indeed, the definitions of writing expertise above would suggest that self-evaluation is the optimal mode of assessment for ESL composition teachers to adopt. Self-evaluation encourages students to gain greater control over their own writing skills and to enhance their personal understanding of what they are writing about or learning—a necessary prerequisite for the development of knowledge-transforming approaches to writing. For someone like Danielle who already has such self-control over her writing processes, self-evaluation may focus on aspects of English that she needs to learn or the purposes which her writing is able to fulfill. For a student like Abdullah, two other kinds of self-awareness are worth developing through self-evaluation.

One aspect is an awareness of the strategies and language forms that more skilled writers use when they compose. In this way, evaluation can take the form of Abdullah systematically comparing his writing performance to relevant texts produced by others—be it peers, skilled native speakers performing the same task, or a teacher (Cohen, 1990; Dudley-Evans; Johns, Leki; all this volume). A second kind of self-awareness is self-monitoring, by which Abdullah can ensure he is learning to use more expertlike composing strategies appropriately and progressively. The goal-setting approach to writing instruction outlined above leads to this sort of self-monitoring and puts Abdullah in the position of judging for himself whether he has achieved the goals that he has chosen to focus on, while making adjustments to his own learning and writing strategies as he sees fit (Cumming, 1986). Numerous other approaches exist to organize self-evaluation in academic settings for language learning (e.g., Cohen, 1990; Dickinson, 1987; Oskarsson, 1989; Riley, 1985).

Self-evaluation can be facilitated through techniques like students making portfolios of their best written work, self-review procedures or check lists, or responses to writing by interested and sympathetic peers. But each of these techniques tends to focus mainly on the textual dimensions of writing, providing little information or criteria for self-assessment of the cognitive or social processes for developing writing expertise (Freedman, 1991). For example, students like Danielle may find self-evaluation of her writing quite straightforward because her knowledge-transforming approach enables her to diagnose her problems in her writing and to act productively on them. But students like Abdullah might not know how to perceive or act productively on self-evaluation of his own writing. Indeed, Abdullah's knowledge-telling approach may prompt him to disregard his written texts once they have been produced, rendering portfolio assessment of little value for development of writing skills unless supplemented by active tutoring, process-oriented check lists, or specific procedures for self-analysis of his writing.

Thus self-evaluation may be helpful in prompting the development of writing expertise, but it cannot be sufficient to explain how students acquire such expertise through ESL composition instruction. Indeed, observation of experienced ESL composition instructors show them to consistently and skillfully use a diverse range of verbal and written strategies for providing evaluative information to students on their writing (Cumming, 1992). Such verbal activity in ESL composition classes might be conceptualized as a Vygotskian dialogic process between teachers and students that permits students to learn how to talk and think about academic writing in more expertlike ways (Scardamalia & Bereiter, 1986; Wells, 1990), to negotiate and appropriate the kinds of knowledge that writing teachers possess (Newman, Griffin, & Cole, 1989; Rogoff, 1990), and to integrate the complex qualities of knowledge needed to develop literate expertise in a second language (Cumming & Gill, 1991; Hornberger, 1989).

## DIRECTIONS FOR RESEARCH AND PEDAGOGY

Following these ideas, my current research is adopting three approaches to understanding how writing expertise might be promoted in second language instruction. Each approach makes explicit use of *procedural facilitation prompts* (Bereiter & Scardamalia, 1987) derived from earlier research on the thinking processes that ESL students with high levels of writing expertise frequently use when they write in their second language (Cumming, 1989, 1990a; Cumming, Rebuffot, & Ledwell, 1989). Five prompts have been selected to encourage ESL students while they compose or revise their writing:

1. *goals*—to set and monitor goals to accomplish specific purposes and to accommodate readers of their writing
2. *word choice*—to choose appropriate words or phrases
3. *L1/L2 comparisons*—to compare equivalent expressions in their first and second languages
4. *rules*—to use relevant grammar and spelling rules
5. *fit*—to assess the coherence between parts of their compositions

Whereas most previous research on second language writing has focused solely on student task performance or the genres of writing to be learned, the present research is attempting to analyze the conceptions, uses, and effects of a specific instructional procedure among ESL teachers and students alike in three different kinds of pedagogical environments. In one environment, tutors are using these prompts printed on strips of paper while they help ESL students compose or revise their writing. Verbal interactions between the tutors and students are being analyzed to determine how people jointly construct attention to these aspects of their writing, as well as the resulting changes in students' performance that emerge. In the second environment, the prompts have been put into a menu on a word-processing program (as in Kozma, 1991). Students are encouraged to use the menu when they are stuck or are revising their writing, and their uses of specific prompts are tracked through a computer file that accounts for each use of the menu prompts and subsequent text changes. The third environment is a conventional classroom setting, where a few teachers are using these prompts while they teach academically oriented ESL composition classes. These teachers' classroom activities and responses to students' writing are being documented and each teacher interviewed on a weekly basis.

This project is still in its preliminary stages, so results are not yet available to determine the effectiveness of these direct approaches to prompting writing expertise in ESL instruction. But several observations can be made on the basis of exploratory case studies with three experienced instructors teaching academically oriented ESL courses at a Canadian university; 18 volunteer ESL students from their classes (with Cantonese, Farsi, Japanese, and Mandarin backgrounds); and 8 tutors/research assistants (who speak 1 of the 4 languages) working with these students and the teachers. These case studies consist of various observational, interview, survey, and discourse-analytic data collected in late 1991 and early 1992 as a means of preparing for more systematic experiments on students' learning and instructional processes in the following year.

On the one hand, these case studies testify to the comprehensive value of the five thinking prompts. That is, all participating teachers, tutors, and students have: (a) appeared able to integrate the prompts productively and easily into their usual teaching, tutoring, or composing routines; (b) consistently rated the usefulness of each of the prompts as high (e.g., about 4 on a scale of 5) in questionnaire surveys; and (c) stated in interviews that the prompts include almost all of the aspects of writing to which they need to attend while teaching, tutoring, or composing in the present contexts. Moreover, many participants have been able to suggest formative changes to the phrasing or uses of the thinking prompts in order to increase their pedagogical or cognitive value.

On the other hand, these case studies reveal the complexity and subtlety of variables to be accounted for when introducing even a simple innovation into natural educational contexts. Like numerous other recent studies closely documenting teachers' and students' conceptions and practices in language education, the present research is generally finding that:

- teachers' individual beliefs shape their pedagogical approaches and concerns differently (Burns, 1991; Richardson, Anders, Tidwell, & Lloyd, 1991; Woods, 1989; Zancanella, 1991; chapters by Leki and Prior, this volume);
- students likewise assume and develop differing perspectives on pedagogical activities according to their backgrounds, interests, intentions, and skills (Cumming, 1986; Prior, 1991; Volet & Lawrence, 1988); and as a consequence,
- the local adoption of a pedagogical innovation depends largely on such conceptions as particular users of that innovation create in specific teaching contexts (Cumming, 1988; Fullan, 1982; Roemer, 1991).

Indeed in the present setting, a single simple innovation — five prompts introduced into only a few ESL writing classes and tutoring sessions at one institution — is proving to vary in its implementation across nearly every situation documented. Although all of the participating teachers, tutors, and students initially received similar orientations, explanations, and demonstrations of the thinking prompts, each person appears to have adapted their uses of the prompts to suit their individual conceptions, practices, and interests. Four factors that appear integral to this variation are differences in teachers' personal beliefs and overall instructional approaches, students' experiences writing in their mother tongue and purposes for writing academic English, the functions of each prompt in specific aspects of the writing process, and the situational constraints of each instructional environment.

## Teachers' Focuses

Interview and observational data indicate that each of the instructors participating in our study hold somewhat different conceptions of ESL writing instruction, and correspondingly adopt different focuses in their teaching — even though each person has taught in the same ESL program for more than 5 years and had earlier pursued graduate studies at the same university. These differences are evident in each teacher's uses of the thinking prompts. For example, one teacher approaches ESL writing instruction by having her students "free write," then edit their compositions individually and in groups for specific audiences and purposes. Her conceptualization of the five thinking prompts has been mainly as a tool for editing, following her belief that "it is only when you edit that the critical side of your mind starts to work."

In contrast, a second teacher focuses her ESL writing instruction on thesis statements and topic sentences. Following her beliefs in a student-centred, developmental approach to adult education, this teacher is urging students to use the five thinking prompts to define and consolidate their ideas prior to composing. At the same time, she uses the five prompts as a code for correcting student compositions and for peer revision, drawing students' attention to aspects of their texts to be revised according to these common points of reference.

The third instructor adopts yet another focus, on rhetorical development in students' writing through analyses of her own and the students' compositions, as well as published essays. Whereas the other two teachers emphasize the uniqueness of individual expression, allowing students to use the thinking prompts more or less as they decide themselves, this third teacher highlights the "goal" and "fit" prompts as a common basis for group analysis, peer editing, and rewriting to improve logical development. As she stated in one class, "I want you to think about the goal, the main opinion, what points the writer uses to support the opinion, and also about how parts fit."

Given these differences in instructional focus, the five thinking prompts, when introduced into these natural classroom contexts, have alternately become a vehicle for individual and peer editing processes (in the case of the first teacher), for clarifying central ideas while preparing to write and for teacher feedback (in the case of the second teacher), or for structuring the rhetorical organization of student writing, as well as teacher modeling and text analysis (in the case of the third teacher).

Each of these emphases appears productive and appropriate in view of the individual instructor's beliefs and teaching approaches, as well as the views of modeling and self-evaluation outlined above, but it would be difficult to say that the same classroom uses of the thinking prompts are taking place. This natural variation poses a challenge to experimentation attempting to determine the effects of cognitive modeling on ESL writing. But such an "ecologically valid" approach to educational innovation may be necessary to integrate cognitive modeling effectively into the diverse bases of knowledge and classroom practice that experienced teachers possess. Indeed, research that ignores these pedagogical variations and individual priorities, such as narrowly defined training studies, may hold little relevance for educational practice.

## Students' Experiences and Purposes

Students also make unique conceptualizations and uses of the thinking prompts. One area of difference emerges in regards to ESL students' previous experiences in writing. Among the students in our tutoring sessions, an extreme contrast appears between students with considerable writing expertise in their mother tongue (i.e., published authors like Danielle) and students with little prior experience in writing or formal writing instruction (i.e., like Abdullah). In particular, learners with considerable writing expertise seek tutor assistance almost exclusively in reference to prompts on word choice and grammar rules. This limited focus seemingly arises because their available expertise enables them to assess the coherence of their discourse, goals for reader response, and cross-linguistic equivalents on their own — not requiring tutor assistance. In contrast, ESL students with little writing experience in either their mother tongue or English make more extensive uses of *all* of the prompts in tutoring sessions, apparently reflecting their knowledge lacks in such aspects of writing skill as setting goals, assessing the coherence of their discourse, or making metalinguistic analyses of relations between their first and second languages.

These tendencies appear to substantiate the pedagogical relevance of novice–expert contrasts of ESL writing processes as documented in previous research (described above). For example, one Japanese participant in our tutoring sessions is a dental researcher on a scientific exchange program who has published numerous articles on his research in Japanese. The compositions he brings to his tutoring sessions have been drafts of research reports or articles to be submitted for publication in English. Typically, he has a very specific audience and context of distribution in mind for these texts, and he has shaped their content and rhetorical organization in a very professional manner — such that a tutor unfamiliar with his field could scarcely criticize their substance or discourse structure. But nearly every sentence in these texts contains either a lexical phrase that he is unsure of an error in English article use, pronoun reference, or clause structure. Consequently in using the five thinking prompts, his attention, as well as that of tutors, is consistently drawn to "word choice" and "grammar rules." However, his substantive knowledge, writing expertise, and awareness of appropriate discourse transfer readily across languages, making any references by tutors to the "goals" or "fit" prompts superfluous as he has already addressed these issues on his own.

In contrast are four students from Iran, each who claims to have received little formal composition instruction in either Farsi or English (apart from high school classes, where compositions were usually copied from other texts and then read aloud, and despite having completed university degrees that required occasional written assignments). For these students, the five thinking prompts reportedly represent their first systematic introduction to formal composition. They say the thinking prompts have broadened their conceptions of what they should attend to while they compose, leading them to use each of the five prompts frequently and consistently and to judge each prompt to be of high value in their learning to write in English:

I think all of the five thinking prompts are useful in my writing. For example, *goals*, I should pay attention to my readers. Or I should be very careful to *fit* the sentences to each other. I also try to find ideas in my mother tongue and then *translate* them into English. I sometimes find it difficult since the *grammar* of the two languages are different. But I know that we do not have articles in our language. *Word choice* is also another problem for me. I know many words, but it is difficult for me to choose the best one. (original interview in Farsi)

Differences across the four language groups selected for the research are difficult to assess given variation in participants' personal backgrounds. However, one distinction appears in Japanese learners' preferences for tutoring through their mother tongue, whereas the Cantonese, Mandarin, and Farsi participants have tended to make more extensive, self-initiated use of English, even with tutors who speak their native language. This distinction may not, however, be a widespread cultural preference but only reflect individuals' past experiences with English-medium education or wider communication, or arise when English has greater prestige in education in their native countries (e.g., in Iran, Hong Kong, or Taiwan, rather than Japan).

## Functions of Each Prompt

The thinking prompts used in the current research vary also in their inherent value and functions for particular aspects of composing. Specifically, *initial drafts* of compositions require more extensive deliberation over the "goals" and "coherence" of units within compositions, whereas *revisions* of subsequent drafts tend to involve less frequent attention to these concerns. Consideration of word choice, grammar rules, and cross-linguistic comparisons, on the other hand, seem to occur more frequently at either the early (drafting) or later (revising) stages of students' writing processes. That is, for most students in our tutoring sessions, the goals and overall discourse structure of compositions are usually determined quickly, then attended to only infrequently in later revisions. As Burtis, Bereiter, Scardamalia, and Tetroe (1983) suggest for mother tongue writing, this tendency may characterize an inexpert, knowledge-telling approach to composing in its reluctance to revise ideas or texts to any great extent once they are written down, or this tendency may suggest that interests related to language accuracy or learning take precedence over the social functions of writing tasks assigned for language learning purposes.

## Situational Constraints

Distinctions that emerge across the three pedagogical environments of classroom, tutorial, and computer-mediated instruction seem to center on the potential for relevant modeling and evaluation to occur in each situation. These differences range on a continuum from one-to-one tutoring (where the most intensive and elaborated uses of the thinking prompts occur), to computer-mediated interventions (where the thinking prompts are studiously attended to but students receive little further elaboration or interpersonal interaction), to classroom settings (where attention to the thinking prompts often lags or is subservient to other concerns).

Differences appear particularly in reference to the potential value of error identification as a learning process, especially in regards to the prompts for grammar rules or word choice. Indeed, participating students, teachers, and tutors all make such extensive, spontaneous use of error identification, and value this process so highly in their ratings of each thinking prompt, that I wonder if a reconceptualization is warranted for the learning potential of this aspect of ESL composition instruction.

In the classroom context, error identification is done mainly through teachers or peers reading over, drawing attention to, or correcting bothersome phrases — largely as an editing process distinct from the immediacy of students' composing processes and concerns for communication or idea formation. In the terms developed in the first portion of this chapter, classroom environments offer little potential for *modeling* that is relevant to the composing processes of individual students, and *evaluation* processes are also typically separated from students' acts of composing. As numerous studies have pointed out, such identification of written errors takes the form of a *feedback* process that may be inconsistent and fail to consider the complexities of particular students' knowledge or emerging writing expertise (Cohen & Cavalcanti, 1990; Cumming, 1990b; Zamel, 1985). The conventional image of this process, whereby a single teacher reads and responds to 15 to 50 compositions weekly per class at home or in an office, would appear to be an artifact of educational systems with large class sizes, frequent class meetings, and little time for teachers to respond individually to students' knowledge or writing development. Moreover, little theory on writing expertise has been available to guide such feedback practices, particularly to provide relevant criteria or modeling strategies for evaluation of student writing.

In contrast, the one-to-one tutoring sessions appear to be more conducive environments for the textual, cognitive, and social dimensions of error identification to be integrated with individual students' composing processes and their immediate concerns about language, ideas, and texts. Either as attention to word choice or grammar rules, the identification of errors appears to create the most frequent point of discussion between students and tutors (typically 3 or 4 times that of attention to other thinking prompts). And, in the terms developed above, these interactions appear in a meaningful combination of *modeling* and *evaluation* where more expert knowledge and skills are displayed by the tutor in a way that is immediately pertinent to a students' self-assessment and personal expression, composing, and learning. As Newman, Griffin, and Cole (1989) put it, in tutoring sessions, assessment and teaching tend to be one and the same process, as teachers implicitly adjust their instruction to the qualities and extent of learning which they judge to be within learners' *proximal zone of development*.

In the computer environment, students also make far more extensive use of word choice or grammar rules than the other three thinking prompts, but none of the potential for immediate response, explanation, or correction appears as in the tutoring sessions. In the terms developed above, the present computer medium appears to offer appropriate prompting of *self-evaluation* processes, but the benefits of relevant *modeling* are not available as they are in tutoring sessions. Indeed, it would be difficult to imagine how such modeling could be made available in a computer environment, given the unpredictable nature of writing, language, or individual concerns.

These observations suggest that tutoring may be the most optimal environment for the development of writing expertise through the approach using thinking prompts described in the present settings of ESL instruction. Tentative support appears for this interpretation in the present case studies through the results of surveys among ESL students who used the thinking prompts either in classroom settings only or in classroom and tutorial settings. On a scale of 5, students who had participated in tutoring sessions rated the usefulness of the thinking prompts as 4.3 on average, compared to students who had not participated in tutoring sessions but used the thinking prompts in classroom environments, who rated the usefulness of the thinking prompts as 3.6 on average. But the precise benefits of tutor–student interactions remain to be assessed. Although the value of student–teacher writing conferences has been proclaimed widely in the professional literature, research in second language writing thus far has tended to assess only structural features of student–teacher discourse in these situations without reference to theories of writing expertise or the effect that such discourse actually has on students' knowledge about writing (e.g., Goldstein & Conrad, 1990).

## Summary

In summary, numerous characteristics of writing expertise have now been documented which can inform ESL composition instruction, and diverse options exist for modeling the cognitive, social, and textual aspects of writing, as well as for promoting knowledge-transforming approaches to composing and student self-evaluation of their composing processes. But considerable research remains to be done to assess, and to come to know how to act appropriately upon, the various factors integral to developing instructional approaches that can foster writing expertise among teachers and ESL learners in educational settings.

By addressing the contextual and pedagogical factors that appear in just a few educational settings, the present case studies are able to point toward some of the factors that will need to be accounted for to implement approaches to instruction which can capitalize on second language students' and teachers' capacities to foster writing expertise. These factors include teachers' beliefs and focus in instruction, students' individual experiences with and purposes for writing, the functions of specific prompts for cognitive modeling in different aspects of composing, and situational constraints in specific pedagogical environments. By attending carefully to these and other considerations, research on the cognitive processes and social conditions of composing in a second language may be able to avoid creating the kind of simplistic, doctrinaire routines for instruction that Applebee (1983) described as commonplace a decade ago in regards to the classroom introduction of "process writing approaches."

## REFERENCES

Applebee, A. (1983). *Contexts for learning to write.* Norwood, NJ: Ablex.

Bereiter, C., & Scardamalia, M. (1987). *The psychology of written composition.* Hillsdale, NJ: Erlbaum.

Brown, A., & Day, J. (1983). Macrorules for summarizing texts: The development of expertise. *Journal of Verbal Learning and Verbal Behavior, 22*, 1–14.

Burns, A. (1991). *Teacher beliefs: The link with classroom practice and professional development.* Unpublished manuscript, Macquarie University, Australia, National Centre for English Language Teaching and Research.

Burtis, J., Beretier, C., Scardamalia, M., & Tetroe, J. (1983). The development of planning in writing. In B. Kroll & G. Wells (Eds.), *Explorations in the development of writing.* New York: Wiley.

Cohen, A. (1990). *Language learning: Insights for learners, teachers, and researchers.* New York: Newbury House/Harper Collins.

Cohen, A., & Cavalcanti, M. (1990). Feedback on compositions: Teacher and student verbal reports. In B. Kroll (Ed.), *Second language writing: Research insights for the classroom* (pp. 155–177). Cambridge, UK: Cambridge University Press.

Cumming, A. (1984). Simulation or reality? A group project in writing. *Carleton Papers in Applied Language Studies, 1,* 147–158.

Cumming, A. (1986). Intentional learning as a principle in ESL writing instruction: A case study. In P. Lightbown & S. Firth (Eds.), *TESL Canada Journal, 1* [Special Issue] 69–83.

Cumming, A. (1988). Change, organization, and achievement: Teachers' concerns in implementing a computer learning environment. *Journal of Educational Technology Systems, 17,* 141–163.

Cumming, A. (1989). Writing expertise and second language proficiency. *Language Learning, 39*, 81–141.

Cumming, A. (1990a). Metalinguistic and ideational thinking in second language composing. *Written Communication, 7,* 482–511.

Cumming, A. (1990b). Expertise in evaluating second language compositions. *Language Testing, 7,* 31–51.

Cumming, A. (1990c). The thinking, behaviors, and participation to foster in adult ESL literacy instruction. In J. Bell (Ed.), *ESL Literacy, TESL Talk, 20* [Special Issue], 34–51.

Cumming, A. (1992). Instructional routines in ESL composition teaching. *Journal of Second Language Writing, 1,* 17–35.

Cumming, A., & Gill, J. (1991). Learning ESL literacy among Indo-Canadian women. *Language, Culture and Curriculum, 4,* 181–200.

Cumming, A., Rebuffot, J., & Ledwell, M. (1989). Reading and summarizing challenging texts in first and second languages. *Reading and Writing, 2,* 201–219.

Cummins, J. (1984). *Bilingualism and special education: Issues in assessment and pedagogy.* Avon, UK: Multilingual Matters.

Cummins, J. (1991). Interdependence of first- and second-language proficiency in bilingual children. In E. Bialystok (Ed.), *Language processing in bilingual children* (pp. 70–89). Cambridge, UK: Cambridge University Press.

Dickinson, L. (1987). *Self-instruction in language learning.* Cambridge, UK: Cambridge University Press.

Durst, R. (1987). Cognitive and linguistic demands of analytic writing. *Research in the Teaching of English, 21,* 347–376.

Early, M. (1990). ESL beginning literacy: A content-based approach. *TESL Canada Journal, 7,* 82–93.

Edelsky, C. (1986). *Writing in a bilingual program.* Norwood, NJ: Ablex.

Flower, L., & Hayes, J. (1984). Images, plans and prose: The representation of meaning in writing. *Written Communication, 1,* 120–160.

Freedman, S. (1991). *Evaluating writing: Linking large-scale testing and classroom assessment* (Occasional paper #27). Berkeley: Center for the Study of Writing.

Fullan, M. (1982). *The meaning of educational change.* Toronto: OISE Press.

Gass, S. (1988). Integrating research areas: A framework for second language studies. *Applied Linguistics, 9,* 198–217.

Goldstein, L., & Conrad, S. (1990). Student input and negotiation of meaning in ESL writing conferences. *TESOL Quarterly, 24,* 443–460.

Hammond, J. (1987). An overview of the genre-based approach to the teaching of writing in Australia. *Australian Journal of Applied Linguistics, 10,* 163–181.

Hornberger, N. (1989). Continua of biliteracy. *Review of Educational Research, 59,* 271–296.

Horowitz, D. (1986). What professors actually require: Academic tasks for the ESL classroom. *TESOL Quarterly, 20,* 445–462.

Krashen, S. (1982). *Principles and practice in second language acquisition.* Oxford, UK: Pergamon.

Kozma, R. (1991). The impact of computer-based tools and embedded prompts on writing processes and products of novice and advanced college writers. *Cognition and Instruction, 8,* 1–27.

Moll, L., & Diaz, S. (1987). Change as the goal of educational research. *Anthropology and Education Quarterly, 18,* 300–311.

Newman, D., Griffin, P., & Cole, M. (1989). Assessment versus teaching. In *The construction zone: Working for cognitive change in schools* (pp. 76–89). Cambridge, UK: Cambridge University Press.

Oskarsson, M. (1989). Self-assessment of language proficiency: Rationale and applications. *Language Testing, 6,* 1–13.

Peyton, J. (Ed.). (1990). *Students and teachers writing together: Perspectives on journal writing.* Alexandria, VAI: TESOL.

Prior, P. (1991). Contextualizing writing and response in a graduate seminar. *Written Communication, 8*, 267-310.

Raimes, A. (1990). The TOEFL test of written English: Causes for concern. *TESOL Quarterly, 24*, 427-442.

Richardson, V., Anders, P., Tidwell, D., & Lloyd, C. (1991). The relationship between teachers' beliefs and practices in reading comprehension instruction. *American Educational Research Journal, 28*, 559-586.

Riley, P. (Ed.). (1985). *Discourse and learning*. London: Longman.

Ringbom, H. (1987). *The role of the first language in foreign language learning*. Avon, UK: Multilingual Matters.

Roemer, M. (1991). What we talk about when we talk about school reform. *Harvard Educational Review, 61*, 434-448.

Rogoff, B. (1990). *Apprenticeship in thinking: Cognitive development in social context*. Oxford, UK: Oxford University Press.

Scardamalia, M., & Bereiter, C. (1986). Research on written composition. In M. Wittrock (Ed.), *Handbook of research on teaching* (3rd ed., pp. 778-803). New York: Macmillan.

Spack, R. (1984). Invention strategies and the ESL composition student. *TESOL Quarterly, 18*, 649-670.

Swain, M. (1985). Communicative competence: Some roles of comprehensible input and comprehensible output in its development. In S. Gass & C. Madden (Eds.), *Input in second language acquisition* (pp. 235-253). Rowley, MA: Newbury House.

Swales, J. (1990). *Genre analysis: English in academic and research settings*. Cambridge, UK: Cambridge University Press.

Uzawa, K., & Cumming, A. (1989). Writing strategies in Japanese as a foreign language: Lowering or keeping up the standards. *Canadian Modern Language Review, 46*, 178-194.

Volet, S., & Lawrence, J. (1988). University students' representations of study. *Australian Journal of Education, 32*, 139-155.

Walsh, C. (1991). *Literacy as praxis: Culture, language, and pedagogy*. Norwood, NJ: Ablex.

Wells, G. (1990). Talk about text: Where literacy is learned and taught. *Curriculum Inquiry, 20*, 369-405.

Woods, D. (1989). Studying ESL teachers' decision-making: Rationale, methodological issues and initial results. *Carleton Papers in Applied Language Studies, 6*, 107-123.

Zamel, V. (1985). Responding to student writing. *TESOL Quarterly, 19*, 79-101.

Zancanella, D. (1991). Teachers reading/readers teaching: Five teachers' personal approaches to literature and their teaching of literature. *Research in the Teaching of English, 25*, 5-32.

# Author Index

# Subject Index

## A

Academic discourse community, 4, 24, 42, 55, 294–295, 340, *see also* Disciplinary community; Discourse community

Academic task portfolios, 283–286

Academic writing surveys, 114–118

Acculturation, 4, *see also* Disciplinary enculturation

Adjunct classes, 126, 281–283, 352, 352n, 353

Argumentation
in scientific and technical texts, 234

Assessment, *see* Criteria; Direct assessment writing tasks; Holistic assessment; Writing assessment issues

Assignments
reading–writing, 156, 159, 284–288
samples, 348
structuring of, 334–335
take home, 116, 118

Audience, 18, 44–45, 116–117, 143–146, 289, 343
of research reports, 355
in technical fields, 324

## C

Case studies, 5, 20, 20n, 88

Chinese speakers
article errors of, 186, 192–194
citation use of, 232–258
rhetorical traditions of, 17, 207, 258–272

Citations, 287–289, *see also* Chinese speakers, citation use of

Classroom activities
in teaching scientific writing, 364–366

Classroom culture, 324–328

Cloze exercises, 339

Cognitive processes, 324, 378–379

Cohen's Kappa coefficients, 215, 219

Collaborative learning, 343

Communicative skills, 9

Composing processes, *see* Cognitive processes; Process approach; Writing process

Contrastive rhetoric, 271–272, 279, 314–316

Criteria
in evaluation of ESL writing
ESL student perceptions, 26–32
faculty understanding and use of, 32–39

Critical writing, *see also* Chinese speakers, citation use of
definition of, 135
student resistance to, 137–138
text structure of, 139–143

Cultural knowledge
as contributor to academic success, 4